D1608713

Foundations of Risk Management and Insurance

Foundations of Risk Management and Insurance

Eric A. Wiening, CPCU, ARM, AU
Assistant Vice President and Ethics Counsel
American Institute for CPCU/Insurance Institute of America

First Edition

American Institute for Chartered Property Casualty Underwriters/
Insurance Institute of America
720 Providence Road, Malvern, Pennsylvania 19355

Foreword

The American Institute for Chartered Property Casualty Underwriters and the Insurance Institute of America are independent, nonprofit organizations serving the educational needs of the risk management, property-casualty, and financial services businesses. The Institutes develop a wide range of curricula, study materials, and examinations in response to the educational needs of various elements of these businesses. The American Institute confers the Chartered Property Casualty Underwriter (CPCU®) professional designation on people who meet its examination, ethics, and experience requirements. The Insurance Institute of America offers associate designations and certificate programs in the following areas:

- Accounting and Finance
- Agent Studies
- Business Writing
- Claims
- Global Risk Management and Insurance
- Information Technology
- Insurance Fundamentals
- Management
- Marine Insurance
- Performance Improvement
- Personal Insurance
- Premium Auditing
- Regulation and Compliance
- Reinsurance
- Risk Management
- Surety Bonds and Crime Insurance
- Surplus Lines
- Underwriting

The American Institute was founded in 1942 through a cooperative effort between property-casualty insurance company executives and insurance professors. Faculty members at The Wharton School of the University of Pennsylvania in Philadelphia led this effort. The CPCU designation arose from the same type of business and academic partnership at Wharton as the Chartered Life Underwriter (CLU) designation did in 1927.

The Insurance Institute of America was founded in 1909 by five educational organizations across the United States. It is the oldest continuously functioning national organization offering educational programs for the property-casualty insurance business. It merged with the American Institute in 1953.

The Insurance Research Council (IRC), founded in 1977, is a division of the Institutes. It is a not-for-profit research organization that examines public policy issues that affect property-casualty insurers and their customers. IRC research reports are distributed widely to insurance-related organizations, public policy authorities, and the media.

The broad knowledge base in property-casualty insurance and financial services created by the Institutes over the years is contained mainly in our textbooks. Although we use electronic technology to enhance our educational materials, communicate with our students, and deliver our examinations, our textbooks are at the heart of our educational activities. They contain the information that you as a student must read, understand, integrate into your existing knowledge, and apply to the tasks you perform as part of your job.

Despite the vast range of subjects and purposes of the more than eighty individual textbook volumes we publish, they all have much in common. First, each book is specifically designed to increase knowledge and develop skills that can improve job performance and help students achieve the educational objectives of the course for which it is assigned. Second, all of the manuscripts for our texts are reviewed widely before publication, by both insurance business practitioners and members of the risk management and insurance academic community. In addition, the revisions of our texts often incorporate improvements that students and course leaders have suggested. We welcome constructive comments that help us to improve the quality of our study materials. Please direct any comments you may have on this text to my personal attention.

We hope what you learn from your study of this text will expand your knowledge, increase your confidence in your skills, and support your career growth. If so, then you and the Institutes will truly be *succeeding together*.

Terrie E. Troxel, Ph.D., CPCU, CLU
President and CEO
American Institute for CPCU
Insurance Institute of America

Preface

This text was written for use, along with the *Code of Professional Ethics* and the *Foundations of Risk Management, Insurance, and Professionalism Course Guide*, as required study material for the gateway course in the educational program leading to the Chartered Property Casualty Underwriter (CPCU®) professional designation. The CPCU 510 course, Foundations of Risk Management, Insurance, and Professionalism, is the first course in a revised CPCU curriculum for examinations given by the American Institute for CPCU beginning in 2003. This course is probably the one that most CPCU candidates will take first. Therefore, it should provide a firm foundation on which other CPCU courses can build.

The CPCU program is designed to provide an advanced education for insurance and risk management professionals. The goals of this text are the following:

- To provide CPCU candidates with a solid understanding of modern risk management principles. Modern risk management takes a somewhat broader, more holistic view than principles taught in traditional courses that tended to focus on insurable risks and insurance as the primary risk management technique.

- To describe current insurance principles, practices, and contracts accurately.

- To enable CPCU candidates to understand and apply the fundamental principles on which the practice of insurance is based.

- To equip CPCU candidates to apply a formal approach in analyzing any property-liability insurance contract, using up-to-date examples and insurance policy extracts.

- To communicate important insurance and risk management principles in a clear, engaging, and interesting manner.

Acknowledgments

Eric A. Wiening, CPCU, ARM, AU, Assistant Vice President and Ethics Counsel, AICPCU/IIA, developed the structure of this textbook and submitted the original manuscript.

The following reviewers contributed substantially to the accuracy and clarity of the text:

Norman A. Baglini, Ph.D., CPCU, CLU

David N. Blakesley, CPCU, ARM

Michael W. Elliott, MBA, CPCU

Karen Epermanis, Ph.D.

Donald S. Malecki, CPCU

Thomas W. Mallin, J.D., CPCU

Dean A. Ockerbloom, CPCU, ARM, AU

Robert J. Prahl, CPCU

George E. Rejda, Ph.D., CLU

Jerome Trupin, CPCU, CLU, ChFC

Jerome E. Tuttle, FCAS, FCIA, CPCU

The Institutes give special thanks to Insurance Services Office (ISO) for its cooperation and help in the preparation and review of the manuscript for this text. Stephen Anderson, CPCU, AIM, coordinated ISO's efforts, which included reviews from the following ISO staff members:

Reid J. Bellanca, CPCU

Jeff DeTurris, CPCU

Gary P. Grasmann

Laurence J. Skelly, J.D.

Contents

Chapter 1

Direct Your Learning

Risk

After learning the subject matter of this chapter, you should be able to:

- Explain each of the following concepts associated with risk:
  - Uncertainty
  - Possibility
  - Probability
  - Loss exposure
  - Perils
  - Hazards
- Explain why each of the four dimensions of a loss exposure is relevant in analyzing risk.
  - List the four dimensions of a loss exposure, and explain the importance of credibly projecting those dimensions.
- Evaluate whether a given risk should be categorized as follows:
  - Subjective or objective
  - Financial or nonfinancial
  - Diversifiable or nondiversifiable
  - Pure or speculative
- Describe the cost-of-risk concept, and explain how it can be used.

Develop Your Perspective

What are the main topics covered in the chapter?

This chapter describes the concept of risk by illustrating the elements of risk, types of loss exposures, classifications of risk, and costs associated with risk.

Identify the risks facing a family or an organization.

- What types of loss exposures are present?
- How would you classify these risks?
- What are the associated costs?

Why is it important to know these topics?

Risk is present in all activities. Identifying risk and its implications, loss exposures, and cost factors will help you to understand why people and organizations must manage risk.

Consider why people and organizations are willing to take certain risks.

- Explain why some loss exposures are more risky or costly than others.

How can you use this information?

Examine how a family or an organization can manage risk.

- What actions could a family or an organization take to minimize risk?
- Why could these courses of action be chosen?

Chapter 1

Risk

Risk is a term regularly used in both business and everyday life. Risk has been defined in numerous ways; even without definition, "risk" is generally understood in context. Virtually every human activity involves some risk. For example, when someone pursues an opportunity for benefit (reward), he or she usually faces threats to its success (risks).

Risk

Someone once said that risk was the sugar and salt of life. This is an excellent definition of what risk is all about. Risk brings sweetness to life and it brings bitterness. Few of us want a world totally free of risk. There is something exciting about risk, an edge which it brings, a dimension which we would not want to give up. The other side is less attractive. The bitter side of risk is one with which we are only too familiar. It is this "downside" of risk which concerns us in our studies and work.[1]

Professor G. C. A. Dickson, *Corporate Risk Management*

Risk management helps persons and organizations to realize the opportunities, and avert the threats, associated with risk. In the safety and insurance fields, risk management focuses on loss prevention and mitigation. In finance, risk management focuses on asset and liability risks in an organization's balance sheet and on such issues as currency and stock market fluctuations that represent opportunity for gain as well as potential for loss. Although risk intuitively seems bad, risk management is increasingly being recognized as a method for addressing positive and negative aspects of uncertainties.[2] The opening chapters of this book explore risk's many facets and its management.

Insurance is one important technique for dealing with some risks. Insurance can be examined and defined in many ways:

- *Risk managers* can view insurance as a risk transfer technique to finance their organizations' insurable risks.
- *Economists* might view insurance as a social device to distribute risks among large numbers of individuals or enterprises.

- *Investors* might view insurance organizations as a favorable or an unfavorable investment opportunity in the financial services sector.

- *Insurance regulators*, on the other hand, define insurance to clarify which activities they are authorized to regulate—and even insurance regulators have not always been consistent in their definitions. The National Association of Insurance Commissioners recently produced a twelve-page draft definition of insurance.[3]

Later chapters of this textbook examine insurance from a variety of perspectives.

RISK AND RELATED CONCEPTS

Risk is a complex concept that is difficult to define concisely and has many terms used as substitutes. Two key elements, discussed in the next section of this chapter, are usually associated with the concept of risk. After examining those so-called elements of risk, this chapter will explore several other closely related terms:

- Uncertainty
- Possibility
- Probability
- Loss exposure
- Perils
- Hazards

Elements of Risk

Elements of risk
(1) An uncertain outcome and
(2) the possibility of loss.

Two generally accepted **elements of risk** are the following:

1. Uncertain outcome
2. Possibility of loss

In his *Risk Management* text, Emmett J. Vaughan details those two elements:

> If we were to survey the best-known insurance textbooks used in colleges and universities today, we would find a general lack of agreement concerning the definition of risk. Although the insurance theorists have not agreed on a universal definition, all the definitions share two common elements: indeterminacy and loss.
>
> - The notion of an indeterminate outcome is implicit in all definitions of risk: the outcome must be in question. When risk is said to exist, there must always be at least two possible outcomes. If we know for certain that a loss will occur, there is no risk....
>
> - At least one of the possible outcomes is undesirable. This may be a loss in the generally accepted sense in which something the individual possesses is lost, or it may be a gain smaller than the gain that was

possible. For example, the investor who fails to take advantage of an opportunity "loses" the gain that might have been made. The investor with the choice between two stocks may be said to "lose" if he or she chooses the one that increases in value less than the alternative.[4]

In other words: Whenever risk exists, what will happen is uncertain, and it might be something bad.

Uncertainty

"Uncertainty" appears to be the same as "indeterminate outcome." In his best-selling college textbook, George E. Rejda notes the following, based on the uncertainty concept:

> [R]isk is defined as uncertainty concerning the occurrence of a loss. For example, the risk of being killed in an auto accident is present because uncertainty is present. The risk of lung cancer for smokers is present because uncertainty is present. And the risk of flunking a college course is present because there is uncertainty concerning the grade you will earn.[5]

To some degree, uncertainty—not being certain—represents a state of mind, based on opinion or emotion, rather than objective risk. As noted in the "Individuals' Risk Evaluation" box, differences in the ways people evaluate objective information regarding risks might actually be beneficial in particular situations.

Individuals' Risk Evaluation

Gut rules the measurement. Ask passengers in an airplane during turbulent flying conditions whether each of them has an equal degree of anxiety. Most people know full well that flying in an airplane is far safer than driving in an automobile, but some passengers will keep the flight attendants busy while others will snooze happily regardless of the weather.

And that's a good thing. If everyone valued every risk in precisely the same way, many risk opportunities would be passed up....Think of what life would be like if everyone were phobic about...flying in airplanes, or investing in start-up companies. We are indeed fortunate that human beings differ in their appetite for risk.[6]

Peter L. Bernstein, *Against the Gods*

Uncertainty resulting from a state of mind cannot easily be measured. However, this text will note later that the effects of such uncertainty clearly contribute to the cost of risk.

The uncertainty associated with risk is sometimes characterized in terms of possibility or probability.

Possibility

Possibility means something could happen.

- Someone could correctly answer a series of questions on a television show and become an instant millionaire.
- Someone could be struck by lightning.
- Someone could be injured in an auto accident—unless he or she is on a lifelong ocean cruise or otherwise isolated from modern civilization.

A possibility either exists or does not exist. Someone could become an instant millionaire—which would probably be a happy outcome. Someone faces undesirable risks of being struck by lightning and being injured in an auto accident. Even though auto-related injuries are much more common than lightning strikes to people, both possibilities exist. Other situations, however, are impossible. Unless one is referring to a fairy tale character, there is no possibility whatsoever that someone will turn into a frog.

Possibility exists, or it does not exist, just as a light switch is either on or off, as Exhibit 1-1 depicts.

EXHIBIT 1-1

Possibility

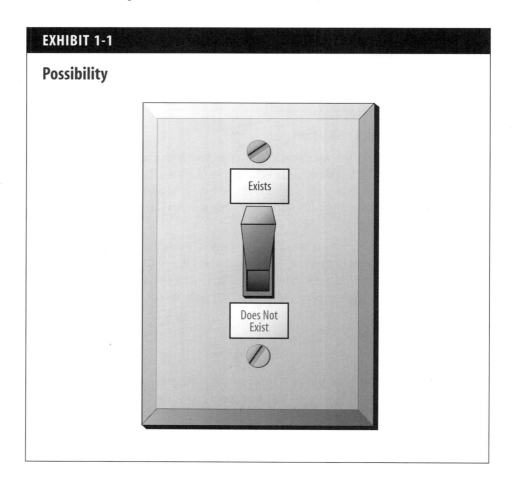

Probability

Probability is the proportion of times that events will occur in the long run. If something can possibly happen at all, its likelihood of happening can be expressed numerically, as a number between zero and one.

Unlike possibility, probability is measurable, as illustrated in Exhibit 1-2. The probability that someone will become an instant millionaire is almost nonexistent, and the probability of being struck by lightning is only slightly greater. The probability of being in an auto accident during the next year, however, is significant. The probability that someone will turn into a frog is zero.

Understanding the probability of various outcomes is a key step in such important matters as prioritizing where risk management attention should be focused, as well as determining what risks can be insured.

Probability
The proportion of times that events will occur in the long run.

EXHIBIT 1-2

Probability—A Hypothetical Illustration

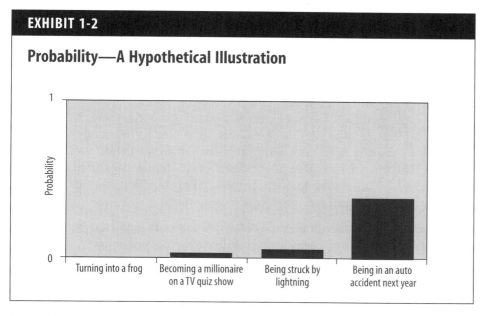

Loss Exposure

Risk involves an uncertain outcome and the possibility of loss. Possibility of loss is the second element of risk. Risks present not only threats—the possibility of losses, but also opportunities—the possibility of rewards. A **loss exposure** is any condition or situation that presents a possibility of loss, whether or not an actual loss occurs.

Loss exposure
Any condition or situation that presents a possibility of loss, whether or not an actual loss occurs.

Evaluating a Loss Exposure

When persons and organizations evaluate a loss exposure's potential effect, they project four loss-exposure dimensions: the frequency, severity, total dollar losses, and timing of a loss. The credibility of these projections is critical to the risk-evaluation process. The greater the credibility (confidence) in the projection, the better the decisions will be about handling loss exposures.

Loss frequency
The number of losses within a specified time period.

Loss severity
The amount, in dollars, of a loss for a specific occurrence.

Total dollar losses
The total dollar amount of losses for all occurrences during a specific time period.

Timing
When losses occur and when loss payments are made.

> ## Four Dimensions of a Loss Exposure
>
> 1. **Loss frequency**—the number of losses (fires, auto accidents, liability claims) within a specified time period.
> 2. **Loss severity**—the amount, in dollars, of a loss for a specific occurrence.
> 3. **Total dollar losses**—the total dollar amount of losses for all occurrences during a specific time period.
> 4. **Timing**—when losses occur and when loss payments are made. The time interval between loss occurrence and a loss payment can be lengthy.

Depending on its use, the term "frequency" may have one of several meanings. For instance, frequency may refer to how often an event occurs, without assigning a numerical value. In this use, "high-frequency losses" are understood to be those that occur more often than others.

A risk manager, an underwriter, or an actuary also might evaluate frequency relative to the number of exposure units. Strictly speaking, this is *relative* frequency. However, the term is commonly simplified to frequency. For example, a company may analyze the frequency of work-related accidents in a year by calculating the number of accidents (100) divided by the number of employees (1,000); relative frequency is 0.10. This text will distinguish frequency when evaluated relative to exposure units.

Credibility
How reliably the frequency, severity, total dollar losses, and timing of a loss can be projected.

After estimating the four dimensions of a loss exposure, a person or an organization should then consider **credibility**, that is, how reliably the frequency, severity, total dollar losses, and timing of a loss can be projected.

Most large organizations experience a high number of relatively small accidental losses, such as those involving minor injuries to employees. Catastrophic losses, such as a large fire and a plant explosion, are more infrequent but have a high severity. Between those two extremes are medium-sized losses that might or might not occur with some regularity.

Types of Loss Exposures

For insurance and risk management purposes, loss exposures can be analyzed in various categories. Those discussed here include the following:

- Property loss exposures
- Liability loss exposures
- Personal or human loss exposures
- Personnel loss exposures
- Exposures to loss of goodwill

- Exposures to loss resulting from failure to perform
- Missed opportunities

Many other categories could, of course, be added to this list.

Property Loss Exposures

Every type of property is exposed to potential losses. Property loss exposures affect both real property (land and any property attached to it) and personal property (all property that is not real property).

A **property loss exposure** is the possibility that a person or an organization will sustain a loss resulting from the damaging, destruction, taking, or loss of use of property in which that person or organization has a financial interest. Damage to property can cause a reduction in that property's value, sometimes to zero. When property is stolen, it might not be damaged, but the owner has still suffered a total loss of that property because the owner cannot use it. In addition to those direct losses, property damage can result in a loss of income because the property cannot be used to generate income or because extra expenses are incurred to continue operations.

Liability Loss Exposures

A **liability loss exposure** is the possibility of a claim alleging a person's or an organization's legal responsibility for injury or damage suffered by another party. Notice the emphasis is on claims, as opposed to the payment of damages. Many liability claims are successfully defended and result in no payment of damages, but defense costs, adverse publicity, and other matters can create a distinct financial loss even for the defendant who prevails.

In practice, risk management and insurance professionals often use shorthand terminology to concisely characterize specific property and liability loss exposures, as shown in the box on the next page.

Personal or Human Loss Exposures

An individual or a family faces risks associated with a family member's illness, death, disability, or unemployment. For example, a family would face a loss of income if the primary breadwinner died. Those individual or family risks are referred to as **personal,** or **human, loss exposures**.

Personnel Loss Exposures

Businesses face similar risks related to key employees' disability, death, retirement, or resignation. These risks are generally referred to as **personnel loss exposures.**

Exposures to Loss of Goodwill

As defined in the dictionary, **goodwill** is an intangible asset that reflects the value added to a business firm as a result of patronage and reputation.[7] Every business, individual, or family is concerned with maintaining its reputation

Property loss exposure
The possibility that a person or an organization will sustain a loss due to the damaging, destruction, taking, or loss of use of property in which that person or organization has a financial interest.

Liability loss exposure
The possibility that a person or an organization will sustain a loss due to a claim alleging legal responsibility for injury or damage suffered by another party.

Personal loss exposure, or **human loss exposure**
The possibility that an individual or a family will sustain a loss due to a family member's illness, death, disability, or unemployment.

Personnel loss exposure
The possibility that an organization will sustain a loss due to a key employee's disability, death, retirement, or resignation.

Goodwill
An intangible asset that reflects the value that reputation and patronage add to an organization. Goodwill is also important to individuals.

Property and Liability Loss Exposure Terminology in Practice

Property

A *property loss* occurs when a person or an organization sustains a loss as the result of the damaging, destruction, taking, or loss of use of property in which that person or organization has a financial interest. The fact that such an event could occur is a *property loss exposure*. The event itself, involving property, cause of loss (peril), and consequences is called a *loss* or, more completely, a *property loss*.

A property loss may be referred to by different labels, depending on whether emphasis is placed on the property, the cause, or the consequences:

- When focusing on the type of property, insurance practitioners often refer to a "building loss" or a "personal property loss," regardless of the peril involved.

- When emphasis is on perils (causes of loss), one might refer to a "fire loss," a "smoke loss," or a "theft loss."

- When focusing on loss consequences, insurance practitioners might refer to a "business income loss," an "extra expense loss," or an "additional living expense loss," regardless of the type of property or perils involved.

- Insurance practitioners might label a loss by referring to the policy providing coverage. Fire damage to a house might be referred to as a "homeowners loss," while concurrent damage to a car in the attached garage might be referred to as an "auto loss."

In practice, these same labels are loosely applied to exposures. One might refer to a building exposure, a fire exposure, a business interruption exposure, or a homeowners exposure.

Liability

Insurance and risk management practitioners loosely refer to specific types of liability losses in many ways, often labeling them according to the type of insurance that might cover the exposure. Consider the following examples:

- A claim for damages arising out of a product defect might be referred to as a "products liability loss," and the possibility of such a claim might be referred to as a "products liability loss exposure."

- The possibility of professional liability claims against a physician might be referred to as a "professional liability exposure" or a "malpractice exposure."

- Losses arising out of an employer's liability under workers compensation statutes might be referred to as "workers compensation losses," and a hazard increasing the potential for loss might be called a "workers compensation loss exposure."

and, for a business, its customers. Goodwill can be lost in many ways, including poor service, obsolete products, or mismanagement.

Goodwill has a monetary value when it increases the value of a corporation or company that is acquired by another. In this context, goodwill might be loosely defined as any premium that a company pays for another company's assets. For a nonprofit organization, goodwill is equivalent to reputation. Every nonprofit understands that its reputation is key to fund-raising, volunteer recruitment, staff retention, and overall good organizational health.

A loss of goodwill can substantially reduce a corporation's value. Goodwill can be lost in connection with property losses or—especially—liability losses. More than one business has been sold at a distressed price because customers lost confidence in a brand after a products liability loss.

Goodwill can be lost in circumstances involving neither loss of one's own tangible property nor a legal liability to pay others for damages. For example, Laurie borrowed her friend's car to run an errand. While the car was legally parked, it was struck by a hit-and-run driver. None of Laurie's own property was damaged, and Laurie was not legally responsible for the damage caused by the hit-and-run driver. However, both Laurie and her friend thought that Laurie had some moral responsibility to pay for the repairs.

Situations of that type often arise when one party has custody of another's property. Similar situations develop when a guest slips and falls, or otherwise sustains injury, while on somebody else's premises under circumstances in which the property owner did nothing to cause or contribute to the injury and is not therefore legally liable for any medical bills.

Many people and businesses pay for damage or injury in such situations because of a sense of obligation or to preserve goodwill. Even though goodwill does not involve traditional property or liability insurance loss exposures, many property and liability insurance policies provide coverages to prevent a loss of goodwill in these situations. Examples include bailees customers insurance in various inland marine forms, "personal property of others" coverages in commercial property forms, and medical-payments-to-others coverages in various liability forms.

Exposures to Loss Resulting From Failure To Perform

Losses occur in a variety of situations that do not involve property damage or destruction, liability claims for damages, or human injury or death. One broad category of risks involves a product's failure to perform as promised. Other examples include a contractor's failure to complete a construction project as scheduled or a debtor's failure to make scheduled payments.

Missed Opportunities

Although most losses involve a direct expense to an organization, some involve a missed opportunity for profit. For example, an organization that delays a decision to modify its product in response to changes in market demand might lose market share and profit that it could have made on that updated product.

Missed Opportunity

Of all sad words of tongue or pen, the saddest are these:

"It might have been!"

John Greanleaf Whittier, "Maud Muller"

Perils and Hazards

Loss exposures involve perils and hazards, and these two risk-related terms are sometimes confused.

Perils

Peril
A cause of loss, such as fire, windstorm, explosion, or theft.

A **peril** is a cause of loss. Fire, windstorm, explosion, and theft, for example, are obvious perils presenting the possibility of loss to property. Other perils are listed in Exhibit 1-3, but even this long list is not exhaustive.

The term "peril" is used when identifying the causes of losses that could occur and when describing the causes of losses that have actually occurred. Although certain measurements indicate the intensity of some perils involving natural events—such as the Richter Scale and the Mercalli Scale applied to earthquakes and the Saffir-Simpson Hurricane Scale, most perils are not measurable. However, the probability of loss or the frequency and severity of past losses by any given peril can often be analyzed statistically.

In practice, "peril" usually refers to a cause of property losses. The causes of liability losses tend to be categorized in other ways, depending on the following:

*   *The legal basis of liability*—for example, common law, statutes, contracts, or
*   *The activity leading to a claim for damages*—for example, owning, operating, maintaining, or using an auto (auto liability exposures); manufacturing or distributing products (products liability exposures); employing workers (workers compensation exposures); or providing professional services (malpractice exposures).

Hazards

Hazard
A condition that increases the frequency or severity of a loss.

A **hazard** is a condition that increases the frequency or severity of a loss. A fire hazard, for example, increases the probability of loss by the peril of fire. Because they increase the likelihood that a loss will occur, hazards tend to *reduce* uncertainty regarding loss; when hazards increase, losses become more likely.

EXHIBIT 1-3

Examples of Property Perils

Aircraft

Animals

Barnacles,
  marine life

Breakage

Burglary

Centrifugal force

Civil commotion

Collapse

Collision or upset

Computer fraud

Computer virus

Condemnation

Confiscation

Contamination,
  pollution

Corrosion

Decay

Delay

Drought

Dust

Earthquake

Electrical overload,
  arcing

Embezzlement

Erosion

Evaporation

Expansive soil

Explosion

Expropriation

Extortion

Falling objects

Faulty design,
  workmanship

Fire

Flood and runoff

Forgery

Fraud

Fungus

Governmental
  seizure

Hail

Human error

Humidity extremes

Hurricane

Insects

Jettison

Labor disturbance

Landslide

Latent defect,
  inherent vice

Lightning

Malicious mischief

Mechanical
  breakdown

Mildew, mold

Misdelivery

Mudslide

Neglect

Perils of the sea

Power outage

Radioactive
  contamination

Rain

Riot

Robbery

Rot

Rust

Sabotage

Shoplifting

Shrinkage

Sinkhole collapse

Smoke

Sonic boom

Spoilage

Sprinkler leakage

Static electricity

Strikes

Subsidence

Temperature
  extremes

Terrorism

Theft

Tidal wave

Tides

Tornado

Trickery

Vandalism

Vehicles

Vibration

Volcanic action

War, military action

Water

Weight of ice,
  snow, sleet

Windstorm

The hazard concept is important to everyone involved in the identification, evaluation, and management of risks. Insurers often identify four hazard categories:

1. Moral hazard
2. Attitudinal hazard (or morale hazard)
3. Physical hazard
4. Legal hazard

Moral hazard
A condition that increases the likelihood that a person will intentionally cause or exaggerate a loss.

Moral hazard is a condition that increases the likelihood that a person will intentionally cause or exaggerate a loss. Some people might tend to act differently once they enter into a contract that shifts the burden of risk to another party. In insurance, moral hazard is a condition that exists when a person tries intentionally to cause a loss, exaggerates a loss that has occurred, or engages in actions that increase the likelihood that a loss may occur. Moral hazard refers not only to outright insurance fraud but also to character weaknesses that present danger signals because they increase the likelihood of fraud.

Most insurance claims are not fraudulent. However, insurance underwriters try to recognize symptoms of moral hazard, such as property that is grossly overinsured. An obsolete building that nobody is willing to buy can quickly be "sold" to the insurance company if it happens to burn while it is insured. Experienced underwriters sometimes joke that the friction between large property insurance policies and undesirable buildings tends to cause fires.

An insured facing serious financial difficulty might present a moral hazard because financial difficulty presents an incentive to commit insurance fraud, sometimes even tempting people who have not previously committed criminal acts. Moral hazard is also considered by an underwriter who is asked to provide employee dishonesty insurance on an employee who has previously stolen from his or her employer. Labor unrest could increase the likelihood of vandalism—or of questionable workers compensation claims.

Insurers are not the only parties affected by moral hazards. Every person or organization must consider the likelihood of vandalism or bodily injury because of crime rates; unsafe business practices; or hostile neighbors, competitors, or employees.

Attitudinal hazard, or **morale hazard**
A condition of carelessness or indifference that increases the frequency or severity of loss.

An **attitudinal hazard** is a condition of carelessness or indifference that increases the frequency or severity of loss. The traditional term, used in most insurance texts, is **morale hazard**. Students always find remembering the difference between moral and morale to be difficult, but the problems associated with a bad attitude cannot be mistaken. That is why the "attitudinal" label is now used. Driving carelessly, failing to lock an unattended building, or failing to clear an icy sidewalk to protect pedestrians are examples of attitudinal (morale) hazard. Emphasis is on carelessness, not the physical condition that sometimes results from carelessness. Physical conditions resulting from carelessness can also be recognized as physical hazards.

A **physical hazard** is a condition of property, persons, or operations that increases the frequency or severity of loss. Inadequate ventilation in a painting area, for example, might increase the likelihood of an explosion. Inadequate ventilation also creates environmental problems for workers and increases the likelihood or severity of workers compensation claims.

Fire safety professionals and property insurance underwriters further distinguish between common hazards and special hazards. *Common hazards* traditionally include smoking and heating hazards—ignition sources encountered in almost every class of property; the smoking hazard might have become less common in recent years. Nearly every building has a heating system, but only an *unsafe* heating system is considered a physical hazard. A safe heating system presents a normal level of risk.

Special hazards are those considered unique to an individual property—such as dip tanks, spray booths, or drying ovens in a metalworking plant.

A **legal hazard** is a condition of the legal environment that increases loss frequency or severity. For example, people in some geographic areas are much more litigious—likely to initiate a lawsuit—than those elsewhere.

A legal hazard can also exist in areas where the courts are considered more likely to hand down an adverse verdict or to grant large damages awards in liability suits. Various trends can also be recognized as legal hazards. For example, an increasing number of decisions against tobacco manufacturers suggests a legal hazard for companies participating in the tobacco industry.

Hazards can have a compounding effect. Compared with the loss probability of a safe driver in a safe car, the probability of an auto accident is increased by either the physical hazard of an unsafe car or the attitudinal hazard of an unsafe driver, and the probability is further increased by the compound effect of an unsafe driver in an unsafe car. Exhibit 1-4 illustrates this relationship.

Physical hazard
A condition of property, persons, or operations that increases the frequency or severity of loss.

Legal hazard
A condition of the legal environment that increases the frequency or severity of loss.

CLASSIFICATIONS OF RISK

Risk can be categorized in several ways. The following classification pairs are discussed in this section:

- Subjective versus objective
- Financial versus nonfinancial
- Diversifiable versus nondiversifiable
- Pure versus speculative

As Exhibit 1-5 shows, these classifications are not mutually exclusive, and all four classification pairs can be applied to any given risk. A later chapter in this book deals with insurable risks, which generally are risks that can be classified as objective, financial, diversifiable, and pure.

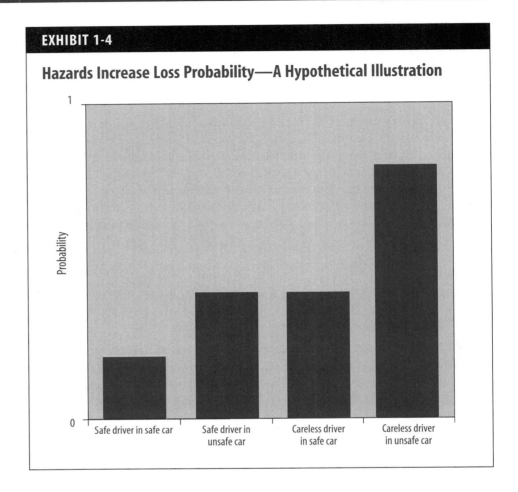

EXHIBIT 1-4

Hazards Increase Loss Probability—A Hypothetical Illustration

Subjective Versus Objective Risk

A person's assessment of the risk in any particular situation can be based on opinions (which are subjective) or facts (which are objective). Emotion, as well as reason, often governs decisions, especially when factual information is elusive and facts clash with perceptions. In theory, at least, rational risk management decisions are based on facts.

Subjective risk
The perceived amount of risk—uncertainty based on a person's opinion.

Subjective risk is the perceived amount of risk—uncertainty based on a person's opinion. Because it is based on opinion rather than fact, subjective risk cannot be measured. However, it is an important factor that contributes to many risk management or other risk-related decisions. Subjective risk can exist even where objective risk does not exist. (See the "Christopher Columbus" box on a following page.)

Objective risk
The measurable variation in uncertain outcomes based on facts and data.

Objective risk is the measurable variation in uncertain outcomes based on facts and data.

EXHIBIT 1-5

Classifications of Risk

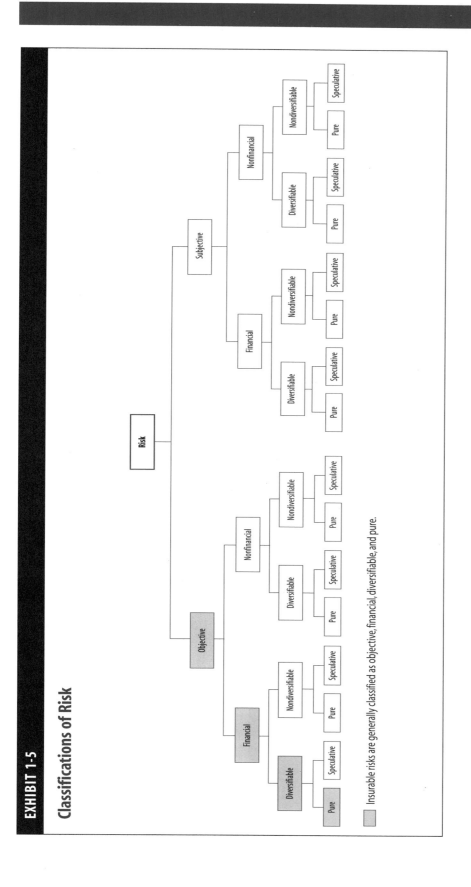

Insurable risks are generally classified as objective, financial, diversifiable, and pure.

Christopher Columbus

Columbus believed that the world was round and that he could reach the Orient by sailing westward. Many of his contemporaries, however, believed that the world was flat and that Columbus's ships would fall off the edge if he sailed too far west. Uncertainty of loss existed when Columbus set sail, even though we now know that there was no possibility of that particular loss.[8]

Herbert S. Denenberg et al., *Risk and Insurance*

The differences between objective risk and subjective risk were vividly illustrated in a United Kingdom study by the Royal Society.[9] Researchers asked a number of people to estimate how many people died in one year from different causes of death. These estimates were compared with the real number of deaths for each cause. Exhibit 1-6 illustrates the results of the study. If an estimate were exactly correct, then the point plotted on the graph would be on the diagonal line. For any point above the line, the number of deaths per year was overestimated (estimated deaths per year is higher than the real number of deaths). For causes below the line, deaths were underestimated. The graph reveals a number of interesting features:

- Dramatic events such as tornado, flood, and botulism are overestimated. One reason for this phenomenon is that certain causes of death seem to receive more media attention than others.

- Medical and less-media-related events involving diabetes, heart disease, and strokes are underestimated by the public. These are common events with which we are all familiar.

- People surveyed tend to overestimate low-frequency events and to underestimate high-frequency events.

For events that are on the same horizontal level, respondents estimated the same number of deaths, but the actual number was quite different. For example, people estimated that pregnancy and diabetes had the same death rate, but in fact diabetes accounted for about eighty times as many deaths as did pregnancy.

Causes of death on the same vertical line imply that the respondents estimated quite different numbers of people dying from causes that actually accounted for the same death rate. Roughly the same number of people die from motor accidents as from diabetes, yet the estimates are far different.

This study illustrates that objective risk and subjective risk can vastly differ, possibly for reasons such as these:

Familiarity—People's perception of risk is influenced by their level of familiarity with the risky event. A person who is very familiar with a risk and possibly faces it daily might understate the real level of risk. Those whose awareness is raised by media exposure might overstate the real level of risk.

Control—People generally understate the level of risk when they feel they are in control. Although many people feel uneasy about air travel, there is a much larger probability of serious injury on the roads. Most people believe they can control their cars, but they have no control over the airplane.

Personal or societal effect—Some people tend to overestimate their own personal risks while understating the risk to society. Others have the "it can't happen to me" syndrome: a general belief, sometimes against all evidence, that "other people" are involved in floods, murders, fires, accidents, and so on. Perhaps some people believe they escape such mishaps because of their own skill and judgment.

EXHIBIT 1-6

Subjective Versus Objective Risk

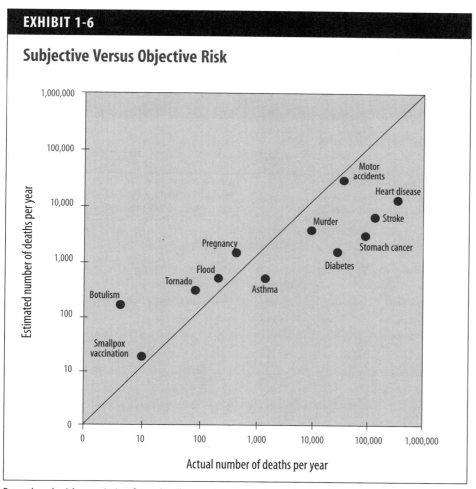

Reproduced with permission from the Chartered Insurance Institute, London.

Frequency and severity—Evidence suggests that some people focus on an event's likelihood, regardless of its severity, while others almost ignore the chance and concentrate on the effect. For example, the probability of a major nuclear event is supposedly low, but what influences most people is the concern that any such event is likely to be a major disaster.

A similar point was made by a survey comparing perceptions with reality regarding the ten leading causes of workplace accidents, shown in Exhibit 1-7. As the exhibit shows, the surveyed executives, who were responsible for workers compensation and commercial insurance at 200 companies in a variety of industries, reported that repetitive motion was the most important cause of workplace accidents and one on which they would focus their resources. However, data show that five other accident causes produced greater direct costs. Sound risk management often seems counterintuitive because it may appear to pay too little attention to the things that concern most people.

Success in both risk management and insurance depends on an ability to objectively identify and analyze risks. Yet, subjectivity is also necessary because risk analysis involves an attempt to predict the future. Sound risk analysis inevitably relies on objective information regarding the past, combined with subjective projections for the future.

EXHIBIT 1-7

Employer Perception Versus Reality

Ranking	Reality — Liberty Mutual Workplace Safety Index—The ten leading causes of workplace accidents ranked by their direct costs.	Est. national workers' comp direct cost:	Perceptions — Liberty Mutual Executive Survey of Workplace Safety—Accident causes ranked by executive concern.
1	Overexertion—injuries from lifting, lowering, pushing or pulling	$9.8 billion	Repetitive motion
2	Falls same level	$4.4 billion	Overexertion—injuries from lifting, lowering, pushing or pulling
3	Bodily reaction—injuries resulting from bending, standing and reaching, but not including slipping and tripping without falling	$3.6 billion	Highway accidents
4	Falls to lower level	$3.6 billion	Bodily reaction—injuries resulting from bending, standing and reaching, but not including slipping and tripping without falling
5	Struck by object	$3.4 billion	Falls to lower level
6	Repetitive motion	$2.3 billion	Becoming caught in or compressed by equipment
7	Highway accidents	$2.1 billion	Falls same level
8	Being struck against an object	$1.9 billion	Struck by object
9	Becoming caught in or compressed by equipment	$1.6 billion	Contact with temperature extremes
10	Contact with temperature extremes	$0.3 billion	Being struck against an object

A gap may exist between risk management executives' perception of the leading causes of workplace accidents and an actual ranking of these accident causes based on their direct cost to companies.

Liberty Mutual Press Release, August 28, 2001.

Financial Versus Nonfinancial Risk

Risk involves an uncertain outcome and the possibility of loss. The gain or loss might or might not involve money.

Financial risk is the risk of change in value, measured in money. It can be measured in dollars, pounds, euros, yen, or some other currency unit. A financial risk involves the possibility of gaining or losing money. Nonfinancial risks are not about money or value. However, the distinction is not as obvious as it seems.

Financial risk
The risk of change in value, measured in money.

The investment risks associated with stocks and bonds are clearly financial. Property loss exposures are financial because they are based on property's intrinsic value and its use value. Even softer values, such as obsolescence, can ultimately be measured in dollar terms. Likewise, liability loss exposures involve money paid to defend against a claim, as well as money paid as damages.

Nonfinancial risks are associated with matters such as health, reputation, and relationships. Although medical bills can be measured in dollar terms, money alone cannot restore mobility to a person paralyzed as the result of an accident. Money does not eliminate pain and suffering. Money does not replace a lost companion. Money does not replace personal or business goodwill lost as the result of adverse publicity, whether the publicity is true or false.

Nonfinancial risk
The risk that is associated with matters such as health, reputation, and relationships.

The distinction between financial and nonfinancial risks might confuse readers who recognize that liability losses often involve the payment of money damages as compensation for pain and suffering and other noneconomic damages. The difference is one of perspective. Every driver faces the *financial* risk that he or she might have to pay damages resulting from an auto accident. Every driver also faces the *nonfinancial* risk that he or she might endure pain and suffering after an accident, thus suffering a noneconomic, *nonfinancial* loss. Another driver who is legally responsible for the same accident might be required to pay *monetary* damages to compensate the innocent, injured driver. Some aspects of no-fault auto insurance are based on the recognition that money is not an exact substitute for painlessness or lack of suffering.

A special form of financial risk is the risk that a firm will not be able to meet its fixed financial obligations, such as the principal and interest payment on its debt. A firm is obligated by contract to meet these commitments, and doing so is often considered an important risk management objective. A firm's exposure to financial risk increases as the firm uses higher levels of debt financing.

Diversifiable Versus Nondiversifiable Risk

Diversification refers to a concept commonly called spread of risk. The usual metaphor is not putting all of one's eggs into the same basket. When a basket containing eggs is dropped, all of the eggs in it are likely to break at the same time. Unless they are hard-boiled eggs, one incident to a basket containing all of one's eggs creates a total loss with little possibility of salvage. Putting the eggs into two or more baskets spreads the risk and reduces the likelihood that all the eggs will be destroyed. But this is an example of risk *management*, which this text will discuss later.

Diversifiable risk
The risk that affects only some individuals, some businesses, or some small groups.

Diversifiable risk, sometimes called *unsystematic risk* or *particular risk*, is the risk that affects only some individuals, some businesses, or some small groups. It means that gains or losses on exposures within a portfolio of risk exposures tend to occur randomly to one another. Take building fires, for example. Unless two buildings are located next to each other or face a common loss by a forest fire or brush fire, usually no direct relationship exists between the two buildings' fire loss exposures. An insurance company can diversify the risks associated with fire insurance by insuring many buildings with different exposures, in different locations. Other diversifiable risks would include the chance of losses from lightning strikes, auto accidents, embezzlement, or disability. A person investing in various businesses might face the possibility that any one of them will not be a successful business venture; this, too, is a diversifiable risk. Investors diversify their holdings hoping those that succeed more than offset those that fail.

Nondiversifiable risk
The risk that affects a large segment of society at the same time.

Nondiversifiable risk, sometimes called *systematic risk* or *fundamental risk*, is the risk that affects a large segment of society at the same time. It means that gains or losses arising from risk exposures in a portfolio are correlated. That is, gains or losses tend to occur simultaneously rather than randomly. For example, under certain monetary conditions, interest rates increase for all firms at the same time. If an insurance company were to insure firms against interest-rate increases, it would not be able to diversify its portfolio of interest-rate risks by underwriting a large number of insureds, because all of them would suffer losses at the same time. Other nondiversifiable risks include potential losses due to hurricanes, floods, war, economic inflation, or widespread unemployment.

Dealing with diversifiable risks is generally considered the responsibility of the individuals or businesses exposed to these risks, who often finance the risks with insurance. Dealing with nondiversifiable risks is generally thought to be the responsibility of society as a whole, often working through social insurance or government programs, as Chapter 6 will discuss.

The distinction between nondiversifiable and diversifiable risks is not always clearcut, and risks can even shift from one category to the other. For example, Mary's unemployment might be the result of her laziness or disability resulting from injury (diversifiable), or it might be the result of an economic downturn (nondiversifiable). A successful products liability claim against a specific manufacturer, such as a tobacco company (diversifiable), might lead to similar claims against all manufacturers in that industry (nondiversifiable). For further examples, see the box on the following page.

Although private insurance tends to concentrate on diversifiable risks, and government insurance is often suitable for nondiversifiable risks, a clear line of demarcation does not exist. Various social insurance programs and government-mandated private insurance plans do address diversifiable risks. Examples include workers compensation plans and compulsory auto insurance programs. Also, private insurers have managed to deal with some nondiversifiable risks, such as earthquakes and hurricanes, by pooling their resources. Insurers also spread such risks through diversification—that is, insuring a variety of exposures not common to a single loss. Upcoming chapters will examine those issues in more detail.

Example: Diversifiable and Nondiversifiable Risk

The owner of a dwelling located in Miami, Florida, faces the risk of windstorm loss to the dwelling. The risk could be reduced through a loss-sharing agreement with other dwelling owners in Miami, but the effectiveness of the pooling arrangement would be limited by the possibility of windstorm damaging a large number of dwellings in the pool at the same time—the aftermath of Hurricane Andrew is a powerful illustration of this point. A pooling agreement with owners of dwellings situated in other cities such as New York or St. Louis would be more effective in reducing their risk. However, even if the pooling arrangement were extended worldwide, the participants in the pool would still face risk; the remaining risk after the pooling agreement is nondiversifiable. Presumably, this nondiversifiable risk would be the risk associated with not being able to predict the *number* of serious windstorms and the resulting damage worldwide in a given year.[10]

Emmett J. Vaughan, *Risk Management*

Pure Versus Speculative Risk

Pure risks involve only the chance of loss or no loss, whereas speculative risks involve the chance of loss, no loss, or gain.

A **pure risk** is the chance of loss but no chance of gain. For example, the owner of a house faces the risk associated with a possible fire loss. If the house burns, the owner will suffer a financial loss. If the house does not burn, the owner's financial condition is unchanged. Pure risks are always undesirable.

Pure risk
The risk with the chance of loss but no chance of gain.

A **speculative risk** is the chance of gain as well as the chance of loss. Gambling is often used as an example of speculative risk (see the following box).

Speculative risk
The risk with the chance of gain as well as the chance of loss.

Every business venture involves speculative risks. For example, an investor who purchases an apartment building to rent to tenants expects to profit from this investment, but the venture could be unprofitable if, for example, tenants find the building unattractive, or if competition or government-imposed rental price controls limit the amount that can be charged.

> ### Gambling Versus Insurance
>
> Gambling, which is a special type of speculation, can exhibit many of the attributes of insurance. Perhaps this is the reason so many uninformed persons think of insurance as gambling and sometimes even feel that they have "lost the bet" if they fail to have a loss equal to the cost of insurance. The distinction is not in the method of operation, which may appear similar, but in the fact that insurance is concerned with an existing risk. Risk as an existing condition is what removes insurance from the category of gambling. **Insurance does not create risk, but it transfers and reduces a risk that already exists. Contrast this to a bet: No risk exists before, but one is created at the time of the gaming transaction**, thus putting values in jeopardy that were not in jeopardy before the bet.[11] [emphasis added]
>
> Burton T. Beam, Jr., et al., *Fundamentals of Insurance for Financial Planning*

The purchase of stocks, as well as other financial investments, involves a distinct set of speculative risks described in Exhibit 1-8. Other business activities can involve speculative risks such as the following:

- *Price risk*—uncertainty over the size of cash flows due to possible changes in the cost of raw materials and other inputs (lumber, gas, electricity), as well as changes in the market for completed products and other outputs.

- *Credit risk*—the risk that customers and other creditors will fail to make promised payments. Although a credit risk is particularly significant for banks and other financial institutions, it can be relevant to every firm with accounts receivable.

Insurance deals primarily with risks of loss, not risks of gain. Traditional insurance textbooks underscore this important, though obvious, point by highlighting the distinction between pure risks and speculative risks. However, the distinction is not as clearcut as one might think. In fact, the earlier examples (home ownership and apartment ownership) should have raised some questions among critical readers.

Many risks have both pure and speculative aspects. Although a homeowner faces a pure risk of loss by fire or other perils, the homeowner also faces the risk that the market value of the house itself might increase or decrease during any year. Meanwhile, the real estate investor faces not only business risks but also property loss exposures. The investor could gain or lose because rental income is adequate or inadequate, and the investor might suffer a loss if the apartment building sustains a fire. To properly manage these investments, the apartment owner must consider both speculative and pure risks. Likewise, the homeowner, while buying insurance or taking other measures to address property loss exposures, should also consider home ownership's business aspects, including obtaining a favorable mortgage and maintaining the property to enhance its resale value.

EXHIBIT 1-8

Investment Risks

Every investment involves certain speculative risks:

*   *Inflation risk*—the risk associated with the loss of purchasing power because of an overall increase in the economy's price level.

*   *Market risk*—the risk associated with fluctuations in prices of financial securities, such as stocks and bonds.

*   *Interest-rate risk*—the risk associated with a security's future value due to changes in interest rates.

*   *Financial risk*—the risk associated with the ownership of securities in a company having a relatively large amount of debt on its balance sheet. If the company defaults on its debt obligations, its creditors might force it into bankruptcy.

*   *Business risk*—the risk associated with the fluctuation in a company's earnings and its ability to pay dividends and interest.

*   *Liquidity risk*—the risk associated with being able to liquidate an investment easily and at a reasonable price.

Although the differences between pure and speculative risks are blurred, distinguishing between a given activity's pure and speculative risks is important because those risks must often be handled differently.

THE COST OF RISK

Because of practical limitations, businesses usually do not measure their risk costs with complete precision. However, every business must recognize the factors affecting risk costs to understand how those costs can be managed.

Pure risks can only reduce an organization's value. The discussion here emphasizes pure risks that can be treated with traditional risk management techniques such as insurance. The cost of risk represents the extent to which an organization's value has been affected by its risks and indicates how much the organization's value might be increased if risks are reduced.

Cost-of-risk measurements indicate not only the current cost of risk for any organization or group of organizations but also how the cost of risk changes over time and by how much. That information can be useful in determining whether to allocate resources to risk management activities.

Such risk-cost calculations can also be used in comparing organizations or operations within an organization. Knowing an organization's risk costs would help the organization to assess whether it controls its risks as well as others in the same industry do.

Cost-of-Risk Data

The year 2000 cost of risk among United States corporations was $4.83 for each $1,000 in revenue, according to the most recent annual cost-of-risk survey.[12] Knowing only that number is not particularly helpful; however, recognizing how the cost of risk has been measured can be useful. Examining how the cost of risk changes over time and how one organization's cost of risk compares with that of other organizations can also be helpful.

The annual study cited here evaluates the cost of risk that applies to three exposure groups, corresponding roughly to exposures that are insurable using property and liability insurance: property, tort liability, and occupational disease or injury. The study considers six types of costs within the three exposures:

1. Insurance premiums
2. Retained losses
3. Internal administration
4. Outside services
5. Financial guarantees
6. Fees, taxes, and similar expenses[13]

The study results are based on information gathered through a survey of several hundred risk managers. In addition to this gross figure, the published survey also compares loss costs over time and presents considerable detailed information specified by industry. This additional information can be used in comparing various organizations' cost of risk.

Hidden Costs of Risk

Long before modern cost-of-risk studies, researchers demonstrated that accident costs are usually underestimated. Several classic loss control studies support the premise that loss prevention has a much larger effect than can usually be measured.

In his classic work on this topic, Herbert W. Heinrich concluded that the cost of industrial accidents is usually stated only in terms of compensation paid the injured employee for lost time and medical expenses. The actual costs, however, are much greater because of "incidental" or "hidden" costs. The following are included among these hidden costs:[14]

- Cost of time lost by injured employee.
- Cost of time lost by other employees who stop work.
- Cost of time lost by foremen, supervisors, or other executives.
- Cost of time spent on the case by first-aid attendants and hospital department staff, when not paid for by the insurance carrier.
- Cost due to damage to the machine, tools, or other property or to the spoilage of material.

- Incidental cost due to interference with production, failure to fill orders on time, loss of bonuses, payment of forfeits, and other similar causes.

- Cost to employee under employee welfare and benefit systems.

- Cost to employer in continuing the wages of the injured employee in full, after his or her return—even though the employee's services may for a time be worth only about half of their normal value.

- Cost due to the loss of profit on the injured employee's productivity and on the idle machines.

- Cost that occurs in consequence of the excitement or weakened morale due to the accident.

- Overhead cost per injured employee—the expense of light, heat, rent, and other items, which continues while the injured employee is a nonproducer.

Following detailed research that attempted to measure the foregoing costs, Heinrich concluded that the indirect costs of industrial accidents are four times as great as the direct costs that are usually measured. Heinrich did not contend that his 4-to-1 indirect-to-direct-cost ratio applied to every accident in every plant.

Other writers have challenged the accuracy of his 4-to-1 ratio, examined other types of accidents, and identified other indirect costs that result from accidents.[15] Except for research purposes, identifying and measuring the indirect costs of every accident are not feasible. The issue here is not the measurement, but the lesson it teaches: Although direct accident costs can easily be measured, they are like the tip of the proverbial iceberg that sticks above the surface. The portion of the iceberg that looms beneath the surface can be much larger, and it is especially dangerous because it cannot readily be seen.

The overall effect of losses is much greater than the direct loss itself. Heinrich and other researchers have identified some of the other cost-producing factors that often are not considered.

Cost-of-Risk Components

In their 1999 textbook, fifty years after Heinrich's classic work, Scott E. Harrington and Gregory R. Neihaus identify five components of the cost of risk:

1. Expected cost of losses

2. Cost of loss control—including the cost of increased precautions and limits on risky activity

3. Cost of loss financing—including the cost of self-insurance, the loading in insurance premiums, and the transaction costs in arranging insurance

4. Cost of internal risk-reduction methods—transaction costs associated with achieving and managing diversification, as well as the cost of obtaining and analyzing information to obtain more accurate cost forecasts

5. Cost of residual uncertainty—including the effect of uncertainty on the price customers are willing to pay for a firm's products or the amount they are willing to pay for its stock[16]

The last item in this list introduces an additional notion, the cost of uncertainty. Because uncertainty is a state of mind involving subjective risk, it is difficult to measure. However, uncertainty coupled with risk aversion can result in missed opportunities. Some risk management techniques improve understanding and therefore help to reduce uncertainty and its related costs.

SUMMARY

This chapter has shown that students of risk management can find many ways to think about risks. But students might also be wondering: What is the value in this analysis?

People in the risk business—and that includes everyone working with insurance and risk management—must recognize risk's many implications. Even though this chapter has not stated a formal definition of "risk," it has viewed it from several angles. While risk sounds negative, risks present not only problems but also opportunities. When risk exists, what will happen is not certain, *and* it might be something bad. That is because risks involve both an indeterminate outcome and a possibility of loss. Those elements present challenges that must be managed, and they can be managed, as upcoming chapters will demonstrate.

Risk is sometimes associated with uncertainty, but uncertainty can be a subjective state of mind that has little relationship to measurable, objective risks. Someone dealing with any risk should recognize the difference between facts and opinions and know which is involved in evaluating the risk.

Many events are possible. Knowing that something can happen is not nearly as useful as recognizing the probability that it will happen. Later chapters will discuss the risk management process that identifies possible losses, analyzes their probability, and develops measures to reduce the risk by removing the possibility of loss or altering its probability. In preparation for this analysis, Chapter 2 will take a close look at the nature of probability.

Loss exposures involve the negative side of risk, the possibility of loss that is not accompanied by the possibility of gain. Insurance deals with loss exposures, but insurance is not the only tool for this purpose. Insurance is often used for property, liability, personal, and personnel loss exposures but is not necessarily suitable for some of the risks involving loss of goodwill or failure of others.

Perils and hazards are often associated with loss exposures, and this chapter has analyzed the distinction between these terms. When persons and organizations attempt to identify loss exposures, they must recognize what perils, or causes, can operate to cause a loss, and they should identify and analyze those conditions (hazards) that can increase the consequences of loss. Often, various risk management techniques can be used to deal with specific perils or to eliminate or reduce specific hazards.

Risks can be categorized in various ways. As this text progresses, it will occasionally refer to the different risk classifications that have been merely identified here. But—to briefly peek ahead—these distinctions are relevant in determining which risks are good candidates for insurance and, conversely, which risks are best handled using other risk management techniques. As noted here, insurance is most often used for risks that are objective, financial, diversifiable, and pure.

Finally, this chapter examined the cost-of-risk concept. Many factors should be considered in evaluating the cost of risk, although many significant risk-associated costs cannot easily be seen or measured.

CHAPTER NOTES

1. G. C. A. Dickson, *Corporate Risk Management* (London: Witherby, 1989), p. 1.

2. International Organization for Standardization (ISO)/TMB Working Group on Risk Management Terminology, "The Second Working Draft of Risk Management Terminology for Comment," Toronto Meeting, April 1999, p. 1, World Wide Web: http://www.airm.org/au/index.cfm?L1=1&L2=2&item=176.

3. National Association of Insurance Commissioners, *Definition of Insurance* (Kansas City: NAIC, Draft: August 4, 2000).

4. Emmett J. Vaughan, *Risk Management* (New York: John Wiley & Sons, 1997), p. 8.

5. George E. Rejda, *Principles of Risk Management and Insurance*, 6th ed. (Reading, Mass.: Addison Wesley, 1998), p. 5.

6. Peter L. Bernstein, *Against the Gods* (New York: John Wiley & Sons, 1996), p. 105.

7. *Webster's New World Dictionary*, Third College Edition (New York: Prentice Hall, 1988), p. 581.

8. Herbert S. Denenberg, Robert D. Eilers, G. Wright Hoffman, Chester A. Kline, Joseph J. Melone, and H. Wayne Snider, *Risk and Insurance* (Englewood Cliffs, N.J.: Prentice Hall, Inc., 1964), p. 5.

9. The presentation here summarizes a discussion in *Risk and Insurance* (with special reference to Lloyds) (London: Chartered Insurance Institute, 1999), pp. 3/5–3/7. Exhibit 1-6 also originates from this material.

10. Emmett J. Vaughan, *Risk Management* (New York: John Wiley & Sons, 1997), p. 8.

11. Burton T. Beam, Jr., David L. Bickelhaupt, and Robert M. Crowe, *Fundamentals of Insurance for Financial Planning* (Bryn Mawr, Pa.: The American College, 2001), p. 12. Copyright 2001. Used with permission.

12. Ernst & Young and Risk and Insurance Management Society, Inc., *2001 RIMS Benchmark Survey* (New York: Risk and Insurance Management Society, 2000). Author's note: Some forecasters project a much higher cost of risk for future years because of losses stemming from the terrorist attacks in the United States on September 11, 2001, and from a hardening insurance market.

13. *1999 RIMS Benchmark Survey* (New York: Risk and Insurance Management Society, 1999), p. 4.

14. Herbert W. Heinrich, *Industrial Accident Prevention*, 4th ed. (New York: McGraw-Hill Book Co., 1949), pp. 51–52. In 1980, a fifth edition of *Industrial Accident Prevention* was published, containing revisions by Dan Peterson and Nester Roos.

15. Examples include R. H. Simonds and J. W. Grimaldi, *Safety Management*, 5th ed. Des Plaines, Ill.: (American Society of Saftey Engineers, 1994) and F. E. Bird and G. L. Germain, *Damage Control* (New York: American Management Association, 1966).

16. Scott E. Harrington and Gregory R. Niehaus, *Risk Management and Insurance*, (Boston: McGraw-Hill, 1999), pp. 22–24.

Chapter 2

Direct Your Learning

Evaluating Risk

After learning the subject matter of this chapter, you should be able to:

■ Interpret the information provided in a simple probability distribution and explain how that information might be used in making basic risk management decisions.

■ Explain how various measures of central tendency and measures of dispersion can be used in evaluating the probabilities associated with risk.

■ Explain why considering the credibility of data used in making risk management decisions is important.

■ Distinguish between correlated and uncorrelated risks.

■ Explain how an individual or organization might apply probability concepts to reduce its risks and make its future more projectable.

Develop Your Perspective

What are the main topics covered in the chapter?

This chapter outlines the process of evaluating risk by describing how probability and the tools for measuring probability help risk managers project outcomes.

Examine the data that your organization manages.

- What tools could you apply to analyze these data to determine the probability of loss?

Why is it important to know these topics?

By contrasting different types of risks and examining the statistical tools used to calculate the degree of risk, you will begin to understand how and why organizations evaluate data and manage risk exposures toward certain outcomes.

Using the data you gathered above, imagine that some of the critical data changed.

- How would your analysis of the risk change?

How can you use this information?

Assess your critical data.

- What changes would you recommend to reduce the uncertainty associated with both risks of loss and opportunity?

Chapter 2

Evaluating Risk

Risk management and insurance are possible because uncertain outcomes tend to follow a pattern based on probability.

When watching or listening to a weather forecast, people receive useful information expressed as a numerical probability. For example, a weather-person might state that a 60 percent chance of rain exists tomorrow. This information is likely to affect some decisions people make, such as what they will wear to work tomorrow or whether they will carry an umbrella. They might apply some judgment based on past experience with weather forecasts. Before tomorrow ends, they will find out whether they should have carried an umbrella. But risk-related decisions like carrying an umbrella must be made before knowing the outcome of a decision. An umbrella is needed before it starts to rain. Likewise, risk managers need to make advance decisions about the future, based on their assessments of what decisions will produce the best outcomes. And insurers need to project what their losses will be to charge an appropriate premium.

Matters of probability usually involve a range of different possible outcomes, each with its own probability. Even the weather forecast with a 60 percent chance of rain implies one of at least two possible outcomes: (1) rain and (2) no rain. An optimistic weather forecaster might predict exactly the same weather by describing a 40 percent chance that it will *not* rain. A more sophisticated forecast might also include the probabilities of other forms of precipitation such as dew, fog, hail, snow, or sleet.

To understand risk management and insurance, one must understand basic probability concepts. The approach in this chapter avoids complicated mathematics, although it does require basic arithmetic and an ability to interpret simple graphs. The chapter begins with an everyday example involving the probability of auto collision losses. Every auto insurance buyer deals with the issues discussed in this example. Next, the chapter will analyze some basic ways in which statistical data—especially data about the past—can be organized, used, and interpreted in making projections about the future. Finally, the chapter will use the City Newspaper case to introduce the principle that risk management can reduce the uncertainty associated with both risks of loss and opportunity.

PROBABILITY DISTRIBUTION: PURE RISK EXAMPLE

To launch the discussion of probability, this chapter uses a case study about a simple probability distribution involving the auto collision damage loss exposure of Justin, a fictitious driver. Because the exposure involves only the possibility of damage to Justin's car, and no possibility of gain,[1] Justin's risk would be categorized as a *pure* risk. Such a risk is also a *financial, diversifiable* risk, meaning that it pertains to a change in value—measured in money—and affects only Justin. Evaluating Justin's risk, or probability of loss, can be either *objective*, based on facts, or *subjective*, based on opinions and emotions. Based on this evaluation, Justin might then purchase insurance to protect against his risks.

As Justin analyzes his auto risks, he must first evaluate the cost of the insurance compared with the losses it would cover. For example, Justin probably would not be willing to pay $20,000 to insure a car worth $20,000.[2] And he would need to weigh the amount he could lose ($20,000) against the chances of losing it. Similarly, if Justin owned a $100,000 home on a mountaintop, the home's value might be at risk, but the risk of flooding is small. Therefore, Justin would probably not buy flood insurance.

Probability distribution
A list of probabilities for a set of values that indicates how the probabilities are distributed.

For his auto insurance, before Justin decides whether to purchase collision insurance at a specific premium or whether to choose a particular deductible on his policy, he could create an estimated probability distribution, shown in Exhibit 2-1, to help him analyze his risk. A **probability distribution** is a list of probabilities for a set of values that indicates how the probabilities are distributed. It is a statistical representation of the chance of a particular event

---

EXHIBIT 2-1

Estimated Probability Distribution Table

Probability of collision damage to Justin's car next year

Severity of Damage	Probability of Damage
$0	0.40
$1–250	0.25
$251–500	0.12
$501–1,000	0.09
$1,001–5,000	0.06
$5,001–10,000	0.05
$10,001–20,000	0.03
Total	1.00

happening, such as an auto collision damage loss to Justin's car. If Justin correctly estimates how many losses he is likely to suffer, and their degree of severity, he will be better prepared to decide whether to purchase insurance and to decide how much insurance would adequately cover his losses.

To interpret the data in the following exhibits, remember the questions behind the probabilities. For Justin, consider the following questions: If Justin had no accidents last year, does that mean he will have no accidents next year? What is the likelihood that Justin will be in an accident next year? What is the probability that he will have a minor accident or a serious one? Because he is a particularly bad driver, Justin is more likely to be involved in a collision next year. Justin is also more likely to have a minor collision (bumper scuffs, parking lot dings, or minor scratches) than he is to have a major accident with serious damage. Keep in mind that the past may serve as a good projection of the future, even though nothing guarantees that the future will be exactly like the past.

For the purposes of this case study, fictitious numbers were created to represent Justin's estimated probabilities of loss to his $20,000 vehicle. In actual situations, most people would not know their exact probabilities of loss, but they could combine estimates with judgment to make informed projections. Insurance companies and risk managers usually have more reliable statistics than those used in this case study, based on several years' experience with many different exposure units (drivers).

Some of the dollar ranges for severity of damage in Exhibit 2-1 reflect the different deductibles that Justin could purchase to cover his collision losses. Collision coverage always includes a deductible, namely, a portion of the loss the insured must pay before the insurer contributes. People generally have a choice of deductibles. If Justin chooses a $250 deductible, for example, his insurance company will pay the cost of any collision damage over $250,[3] after Justin pays the first $250. For collisions in which the damage is less than $250, Justin must pay all losses and receives no insurance payment.

The information in Exhibit 2-1 also appears in Exhibit 2-2. However, Exhibit 2-2 depicts these probabilities in a bar graph to better illustrate the patterns in the relationship between the probability of damage occurring and the severity of damage.

The probabilities shown in the exhibits indicate the likelihood of each outcome. For example, there is a 0.40 probability that Justin's car will have no collision damage next year. The probability distribution also implies a 60 percent chance that Justin's car will have some damage. (See the "Expressing Probability" box.)

Expressing Probability

What does it mean to say there is a 0.40 probability that someone's car will have no collision damage next year?

- *Percentage*: Because 0.40 is just another way of saying 40%, it means that a person has a 40% chance of having no collision damage next year. It also means he or she has a 60% chance of having some collision damage next year because probabilities must always add up to 100% or 1.

- *Fraction*: Expressed as a fraction, 0.40 is the same as 40/100, 4/10, or 2/5.

- *Odds*: A gambler might say the person has 4 to 6 odds of not having collision damage next year.

Specifically, what do Justin's data show? Because the collision damage to Justin's car will never be less than $0 or greater than $20,000, the probability distribution chart shows all possible outcomes.[4] This is because the sum of the probabilities listed equals 1. (0.40 + 0.25 + 0.12 + 0.09 + 0.06 + 0.05 + 0.03 = 1.00.) With a probability of 1.00, it is 100 percent certain that one of these outcomes will occur. This point is depicted in Exhibit 2-3, which takes the same data from Exhibits 2-1 and 2-2 and displays them vertically instead of horizontally.

How can Justin interpret these data? The data in the probability distributions imply a 0.60 probability that Justin will have some collision damage next year. They also suggest a 0.65 probability that Justin will not have collision damage greater than $250. This is because the probability of no collision damage is 0.40, and the probability of collision damage between $1 and $250 is 0.25. When those numbers are added, the probability equals 0.65. So with a $250 deductible, there is a 0.65 probability, a 65 percent chance, that Justin will not have a collision claim next year that his insurer would pay.

Similarly, a 0.35 probability (a 35 percent chance) that Justin will have a covered claim exceeding $250 next year exists. How was that figure determined? It was calculated by adding all the probabilities in the chart over $250 (0.12 + 0.09 + 0.06 + 0.05 + 0.03 = 0.35, or 35 percent). Another way to reach this same result is to add the probabilities of losses under $250, which is 0.65, and subtract that number from 1.00 (the probability of all possible outcomes).

What would Justin pay to insure his car next year with a $250 deductible? What would he pay for insurance with a $500 deductible, or with a $1,000 deductible? The cost would be lower with a higher deductible, but is it worth the premium savings to put more of Justin's money at risk?

Although Exhibits 2-1, 2-2, and 2-3 illustrate the probabilities of collision damage to Justin's car in just one year, they could also be used every year to

EXHIBIT 2-2

Estimated Probability Distribution of Justin's Auto Collision Losses Next Year

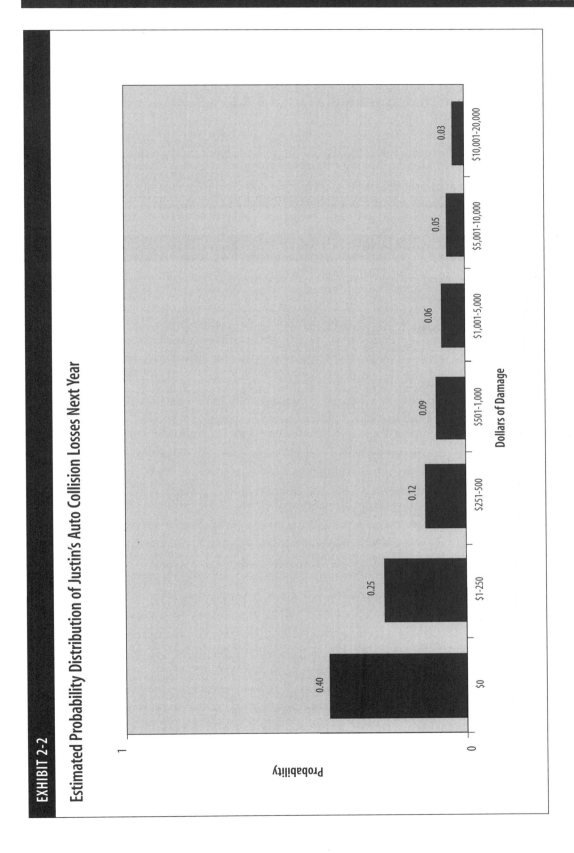

analyze the probability of collision damage to Justin's car, provided that nothing else would change.[5] For example, notice in Exhibit 2-1 that there is a 0.60 probability of his car's sustaining collision damage next year. Assuming this probability remains constant from year to year, 40 percent of the time, on average, Justin will get through a year with no collision damage. This does not necessarily mean that Justin will actually then have an accident during three of the next five years. Nor does it mean that if Justin has an accident during the next three years, he will not have an accident for the following two years. It does not even mean Justin will have accidents during six out of the next ten years. Even if these estimated probabilities are completely accurate, Justin might or might not have an accident every year for some or all of the next ten years.

EXHIBIT 2-3

Stacked Probability Bars

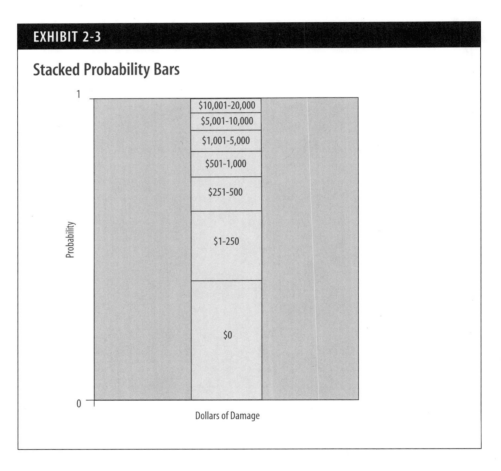

Likewise, the estimated probabilities in Exhibits 2-1, 2-2, and 2-3 would also apply to every other car-owner whose situation is exactly like Justin's. In fact, the best way to develop a realistic probability distribution for Justin would be to analyze past accident statistics involving a large number of other drivers similar to Justin. Many insurance companies use that method to determine premiums. Real-world risk management decisions are often based on a combination of objective data, subjective opinions, and a knowledgeable professional's informed judgment.

TOOLS FOR ANALYZING PROBABILITY

The raw data in any probability distribution can be analyzed by using descriptive statistics. A **descriptive statistic** is a number describing a characteristic of a set of values. The most familiar descriptive statistic is the average. A risk manager reviewing workers compensation loss data, for example, might be interested in knowing the average size of losses incurred during the past year.

Measures of central tendency, such as the average, indicate the middle or center of a set of values. **Measures of dispersion** indicate how spread out the values are or how much variability there is among the values. Because they summarize such important characteristics of the values, both types of statistics are extremely useful for making decisions and projections.

Organizing the Data

Raw data are a collection of values that has not been organized into a useful form. Exhibit 2-4, for example, lists Allied Manufacturing Company's property losses from last year.

Descriptive statistic
A number describing a characteristic of a data set.

Measures of central tendency
Descriptive statistics that indicate the middle or center of a set of values; include the *mean* (or *numeric average*), *median*, and *mode*.

Measures of dispersion
Descriptive statistics that indicate the variability among the values; include the *range*, the *standard deviation*, and the *coefficient of variation*.

EXHIBIT 2-4

Property Losses Last Year

Allied Manufacturing Company

Date	Loss Amount
March 4	$ 1,650
December 9	1,250
January 10	3,500
July 4	1,500
February 27	1,650
October 6	1,100
August 1	50,000
October 18	2,000
February 26	2,000
January 30	1,000
May 28	1,800
September 5	2,000
February 4	1,500

Before raw data can be analyzed, they must be organized into a useful form such as an *array* or a *frequency distribution*.

Array

An array is a list of values arranged in a specified order. Exhibit 2-1 presented an array. Exhibit 2-5 also shows an array; it uses the same data as Exhibit 2-4, but with the losses listed in order of size. That array would be useful, for example, in analyzing a deductible's effect. If Allied had a $2,500 per loss deductible, how would that deductible affect Allied's retained losses? Because eleven of the thirteen losses involve $2,500 or less, these eleven losses would be entirely retained by Allied, and the remaining two losses would be partially retained.

EXHIBIT 2-5

Property Losses Last Year—Array Arranged by Amount of Loss
Allied Manufacturing Company

Date	Loss Amount
January 30	$ 1,000
October 6	1,100
December 9	1,250
February 4	1,500
July 4	1,500
February 27	1,650
March 4	1,650
May 28	1,800
February 26	2,000
September 5	2,000
October 18	2,000
January 10	3,500
August 1	50,000

Frequency Distribution

Frequency distribution
A list that indicates the number of times each value in a data set occurs.

Exhibit 2-6 shows a frequency distribution table containing the same values as those in Exhibits 2-4 and 2-5. A **frequency distribution** indicates the number of times each value in a data set occurs. A *probability distribution* indicates the probabilities of each value in a data set. Probability is often estimated using relative frequency. *Relative frequency* is the number of occurrences divided by the number of observations. For example, if a car's ability to start is tested ten times (observations), and if the car starts two times (occurrences), then the relative frequency that the car will start is 0.20 (2 divided by 10). Relative frequencies can be expressed as percentages. If enough observations are available over time, the relative frequency of occurrence may provide an accurate estimate of the probability of occurrence. Probabilities range between 0 and 1 and can be expressed in percentages. The sum of all probabilities in a probability distribution must equal 1.00.

Exhibit 2-1 is an estimated probability distribution that lists the *probability* that losses of a certain size would occur. The frequency distribution in Exhibit 2-6 lists the *frequency* with which losses of a certain size have occurred.

Exhibit 2-6   ·

Property Losses Last Year—Frequency Distribution

Allied Manufacturing Company

Loss Amount	Frequency
$1–999	0
$1,000–1,999	8
$2,000–2,999	3
$3,000–3,999	1
$4,000–4,999	0
$5,000–7,499	0
$7,500–9,999	0
$10,000–14,999	0
$15,000–49,999	0
$50,000–99,999	1
$100,000–500,000	0

Many insights can be gained by examining data arranged in an array or in a frequency or probability distribution. For example, Exhibit 2-5 shows how an array can be used in analyzing a deductible's effect.

Measures of Central Tendency

Summarizing important characteristics of a data set is often especially useful. For example, even if many pages of raw data are available, for some purposes it is helpful for the manager of a large fleet of school buses to know one specific number that summarizes the data—the amount of dollar losses that have "typically" occurred in each of the past several years because of collisions. As a starting point, at least, this "typical-year" information would be used in projecting the dollar amounts of losses for future years. The information would also be useful in determining whether to purchase insurance and at what price. The most useful "typical" figure might be the average or one of the other measures of central tendency.

The typical value of losses can be determined in three different ways:

1. The *average* or *mean*—the sum of observed values divided by the number of observations
2. The *median*—the middle value in a group of sequential values
3. The *mode*—the value occurring most frequently

Average (Mean)

Average, or mean
The numeric average; calculated by summing all observed values and dividing by the number of observations. When used to project a likely outcome, the average (or mean) might also be referred to as the **expected value**.

To calculate the **average** (or **mean**), add all the observed values and divide that sum by the number of observations:

$$\text{Average} = \frac{\text{Sum of all observed values}}{\text{Number of observations}}$$

Exhibit 2-7 shows the average loss, or severity, calculation for Allied Manufacturing Company.

EXHIBIT 2-7

Average Loss Calculation
Allied Manufacturing Company

	Date	Loss Amount (Observed Values)
1	January 10	$ 3,500
2	January 30	1,000
3	February 4	1,500
4	February 26	2,000
5	February 27	1,650
6	March 4	1,650
7	May 28	1,800
8	July 4	1,500
9	August 1	50,000
10	September 5	2,000
11	October 6	1,100
12	October 18	2,000
13*	December 9	1,250
	Total losses	$70,950

$$\frac{\$70,950}{13} = \$5,458 \text{ (Average Loss)}$$

*Number of observations equals 13.

The average (mean) has two advantages:
- It is simple to calculate.
- It uses all the values in the data set.

One major disadvantage of the average is that it is unduly affected by extreme values. A single very large or very small value can greatly change the average's size. This is the case with the Allied Manufacturing loss distribution. Allied had thirteen losses with a mean of $5,458. However, one large loss of $50,000 tremendously affected the average by driving it up. Fortunately, all but one of the losses were much smaller than the "average loss," and those smaller losses helped the average loss amount go back down. Without the one very large loss, the average would have been $1,746.

One way to offset extreme data's effects on averages is to use weighted averages, which reflect each value's relative importance. The **weighted average** is the average of the relative values in a data set. As another example, Zeta Manufacturing has three insurance policies: one with a $100,000 premium and two with a $1,000 premium. Exhibit 2-8 shows how the premium on those policies has increased.

Weighted average
The average of the relative values in a data set.

EXHIBIT 2-8

Weighted Average Example

Zeta Manufacturing Premium Increases

Policy	Original Premium	Premium Increase	Original Premium × Premium Increase
Policy 1	$100,000	5%	$5,000
Policy 2	1,000	10%	100
Policy 3	1,000	15%	150
	Total premium:	Average premium increase:	Total premium increase:
	$102,000	10%	$5,250

Weighted Average Premium Increase

$$\frac{\$5,250}{\$102,000} = 5.1\%$$

The *average* premium increase is 10 percent. This information is misleading because the calculation gives equal weight to the premium-increase values of the $1,000 policies and the premium-increase values of the $100,000 policy. The weighted average of 5.1 percent reflects the amount by which Zeta's premiums have increased as a whole. Weighted averages may also affect expected value and can be used in other situations in which the data are not all of equal importance.

For a different example, refer again to Exhibits 2-1 and 2-2. What is the expected value of Justin's auto collision losses during the coming year? Although $0 is the most likely outcome during any given year, it is not the expected value on the average and in the long run. Although the chapter has not provided enough information to calculate the expected value with any precision, it would appear to be near $1,150. This amount is calculated by using a weighted average approach and assuming that the actual dollar losses within each range lie near the middle of the range. The $1,150 expected value balances the very small 0.03 probability of a large $20,000 loss with the much greater 0.65 probability that losses will be $250 or less, as well as all other loss possibilities identified in the exhibits.

Using such a weighted average approach can help persons and organizations decide how to handle their risks. For example, if the estimates shown above are accurate and do not change from year to year, Justin could pay for his auto collision losses himself by setting aside $1,150 per year into a separate fund. Of course, this assumes that Justin does not have a major accident until several years have passed and that the fund has accumulated enough money to replace his car when it is damaged. Or Justin could pay, say, $1,400 per year to an insurance company and remove the uncertainty that he might have an accident he cannot afford.

Median

Median
The midpoint of a sequential set of values. For an even number of values, the median is the average of the two middle values.

Another measure of central tendency is the median. The **median** is the midpoint of a sequential set of values. Half of the values are less than or equal to the median, and the other half are greater than or equal to the median. Exhibit 2-9 contains the same data as Exhibit 2-5 but indicates both the median of $1,650 and the mean of $5,458. Six values are lower than or equal to the median, and six values are higher than the median.

Because the median is determined only by its position in a set of sequential values, it is not affected by the values above and below it. The median is easy to identify, but it does not use all of the information contained in a data set. For arrays containing an extreme value, the median can be better than the average (mean) in providing a useful estimate of the "typical" value.

Mode

Mode
The most frequently occurring value in a data set.

The **mode** is the most frequently occurring value in a data set. In a probability distribution, the mode is the value with the highest probability of occurring. For most loss distributions, the mode is zero because the most likely outcome is for no losses to occur. If someone looks only at Allied Manufacturing's actual losses, the mode is $2,000 because that value occurred more frequently than any other. This is not an unlikely outcome if, for example, Allied has a large number of loss exposure units.

EXHIBIT 2-9

Property Losses Last Year, Showing Median Value

Allied Manufacturing Company

	Date	Loss Amount (Observed Values)
1	January 30	$ 1,000
2	October 6	1,100
3	December 9	1,250
4	February 4	1,500
5	July 4	1,500
6	February 27	1,650
7	March 4—Median—>	**1,650**
8	May 28	1,800
9	February 26	2,000
10	September 5	2,000
11	October 18	2,000
12	January 10	3,500
13*	August 1	50,000
	Total losses	$70,950
	Mean loss ($70,950/13)	**$5,458**

*Number of observations equals 13.

Shape of the Distribution

The "shape" of a particular relative frequency or probability distribution can be seen by graphing a curve of the data. The relationships among the mean (average), median, and mode for any data set are illustrated in the distribution's shape.

In a symmetrical distribution, one side of the curve is a mirror image of the other. For example, someone could fold the graph of a symmetrical curve along its center line, and both sides would match. Exhibit 2-10 illustrates three symmetrical distributions. Distribution (a) is the standard (normal) distribution commonly referred to as a "bell-shaped curve," but all three distributions are symmetrical.

If a distribution is asymmetrical, it is **skewed**. Exhibit 2-11 shows two skewed distributions. Many loss distributions are skewed because the probability of small losses is large while the probability of large losses is small.

Skewed
A distribution that is asymmetrical, that is, has the bulk of values at either the distribution's high or low end.

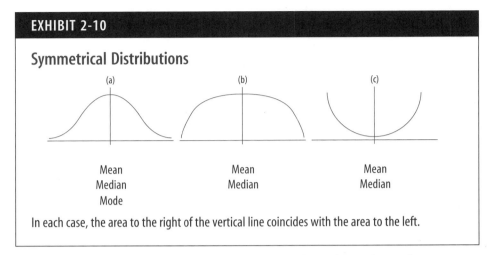

EXHIBIT 2-10

Symmetrical Distributions

In each case, the area to the right of the vertical line coincides with the area to the left.

In a symmetrical distribution, the mean and median always have the same value. In a standard "bell-shaped" distribution, the mode has the same value as that of the mean and the median.

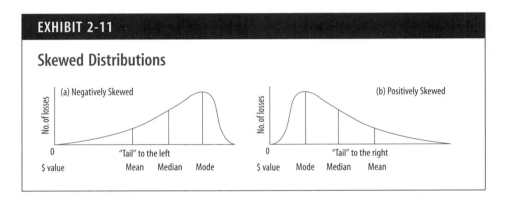

EXHIBIT 2-11

Skewed Distributions

Analyzing Loss Distributions

Three issues are important when analyzing loss distributions. First, the average tends to be unduly influenced by extreme values. Knowing that the average loss amount, or severity, has been $5,458 is not very helpful unless the other characteristics of the distribution on which it is based are known. Was the distribution highly skewed? What were the median and mode values? This information provides a clearer picture of what outcomes might be in a "typical" future time period.

Second, the number of values from which average frequency or severity has been calculated must be of sufficient size. When the number of values is small, judging whether the data demonstrate a pattern is difficult—or impossible. When the number of observations is small, industry data can supplement company data and improve credibility of a projection.

Third, reaching too far into the past for data can also cause problems; the more-distant past might be more dissimilar to the future than the recent past would be. Past loss data generally have a somewhat limited value because future losses are unlikely to be precisely like past losses.

Measures of Dispersion

The mean, median, and mode provide information about where the center of a group of values tends to be located. Measures of dispersion provide information about the values' degree of variability.

Dispersion is the extent to which values differ from one another. More precisely, **dispersion** is defined as the variability, or scatter, among the values of the observations in a data set. Think of the bull's-eye on a shooting gallery target. An expert marksman might be able to place a number of shots into the bull's-eye, while an amateur's shots would be dispersed all over the target, with some shots entirely missing the target.

Dispersion
The variability, or scatter, among the values of a data set.

Given a sufficient number of observations, a tighter clustering of values leads to more reliable estimates of expected values. When one assumes that the conditions of the past do continue into the future, the degree of variation in past values may indicate the degree of variability that should be expected in the future. Consequently, measures of dispersion provide useful risk analysis information in such a case.

Three measures of dispersion considered here are the range, the standard deviation, and the coefficient of variation. This chapter discusses the standard deviation, but not its calculation, a subject that can be found in any standard statistics text.

Range

The **range** is the difference between the lowest and the highest value in a data set. For example, the range between 1 and 10 is 9. The range of the data in Exhibit 2-4 is $49,000, the difference between the highest value ($50,000) and the lowest value ($1,000).

Range
The difference between the lowest and the highest value in a data set. When the highest value is unknown, the range is open-ended.

The range can be very useful for some purposes. For example, highway department employees in the snowbelt who must know how much salt to stockpile should know the maximum amount of salt that was used on the roadways during the most severe winter on record, rather than base their decisions on the amount used in an average winter—or, worse, the amount that was used last year, both of which might lead to an inaccurate projection for the next year. Of course, the coming winter could be more severe than any previous winter on record, but the range at least provides a good starting point. For risk management purposes, loss data can often be similarly analyzed. Knowing the past range of losses and the past worst year can guide planning.

Sometimes the range cannot be calculated, because the highest value is unknown. The range of potential liability losses for many organizations is open-ended because the extent of their loss exposures is unknown.

The range provides a rough measure of the degree of dispersion, but its value for many purposes is limited because it ignores all values except the two extremes.

Standard Deviation

Standard deviation
A measure of dispersion that indicates the variability between each value in the data set and the data set's mean.

The **standard deviation** is a measure of dispersion that indicates the variability between each value in the data set and the data set's mean. The standard deviation uses all of the information in the data set. Because it is calculated from the deviations of all the values from the mean, it is a powerful indication of the degree of variability. When two distributions with the same mean are compared, the distribution with the larger standard deviation has a larger degree of dispersion. The distribution with the smaller standard deviation provides a stronger basis for projecting future occurrences.

The data in Exhibit 2-5 are shown again in Exhibit 2-12, but with some added features. As calculated with the aid of Microsoft Excel®, using the Excel function STDEV, the standard deviation of all values, with a range from $1,000 to $50,000, is $13,398 (rounded to the nearest dollar). If the $50,000 loss had not occurred, the standard deviation of losses ranging from $1,000 to $3,500 would be $649, a much smaller number.

The standard deviation is easiest to interpret when the distribution from which it has been calculated is normal, or bell-shaped. In a normal distribution, roughly two-thirds (68 percent) of the values are found in the area that is within one standard deviation on either side of the mean. Plus or minus two standard deviations encompasses slightly more than 95 percent of the values, as Exhibit 2-13 shows. Thus, the greater the standard deviation of a data set, the wider the range of values necessary to encompass any given percentage (say 50 percent, 90 percent, or 99 percent) of the observed values of the data.

How might information about standard deviation be useful? Suppose that insurers were required to base auto insurance rates primarily on the annual mileage driven. Knowing that the average annual mileage for one insurer's covered autos is, say, 15,000 and that the range is from 1,200 to 85,000 would be helpful. But even more helpful would be knowing how "spread out" the mileage is among the population. If the standard deviation of annual mileage were determined to be 3,000 miles, and if the distribution were assumed to be normal and bell-shaped, several conclusions could be made. First, about 68 percent of this insurer's drivers drive between 12,000 and 18,000 miles per year (that is, plus or minus one standard deviation from the mean; 15,000 plus or minus 3,000). About 95 percent of the drivers drive between 9,000 and 21,000 miles per year, and nearly all of this insurer's drivers drive between 6,000 and 24,000 miles per year.

EXHIBIT 2-12

Property Losses Last Year, Showing Measures of Dispersion

Allied Manufacturing Company

	Date	Loss Amount
1	January 30	$ 1,000
2	October 6	1,100
3	December 9	1,250
4	February 4	1,500
5	July 4	1,500
6	February 27	1,650
7	March 4–Median—>	**1,650**
8	May 28	1,800
9	February 26	2,000
10	September 5	2,000
11	October 18	2,000
12	January 10	3,500
13	August 1	50,000
	Total losses	$70,950
	Mean of all losses ($70,950/13)	**$5,458**
	Mean of losses 1–12 ($20,950/12)	**$1,746**
	Standard deviation of all losses	**$13,398**
	Standard deviation of losses 1–12	**$649**
	Coefficient of variation of all losses	**2.45**
	Coefficient of variation losses 1–12	**0.372**

This information could be very helpful to the insurer in deciding where to draw the dividing lines between different rate classifications. For example, the information would be useful in estimating how many people would fall into each classification and how much premium would be generated.

Both the mean and the standard deviation use all of the information in the distribution, and both are greatly affected by extreme values. Even one large observation can make the standard deviation quite large. Exhibit 2-12 noted that the standard deviation of all thirteen observations is $13,398. However, if the "extreme value" of the $50,000 loss were not a part of the loss history, the standard deviation of the other twelve observations would be only $649.

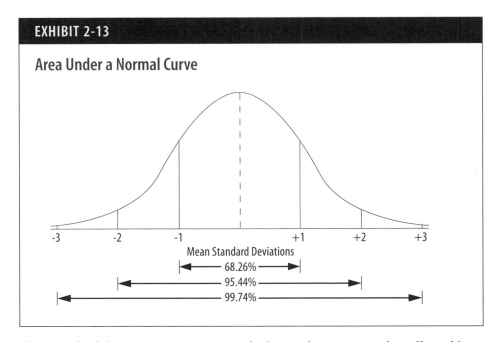

EXHIBIT 2-13

Area Under a Normal Curve

The standard deviation is a measure of relative dispersion and is affected by the size of all values in the distribution. Therefore, when the standard deviations of two distributions are compared to see which has the greater dispersion, direct comparisons can be made only if the means are the same or approximately the same. If the means are not the same, then another statistic, such as the coefficient of variation, must be used.

Coefficient of Variation

Coefficient of variation
A measure of dispersion that compares two data sets with substantially different means (averages). The coefficient of variation is calculated by dividing the standard deviation by the mean.

The **coefficient of variation** is a measure of dispersion that compares the degree of dispersion between two data sets with substantially different means. The coefficient of variation is calculated by dividing the standard deviation by the mean. The coefficient of variation for the data in Exhibit 2-12 is 2.45. ($13,398 is divided by $5,458.) If the $50,000 loss had not occurred, the coefficient of variation would be 0.372. ($649 is divided by $1,746.) The distribution with the larger coefficient of variation has a larger degree of dispersion.

Credibility

One of the most important issues regarding probability-related statistics—whether they analyze loss exposures or are used for other purposes—is deciding when to apply them. The rule is deceptively simple. One can apply statistical computations to make projections in situations in which the number of observations is sufficiently large. The trick, of course, lies in determining when that condition exists.

Statisticians use various sophisticated measures to quantify the degree of *credibility*, the extent to which past data accurately project future data. Credibility is then a measure of the predictive value that the analyst attaches to the data. Generally, credibility increases as the number of values increases. This phenomenon is closely related to the **law of large numbers**. In the context of projecting losses, this mathematical law states the following: When the number of similar independent exposure units increases, the relative accuracy of projections about future outcomes (such as losses) based on these exposure units also increases. Projections that are completely unreliable are useless for risk management or insurance, and they can even be misleading and harmful. Chapter 6 will demonstrate that the law of large numbers provides the basis for one of the ideal characteristics of an insurable exposure: a *large number* of homogeneous, uncorrelated (independent) exposure units.

When results differ from expectations, one of the most common reasons is that the projection is based on an inadequate number of exposure units. When the number of past observations is very small, the difference between actual and expected results can be extremely large.

Credibility is also affected when the underlying phenomenon being studied changes. For example, consider the legal hazard discussed in Chapter 1. Changes in laws can make lawsuits more or less likely and the damages recoverable in such suits greater or smaller. Upon such changes in laws, predictions of future suits and damages based on past data might not be credible.

Projections and credibility depend on homogeneity, or similarity in the exposures on which the projection is based. One should not compare apples and oranges (the common metaphor for describing a lack of homogeneity). For example, projecting the accident rates of sports utility vehicles based on the accident rates of private passenger sedans might not yield accurate information.

For more accurate projections, exposure units should also be independent, or uncorrelated. That is, the occurrence of one loss should not affect the likelihood of another, similar loss. In contrast, when the occurrence of a loss affects the likelihood of another similar loss, the exposure units are correlated. Statistical inference is based on the premise that possible outcomes occur more or less randomly. Thus, projections of all theft losses to homeowners' property tend to be more accurate than projections of all hurricane losses to homeowners' property. Theft losses are substantially uncorrelated, whereas hurricane losses are correlated because they tend to occur to tens of thousands of buildings at once, or not at all.

Law of large numbers
A mathematical principle stating that when the number of similar independent exposure units increases, the relative accuracy of projections about future outcomes (such as losses) based on these exposure units also increases.

PROBABILITY DISTRIBUTION: SPECULATIVE RISK EXAMPLE

This chapter began with an example based on auto collisions that, as noted, involve only the pure risk of having a loss. The City Newspaper example presented in this section of the chapter involves not only risks of loss but also opportunities for gain—in other words, speculative risks.

City Newspaper faces a number of major risks during the year ahead. The newspaper faces some risks relating to the variation in newsprint (paper) prices. Newsprint prices could rise or fall for many reasons, including government regulation of forestry or paper mills, labor union negotiations, technological changes, and energy costs. Other risks exist because of an uncertain demand for newspapers. The newspaper might face increased or decreased competition not only from other newspapers but also from news magazines, local and national radio and television news programs, and the Internet. Investigative reporters might receive awards for their work, enhancing the newspaper's reputation and increasing its sales. Or, while pursuing a dangerous assignment, reporters might be threatened, injured, or even killed—resulting in workers compensation claims against the paper or the loss of valued, talented individuals. Customers can sue the newspaper, alleging damages from libel and misinformation. The newspaper faces these and many other risks.

How should the newspaper address those risks? Can some risks be controlled? Should it retain some risks of loss and insure others? Decisions must be made. A starting point involves identifying and measuring the risks, as well as assessing the costs and benefits of different risk management alternatives and their likely effect on the newspaper's profitability.

Suppose last year the newspaper generated a profit of $3 million. Assuming that last year was a reasonably normal year and that no major changes—such as merging with another newspaper—occurred, someone could reasonably assume that next year's profits would also be somewhere around $3 million—if next year is also a normal year. But next year's results are difficult to project. The newspaper might determine that the worst possible outcome would be a $3 million loss rather than a $3 million profit. Of course, next year might be a very good year, in which the best possible outcome would be a $9 million profit. But are all these outcomes equally likely? Certainly not.

An economist or a statistician associated with the newspaper might have enough information on all the risks to develop a sophisticated analysis. For the sake of this discussion, assume that the various risks affecting profitability are truly random variables, as they are in many instances, and that the desirable outcomes are equally balanced with undesirable outcomes. In that case, the likelihood of various profitability levels can be represented by a probability chart similar to the one in Exhibit 2-14. This kind of chart is commonly referred to as a normal distribution, or a bell-shaped curve, described earlier, for the obvious reason that it resembles a bell's shape.

The first charts in this chapter indicated the probability of *loss* from one cause: collision. The bars in Exhibit 2-14 indicate the probability of any given level of loss or *profit*, the combined effect of many different risks and opportunities.

The newspaper's most likely profit next year is $3 million. Although a little less likely than a $3 million profit, the chance of a $2.5 million profit is as good as the chance of a $3.5 million profit. And the chance of a $2.0 million profit is the same as the chance of a $4.0 million profit. The graph in Exhibit 2-14 could

EXHIBIT 2-14

City Newspaper Profits—Normal Probability Distribution

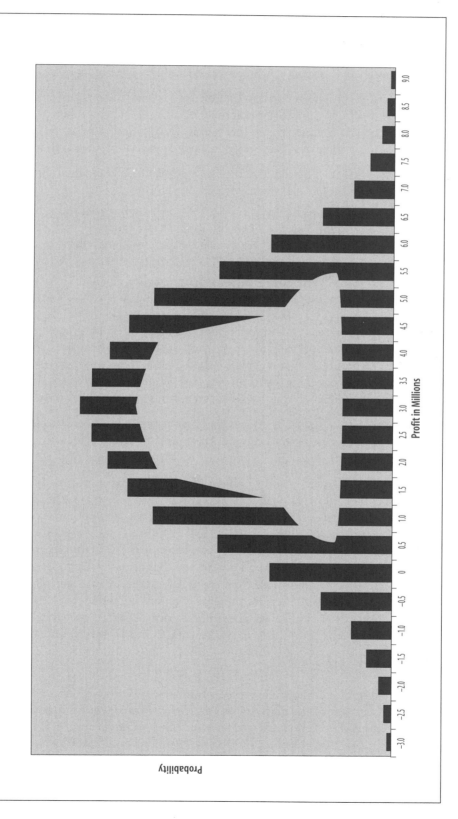

Probability

Profit in Millions

also be used to determine the likelihood that profits will be between $2 million and $4 million, or between any other two figures. The graph also shows that chances are almost—but not quite—zero that the newspaper's profits will be as high as $9 million or as low as –$3 million (a $3 million loss).

The bell-shaped curve in Exhibit 2-14 is referred to as a normal distribution. Probability distributions often take this shape when random variables are involved. The newspaper's probability distribution provides an opportunity to review some very basic statistical concepts that professionals use to examine risks.

- *Mode*. The mode is the most probable outcome in a normal distribution. In Exhibit 2-14, the mode is $3 million.[6]

- *Median*. The median is the middle number in a data set. The median of a normal distribution is the same as the mode or, in this case, $3 million. Half of the time, on average, the newspaper will have net profits of more than $3 million, and half of the time profits will be less than $3 million.

- *Mean*. The mean is the arithmetic average of a group of numbers. For a normal distribution, the mean (also known as the "expected value") is always the same as the median and the mode. If nothing changes, the newspaper's net profits will most likely be $3 million every year, although some years might be better and others might be worse. The mean ($3 million profit) is what would be expected, and if the newspaper's net profits had to be projected for planning purposes, $3 million would probably be used. But it is understood that the actual result might never be *exactly* $3 million.

A normal distribution has some additional characteristics that make it useful as a forecasting tool. One of the most important forecasting tools of a normal distribution is standard deviation, illustrated in Exhibit 2-15.

The statistical power behind the standard deviation is the fact that roughly two-thirds of the time (68.26 percent, to be exact), the actual outcome is within one standard deviation of the expected outcome or mean. Assume that the probability distribution in Exhibit 2-15 has a standard deviation of $2 million. The coefficient of variation is 0.67 (that is, a standard deviation of 2.0 divided by the mean of 3.0). That means that even though the newspaper could lose $3 million, or it could earn a net profit of $9 million, two-thirds of the time the earnings will be between $1 million and $5 million. That is because $1 million is one standard deviation ($2 million) below the $3 million expected value, and $5 million is one standard deviation above $3 million. ($3 million – $2 million = $1 million; $3 million +$2 million = $5 million.)

Estimates that are accurate more than two-thirds of the time are quite satisfactory for many purposes. But it gets better because 95.44 percent of the time, results are within two standard deviations of the expected value. In the newspaper's case, its management could be 95 percent confident that financial results would be no worse than a $1 million loss, and possibly as good as a $7 million profit.

EXHIBIT 2-15

City Newspaper Profits—Probability Distribution Showing Standard Deviations

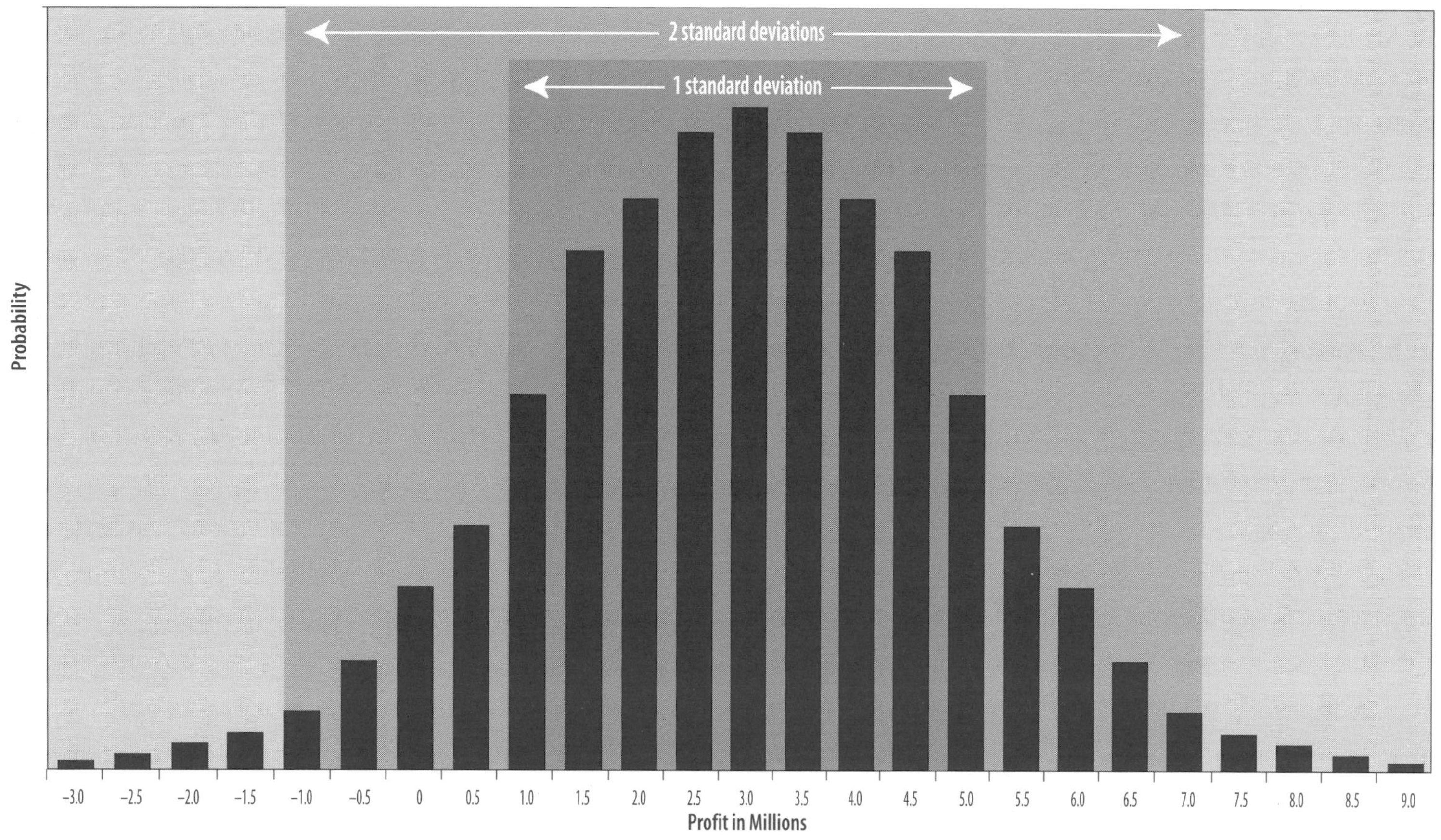

What else could the newspaper do to make its future more projectable? Basically, anything that reduces its risks. Anything that reduces risk will make the probable results "less spread out"; that is, it will reduce the amount of dispersion, resulting in a lower standard deviation. For example, the newspaper might do the following:

- Enter into a long-term contract with paper suppliers to buy newsprint at a fixed price. The fixed price might turn out to be higher or lower than the market price, which varies, but the negotiated price will be stable.

- Sign a labor union contract that makes labor costs projectable for the contact's duration and also reduces the likelihood of a strike.

- Purchase workers compensation insurance to cover the newspaper's obligations for employees injured on the job. The cost of insurance might be higher or lower than the value of insured losses, but it is projectable.

- Institute fleet-safety programs to reduce the number of auto accidents involving newspaper delivery vehicles and their operators.

- Purchase broad liability insurance coverage that would protect the newspaper against claims of libel and slander.

- Buy competing newspapers to reduce competition.

All of these measures would probably cost money, reducing the newspaper's potential profits. But they might also reduce the newspaper's potential losses. The result might be a probability distribution shaped more like the one in Exhibit 2-16. The chart shows that the values are clustered more closely around the mean, or expected value, which, in this case, has dropped from $3 million to $2.8 million as a result of the risk control measures. The standard deviation has shifted to 1.4, and the coefficient of variation has become 0.50 (that is, a standard deviation of 1.4 divided by the mean of 2.8). Two-thirds of the time, the newspaper's net profits would be between $1.4 million and $4.2 million. Better yet, there is a 95 percent probability that the newspaper will at least break even with a profit of $0 and that profits could range as high as $5.6 million.

This example illustrates that measures that reduce risk also increase confidence in the projections. It also illustrates the relationship between risk and reward. Reducing the newspaper's risk has all but eliminated the chance that the newspaper will operate at a loss. However, it has also reduced the newspaper's opportunities for gain—potential profits.

For Further Thought

Should an insurer sell City Newspaper an insurance policy reimbursing a loss in excess of $1 million? Should the newspaper buy such a policy?

Various measures could be initiated to increase the newspaper's likely profits, perhaps by reducing its losses. For example, investing in a new automated typesetting system might be expected to increase the newspaper's efficiency.

EXHIBIT 2-16

City Newspaper Profits—Probability Distribution With Risks Reduced

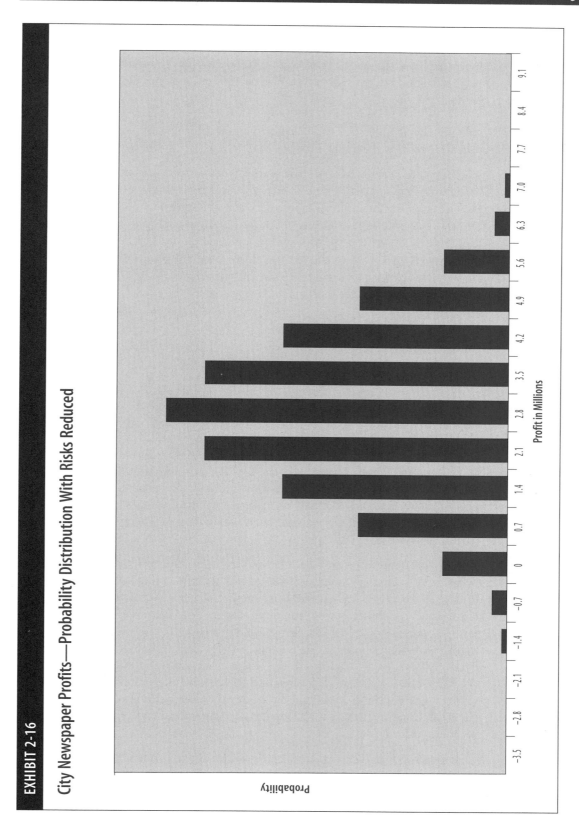

Or an improved fleet-safety program might be expected to reduce the number of delivery truck accidents. Anything that can be done to shift the probability distribution shown in Exhibit 2-16 by moving the bell-shaped curve to the right will increase the $2.8 million expected value of the newspaper's annual profits. Anything that is projected to improve the newspaper's expected profits will generally increase the newspaper's value to its stockholders. This increased value results from an increased expectation of future profits, not a guarantee that the profits will actually occur.

The opposite is also true. Anything that is likely to decrease expected profits reduces the newspaper's value. For example, if the newspaper faces a libel lawsuit claiming $1 million as damages, the newspaper's profits might be reduced by $1 million—unless, of course, the newspaper has liability insurance including coverage for libel. Unless or until the claim is resolved in the newspaper's favor, the uncertainty will have a depressing influence on City Newspaper's stock value.

SUMMARY

Using concrete examples rather than abstract statistical rules, this chapter examined some fundamental probability concepts used in evaluating risk. Later chapters will make further use of those concepts.

The chapter began with a simple example involving the risk of collision damage to a car next year. This is a pure risk, involving no possibility of gain but only the possibility of loss. A probability distribution estimated the probability of damage in various amounts. The same information was then shown in a bar graph. By stacking the bars in another graph, the chapter showed that the probability distribution included the probability of every possible outcome, ranging from no loss to a total loss of the car. By the end of next year, the car will either have been totally destroyed, it will have had partial damage, or it will have had no damage. No other possibilities exist.[7]

The chapter then presented some tools for analyzing probability using descriptive statistics—measures of central tendency that indicate the middle point of a data set, and measures of dispersion that indicate the amount of variability among the data values. The measures of central tendency are the "m"-words: the mean (or average), the median, and the mode, and this chapter defined each of them and explained their relevance. The measures of dispersion are the range, the standard deviation, and the coefficient of variation. The standard deviation is especially useful in analyzing the data in a normal distribution. The coefficient of variation is used to compare two distributions involving substantially different means, or averages.

This chapter also discussed credibility, which is the concept that data about the past should be used to project the future only when enough data for meaningful analysis are available. The law of large numbers states that more data make for more meaningful projections.

Data about the past can most successfully be used to project the future when the observations are independent (uncorrelated) and the underlying conditions have not changed. The importance of this distinction will become clearer in upcoming chapters that will discuss why insurance is most suitable for independent, uncorrelated exposure units.

The chapter concluded by applying probability concepts in the City Newspaper case, an example involving speculative risks of either loss or gain. This example demonstrated that City Newspaper can, if it chooses, manage its risks in ways that make its future more predictable. The ideas developed in this example set the stage for Chapter 3, which more closely examines risk management.

CHAPTER NOTES

1. Perhaps a slight opportunity for gain exists. If the car's scratched fender is struck by another driver whose insurance pays for a new, unscratched fender, the car could actually receive some "betterment" as the result of an accident. Generally, insurance companies avoid paying for betterment.

2. In some circumstances, paying a premium larger than the amount of any single loss can make sense. For example, it could be reasonable to pay, say, $2,500 for $1,000 of robbery insurance on a twenty-four-hour convenience store during a one-year policy period. Why? Because convenience stores are vulnerable, and more than one robbery could easily occur during the course of a year.

3. The insurer will not pay more than the car's current value.

4. To keep this example simple, it assumes that Justin could not have more than one collision next year. Unfortunately, real-world situations are not quite that simple.

5. The car's value will usually decline because of depreciation, even if nothing else changes. Although the changing value would not affect the probability of loss, it could affect the value of any loss, particularly a total loss.

6. Since the example said the most likely outcome is $3 million, this text should clarify that it ignores the possibility of a profit of *exactly* $3,000,000.00. The actual dollars-and-cents amount will inevitably be above or below that expected outcome, even if it is very close to the projected $3 million mean.

7. For simplicity's sake, the example ignored the possibility of having more than one collision next year.

Chapter 3

Direct Your Learning

Managing Risk

After learning the subject matter of this chapter, you should be able to:

- Explain the types of risk management objectives an organization might have.

- Describe in detail each of the steps in the risk management process, and apply them to a case situation.

- Explain how the risk management function operates in businesses and families.

- Explain risk management's benefits.

Develop Your Perspective

What are the main topics covered in the chapter?

This chapter describes risk management objectives, the risk management process, the risk management function, and risk management benefits.

Evaluate the loss exposures facing your organization.

- What data might your organization collect to assess those risks?

Why is it important to know these topics?

Knowing these topics will help you understand how and why organizations and individuals strategically manage their risks.

Consider the loss exposures your organization manages.

- Why is your organization willing to assume those risks?
- Who within your organization has responsibility for performing risk management functions?

How can you use this information?

Imagine that you perform the risk management function within your organization.

- What data might you need to analyze risks?
- How might the data affect the risk control or risk financing techniques you choose?

Chapter 3

Managing Risk[1]

For most businesses, risk management's overall objective is to maximize the organization's value. For a corporation, maximizing value means maximizing shareholders' financial return, such as favorably affecting stock prices and/or dividends. Exhibit 3-1 explains why business managers care about shareholder returns.

EXHIBIT 3-1

Why corporate managers care about shareholder returns

- Stock represents a portion of ownership in the company; shareholders can vote at annual meetings.

- Shareholders sometimes own enough shares to cast deciding votes about management.

- Higher stock prices mean more compensation or more stock options for executive stockholders.

- Managers who raise shareholder value command higher salaries.

- Low stock prices could lead to a takeover.

For nonprofit or government entities, which do not have shareholders, the risk management objective generally is to maximize their financial situation and minimize the cost of risks so that these entities can deliver their products or services. For individuals or families, important risk management objectives include maximizing financial and physical well-being. In any case, risk management should foster the individual's or organization's overall goals.

THE OBJECTIVES OF RISK MANAGEMENT

Risk management objectives can be classified into two categories, as shown in the following box.

Pre-loss risk management objectives
The objectives that should be met even if no losses occur, generally relating to efficiency, tolerable uncertainty, legal requirements, and ethical conduct.

Post-loss risk management objectives
The objectives that should be met after a loss occurs and that relate to survival, continuity of operations, profitability or earnings stability, growth, and ethical conduct.

Two Categories of Risk Management Objectives

1. **Pre-loss objectives**, which should be met even if no losses occur. These objectives relate to efficiency, tolerable uncertainty, legal requirements, and ethical conduct.

2. **Post-loss objectives**, which should be met after a loss occurs, even the most severe foreseeable loss. These objectives relate to survival, continuity of operations, profitability or earnings stability, growth, and ethical conduct.

Pre-Loss Objectives

Most risk management activity involves preparing for major losses that, ideally, will never occur. Even if no losses occur, risk management should meet certain pre-loss objectives, which typically include efficiency, tolerable uncertainty, legality, and ethical conduct.

Efficiency

A risk management program must be designed to efficiently protect the organization. These risk management programs should not incur significant costs to gain only slight benefits and should use the organization's resources economically. The efficiency of any organization's risk management program can sometimes be evaluated by using published studies to compare its cost of risk with that of other similar organizations.

Tolerable Uncertainty

Another pre-loss objective of risk management is maintaining a tolerable level of uncertainty. A good risk management program should identify loss exposures and appropriate risk control and risk financing measures to address these exposures. The organization must then determine which of those measures to implement by using cost-benefit analysis. The benefits of a risk control or risk financing technique should be greater than the costs of the techniques. Effective pre-loss risk management enables managers to concentrate on other matters, without excessive worry about the uncertainty of accidental losses.

Legal Requirements

Externally imposed legal requirements can determine risk management programs by mandating specific treatment of some loss exposures. For example, corporations engaging in government contracts are often legally required to purchase insurance and surety bonds. Most states' laws require individuals and organizations to purchase liability insurance for their vehicles or, alternatively, to qualify as self-insurers by posting a surety bond and meeting other requirements.

Failure to meet legal requirements can create a loss exposure because violations can result in fines or court orders that cost money, require a change in business practice, and seriously affect goodwill. Breaking the law in ways that contribute to an injury can compound the costs of a loss. Therefore, risk managers should consider all legal obligations and related costs in risk management.

Ethical Conduct

Risk management objectives can be presented in purely financial terms, but sound risk management also requires a firm commitment to ethical conduct. Ethics involves not only complying with the law but also doing what is right. Ethical conflicts often arise because of financial considerations. For example, a manufacturer might pollute a stream by dumping a chemical by-product into it, rather than safely dispose of the by-product at a higher cost.

Efficiency, tolerable uncertainty, legal requirements, and ethical conduct are important pre-loss objectives of a risk management program.

Post-Loss Objectives

Post-loss risk management objectives describe the organization's desired condition after a loss occurs. Possible post-loss objectives include survival, continuity of operations, profitability, stability of earnings, growth, and ethical conduct.

Survival

Survival is a fundamental post-loss objective. For individuals, survival usually means staying alive. For businesses, survival means to resume operations in some manner after an adverse event. Survival does not necessarily mean returning to the condition that existed before loss.

Continuity of Operations

For many organizations, a key post-loss objective is continuing operations without interruption. Continuity requires committing more resources to sustaining operations than those required to merely survive the loss.

Some organizations require only that certain activities continue to sustain the business. Such organizations must identify these key activities, identify the exposures that could disrupt the activities, and ensure that appropriate measures have been taken to eliminate or mitigate the possibility of an interruption. Frequently, committing standby resources and duplicating some activities are required to maintain adequate continuity of operations.

Profitability or Earnings Stability

Profitability is an organization's ability to generate net income or, for a nonprofit, to operate within its budget or generate a surplus. In either case, a minimum acceptable amount of profit or surplus might be essential. To maintain its profitability, the organization will probably rely heavily on insurance and other techniques to manage the financial consequences of loss. Restoring profitability usually requires committing more resources than does survival.

Although some organizations attempt to maximize current short-term earnings, others place the highest priority on maintaining stable earnings over time. A focus on stability tends to favor using risk management techniques that have fairly determinable costs. Although insurance markets have demonstrated volatility in some cases, one of the advantages of insurance has been its ability to stabilize earnings over time.

Growth

Post-loss objectives related to growth may vary according to the level of risk that the organization is willing to accept. For example, because aggressive growth objectives are usually accompanied by high risks, the owners and managers of a growth-oriented organization might have a relatively high risk tolerance. Therefore, they might be willing to accept a serious setback resulting from an uncontrolled loss. For other organizations, the growth objective implies maintaining the organization's orderly rate of expansion at all costs. Under these circumstances, little tolerance for loss might exist, suggesting high reliance on risk control and risk financing measures.

Ethical Conduct

Ethical conduct objectives relate to operating in a legal and humanitarian manner. These objectives affect both pre-loss and post-loss risk management planning. Fulfilling ethical responsibilities can involve post-loss expenses that would not otherwise be incurred. Products liability cases provide an illustration. Upon discovering a product defect, some organizations have taken extraordinary measures to recall outstanding products to prevent injuries.

Risk management objectives, whether accomplished before or after a loss, should advance an organization's goals.

THE RISK MANAGEMENT PROCESS

Risk management process
A series of six steps taken to meet risk management objectives.

The **risk management process** is a series of six steps taken to meet risk management objectives. This process may be applied to any set of loss exposures. In large businesses, the risk management process is applied by a *risk manager* or other individuals performing the risk management function, possibly as part of a *risk management department*. In small businesses and in families, risk management is often a less formalized process usually performed by someone with responsibilities in addition to risk management. Anyone undertaking the risk management process should have a sound grasp of the organization's or family's objectives and be able to recognize which risks pose the most dire financial consequences, should they occur.

Six Steps in the Risk Management Process

1. Identifying loss exposures

2. Analyzing loss exposures

3. Examining the feasibility of risk management alternatives

4. Selecting the best risk management techniques

5. Implementing risk management techniques

6. Monitoring results

The risk management process has six steps, which this text describes in sequence. However, experienced risk management professionals might deal with several steps simultaneously.

1. Identifying loss exposures
2. Analyzing loss exposures
3. Examining the feasibility of risk management alternatives
4. Selecting the best risk management techniques
5. Implementing risk management techniques
6. Monitoring results

For example, Mary, an experienced risk management professional, is identifying and analyzing the property loss exposures of a newly acquired $5 million building financed with a bank loan. Based on experience, Mary realizes that the most practical way to finance these exposures is to purchase special-form open-perils ("all-risks") property insurance with an appropriate limit and deductible. Mary could spend much time and effort identifying all the various perils—such as fire, lightning, windstorm, and vandalism—that could result in building damage. However, she knows that her time is better spent on matters that require special treatment such as evaluating exposures subject to pollution, contamination, or flood damage. Even though insurance will be purchased on the building, Mary does not completely disregard exposure identification and analysis, because she realizes that property risk control measures should also be considered.

The risk management process is continuous because the last step in the process, monitoring results, leads to identifying new or additional loss exposures. However, the risk management process can also be initiated by events such as the following:

• A pending insurance renewal might suggest a thorough risk analysis.

- A serious claim might spur a review of the organization's risk management activities.
- Merger or acquisition activity might create a new organization whose risks require reevaluation.
- New laws or regulations might affect the organization.

Step 1: Identifying Loss Exposures

The first step in the risk management process is identifying all the possible loss exposures. How do risk managers begin identifying loss exposures? Because no single technique identifies all loss exposures, many risk managers use one or more of the following:

- Checklists or questionnaires
- Financial statement analysis
- Contract and lease analysis
- Flowchart analysis
- Loss analysis
- Hazard analysis
- Personal inspections
- Interviews

These techniques offer a systematic approach to identifying loss exposures. They also may enable risk managers to identify missed opportunities. A systematic approach helps to ensure a thorough risk analysis.

Checklists or Questionnaires

Many loss exposures can be identified with a *checklist* that can be checked "yes" or "no." A *questionnaire* captures descriptive information, amounts, or values. Various exposure-related checklists and questionnaires have been published by insurers, the American Management Association (AMA), the Risk and Insurance Management Society (RIMS), the International Risk Management Institute (IRMI), and others. Some organizations or trade associations have developed specialized checklists or questionnaires for their members. Many checklists or questionnaires can be categorized as either insurance surveys or risk management surveys.

Insurance Surveys

Insurance survey questionnaire
A survey that identifies insurable loss exposures and that provides underwriting and ratemaking information.

Many insurers supply **insurance survey questionnaire** forms to their producers. Most insurance survey questionnaires identify insurable loss exposures and provide underwriting and ratemaking information. An insurance survey can provide information needed to design a sound insurance program. However, because they are insurance-oriented, insurance surveys can lead to the use of insurance when other risk management techniques might better meet the organization's risk management objectives.

Insurance survey questionnaires focus on insurable loss exposures. To discover uninsurable loss exposures, the insurance survey should be supplemented with other sources of information, such as a risk management survey.

Risk Management Surveys

Because **risk management survey questionnaires** address both insurable and uninsurable loss exposures, they overcome the major limitation of insurance survey questionnaires. However, a risk management survey can be completed only with considerable expense, time, and effort, and the survey might not identify all possible loss exposures.

Most risk management questionnaires are generic, designed for use by many different organizations. Therefore, a standardized questionnaire might not uncover the exposures peculiar to a given industry or organization.

Risk management survey questionnaire
A survey that identifies both insurable and uninsurable loss exposures.

Using Checklists and Questionnaires

Even a thoroughly completed checklist or questionnaire does not ensure that all loss exposures have been recognized. The value of any checklist or questionnaire varies according to its user's skill. Experienced insurance and risk management professionals often follow up some answers with additional questions that are not on the prepared document. For example, a questionnaire used by an insurance agent for an auto body shop asked whether the shop had a spray-painting booth. The answer was "no," which was surprising for a modern body shop. The agent asked a few more questions and learned that this shop was using a newly developed air filtration system that was even better than the standard spray-painting booth. Moreover, rather than rejecting this account because of the "no spray-painting booth" response on the questionnaire, the property underwriter also visited the shop. The underwriter then granted a preferential rate based on information he uncovered that was not on the questionnaire as well as the agent's information about the new air filtration system.

Financial Statement Analysis

Professionals with accounting or finance expertise sometimes begin the loss exposure identification process by analyzing financial statements, such as an organization's balance sheet, income statement, budget, and supporting documents. Each financial statement is scrutinized to determine what loss exposures it reveals. For example, an entry for "finished goods inventory" in a manufacturer's balance sheet indicates a property loss exposure and provides information about the exposure's potential loss severity. Moreover, this entry might trigger questions about the damageability of the inventory items, inventory location, and any related hazards.

Financial statements can also reveal that an organization is subject to significant financial risks, such as fluctuations in the value of financial investments, interest rate swings, foreign exchange exposures, or commodity price swings.

Contract and Lease Analysis

Another technique for identifying loss exposures is contract and lease analysis. Almost every organization has contractual agreements. Loss exposure identification might require analyzing the contracts affecting an organization's property and liability exposures to determine who has assumed responsibility for which loss exposures. Legal expertise is often necessary to interpret such agreements.

Ongoing contract evaluation is part of monitoring and maintaining a risk management program. Hold-harmless and indemnification clauses are common in many contracts and can create significant exposures. Although reviewing every contract before it is signed might be impractical for risk management professionals, they should determine what contractual elements require a risk management review. For example, a risk manager might insist on reviewing any agreement to purchase real property to ensure that the organization is not becoming responsible for contaminated or polluted land with severe environmental liability implications.

Flowchart Analysis

Loss exposures can be uncovered by analyzing flowcharts. Flowchart diagrams show the sequence and relationships of operations or processes by illustrating what an organization does, the sequence in which activities occur, and the nature and use of the resources involved.

A manufacturer's flowchart might start with raw material acquisition and end with the finished product's delivery to the ultimate consumer. Individual entries on the flowchart, the processes involved, and the means by which products move from one process to the next can help identify loss exposures, particularly critical exposures. For example, a flowchart might illustrate that every item produced by a certain manufacturer must be spray painted during the production process. This activity presents a critical property loss exposure. An explosion at the spray-painting location might disable the entire production line. A shutdown could also occur if the spray-painting operation is closed because it fails to meet environmental standards.

The flowchart in Exhibit 3-2 reveals that a minor amount of damage to Process AB could stop the production of both processes A and B. Another flowchart might reveal that most operations depend on a single computer system and that a small mishap in the computer room could close an entire plant.

Loss Analysis

Loss analysis
The process of examining the records of past losses to identify loss exposures.

Loss analysis is the process of examining the records of past losses to identify loss exposures. Loss analysis identifies only loss exposures that have actually sustained a loss or, in some cases, led to a lost opportunity.

Airplane "black boxes," or flight recorders, illustrate a special loss analysis tool. Although a black box does nothing to prevent the airplane from crashing, a

EXHIBIT 3-2

Flowchart Covering Internal Flow

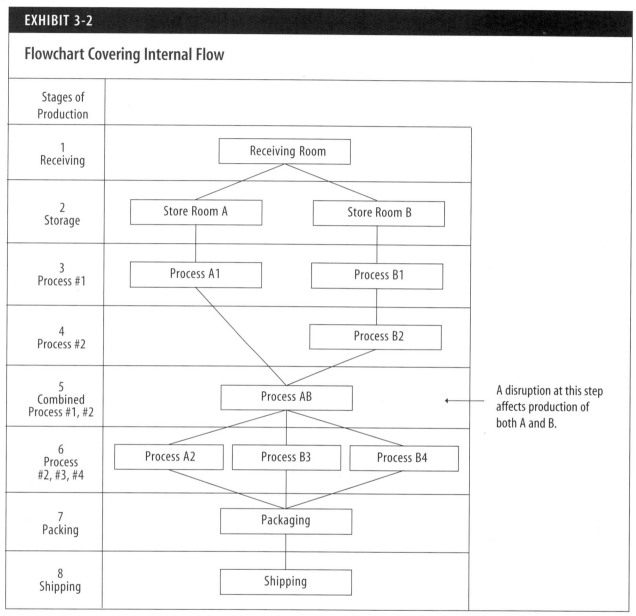

Adapted with permission from POA Publishing, LLC, *The Merritt Risk Management Manual* (Los Angeles: POA Publishing, LLC, 1993), p. 17.

black box recovered from a crashed airliner sometimes provides information that is extremely useful in preventing future crashes.

Hazard Analysis

Identifying loss exposures can include **hazard analysis**, which identifies conditions that increase the estimated frequency or severity of loss.

Hazard analysis often requires the services of a specialist. A business consultant might identify conditions that cause the organization to overlook opportunities

Hazard analysis
The process of identifying conditions that increase the estimated frequency or severity of loss.

for growth. Likewise, concerns over environmental hazards might require a specialist to take air or water samples and a specialized laboratory to analyze them. However, even a person without special expertise can identify some hazards by conducting a personal on-site inspection.

For example, one might notice that seat belts in a company-owned vehicle are stuffed under the seat cushion and obviously not being used. Or one might notice that a drill press operator's long hair is dangling dangerously close to machinery with moving parts—an accident waiting to happen.

Personal Inspections

Whenever possible a personal inspection or an on-site visit is highly desirable. Personal inspections often reveal loss exposures that would not appear in written descriptions. For example, an on-site inspection might reveal that an organization has two pickup trucks in addition to the fleet of cars identified through a checklist.

Interviews

While an inspection can only reveal what is currently happening, interviews can elicit information about what occurred before the inspection or what might be planned for the future. Worthwhile interviews might be conducted with anyone in the organization, ranging from the president to the janitor. The proper questions can elicit extremely useful risk management information that might not otherwise be available.

Identifying loss exposures should be done thoroughly and systematically. The techniques mentioned above help risk managers document the loss exposures that will drive risk management activities.

Step 2: Analyzing Loss Exposures

Analyzing loss exposures is the next step in the risk management process after *identifying* loss exposures. The analysis step involves considering the four dimensions of a loss exposure:

1. *Loss frequency*—the number of losses (fires, auto accidents, liability claims) within a specific time period.
2. *Loss severity*—the amount, in dollars, of a loss for a specific occurrence.
3. *Total dollar losses*—the total dollar amount of losses for all occurrences during a specific time period.
4. *Timing*—when losses occur and when loss payments are made. The time interval between loss occurrence and loss payment can be lengthy.

Analyzing loss exposures is, in itself, a costly endeavor. The cost of risk includes the cost of acquiring risk-related information used in loss forecasts, estimates of future cash flows, and other planning activities. In some cases, this information can actually reduce losses. Recent satellite technology, for example, provides advance warning that enables people in a hurricane's path to board up windows, evacuate, and implement other loss reduction measures. Such detailed information improves forecast accuracy and reduces variability. In short, more information is worth its costs because it can lead to better risk management decisions.

Analyzing loss frequency and severity data helps to develop projections. Frequency and severity projections help prioritize loss exposures so that risk management resources can be concentrated where needed most. The law of large numbers indicates that the larger the number of exposure units are for a given loss exposure, the more credible the projections are.

Loss Frequency

The first dimension in analyzing loss exposures is loss frequency. Loss frequency is the number of losses—such as fires, thefts, floods—that occur within a specified time period. The relative frequency of theft losses at a particular building might be one in every two years (0.50 per year), while flood frequency might be one every hundred years (0.01 per year). Frequency can be estimated based on experience, on the average, over many cases.

Generally, loss frequency is more easily projected than loss severity. In fact, loss frequency can be projected with a fairly high degree of confidence for some exposures in large organizations. For example, a mail-order house that ships thousands of parcels each day probably can accurately project the number of transit losses it will sustain in a year, based on past experience and adjusted for any expected changes in future conditions.

Most organizations do not have enough exposure units to accurately project low-frequency, high-severity events. However, an estimate with a margin for error is better than no estimate at all, as long as its limitations are recognized.

Loss Severity

The second dimension in analyzing loss exposures is loss severity. The purpose of analyzing potential loss severity is to assess how serious a loss might be. How much of a building could be damaged in a single fire? How long before operations can resume after a fire?

Knowing the size of the most likely loss is useful in managing risk. However, knowing that the most likely amount of loss was $25,000 is of little value if a $1 million loss has actually occurred. Therefore, also knowing the size of the largest loss that could occur (maximum possible loss), as well as the largest loss likely to occur (probable maximum loss), is helpful in measuring loss exposures.

Considering Loss Frequency and Loss Severity Jointly

To evaluate the significance of a particular loss exposure, someone must consider its expected loss frequency and loss severity jointly. One method of considering possible combinations of loss frequency and loss severity, known as the Prouty Approach, identifies four broad categories of loss frequency and three broad categories of loss severity.[2] As shown in Exhibit 3-3, the four categories of loss frequency are as follows:

1. Almost Nil: extremely unlikely to happen; virtually no possibility.
2. Slight: could happen but has not happened.
3. Moderate: happens occasionally.
4. Definite: happens regularly.

The three categories of loss severity are as follows:

1. Slight: The organization can readily retain each loss.
2. Significant: The organization cannot retain the loss, some part of which must be transferred.
3. Severe: The organization must transfer virtually all of the loss or endanger its survival.

These broad categories of loss frequency and loss severity are somewhat subjective. However, it is easy to understand them and to infer the financial significance of losses in each of the frequency/severity cells of Exhibit 3-3.

Loss frequency and loss severity tend to be inversely related for any given exposure. In other words, the more severe a loss tends to be, the less frequently it tends to occur. And the more frequent a loss to a given exposure, the less severe the loss tends to be. Losses that are slight but almost definitely will occur are so routine that good managers budget for them through depreciation allowances. At the other extreme, an activity that would generate intolerable

---

EXHIBIT 3-3

The Prouty Approach To Analyzing the Significance of Loss Exposures

Severity Frequency	Slight	Significant	Severe
Almost Nil			
Slight			
Moderate			
Definite			

loss severity is typically avoided; good risk managers recognize that the activity is too risky to undertake. So, most risk management decisions concern loss exposures for which individual losses, while tolerable, tend to be either significant or severe and have a moderate, slight, or almost nil chance of occurring.

A given loss exposure might generate financially serious results because of either high individual loss severity or high-frequency, low-severity losses that aggregate to a substantial total. Perhaps too often, an organization's risk management efforts focus too narrowly on the sudden, large "shock loss," such as the major fire, violent explosion, or huge liability claim. However, much smaller losses, which happen so frequently that they become routine or "normal," can eventually produce much larger total losses than the single dramatic event. For example, many retailing firms suffer greater total losses through shoplifting or pilferage, which happens every day, than they do through the large fire that might happen every twenty years. Minor, cumulatively significant losses usually deserve as much risk management attention as do large individual losses.

Maximum Possible Loss

Effectively managing risk requires identifying the worst possible outcome. The **maximum possible loss**, sometimes called the **amount subject**, is the total value exposed to loss at any one location or from any one event. In the case of fire damage to a building and its contents, the maximum possible loss is usually the total building and contents values exposed to loss within any one building or fire division.

Maximum possible loss, or amount subject
The total value exposed to loss at any one location or from any one event.

Risk managers might ask questions such as these: What is the maximum possible loss for a fleet of motor vehicles? Is it the value of the most expensive unit? Do the vehicles travel together, and might two vehicles in the fleet collide with one another or participate in a chain collision? Are several vehicles stored in the same building at night and therefore subject to a common loss? What are the chances of flood or tornado damage at the company's parking area? The answers to such questions should be considered in the risk management process.

Although maximum possible *property* losses can be estimated based on the values exposed to loss, assessing the maximum possible *liability* loss is usually difficult or impossible.

If statistical analysis is possible, then assuming that the maximum possible loss severity represents an amount that will not be exceeded, say, 95 percent or 98 percent of the time might be practical.

Probable Maximum Loss

The value of the largest loss *likely* to occur might be much less than the value of the maximum possible loss. The probable fire loss will be limited by fire protection available. The probable liability loss can be estimated based on a firm's own experience or other organizations' experience. If statistical data are available, assuming that the probable maximum loss lies within, say, one standard deviation of the average past loss might be practical.

Total Dollar Losses

The third dimension of analyzing loss exposures is total dollar losses. Total dollar losses are calculated by multiplying loss frequency times average loss severity. Expected dollar losses can be projected by multiplying expected loss frequency times expected average loss severity, and worst-case scenarios can be calculated by assuming both high frequency and the worst possible severity. However, in such projections, one should not overlook the possibility of a loss involving exposures of more than one type.

For example, a severe explosion in a manufacturing plant can decrease the affected property's value, involve a substantial interruption of business, involve personnel losses and employee injuries, and result in liability claims for injury to members of the public or damage to neighboring property. Inability to fulfill contracts because the plant is shut down might result in additional penalties and decrease the opportunity for future contracts or, at minimum, a loss of goodwill. For these reasons, it is important to consider the maximum loss that could result from a single event or a series of related events.

Timing

The fourth dimension of analyzing loss exposures is timing of losses. Sound risk analysis takes into account not only (1) when losses are likely to occur, but also (2) when payment for those losses will likely be made. The timing dimension is significant because money held in reserve to pay for a loss can earn interest until the actual payment is made. Whether a loss is counted when it is incurred or when it is paid is also significant for various accounting and tax reasons.

Some losses, such as earthquake losses, have an equal probability of occurring at any time during the calendar year or business cycle, while others—such as hurricane or flood losses—have a distinct seasonal factor.

Funds to pay for property losses are generally disbursed relatively soon after the event occurs. Liability losses, alternatively, often involve a long delay among the time of the adverse event, the time when an occurrence is recognized, the period of possible litigation, and the time when payment is actually made. Disability claims, for example, might then be paid over a long period of time. In some cases, especially those involving environmental exposures or health risks, the delay can span several decades.

Credibility

The term "credibility" is often used in risk management to mean the level of confidence that one can properly have that available data are capable of being used as accurate indicators of future losses. After estimating the four dimensions of a loss exposure, a risk manager then evaluates the credibility of the projections of loss frequency, loss severity, total dollar losses, and timing.

The pattern shown in Exhibit 3-4 might illustrate the expected transportation losses for a large shipper in business for ten years and with a steadily increasing volume of transportation services. A risk manager might project that average losses during the coming years would fall along the line labeled "expected" and that the probable maximum loss would lie along the line labeled "maximum." Probable minimum loss levels might also be projected, as shown by the "minimum" line. If such projections can be made with a high degree of confidence, actual losses will be expected to follow a pattern like the "actual" line on the graph, deviating from the average from one year to the next but in no case exceeding the maximum or falling below the minimum. Because the shipper faces little uncertainty, it may choose to retain these losses instead of insuring them.

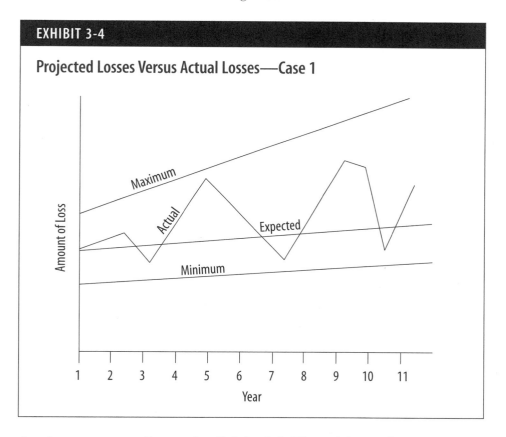

EXHIBIT 3-4

Projected Losses Versus Actual Losses—Case 1

Another situation is illustrated in Exhibit 3-5. This exhibit might represent products liability losses experienced by a large manufacturer. A few losses usually occur each year. In Year 4, however, almost no losses occurred, while in Year 8 at least one major loss occurred. (The losses in Year 8 are so high that the scale is not continuous, as indicated in the exhibit by the breaks in the actual line.) These losses might have been projectable to a certain extent at lower levels, but possibilities existed for substantial losses above the normal loss levels. It might be disastrous to attempt to finance such losses out of the organization's operating budget.

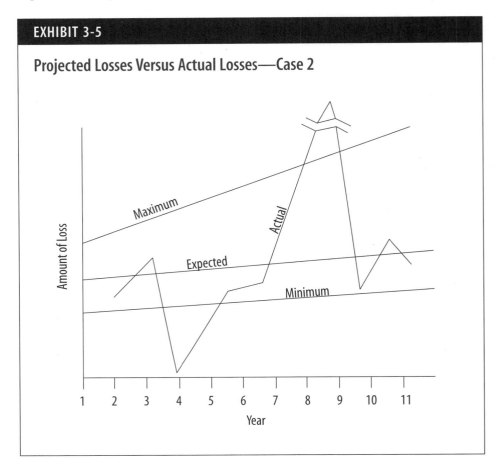

EXHIBIT 3-5

Projected Losses Versus Actual Losses—Case 2

Step 3: Examining The Feasibility of Risk Management Alternatives

The third step in the risk management process is evaluating risk management alternatives. The most effective risk management technique for handling any loss exposure is simple: Avoid the exposure, completely eliminating any risk. Complete avoidance usually is not feasible or desirable. Loss exposures arise from activities and circumstances that are essential to individuals and to organizations. Risks that are not avoided must be addressed through a combination of risk control techniques and risk financing techniques.

- *Risk control techniques* minimize the estimated frequency or severity of accidental losses.
- *Risk financing techniques* generate the funds to pay for or offset losses that occur despite risk control efforts.

These three broad categories (exposure avoidance, risk control, and risk financing) are illustrated in Exhibit 3-6.

EXHIBIT 3-6

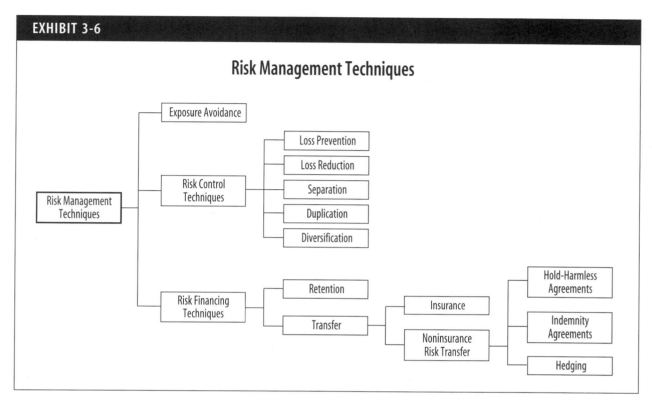

Risk management techniques should not be evaluated or used in isolation. Unless the exposure is avoided, an organization should apply at least one risk control technique *and* one risk financing technique to each of its significant exposures. The control technique minimizes the estimated frequency and severity of loss, and the financing technique addresses losses that occur despite the controls. Any risk control or risk financing technique can generally be used together with any other control or financing technique.

Exposure Avoidance

Exposure avoidance, also called **avoidance**, is the risk management technique used when a party decides not to incur a loss exposure in the first place or to eliminate one that already exists. These are examples:

- *Proactive avoidance:* Some medical students choose not to become obstetricians because they want to avoid the large professional liability (malpractice) claims associated with that profession.
- *Abandonment:* Manufacturers of hand-held hair dryers stopped using asbestos insulation in their dryers once the cancer-causing properties of asbestos became known. Consequently, the users of the new dryers were not being exposed to asbestos.

Exposure avoidance, or avoidance
The risk management technique used when a party decides not to incur a loss exposure or to eliminate one that already exists.

Nest Heads™, Copyright, Copley News Service, September 14, 2000. Reprinted with permission of Copley News Service. All rights reserved.

Exposure avoidance reduces the *probability* of loss from the avoided exposure to zero. If the probability of loss is not zero, the exposure has not been avoided.

Often, discontinuing an existing activity (abandonment) avoids exposures from future activities but does not eliminate exposures from past activities. For example, a child car seat manufacturer might stop making seats because of claims for injuries associated with their use. Products liability losses arising out of the exposures of future car seat sales are avoided, but claims could still arise from the defective seats already in use.

Risks do not exist in a vacuum, and avoiding one risk can actually create or enhance another. For example, a jewelry store might put secure bars on its windows and doors to eliminate the possibility that burglars could enter through the windows and steal merchandise. Burglars might still enter through other means; the loss exposure is not avoided entirely. Although they eliminate one exposure, these same bars might make the store less attractive to potential shoppers, might make it impossible for firefighters to enter the building through the windows if they are called to extinguish a fire, and might trap employees inside the store if a fire occurs.

Exposure avoidance is the first risk management technique to consider. However, avoidance is usually not a practical option because going out of a line of business is the only way many firms could effectively implement avoidance.

Risk Control Techniques

Risk control technique

A risk management technique that minimizes the estimated frequency or severity of accidental losses.

Another risk management alternative to consider is risk control. **Risk control techniques** actually modify the exposure by reducing the estimated frequency or severity of accidental losses. Risk control techniques include the following:

- Loss prevention
- Loss reduction
- Separation of loss exposures
- Duplication
- Diversification

These risk control techniques can be implemented separately or in any combination.

Loss Prevention

Loss prevention lowers the expected *frequency* of loss from a particular loss exposure. For example, pressure relief valves on a boiler are intended to "prevent" explosions by keeping the pressure in the boiler from reaching an unsafe level. The valve is an example of loss prevention, not exposure avoidance; an explosion could still occur if the valve should malfunction.

Loss prevention
A risk control technique that lowers the expected *frequency* of loss from a particular loss exposure.

Loss Reduction

The **loss reduction** risk control technique aims to lower the *severity* of losses from a particular loss exposure. Automatic sprinkler systems are a classic example of loss reduction measures. Sprinklers do not prevent fires from starting, but they are intended to limit or extinguish fires that have already started.

Loss reduction
A risk control technique that lowers the expected severity of losses from a particular loss exposure.

Some risk control measures both prevent and reduce losses. For example, using burglar alarms is generally considered a loss reduction measure because an alarm is activated only when a burglary occurs and because it tends to minimize the amount of property stolen. Burglars tend to avoid breaking into buildings that have an alarm; therefore, a burglar alarm also plays a loss prevention role.

Disaster planning is a specialized aspect of loss reduction. A **disaster plan**, also known as a **catastrophe plan** or a **contingency plan**, involves formally identifying possible crises that might occur and developing a detailed, formal response plan. For many organizations, disaster planning is especially important in addressing the risks associated with those systems without which the entire organization could not function.

Disaster planning
A specialized aspect of loss reduction. A **disaster plan**, also known as a **catastrophe plan** or a **contingency plan**, involves formally identifying possible crises that might occur and developing a detailed, formal response plan.

Separation

The **separation** risk control technique isolates loss exposures from one another to minimize the adverse effect of a single event. For example, instead of placing all inventory in one large warehouse where it is all subject to loss caused by the same occurrence, a business might use several smaller warehouses at different locations.

Separation
A risk control technique that isolates loss exposures from one another to minimize the adverse effect of a single event.

Duplication

The **duplication** risk control technique uses backups, spares, or copies of critical property, information, or capabilities. Copies of key documents and information can be inexpensively made and—using the separation technique—stored in a remote, protected location. Critical repair parts or duplicate machines can be kept on hand for immediate replacement. An electric generating plant might keep one functioning generator off-line and ready for immediate use if another generator should fail, so that power can be provided virtually without interruption. Duplication plans such as these are often part of disaster plans.

Duplication
A risk control technique that uses backups, spares, or copies of critical property, information, or capabilities.

Separation and duplication often go together. Placing the *same types of inventory* in two different warehouses is an example of separation and duplication. Usually, simultaneously operating several identical warehouses strictly for risk management reasons would not be cost-effective. However, a business might also have other reasons for such an operation. For example, rather than have a single warehouse in Philadelphia, a produce wholesaler might operate parallel warehouses in Baltimore and New York, reducing the distance between the warehouse and local stores and restaurants. If it became necessary, one of these warehouses could continue to fill orders in both areas, despite some extra transportation expense. In this case, duplication and separation serve as risk control techniques and fulfill another operational purpose.

Diversification

Diversification

A risk control technique that spreads loss exposures over different categories of risk.

Diversification closely resembles the risk control techniques of duplication and separation. However, diversification is more commonly applied to managing speculative risks, or risks with the possibility of gain or loss. **Diversification** is a risk control technique that spreads loss exposures over different categories of risk.

Businesses engage in diversification of loss exposures when they provide a variety of products and services that are used by a range of customers. An insurer might diversify its exposures geographically and by type of business by selling both personal and commercial insurance or both property-casualty and life insurance.

Investors employ diversification when they allocate their assets among a mix of stocks and bonds from companies in different industry sectors. An investor might diversify investments by purchasing stock in a bank and a pharmaceutical manufacturer. Because these are unrelated industries, the investor hopes that any losses in one stock might be more than offset by profits in another.

Risk Financing Techniques

Risk financing technique

A risk management technique that generates the funds to pay for or offset losses.

A **risk financing technique** is a risk management technique that generates the funds to pay for or offset losses. Risk financing techniques can be classified into two groups:

1. Transfer, which includes insurance and noninsurance techniques to shift the cost of loss to another party.
2. Retention, which includes retaining the loss by generating funds within the organization to pay for the loss.

Risk financing techniques are not necessarily used in isolation. Many measures involve elements of both retention and transfer. For example, insurance with a deductible involves retention of the deductible amount and transfer of losses above the deductible.

Applying Exposure Avoidance and Risk Control Techniques

Yellow Bus Company operates a fleet of school buses for several local school districts, as well as a charter bus service. Any accident involving a loaded bus could be very serious and costly. Yellow could consider these risk management techniques:

Exposure avoidance could be achieved if Yellow were to sell its buses and use the proceeds to purchase certificates of deposit (CDs) from a bank. However, complete avoidance probably is not practical.

Risk prevention measures could include driver screening, driver safety training, and equipment maintenance practices.

Risk reduction measures could include first-aid training and kits, fire extinguishers, flares, and two-way radios.

Duplication measures could include having some spare buses that would be immediately pressed into service if needed.

Separation measures could include storing buses at two or more locations so that the entire fleet is not subject to damage from a single occurrence.

Diversification measures could include operating or investing in different types of businesses, other than bus and charter service.

Insurance

Although insurance is one approach to risk financing, it is a vital component of a risk management program and will be discussed in depth in subsequent chapters. **Insurance** is a risk management technique that transfers the potential financial consequences of certain specified loss exposures from the insured to the insurer. The insurance buyer substitutes a small certain financial cost, the insurance premium, for the possibility of a large financial loss paid by the insurer.

Insurance is a funded risk transfer. By accepting a premium, the insurer agrees to pay for all the organization's losses that are covered by the insurance contract. The insurer also agrees to provide necessary services, such as claim handling and defense of liability claims.

Noninsurance Risk Transfer Techniques

In addition to insurance policies, other contracts transfer loss exposures. Such contracts include hold-harmless and indemnity agreements. Hedging is also considered a **noninsurance risk transfer technique.**

Hold-Harmless Agreements and Indemnity Agreements   Some contracts deal solely with the responsibility for losses arising out of a particular relationship or activity. Noninsurance transfers are often expressed in a *hold-harmless agreement* or an *indemnity agreement.*

- Under a **hold-harmless agreement**, one party (the indemnitor) agrees to pay specified types and amounts of losses *on behalf of* a second party (the indemnitee).

Insurance
A risk management technique that tranfers the potential financial consequences of certain specified loss exposures from the insured to the insurer.

Noninsurance risk transfer technique
A risk management technique that transfers all or part of the risk of loss to another party, other than an insurer.

Hold-harmless agreement
A contract under which one party (the indemnitor) agrees to pay specified types and amounts of losses on behalf of a second party (the indemnitee).

Indemnity agreement
A contract under which one party (the indemnitor) agrees to reimburse a second party (the indemnitee) for losses that the indemnitee has already paid.

- Under an **indemnity agreement**, one party (the indemnitor) agrees *to reimburse* a second party (the indemnitee) for losses that the indemnitee has already paid. Therefore, the indemnitor has no obligations until the indemnitee has already paid for the loss.

Indemnity and hold-harmless agreements are often combined into an "indemnity-and-hold-harmless agreement," such as the one in Exhibit 3-7.

EXHIBIT 3-7

Sample Indemnity and Hold Harmless Agreement for Use in Contracts With State Government Agency

To the fullest extent permitted by law, Contractor shall indemnify, defend and hold harmless State, agencies of State and all officials, agents and employees of State, from and against all claims arising out of or resulting from the performance of the contract. "Claim" as used in this agreement means any financial loss, claim, suit, action, damage, or expense, including but not limited to attorney's fees, attributable for bodily injury, sickness, disease or death, or injury to or destruction of tangible property including loss of use resulting therefrom. Contractor's obligation to indemnify, defend, and hold harmless includes any claim by Contractors' agents, employees, representatives, or any subcontractor or its employees.

Contractor expressly agrees to indemnify, defend, and hold harmless State for any claim arising out of or incident to Contractor's or any subcontractor's performance or failure to perform the contract. Contractor's obligation to indemnify, defend, and hold harmless State shall not be eliminated or reduced by any actual or alleged concurrent negligence of State or its agents, agencies, employees and officials.

Washington State Department of General Administration, Division of Transportation, Risk, and Mail, *Contracts: Transferring and Financing Risk*, May 1999, p. 22, http://www.ga.wa.gov/risk/riskcont.pdf

---

Hedging
A financial transaction in which one asset is held to offset the risks associated with another asset.

Hedging A financial transaction in which one asset is held to offset the loss exposure associated with another asset is **hedging**. Hedging often involves speculative rather than pure risks. A simple example: If Bob has a bet with Jim that the Blue team will win a sporting event, he could offset this risk by betting with Mary that the Blue team will lose.

Hedging is practical when it is used to offset loss exposures to which one is naturally, voluntarily, or inevitably exposed. For example, City Newspaper might enter into a futures contract with its paper supplier to purchase a fixed quantity of newsprint paper over the coming year at today's market price. City Newspaper inevitably has to acquire newsprint over the coming year, and it faces the loss exposure of its price variability. A futures contract for newsprint offsets this loss exposure. If the market price of paper increases over the next year, City Newspaper will save money by buying paper below the prevailing price. If the market price drops, City Newspaper will pay more than the new prevailing lower price for its paper. Either way, City Newspaper's loss exposure is reduced because the variability in the newsprint's cost is eliminated—*from the standpoint of City Newspaper*. Notice that the risk is increased for the paper supplier, who now faces the possibility of increased or decreased profits depending on the newsprint's prevailing market price. City Newspaper's loss exposure has, in effect, been transferred to the supplier.

Retention

Because **retention** can be the most efficient risk financing technique available, it is sometimes preferred even when insurance is available. Retention can also be the risk financing technique of last resort; the financial burden of any losses that cannot be insured or otherwise transferred *must* be retained.

Retention
A risk management technique by which losses are retained by generating funds within the organization to pay for the losses.

"Self-Insurance" Versus Retention

The term "self-insurance" sometimes describes any type of plan for which a person or an organization retains its own losses—or simply decides not to buy insurance. Used this way, "self-insurance" is interchangeable with the term "retention."

Some people assert that certain forms of "self-insurance" are not insurance at all and that the label "self-insurance" should be applied only to a formal program in which an organization keeps records of its losses and maintains a system to pay for them.

Some people refuse to use the term "self-insurance," claiming it is an inaccurate term because insurance involves a transfer of risk, thereby making it impossible to insure one's self.

Risk and insurance professionals cannot completely avoid the issue because some statutes, regulations, or contracts refer to "self-insurance."

The term "self-insured" remains ambiguous unless it is further defined as "funded" or "unfunded."

Retention can be planned or unplanned; complete or partial; or funded or unfunded.

- **Planned retention** is a deliberate retention of a loss exposure that has been identified and evaluated. Planned retention might be chosen because it is most cost-effective, because it is most convenient, or because no other alternatives are available.

- **Unplanned retention** is the retention of a loss exposure because it has not been identified or accurately evaluated. For example, many people in North Carolina did not have flood insurance when the floods that followed Hurricane Floyd destroyed 3,680 homes and damaged 12,000 others.[3]

    Many of these North Carolina residents probably identified the possibility of flood but underestimated the probability of a serious flood at their location.

- **Complete retention** is the assumption of the full cost of any loss that is retained by the organization.

Planned retention
A deliberate assumption of a loss exposure that has been identified and evaluated.

Unplanned retention
An inadvertent assumption of a loss exposure that has not been identified and evaluated.

Complete retention
The assumption of the full cost of any loss that is retained by the organization.

Partial retention
The assumption of a portion of the cost of a loss by the organization and the transfer of the remaining portion of the cost of the loss.

Funded retention
The pre-loss arrangement to ensure that funding is available post-loss to pay for losses that occur.

Unfunded retention
The lack of advance funding for losses that occur.

Pre-funding
A funded retention arrangement that sets aside funds in advance of losses to pay for losses that occur.

Current funding
A funded retention arrangement that provides funds to pay for losses when losses occur.

Post-funding
A funded retention arrangement that provides funds to pay for losses sometime after losses occur, using borrowing (or some other method of raising additional capital) in the meantime.

- **Partial retention** is the assumption of a portion of the cost of a loss by the organization and the transfer of the remaining portion of the cost of the loss.
- **Funded retention** is the pre-loss arrangement to ensure that funding is available post-loss to pay for losses that occur.
- **Unfunded retention** is the lack of advance funding for losses that occur.

Methods of Funding Retained Losses

Three general methods can be used to pay for retained losses: pre-funding, current funding, and post-funding.

1. With **pre-funding**, the money to fund retained losses is set aside in advance of losses. The principal advantage of pre-funding is that the money needed to fund losses can be saved over several budget periods. The principal disadvantage is that it ties up money that could otherwise be used to promote productivity. This loss of productivity is the difference between what fully employed funds can produce for the organization and what can be earned on readily marketable securities. This loss of productivity keeps pre-funding from being widely used except in one form: captive insurers. Chapter 5 takes a closer look at captive insurers.

2. With **current funding**, money to fund retained losses is provided at the time of the loss or immediately after it. Current funding is the most popular and often the least expensive form of retention. Its big advantage is that it commits no funds before they are actually needed. Its principal disadvantage is that only as much money as can be spared from a single budget period can be devoted to it.

3. With **post-funding**, the organization pays for its retained losses sometime after losses occur, using borrowing (or some other method of raising additional capital) in the meantime. Suppose an uninsured building is so badly damaged that it has to be rebuilt. The owner might obtain a mortgage loan to fund the cost of reconstructing the building—and thus engage in post-funding.

Post-loss funding has at least two advantages:

1. The cost of retained losses may be paid over several years instead of all at once.
2. Only the amount of money needed to pay for retained losses is used.

Post-loss funding has at least four disadvantages:

1. The organization using post-loss funding must pay interest on the debt.
2. The same loss event that produces the need to borrow might also reduce the organization's creditworthiness, thus increasing the loan's cost. This disadvantage can be overcome by making pre-loss arrangements for a credit guarantee.
3. When post-loss credit is guaranteed, that guarantee involves a pre-loss fee.

4. Guaranteeing post-loss credit might reduce the organization's capacity to borrow pre-loss funds that can be used for operations.

Under current income tax and financial accounting rules, a corporation cannot deduct loss costs from income until the amount is certain, which means that no deduction can be made before the loss has actually occurred, even if the loss can be projected with a high degree of confidence. The timing of the accounting charge, known as "current expensing," applies regardless of whether the funding occurs before, at the time of, or after the loss.

Step 4: Selecting the Best Risk Management Techniques

The fourth step in the risk management process is selecting the best risk management techniques to use. This occurs after an organization identifies and analyzes loss exposures and considers the various risk management techniques that *might* be applied. Risk managers must identify techniques that will prevent or reduce losses, as well as techniques to finance losses that occur despite the prevention/reduction efforts.

Some loss exposures can adequately be treated with a single risk management technique, but many require a combination of techniques to adequately address the loss exposure. Consider these examples:

• Retention and insurance techniques are in effect when insurance with a deductible is used.

• Insurance and duplication (records also kept at another location) might be combined to protect against losses of key records.

Selecting the mix of risk management techniques that best meets an organization's risk management objectives should be based on quantitative financial considerations and qualitative, nonfinancial considerations.

Financial considerations are an important part of selecting a risk management technique. A thorough financial analysis might be based on the following:

• A credible projection of the dimensions of expected losses (frequency, severity, and timing of payment).

• A forecast, for each feasible combination of risk management measures, of the effect on the frequency, severity, and timing of these expected losses.

• A projection of the after-tax costs involved in applying the various risk management techniques. These costs include, for example, the cost of insurance premiums or the expenses associated with installing and maintaining various risk control devices.

Based on the above considerations, an organization can perform a cost/benefit analysis that identifies the risk management technique, or combination of techniques, that will maximize the organization's value. An organization's objective should be to determine an optimal level of risk management that maximizes value. An organization's value may also include ethical and other nonfinancial considerations as discussed below.

Data based on objective risk factors usually are not the only criteria considered in determining appropriate risk management techniques. An organization might also place a great deal of value on keeping the business in operation at all costs and/or peace of mind.

However, the risk management technique that produces the best financial result might be ethically unacceptable and must therefore be rejected. Recognizing the ethical constraints involved in risk management decisions and determining the most ethical course of action are not always easy. See the "Johnson Controls" box for an example.

Johnson Controls

The environment in Johnson Controls' battery manufacturing operation contained high concentrations of ambient lead. Eight pregnant employees had lead blood levels exceeding Occupational Safety and Health Administration (OSHA) standards for a worker planning to have a family. In response, Johnson decided to establish a policy barring women, except those whose infertility was medically documented, from jobs involving actual or potential lead exposure exceeding the OSHA standard.[4]

The basis for this decision might not have been entirely altruistic or nonfinancial. In addition to preventing possible birth defects, the decision also tended to prevent future claims by these women or their children. Was it an ethical decision? Perhaps. But the court ruled that it constituted illegal sexual discrimination against the women who wanted these jobs.

This case illustrates the ethical difficulties involved in making some risk management decisions.

Determining an Optimal Retention Level

An organization's risk financing program should balance transfer and retention, addressing specific factors that affect uncertainty of its retained loss outcomes and the long-term cost of its loss exposures. Also, the organization should retain losses only up to a tolerable uncertainty level. Determining an optimal retention level is usually more of an art than a science. Generally, the retention level should be based on several factors, including the organization's:

- Risk tolerance,
- Financial condition,
- Ability to diversify its retained loss exposures,
- Ability to obtain a gain,
- Ability to administer a loss retention program,
- Ability to control losses in an efficient, cost-effective manner, and
- Ability to transfer its loss exposures in a cost-effective manner.[5]

Determining the optimal retention level helps risk analysts balance the risk financing program between transfer and retention.

Step 5: Implementing Risk Management Techniques

After an organization decides which risk management technique(s) to use, the next step is to implement the decision, which requires cooperation among an organization's departments. Purchasing loss reduction devices or contracting for loss prevention services might be necessary. Contracts must be written or revised. Retention programs might need funding. Loss control programs must be implemented and then continually reinforced. Agents or brokers, insurers, third-party administrators, and other providers might need to be selected for insurance programs. Insurance policies must be requested and premiums paid.

The process of identifying and evaluating alternatives leads to many techniques that must then be implemented. For example, if a small firm owns a large building, it almost certainly will purchase property insurance. Remaining details, such as the exact placement of fire extinguishers, the terms and cost of insurance and noninsurance contract revisions, which insurer to use, the timing of insurance premium payments, or the actual deposit of funds for a retention program, must be addressed as the program is implemented.

Step 6: Monitoring Results

The last of the six steps in the risk management process is ongoing monitoring. The risk management process is continual and requires attention to both activities and results. Have the selected measures actually been implemented? Have they produced the expected results? Are the results meaningful?

To monitor a risk management program, one must establish performance standards, check adherence to these standards, and determine whether changes are needed.

If a risk management change is required, repeating all or part of the risk management process is necessary.

Identifying and evaluating any changes in internal and external conditions is part of this process. These changing conditions might indicate any of the following:

- New exposures have developed. For example, the organization might be manufacturing new products or conducting operations at new locations.
- Existing exposures have become more significant. For example, a product defect might be uncovered, leading to higher liability exposure.
- Different risk management techniques have become more appropriate. For example a significant increase in insurance premiums might make a retention program feasible.

THE RISK MANAGEMENT FUNCTION

The risk management process is not merely a theoretical list of steps. Somebody actually performs the *function* of risk management.

Risk Management in a Large Business

Many large businesses operate highly skilled, specialized risk management departments, headed by a full-time risk manager. These departments examine the key information and make risk management decisions. The risk management philosophy and practices are conveyed through measures including the following:

- Risk management policies
- Risk management manuals
- Risk management information systems

Risk management is not an isolated activity. A successful risk management department must develop and maintain relationships with every other department within an organization to ensure that risk management decisions effectively support the organization's goals. Successfully implementing risk management techniques requires coordination with accounting, finance, and human resources departments, as well as top management's approval and support.

The recent trend toward insurance rate and form deregulation in commercial insurance underscores the significance of knowledgeable risk management professionals. In many states, if businesses employ full-time risk managers with certain credentials and/or meet specified size requirements, then the level of state insurance regulation affecting the insurance contracts they purchase is reduced. These businesses presumably have sufficient expertise to determine their insurance needs and negotiate appropriate contractual terms and price without regulatory oversight.

Risk Management in a Small or Medium-Sized Business

Separate risk management departments are not common in small businesses. Primary responsibility for risk management is often assigned to a treasurer, an accountant, or a human resources manager who devotes only part of his or her time to risk management. In sole proprietorships or small businesses, the owner might make all management decisions, including those about risk.

Part-time risk managers tend to rely heavily on producers as their primary source of risk management information. Risk management consulting firms also provide risk management services for a fee.

Risk Management by Individuals or Families

Individual or personal risk management is often viewed as part of the financial planning process that encompasses broader matters such as capital accumulation, retirement planning, and estate planning.

Families, like small businesses, are typically unfamiliar with the risk management process, so they tend to rely on the services of insurance producers and financial planners.

Individuals and families often practice risk management informally without explicitly following the six steps in the risk management process. Also, certain risk management techniques may be mandated. For example, auto insurance is required in nearly every state, and homeowners insurance is usually required by a home loan lender, so most individuals and families purchase insurance to finance their major property and liability loss exposures. For families and businesses, the level of formality in the risk management process depends on the size of the entity, the complexity of operations, and the resources available to devote to the process.

THE BENEFITS OF RISK MANAGEMENT

Sound and effective risk management ensures that losses or missed opportunities do not prevent an organization from meeting its pre-loss and post-loss objectives.

Risk Management's Benefits

Effective risk management can increase an organization's value in the following ways:

- Risk management can contribute directly to profit by reducing the cost of risk and increasing efficiency.

- Risk management can improve an organization's capacity to engage in speculative risks (risks of profit or loss) by minimizing the adverse effect of pure risks (risks of loss only).

- Risk management enables management to plan the organization's future with greater confidence and predictability.

SUMMARY

By examining risk management objectives, the risk management process, the risk management function, and the benefits of risk management, this chapter has shown how and why risks can and should be managed by both business organizations and families.

Risk management objectives are divided into two categories: pre-loss and post-loss. Pre-loss objectives include efficiency, tolerable uncertainty, legal requirements, and ethical conduct. Post-loss objectives include survival, continuity of operations, profitability or earnings stability, growth, and ethical conduct.

The persons performing the risk management function follow a six-step process to meet pre-loss and post-loss objectives:

1. Identifying loss exposures
2. Analyzing loss exposures
3. Examining the feasibility of risk management alternatives
4. Selecting the best risk management techniques
5. Implementing risk management techniques
6. Monitoring results

Risk identification can use many tools, including checklists or questionnaires, financial statement analysis, contract and lease analysis, flowchart analysis, loss analysis, hazard analysis, and personal inspections.

Risk management alternatives fall into three categories:

1. Exposure avoidance
2. Risk control techniques (loss prevention, loss reduction, separation, duplication, noninsurance contracts, and diversification)
3. Risk financing techniques (transfer—either through insurance or noninsurance contracts—and retention)

Selecting the best combination of risk management techniques should include both financial and nonfinancial considerations, including ethical considerations. Determining an optimal retention level is also necessary.

Large businesses usually have a risk management department and one or more risk managers who spend most of their time performing the risk management function. In smaller businesses and in families, the risk management process is much more informal and can rely on the advice and counsel of agents, brokers, and consultants.

The next chapter examines one specific risk management technique—insurance—and explains why insurance works as a risk management technique.

CHAPTER NOTES

1. Portions of this chapter are adapted from Robert J. Gibbons, George E. Rejda, and Michael W. Elliott, *Insurance Perspectives* (Malvern, Pa.: American Institute for CPCU, 1992); Chapter 2, George L. Head and Stephen Horn II, *Essentials of Risk Management*, 3d ed., vol. 1 (Malvern, Pa.: Insurance Institute of America, 1997); and Jerome Trupin and Arthur L. Flitner, *Commercial Property Insurance and Risk Management*, 6th ed., vol. 1 (Malvern, Pa.: American Institute for CPCU, 2001).

2. C. Arthur Williams, Jr., and Richard M. Heins, *Risk Management and Insurance*, 5th ed. (New York: McGraw-Hill Book Company, 1985), pp. 55–56.

3. World Wide Web: http://www.redcross.org/news/inthnews/99/10-8-99.html.

4. Alice Ann R. Head and George L. Head, "On Risk Management: The Power of Politics in Safety," *National Underwriter* (Property & Casualty), July 22, 1991, p. 17.

5. Michael W. Elliott, *Risk Financing*, 1st ed. (Malvern, Pa.: Insurance Institute of America, 2000), pp. 1–19.

Chapter 4

Direct Your Learning

Insurance as a Risk Management Technique

After learning the subject matter of this chapter, you should be able to:

- Explain how pooling of both uncorrelated and correlated losses affects risks for each participant.

- Explain the similarities and differences between pooling and insurance.

- Explain how reinsurance helps insurers reduce risks, increase capacity, and remain solvent.

Develop Your Perspective

What are the main topics covered in the chapter?

This chapter details the similarities and differences between pooling (risk reduction) and insurance (risk transfer) and how reinsurance uses both to reduce the risks insurers assume for their policyholders.

Identify the types of loss exposures that are difficult to project.

- What makes them more difficult to project?
- How can reinsurance reduce the consequences of risk for insurers?

Why is it important to know these topics?

Knowing how pools and insurance work will help you understand why insurers purchase certain types of reinsurance arrangements, when alternatives to reinsurance may be appropriate, and how reinsurance strengthens the insurance system.

Compare and contrast reinsurance pools, facultative reinsurance, and treaty reinsurance.

- Under what conditions might an insurer or a group of reinsurers choose each type of arrangement?

How can you use this information?

Investigate how your insurer or your employer handles risk financing.

- What types of reinsurance arrangements have they chosen?
- How do those arrangements strengthen the organization?

Chapter 4

Insurance as a Risk Management Technique

This chapter explains *why* insurance works. It begins by examining a fundamental risk management concept: pooling. The second major section of this chapter explains how insurance uses pooling to transfer risk and describes the basic concepts that make it possible for insurance to work. The final section of this chapter explains the important role of reinsurance and shows how reinsurance strengthens the insurance system.

The next chapter examines *how* insurance works by describing major insurance functions.

POOLING[1]

Pooling is a fundamental risk management concept. Pooling arrangements reduce risk without transferring it. Generally, a pool is an association of persons or organizations formed to combine their resources for a common advantage. In a car pool, for example, several commuters use one vehicle to get to work more efficiently than if each drove a separate car. In the context of risk financing, a **pool** is an association of persons or organizations that combines their resources to economically finance recovery from accidental losses. Two examples are used to present the concept of pooling and to show how it works with uncorrelated and correlated losses.

Pool
An association of persons or organizations that combines their resources to economically finance recovery from accidental losses.

Pooling Arrangements With Uncorrelated Losses

Pooling arrangements reduce risks when the pooled losses are independent, or uncorrelated. Losses are independent—that is, uncorrelated—when each loss occurs independently and the losses are not subject to the same risks. For example, windstorm losses of a building in California and a building in Minnesota are uncorrelated. However, the windstorm exposures of two adjacent buildings are correlated because both could be damaged by the same windstorm.

The following examples demonstrate how pooling arrangements actually serve to reduce risk, even though no risk is transferred.

How Pooling Reduces Risks

Suppose that Emily and Samantha are each exposed to the possibility of an accident in the coming year. Assume that each has a 20 percent chance of an accident that will cause a $2,500 loss and that each has an 80 percent chance of no accident. Also assume that Emily's and Samantha's accident losses are uncorrelated. Finally, assume that neither woman can have more than one accident during the year.

Exhibit 4-1 summarizes the probability distribution for each woman's accident losses.

EXHIBIT 4-1

Probability Distribution of Accident Losses for Each Person (Emily and Samantha) Without Pooling

Outcomes	Probability
$ 0	0.80
$2,500	0.20

Because Emily and Samantha each face a 20 percent chance of having an accident that causes $2,500 in losses, the expected costs for each person *without* a pooling arrangement are $500, calculated as follows:

$$\text{Expected cost} = (0.80 \times \$0) + (0.20 \times \$2,500) = \$500$$

The expected cost is the average cost per year over the long run. Four years out of every five—that is, 80 percent (or 0.80) of the time, expected cost is $0. Over the long pull, one year out of every five—that is, 20 percent (or 0.20) of the time, accident costs are expected to be $2,500.

The variability in accident costs can be measured using the standard deviation. In this example without pooling, the standard deviation is $1,000.[2]

Suppose Emily and Samantha agree to *evenly split any accident costs that the two might incur*. That is, they agree to share losses equally, each paying the average loss. This is a pooling arrangement (or risk pooling arrangement), because Emily and Samantha are pooling their resources to pay the accident costs that may occur.

Exhibit 4-2 lists the four possible outcomes and shows how the pooling arrangement will affect the distribution of costs for each person participating in the pool.

The last column in this exhibit shows the probability that each of the four outcomes will occur. Because Emily's losses are independent of Samantha's losses, the probability that neither woman will have an accident is simply the probability that Emily does not have an accident multiplied by the probability that Samantha does not have an accident. Thus, the probability of the first listed outcome is $0.8 \times 0.8 = 0.64$.

An analogy might help reinforce this result. Consider flipping a coin twice. The result of the second coin flip is independent of the result of the first coin flip. The probability of obtaining two heads is the probability of heads on the first coin flip multiplied by the probability of heads on the second coin flip, or $0.5 \times 0.5 = 0.25$. Proof that this is true is the fact that four outcomes are possible in two coin flips: heads-heads, heads-tails, tails-heads, and tails-tails. Each of those four outcomes has a 0.25 probability (1-in-4 odds) of occurring.

EXHIBIT 4-2

Probability Distribution of Accident Costs Paid by Each Person (Emily and Samantha) With Pooling

Possible Outcomes	Total Cost	Cost Paid by Each Person Person (Average Loss)	Probability
1. Neither Samantha nor Emily has an accident.	$ 0	$ 0	(0.8)(0.8) = 0.64
2. Samantha has an accident, but Emily does not.	$2,500	$1,250	(0.2)(0.8) = 0.16
3. Emily has an accident, but Samantha does not.	$2,500	$1,250	(0.2)(0.8) = 0.16
4. Both Samantha and Emily have an accident.	$5,000	$2,500	(0.2)(0.2) = 0.04

Returning to the accident costs example, find the probability of the second and third outcomes in Exhibit 4-2 (in which only one of the two women has an accident). The probability that Samantha has an accident but Emily does not, equals $0.2 \times 0.8 = 0.16$. The probability that Emily has an accident but Samantha does not is also 0.16. Thus, the probability that only one of the women (either one of them but not both) has an accident equals $0.16 + 0.16 = 0.32$. The probability of the fourth outcome (they both have an accident) is $0.2 \times 0.2 = 0.04$.

As this example demonstrates, *the pooling arrangement does not change accident frequency or severity, but it changes the probability distribution of accident costs facing each person.* The probability that Emily will pay accident costs equal to $2,500 is reduced from 0.20 to 0.04. This is because Emily will not need to pay $2,500 unless *both* Emily and Samantha experience an accident. Given that their accidents are independent, or uncorrelated, the probability that both Emily and Samantha will have an accident is lower than the probability that only Emily, or only Samantha, will have an accident.

Although the probability that either woman will face a $2,500 expense is reduced, the probability that neither woman will have a loss is also reduced from 0.80 to 0.64. Even if Emily does not have an accident, Samantha might have one, and vice versa.

Although both Samantha's risk and Emily's risk are reduced by pooling, each person's expected accident cost is unchanged. It still equals $500, based on calculations shown in Exhibit 4-3.

EXHIBIT 4-3

Expected Cost of Accident Losses Paid by Each Person (Emily and Samantha) With Pooling

(a) Cost Paid by Each Person (Average Loss)	(b) Probability	(a) × (b)
$ 0	0.64	$ 0
$1,250	0.16	$200
$1,250	0.16	$200
$2,500	0.04	$100
Total	**1.00**	**$500**

Because the pooling arrangement reduces the probabilities of the extreme outcomes, the standard deviation of accident costs paid by both Emily and Samantha is reduced. Recall that, without pooling, the standard deviation of accident costs in this example is $1,000. With pooling, the standard deviation of accident costs declines to $707.[3] Accident costs have become more predictable.

In summary, the pooling arrangement does not change either person's expected cost, but it makes the actual cost more consistent and less variable. This pooling arrangement therefore reduces each individual's risk or uncertainty.

Additional risk reduction can occur by adding more people to the pooling arrangement. To illustrate, suppose that Anne, who has the same probability distribution for accident costs as Samantha and Emily, joins the pooling arrangement. At the year's end, each woman will pay one-third of the total losses (the average loss). The addition of a third person whose losses are independent of the other two further reduces the probability of extreme outcomes ($0 or $2,500). For example, for Samantha to pay $2,500 in accident costs, all three individuals must experience a $2,500 loss. The possibility of this occurring is 0.02 × 0.02 × 0.02 = 0.008. As a consequence, the standard deviation for each individual decreases with the addition of another participant. While risk (standard deviation) decreases, each individual's expected accident cost remains constant at $500.

The probability distribution of each person's accident cost will continue to change as more people are added to the pool. Exhibit 4-4 compares the probability distribution for average accident costs when four and twenty participants are in the pooling arrangement. Note that as the number of participants in the pooling arrangement increases, the probability of extreme outcomes (very high average losses and very low average losses) goes down. Stated differently, the probability that average losses (the amounts paid by each participant) will be close to $500 (the expected loss) increases. Also, as the number of participants increases, the probability distribution of each person's cost (the average loss) becomes more bell-shaped.

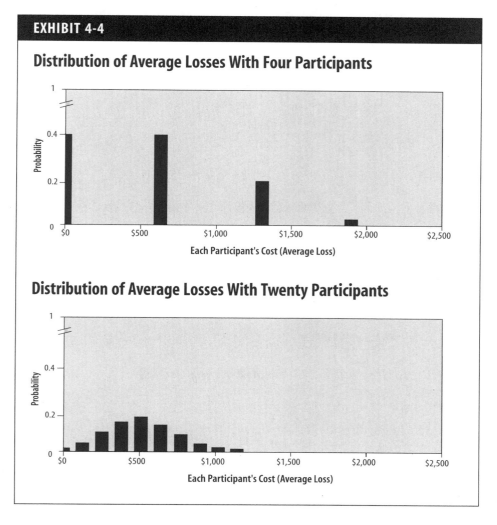

EXHIBIT 4-4

Distribution of Average Losses With Four Participants

Distribution of Average Losses With Twenty Participants

In summary, pooling makes the amount that each person must pay for accident losses less risky (more predictable), because pooling reduces the variability of the average loss for all the participants. Thus, the pooling arrangement reduces each participant's risk. As even more participants are added, the probability distribution becomes more and more bell-shaped.

As a more realistic illustration, consider the case of a large number of small businesses, with uncorrelated property losses. The solid line in Exhibit 4-5 presents the probability distribution for each business's property losses without a pooling arrangement. Each business's property losses could be any number between $0 and $100,000, and although not obvious from the graph, the expected loss is $20,000. Without pooling, the distribution is skewed and has fairly high variability in losses (standard deviation). When these businesses enter into a pooling arrangement, the distribution of property losses for each business changes to that shown by the dashed line in Exhibit 4-5.

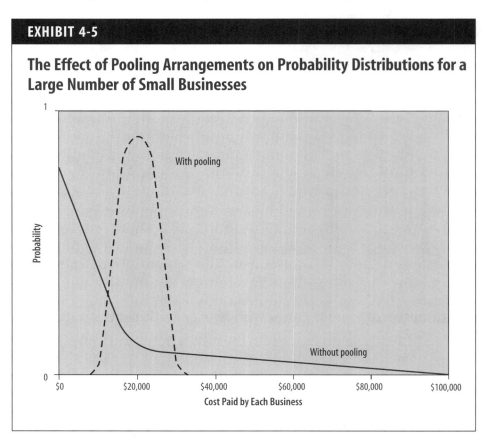

EXHIBIT 4-5

The Effect of Pooling Arrangements on Probability Distributions for a Large Number of Small Businesses

The exhibit highlights pooling arrangements' two important effects on each participant's probability distributions.

1. As more participants join the pool, the variability of property losses is lower, and each participant is more likely to pay an amount approximating the average, expected loss.

2. The distribution of property losses becomes less skewed and more bell-shaped around the expected loss.

Notice in all of these examples that the participant is *not* transferring risk to someone else. Instead, each individual reduces his or her risk. This is the beauty of risk pooling arrangements: *Risk can be substantially reduced for all participants. Although pooling arrangements do not prevent losses or transfer risk, they do reduce the amount of risk borne by each participant.*

Pooling Arrangements With Correlated Losses

Many losses are positively correlated; this part of the chapter examines risk reduction through pooling of correlated losses. This discussion will demonstrate that the essential point—pooling arrangements reduce risk for each participant—continues to hold provided losses are *not* perfectly positively correlated. (Perfect positive correlation means that if one pooled loss occurs, the others will always occur.) However, *the magnitude of risk reduction is lower when losses are positively correlated than when they are independent (uncorrelated).*[4]

Losses across many different businesses or individuals might be positively correlated for several reasons. The occurrence (frequency) of a loss is often due to events that are common to many people. Catastrophes, such as hurricanes and earthquakes, cause property losses to increase for many individuals at the same time. Consequently, property losses in certain geographical regions during a given time period are positively correlated.

Loss severity also is often influenced by common factors. For example, unexpected inflation can cause everyone who needs health care to pay more than expected. The probability of receiving medical care might be independent across people, but the magnitude of the medical costs incurred by different people is related to a common underlying factor: inflation.

How do positively correlated losses affect pooling arrangements? Intuitively, positively correlated losses imply that when one person (or business) has a loss that is greater than the expected loss, then other people (or businesses) will also tend to have losses that are above the expected loss. Similarly, when one person has a loss that is less than the expected loss (perhaps even no loss), then other people will also tend to have losses below the expected value. Thus, when losses are positively correlated, there is a greater chance that many people will have high losses and there is a greater chance that many people will have low losses, as compared with the case of uncorrelated losses. Consequently, average losses are more difficult to predict when losses are positively correlated.

To reinforce this idea, with uncorrelated losses, there is a relatively high probability that one person's unexpectedly high losses will be offset by other participants' unexpectedly low losses. Thus, the average loss becomes more predictable. When losses are positively correlated, similar losses are incurred by more participants, and one person's unexpectedly high losses are less likely to be offset by another person's unexpectedly low losses.

Consider the effect of positive correlation between Emily's and Samantha's losses. Correlation does not change Emily's or Samantha's initial probability distribution for accident costs. As the year begins, the probability of an accident is 0.2 for both Emily and Samantha. Suppose that Emily then has an accident but that it is unknown whether Samantha has had an accident. What is the probability that Samantha will have an accident? If the accidents are assumed to be independent, then the probability assessment will not change; the probability of Samantha's having an accident will still be 0.2.

However, if accidents are assumed to be positively correlated, then knowing Emily has had an accident will raise the assessment of Samantha's accident probability above 0.2.

Positive correlation between Emily's and Samantha's accident costs implies that the probability of both women's having an accident is greater than 0.04. Similarly, positive correlation implies that the probability of neither woman's having an accident is greater than 0.64. Unless more assumptions are made, the exact probabilities of the various outcomes cannot be specified. The critical point, however, is that positive correlation between Emily's and Samantha's accident costs implies that the probability of the extreme outcomes (i.e., that either both or neither will have an accident) is higher than if accident costs were independent.

The maximum degree of positive correlation is perfect positive correlation. In this case, if Emily has an accident, so will Samantha, and if Emily does not have an accident, neither will Samantha. Perfect positive correlation implies that whatever happens to Emily also happens to Samantha. As a result, the probability that both women will have an accident is the same as the probability that either one of them will have an accident (0.2), and the probability that neither woman will have an accident is the same as the probability that one of them will not have an accident (0.8).

The effect of positively correlated losses on the distribution of average losses is summarized in Exhibit 4-6, which presents two cases. In both cases,

EXHIBIT 4-6

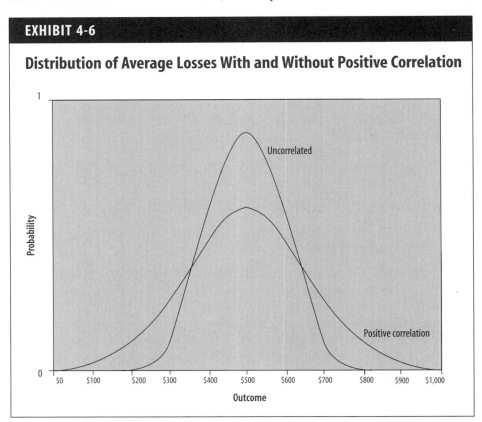

Distribution of Average Losses With and Without Positive Correlation

1,000 participants are in the pooling arrangement and each participant has an expected loss of $500. In one case, each participant's losses are uncorrelated; in the other, they are positively correlated. As illustrated, when losses are positively correlated, the distribution of losses has a greater variability (higher standard deviation) so that losses are less predictable.

Correlation in losses has important implications for risk management and insurance. For example, most insurance policies exclude coverage for losses resulting from war or nuclear reaction. Why? Because losses resulting from either event are positively correlated. Simply stated, both war and nuclear incident have the potential of causing simultaneous loss to large numbers of insurance buyers, defeating the spread-of-risk principles on which insurance is based.

INSURANCE COMPARED WITH POOLING

Pooling is a mechanism for sharing costs; it is not a mechanism for transferring risks. Insurance, although it is based on loss-sharing principles, is a risk-transferring technique. Insurance provides stronger guarantees that sufficient funds will be available in the event of a loss than does a pooling arrangement.

Operating a Pool

The preceding discussion explained how pooling reduces risk for each participant in the pool and how this effect increases as additional members are brought into the pool. *However, pooling is simply a loss-sharing arrangement and does nothing to increase the resources available to finance losses.* In fact, just operating a pooling mechanism would generally create additional costs such as marketing, underwriting, claim administration, and information systems expenses for participants. Therefore, to be economical and effective, a risk pool should have many participants.

Recruiting new participants requires *marketing* and other distribution costs. Pool members would not want to automatically include any new participant, but only those whose risks are comparable to the risks of members already in the pool. If the risks are somewhat different, it is possible to change the way risks are shared among members. *Underwriting* expenses would be incurred in identifying and evaluating each potential participant's risks.

Pools must also pay losses that its members incur. Losses must be verified, and their costs must be determined. The claim administration process might also include collecting funds from other pool members to pay a claim. If each claim is paid by an assessment against all pool members, the pooling mechanism adds no financial resources and probably introduces a time lag in claim payments. In addition to having marketing, underwriting, and claim administration expenses, a pool incurs various other administration expenses and information systems expenses.

Each pool member continues paying its share of losses borne by all pool members. Ideally, this share reflects the member's own average losses over time. In exchange for the added expense of operating the pool, the member receives reduced risk due to reduced variation in losses over time.

The following discussion provides some insights into the operation of a municipal risk pool.

How Municipal Pools Are Formed and Operated[5]

There is no "typical" pool; the structure and organization of individual pools are influenced by the type of state regulation governing pooling (if any), the type of coverage and services offered, financing mechanisms employed, the philosophy and objectives of the pool's members, and other factors.

Pools generally have policymaking boards composed of representatives elected or appointed by their member agencies. When one governmental agency sponsors a pool, its board may serve as the pool board as well. Day-to-day operations may be conducted by a third-party administrator (TPA) and staff hired for that purpose, or by a TPA on a contract basis. A TPA is a person or an organization that manages its clients' claims, acting in each client's interest. Some small pools, especially those that provide only excess coverage, may be run entirely by their boards, with or without external consultants' assistance. Pools may be highly structured nonprofit corporations or simply unincorporated entities that implement an interlocal or a cooperative agreement. Pool boards may arrange for needed administration services through staff, employees, or contracts with outside service firms.

Pool administrators are usually in charge of arranging services that the pool requires, both internally for administering the pool itself and externally for members. The services vary with the types of coverage the pool provides but often include procuring excess insurance or reinsurance, funding to pay for accidental losses, claim handling, loss control and safety consulting, legal defense, actuarial studies, investment of funds, general risk management advice, property appraisals, medical cost-containment programs, wellness programs, and pre-employment physical programs.

Pools are almost always initially capitalized through contributions made by members. Generally the payment of a sum equivalent to (or sometimes less than) what the public entities as individual insureds have been paying as commercial insurance premiums is sufficient to fund the pool. Some established pools may levy an initial capitalization surcharge to strengthen their capital base as they grow and to allow new members to "buy into" the pool's equity. Most pools purchase commercial insurance or reinsurance to provide excess insurance over retentions within their pools, which may be $1 million or more. Other pools are entirely self-funded. They may have accumulated enough funds to pay anticipated claims or have established other arrangements. One method of accumulating these funds is to include retrospectively charged assessments to their members when funds are needed. Another is to issue debt instruments to develop a loss fund. The opportunity that pooling provides to accumulate funds to pay anticipated losses is often particularly important to public entities that, outside the pooling mechanism, would face legal, budgetary, or political barriers to accumulating funded reserves for anticipated losses that may not happen for years (if ever).

Pools build up their reserves by incorporating into their rates a factor for that purpose. Most pools strive to be sufficiently funded to meet their obligations as established by the claim administrator and the actuary. Pools have two types of reserves: case reserves (established by their claim administrator for claims that have been reported to the pool) and actuarial reserves (or bulk reserves) for claims that have been incurred but not reported (IBNR reserves) and for loss development (that is, claims in the aggregate, which tend to settle at amounts higher than reserved). Some pools also establish an amount above those reserves as a contingency margin, called a surplus target. This amount is expected to serve as a cushion if projections regarding loss payouts are less than the actual payouts, to ensure that the pool remains solvent.

Many pools may return excess funds as dividends to their members, provide credits on future contribution billings, or fund new programs. Some pools may keep accumulating surplus funds indefinitely, investing them not only in traditional securities but also in real estate, both to provide office space for their administrative staff and to generate rental income by leasing space to others.

Key Differences Between Pooling and Insurance

Insurance companies are much like large risk pools, and vice versa.

Although an insurance company fundamentally resembles a formal pooling mechanism, they are distinct in two important ways.

1. An insurance company transfers the risk from the insured to the insurer in exchange for premiums, rather than simply serving as a conduit for passing along its costs to other insurance buyers.

2. The insurer introduces additional financial resources, which enables the insurer to provide a stronger guarantee that sufficient funds will be available in the event of a loss, further reducing risk.

The insurer's additional resources are derived from three principal sources:

1. Initial capital
2. Insurance premiums
3. Retained earnings

The initial capital is the money that investors must provide to establish an insurance company. The minimum amount of initial capitalization is required by law in the state where the insurance company is chartered. This startup fund might be provided by stockholders who expect a return on their investment or by policyholders who want to establish an insurance company that will provide a market for their particular insurance needs.

An insurance premium is a periodic sum of money collected from each policyholder. Each premium should be sufficient to cover that policyholder's fair share of claims and expenses—and to provide a profit for the insurer. The premium might also include an amount to cover contingencies (a "risk loading") to pay claims when aggregate loss experience is worse than expected, without impairing the insurer's solvency.

Retained earnings are derived from premiums in excess of amounts used to pay claims and expenses, and from earnings on invested money. The money available for investment includes the initial capital and the "float" on any premiums that have not yet been spent to pay claims or expenses.

Pooling Versus Insurance

- With pooling, losses are shared among all pool members, thereby reducing the financial risks of a member's individual loss.

- With insurance, risks and losses are transferred to an insurer.

Pooling reduces each participant's risk because the pool members' loss experiences tend to cancel each other. The pool as a whole faces a diversified set of risks: One member's unlucky year is offset by another member's lucky year. When many similar members participate, every member's annual share approximates the average loss of all group members. Additional costs might be involved in pool administration. Although losses are shared among all pool members, losses are not transferred to the pool.

With insurance, risks and losses are transferred to an insurer. Because the premiums charged are greater than the expected average loss costs and expenses, and because the insurer begins with an initial capitalization, the insurer is on solid ground in agreeing to accept the transfer of risks from its policyholders—provided the risks it accepts are within its capacity. Chapter 5 more closely examines insurer capacity.

Every insurer's capacity is limited by its financial resources, and its ability to fulfill its obligations is based on remaining solvent. Solvency can be impaired if, for example, many policyholders have an unlucky year and the insurer experiences larger-than-anticipated losses. For example, a widespread hurricane might simultaneously damage much insured property, even if the property is somewhat dispersed geographically. A regional auto insurer could experience a bad year if an unusually severe winter causes a major increase in auto accidents' frequency and severity. Or a specialty insurer such as a medical malpractice insurer could find its solvency is threatened by a widespread increase in large liability judgments against obstetricians who followed previously acceptable practices that nonetheless resulted in adverse medical outcomes.

Insurance buyers transfer risks they are unwilling to retain to insurers. Through reinsurance, primary insurers pool or transfer risks, thus staying within capacity constraints and helping to ensure their solvency. *Reinsurance helps to reduce risk for insurers that accept risks transferred by insurance buyers.*

THE ROLE OF REINSURANCE

Reinsurance is an insurance contract under which one insurer, the **primary insurer**, transfers to another insurer, the **reinsurer**, some or all of the loss exposures accepted by the primary insurer under insurance contracts it has written or will write.[6] In most reinsurance agreements, the primary insurer keeps a portion of the loss exposures.

The next sections of the chapter examine how reinsurance agreements can be structured and how reinsurance reduces risks and increases capacity.

Reinsurance
An insurance contract in which one insurer (the **primary insurer**) transfers to another insurer (the **reinsurer**) some or all of the primary insurer's current or future loss exposures.

Types of Reinsurance Arrangements

Reinsurance arrangements range from simple pooling agreements to complex agreements among insurers.

Reinsurance Pools

Insurers can enter into a simple pooling arrangement similar to the one formed by Emily and Samantha earlier in this chapter. Two primary insurers might each agree to pay one-half—or some other proportion—of the other insurer's claims. As explained previously, this arrangement reduces risks for each insurer by reducing the likelihood of extreme outcomes.

Most reinsurance arrangements are substantially more complex than the simple pooling arrangement just described. A **reinsurance pool** or reinsurance association generally consists of several unrelated insurers or reinsurers that agree to insure risks that the members are unwilling to individually insure. For example, losses at a large nuclear power plant could reach several billions of dollars from liability and property damage claims. Because very few individual insurers are able to assume a loss that large, nuclear energy pools were formed, consisting of many member insurers.

Reinsurance pool
A reinsurance association that generally consists of several unrelated insurers or reinsurers that have joined to insure risks the individual members are unwilling to individually insure.

Facultative Reinsurance

Facultative reinsurance is a reinsurance agreement in which a primary insurer and a reinsurer agree to share losses arising from one specific risk. Facultative reinsurance involves an offer and acceptance for each individual risk. The reinsurer retains the "faculty" (power) to accept or reject each risk. In exchange for the facultative reinsurance agreement, the primary insurer pays a premium to the reinsurer.

Facultative reinsurance
A reinsurance agreement to share premiums and losses on one specific risk.

Treaty Reinsurance

When a primary insurer and a reinsurer agree to share losses arising from a group of policies, usually a whole line or book of business, the agreement is known as **treaty reinsurance**. The ceding of individual risks under a treaty is usually automatic and does not require the reinsurer's acceptance if the

Treaty reinsurance
A reinsurance agreement to share losses arising from more than one risk, usually a whole line or book of business; individual risks are automatically ceded to the reinsurer under the treaty's terms.

individual risk falls within the category of risks covered by the treaty. As with facultative reinsurance, the ceding insurer pays a premium to the reinsurer, reflecting the portion of the risk that is reinsured.

Methods of Sharing Losses

In both facultative and treaty reinsurance, a reinsurer may agree to share losses with the primary insurer using either a pro rata method or an excess of loss method, as shown in Exhibit 4-7.

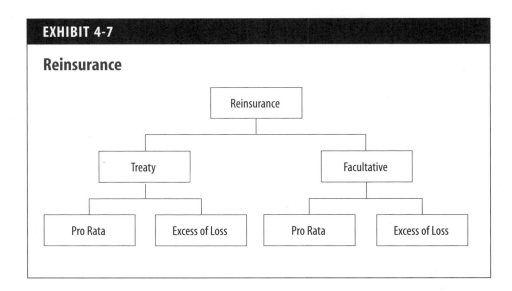

EXHIBIT 4-7

Reinsurance

Pro Rata Method

Pro rata reinsurance agreement
A reinsurance agreement that divides the amount of insurance, the premium, and the losses between the primary insurer and the reinsurer in the same agreed proportions for each risk.

When the reinsurer agrees to pay a percentage of every loss, the agreement is called a **pro rata reinsurance agreement** or, sometimes, a *proportional agreement* or a *quota share agreement*. Under this type of agreement, the amount of coverage, the premium, and the losses are divided between the primary insurer and the reinsurer in the same agreed proportions for each risk. For example, if the reinsurer is obligated for 30 percent of the coverage under a given policy, the reinsurer also receives 30 percent of the premium and pays 30 percent of the loss. The reinsurer usually pays a ceding commission to the primary insurer to cover its expenses (for example, distribution, underwriting, and claim handling expenses) and may also pay the primary insurer an additional commission for the profit generated under the reinsurance agreement.

Excess of Loss Method

Excess of loss reinsurance agreement
A reinsurance agreement that requires the primary insurer to pay losses up to the attachment point and the reinsurer to pay the amount of any loss exceeding the attachment point.

When the reinsurer agrees to pay the portion of a loss that exceeds a specific dollar amount, or "attachment point," the agreement is called an **excess of loss reinsurance agreement**. The attachment point can apply on a per risk basis or on a per occurrence basis. The primary insurer pays losses up to the attachment point, and the reinsurer pays the losses that exceed the attachment point. The reinsurance premium is usually a percentage of the primary insurer's premium income for the covered lines of business, but the percentage is negotiable and varies by type of insurance and by insurer. Generally, ceding commissions are not paid under excess of loss treaties.

Why Reinsurance Is Used

It might seem odd that an insurer goes to all the trouble and expense of selling a policy and collecting a premium and then pays some of its premium to a reinsurer to handle some of its exposures. However, primary insurers purchase reinsurance for sound business reasons, as the following box shows.

Benefits of Reinsurance

Reinsurance can help insurers remain financially sound by:

1. Increasing the primary insurer's capacity, especially for large accounts

2. Stabilizing loss experience, thereby stabilizing the insurer's financial results

3. Providing catastrophe protection

Increase Capacity

Seemingly, every insurer would simply want to sell as much insurance as possible. But it does not quite work that way because an insurer's capacity to write more business is limited by its risk-bearing capacity. This risk-bearing capacity takes two forms:

- *Large-line capacity* is an insurer's ability to provide a high limit of insurance for a single risk, such as for a $30 million jet airliner. Even if the insurer were interested in taking such a risk, most state regulations would prohibit an insurer from retaining a risk of loss that exceeds 10 percent of its policyholders' surplus.[7] A primary insurer can, however, write high limits of insurance if the insurer retains only a portion of the limit and cedes the remainder to a reinsurer. For example, a primary insurer could retain $6 million of the jet risk and cede the remaining $24 million to a reinsurer.

- *Premium capacity* is the aggregate premium volume a primary insurer can write in light of regulations that limit the ratio of net written premium to policyholders' surplus. Financial analysts and insurance rating organizations become concerned if the ratio is higher than a certain figure, generally 2 or 3 to 1. A primary insurer could limit its net written premium volume by ceding a portion of its gross premiums, and a proportionate part of its potential losses, to a reinsurer.

The concept of capacity is explored further in Chapter 5.

Stabilize Loss Experience

Like any other business, an insurer must have a reasonably steady flow of profits to attract and retain capital for growth. Insurance losses sometimes fluctuate widely because of demographic, economic, social, and natural forces, as well as simple chance. Smoothing the peaks and valleys of a primary insurer's random variation in loss experience helps ensure steady profits. Reinsurance helps primary insurers to stabilize results by limiting the amount of any one large loss—even if the potential loss does not exceed the insurer's capacity to absorb losses.

Provide Catastrophe Protection

Property and liability insurers in particular are subject to major catastrophe losses from earthquakes, hurricanes, tornadoes, industrial explosions, plane crashes, and similar disasters. A single event might result in many property and liability claims against a single insurer.

Catastrophe reinsurance
A reinsurance agreement that protects the primary insurer against the adverse effects of catastrophes and limits the primary insurer's loss from catastrophes to a predetermined amount.

Special forms of reinsurance, called **catastrophe reinsurance**, protect the primary insurer against catastrophes' adverse effects and limit the primary insurer's loss from catastrophes to a predetermined amount. A distinguishing feature of catastrophe reinsurance is that it covers multiple losses under many policies issued by a primary insurer but arising from a single event.

Alternatives to Reinsurance

Reinsurance reduces an insurer's retained risks by transferring some or all of specific insured risks. Recently, certain types of agreements have been used instead of reinsurance to reduce an insurer's retained risks.

The risk of earthquake loss to property is an example illustrating how these agreements might work. By selling insurance, the insurance company has already made some big "bets" that certain losses—such as earthquake losses to covered property—will not occur. The word "bets" is in quotation marks here to emphasize that insurance is not gambling (a mechanism to create risk). To be more precise, the insurer accepts calculated transfers of risk—risks that existed even without the insurance contract—believing the odds to be in its favor.

The earthquake risk to property challenges insurers' risk-bearing capacity because it is a low-frequency, high-severity risk that can simultaneously affect insured property at many locations. Although an insurer writing earthquake coverage is most likely to purchase reinsurance, it also has at least two other options:

1. The insurer's risks could be pooled through diversification.
2. The insurer's risks could be offset through hedging.

Diversification

Diversification is an intentional spreading of risks. An innovative example of earthquake risk diversification occurred in an arrangement between

State Farm and Tokio Marine. The insurers exchanged $200 million of earthquake risk. State Farm was exposed to earthquake risk in the central United States, while Tokio Marine was exposed to earthquake risk in Japan.

Earthquake risk is financially measured before any losses occur. If an earthquake in the New Madrid fault area measures 7.1 or higher on the Richter scale, Tokio Marine will pay State Farm $200 million. For quakes between 6.5 and 7.1, lesser amounts will be paid according to a sliding scale. A similar arrangement applies to Tokio, although a different earthquake-severity scale is used.

The effect of this agreement is that even though State Farm does not sell insurance in Japan, a major earthquake in Japan will result in a substantial payment by State Farm. Meanwhile, a major earthquake in the central United States will result in a substantial payment by Tokio Marine. Although these payments would help each insurer offset its potential insurance losses, the arrangement is not directly and specifically linked to the value of insurance claims.

Hedging

Hedging is a financial transaction in which one asset is held to offset the risks associated with another asset. Chapter 3 illustrated hedging with the example of placing a bet that one athletic team will win and placing another bet, in the same amount, that it will lose. Obviously, offsetting bets are pointless because the bettor will break even. However, an earthquake insurer that has already made a "bet" that an earthquake will not occur can offset some of the associated risk if anybody is willing to make an opposing bet.

Some investors are willing to make just such a bet, which is accomplished through catastrophe bonds. By purchasing a catastrophe bond, an investor lends money to the insurer. The insurer agrees to pay a stated, attractive bond interest rate. However, if a specified event—such as an earthquake of a certain magnitude—occurs, the insurer's obligation to pay interest, and possibly also the bond principal, terminates, thus saving the insurer money that can offset earthquake losses. The theory behind catastrophe bonds is that investors appreciate a relatively high return on their investments in exchange for the risk that an earthquake might occur. Catastrophe bonds also diversify an investor's portfolio of investments because the risk of a catastrophe is not closely correlated with the risks affecting other investments. Alternatively, for the insurer, catastrophe bonds provide an automatic source of capital when it is sorely needed to pay claims. Because catastrophe bond payment is triggered by the event and is not linked to the payment of specific insured losses, it is also an uncomplicated source of capital. Various accounting, finance, and regulatory features affecting the use of catastrophe bonds are beyond the scope of this text.

As with the State Farm/Tokio Marine diversification example, no direct link exists between earthquake claims and the funds available from catastrophe bonds. However, a distinct correlation exists because the need to pay claims and the opportunity to cash these bonds are both triggered by an earthquake. Catastrophe bonds use the hedging technique because they produce opposing results—a loss (claims paid) and a gain (catastrophe bond recovery)—from the same event. However, insurers pay an offsetting cost. For catastrophe bonds, the cost is the interest that must regularly be paid to the investors who purchase catastrophe bonds, even when no earthquake occurs.

Interest on catastrophe bonds, the cost of offsetting risks through hedging, can be compared to the premiums charged by reinsurers, the cost of transferring risks to a reinsurer. In either case, various overhead expenses are also involved.

SUMMARY

This chapter has shown *why* insurance works as a risk financing technique.

The chapter began by examining what would happen if two people, Emily and Samantha, agreed to pool their losses. Pooling these two women's *uncorrelated* losses would not affect whether those losses occur, but it would change the probability distribution of the accident costs faced by each woman. Adding more people to the pool would further reduce the variability in each participant's costs.

The chapter then examined pooling's effect on correlated losses. Pooling is much less effective when losses are *correlated*, and it is entirely ineffective when losses are perfectly correlated.

Operating a formal pool and operating an insurance company have many similarities. For example, pool operation requires activities relating to the pool's marketing, underwriting, claims, and administration, and these activities all add costs to the system, similar to costs insurers pay. While pooling is a system for sharing losses with other members of the pool, insurance is a system for transferring losses and risks to an insurance company that also provides additional financial resources. The insurer's resources are derived primarily from its initial capital, its collected insurance premiums (which exceed its expected loss costs), and its retained earnings. Pooling losses enables an insurer to predict its losses with some degree of confidence, and the additional resources from pooling provide an extra cushion that enables the insurer to absorb the risks it accepts, provided that it remains solvent.

Finally, the chapter showed that reinsurance helps insurers remain financially sound, or solvent. Reinsurance arrangements range from simple pools to complex arrangements involving facultative insurance (on specifically reinsured risks) and treaty reinsurance (on a package of risks automatically ceded to the reinsurer). Loss sharing through reinsurance can take one of two primary forms, either pro-rata or excess of loss. Insurers purchase reinsurance to increase the ceding insurer's capacity, stabilize loss experience, and add catastrophe protection. Some of the functions of reinsurance can also be addressed through other types of agreements, such as diversification and hedging.

Now that this chapter examined *why* insurance works, Chapter 5 will show *how* insurance works.

CHAPTER NOTES

1. Discussion here is from *Risk Management and Insurance* by Scott E. Harrington and Gregory R. Niehaus, Copyright 1999, McGraw-Hill, New York. Adapted by permission; all rights, including electronic rights, reserved.

2. Standard deviation $= \sqrt{0.8(\$0 - \$500)^2 + 0.2(\$2,500 - \$500)^2} = \$1,000$

3. Standard deviation $=$

    $$\sqrt{0.64 \times (\$0 - \$500)^2 + 0.32 \times (\$1,250 - \$500)^2 + 0.04 \times (\$2,500 - \$500)^2} = \$707$$

4. The discussion refers to losses that are positively correlated—if one loss occurs, other pooled losses are also likely. It is possible for losses to have a negative correlation—if one loss occurs, other pooled losses are less likely.

5. Adapted from George L. Head and Kwok-Sze Richard Wong, *Risk Management for Public Entities* (Malvern, Pa.: Center for the Advancement of Risk Management Education, 1999), pp. 376–378.

6. Bernard L. Webb, Connor M. Harrison, and James J. Markham, *Insurance Operations*, 2d ed., vol. 2 (Malvern, Pa.: American Institute for CPCU, 1997), p. 1.

7. Policyholders' surplus, discussed in more detail in Chapter 5, refers to the owners' equity of an insurance company. Assets minus liabilities equals policyholders' surplus.

Chapter 5

Direct Your Learning

How Insurance Works as a Business

After learning the subject matter of this chapter, you should be able to:

- ■ Explain factors currently affecting the supply of insurance and the demand for insurance.

- ■ Identify and explain the key financial aspects of insurance.

- ■ Identify the six ratios used to measure insurer performance, and explain the results that each ratio provides.

- ■ Describe the core functions performed by insurance companies.

Develop Your Perspective

What are the main topics covered in the chapter?

This chapter describes the business of insurance by outlining some of its economic, financial, and functional components, such as supply and demand, balance sheets, insurer performance, stakeholders, and the core functions insurers perform.

Identify some economic pressures facing your organization.

- How is your organization responding to those forces?

Why is it important to know these topics?

By examining the insurance industry's economic, financial, and functional components, you will begin to understand how and why insurers are able to assume much risk while still meeting their financial and nonfinancial goals.

Examine the different ratios insurers use to measure performance.

- What do these ratios tell the insurer about its performance?

How can you use this information?

Consider the strategies an insurer might use to combat inadequate company performance.

- Which functional areas within the company might implement the strategies?
- How are the other areas affected?

Chapter 5

How Insurance Works as a Business

Previous chapters examined risk, probability, and risk management and showed how pooling can reduce risk and how insurance can transfer risk. This chapter examines risk from a different perspective, that of the insurer. How can insurers successfully accept the risks of businesses, individuals, and families? This question will be answered by looking at the economic, financial, and functional aspects of insurance.

ECONOMIC VIEW OF INSURANCE

The insurance system operates efficiently when responding to the fundamental economic law of supply and demand. Insurance promotes efficiency when it increases value for the insured by reducing the cost of risk while simultaneously enabling the insurer to earn a profit. This phenomenon can occur only when the cost of insurance is both low enough to appeal to an insurance buyer and high enough to produce a profit for the insurer. Examining how supply and demand work in the insurance business helps one to understand how insurers contribute to social well-being while pursuing their own self-interests.

Supply and Demand

In markets where buyers and sellers interact freely, prices for any goods tend to rise as long as demand exceeds supply, and prices tend to fall as long as supply exceeds demand. At some point, the quantity supplied and the quantity demanded are equal, which creates the **equilibrium price**. A free market, in which the market mechanism operates without constraints, automatically produces a price at which supply equals demand. See the following box for an example of how a market works.

Equilibrium price
The price at which the quantity supplied equals the quantity demanded in a free market that is operating without constraints.

Supply and Demand in the Car Market

Mark wants to buy a new car and is seriously considering a new Hozdota 500. Not many cars of this model are available. Local Hozdota, a nearby dealer, does have the Hozdota 500.

Continued on next page.

Supply

Local Hozdota wants to maximize its profits. It wants to sell as many cars as possible for as high a price as possible and to minimize the costs of keeping cars in inventory. However, car buyers want low prices, and the lower the price for any given model, the more cars that people are likely to buy. Local Hozdota will seek a price that maximizes sales revenue at its lowest cost for the number of units sold.

Demand

Mark can only afford to spend a certain amount of money for a car. If he believes the price Hozdota is charging is reasonable, Mark might buy the car. If he thinks the price is too high, he will shop elsewhere, delay his purchase until the price is reduced, or consider a different brand of car. Each buyer determines what cost is within his or her price range.

Combining Supply and Demand

Hozdota must sell the 500s at a price exceeding its cost to make a profit, which is why it is in business. On the other hand, Mark and other customers are only prepared to buy the vehicles at a certain price level. The lower the price of the vehicles, the more people will want to buy.

What price is appropriate for selling or buying a Hozdota 500? Mark is not willing to pay more than a certain amount, and Local Hozdota is not willing to sell cars for less than a certain amount. If Local's minimum price is lower than Mark's maximum price, the parties will probably be able to negotiate a price that is acceptable to both of them.

Competition

Competition has a bearing on the supply and demand for a particular product. If a satisfactory substitute is available at an equal, or a better, price, a buyer can always decide to purchase the substitute. The presence of competition reduces the amount buyers like Mark are willing to pay for a Hozdota (that is, reduces the demand), and this, in turn, forces sellers like Local Hozdota to lower their prices—increasing the supply of cars for sale at lower prices. Generally, competition among suppliers tends to keep prices down.

Supply and Demand in Insurance

Numerous factors affect both the supply of, and the demand for, insurance. These factors influence how well insurance can operate as a business. When supply and demand are not balanced, the insurance system cannot operate as efficiently. See the box on the following page.

Supply

The supply of insurance might seem to be virtually unlimited. And the more insurance a company sells, the more money it has to invest. From this limited perspective, it seems insurance companies would want to sell just as much insurance as they can. More business should mean more profits, as well as greater diversification through a wider spread of risks that improves predictability. Moreover, insurers who sell more insurance than they can handle are able to control the amount of risk they retain by transferring some of the risk to reinsurers. Overall, the supply of insurance is limited by (1) the amount of risk the insurer is willing to accept in exchange for the premium it receives and (2) the insurer's capacity to assume new business.

Factors Affecting Supply and Demand in Insurance

Supply (Insurers)

- Amount of risk versus premium
- Capacity to assume new business

Demand (Consumers)

- Size of the overall insurance market
- Insurance mandates
- Consumer attitudes toward risk
- Financial status of consumers
- Price of insurance
- Tax incentives

Amount of Risk Versus Premium

The supply of insurance depends on insurance company perceptions of likely risk and profit. Insurance companies might not be willing to accept business for which they do not expect a reasonable profit or that involves unpredictable levels of risk that cannot properly be priced. The opportunity for reasonable profit might also be limited by the premiums the insurer can charge. Premium levels are often affected not only by price controls imposed by insurance regulators but also by competition.

Capacity To Assume New Business

An insurer's **capacity** to assume new business is limited by several factors.

- *Financial capacity.* Insurance regulators pay close attention to an insurer's premium-to-surplus ratio, also called a capacity ratio. This ratio provides a crude measurement of how adequate available funds are to pay claims. Capacity constraints limit an insurer's ability to grow rapidly, because a rapid increase in new business tends to increase an insurer's obligations more rapidly than it increases surplus.

- *Physical and human resources.* An insurer cannot, or at least should not, write business unless it has the physical and human capacity to handle that business. Physical resources—such as information systems—are relevant, and human resources can be even more important. An insurer must not only have enough people to handle the business it accepts but must also have the right people, equipped with the right knowledge and skills to fulfill the insurer's promises to pay claims and provide other services.

Capacity
The amount of insurance an insurer—or the entire insurance industry—is able to write.

- *Reinsurance.* A primary insurer's capacity is limited partly by its ability to reinsure some of its risks. The supply of reinsurance is limited by the same factors affecting the supply of primary insurance, as well as factors peculiar to the reinsurance business.

- *Marketing strategy.* Each insurer must decide what business it wants to be in, where it will specialize, and how it will invest its resources. An insurer will compete vigorously for increased business that fits its current marketing strategy, and it may decline an opportunity to write business in a category in which further growth is not a part of the strategy.

Hurricane Andrew illustrated the importance of several of the issues discussed in this text (see the following box).

Hurricane Andrew and the Supply of Property Insurance

After Hurricane Andrew struck in 1992, inflicting $15½ billion in insured damage, many Florida residents found it nearly impossible to purchase property insurance. The *supply* of property insurance was dramatically reduced, even as the *demand* was increased, because people became acutely aware of their exposure to severe windstorms. These changes in supply and demand were especially interesting because the underlying risk, the probability of hurricane damage to property, was essentially the same after Andrew as before the hurricane.

What was it that so dramatically affected the supply of windstorm insurance without changing the possibility of loss due to windstorm?

First, a change occurred in the subjective risk. Although insurance company managers, actuaries, and underwriters had previously recognized that a catastrophic hurricane was *possible*, they now realized that it was a possibility that had happened once and could happen again, and they had a more acute recognition of its consequences.

Second, because most property insurance companies had to tap their policyholders' surplus to pay the claims from Andrew, the catastrophe reduced primary insurers' financial capacity to write new business.

Third, Hurricane Andrew affected insurers' marketing strategies. Many insurers that had aggressively been marketing property insurance in Florida decided they were no longer interested in expanding their market shares, and most wished to reduce their share of the Florida market.

Fourth, the supply of windstorm reinsurance decreased dramatically and for similar reasons. A catastrophe like Andrew has a major effect on companies writing property reinsurance. A decrease in reinsurance market capacity reduces, in turn, the capacity of primary insurers who deal directly with the insurance buyer.

Demand

Several significant factors affect the demand for insurance, including the following: size of the overall insurance market, insurance mandates, attitude toward risk, financial status, price of insurance, and tax incentives.

Size of the Overall Insurance Market

Drastic changes in the overall demand for insurance seem unlikely, and the overall property-casualty insurance market presents limited growth potential. The existing base of loss exposures (houses, cars, commercial buildings, business receipts, and so forth) is very large. Additions to the existing stock of insured exposures tends to closely follow growth of the overall economy. In a 1998 speech published in March 2000, Arthur Snyder, publisher of *Best's Review*, noted that the average annual growth rate of the insurance industry as measured by premium revenue is declining. For the 1946–1990 period it was 9.4 percent, and the average annual growth rate from 1990 to 1997 was 4.8 percent. However, for 1997–2002, the outlook for average annual growth in premium revenue was 4.7 percent (3 percent for property-casualty and 6 percent for life/health). The following factors contribute to this decline:

1. Saturation of the market demand for insurable products such as autos, houses, and life insurance
2. Decline in the average annual growth rate of [the] population
3. Decline in inflation
4. Competitive market conditions caused by capacity, which has restrained price increases[1]

The growth of alternative risk financing tools—the alternative risk transfer market discussed in Chapter 7—is another factor limiting the demand for traditional property-liability insurance.

Insurance Mandates

Another factor affecting the demand for insurance is insurance mandates. Much of this text's discussion about risk management alternatives assumes that insurance is an optional technique for financing risks. Often, insurance is not optional, or going without insurance is not a feasible option.

For example, states impose financial responsibility requirements on auto owners or operators. Those requirements are almost always satisfied by purchasing auto liability insurance. Theoretically, the question is not whether to buy insurance, but from whom. In practice, alternatives are available. Self-insurance is usually permitted: A person or an organization with sufficient financial resources might post a bond, demonstrating to the state that adequate financial resources exist to pay for any losses resulting from an auto accident. Mandates aside, many motorists who believe they cannot afford insurance weigh the risks of being caught and choose to go without insurance, violating the law.

Most employers are required to provide workers compensation benefits prescribed by law. Although self-insurance alternatives might be permitted for large employers, smaller employers who wish to remain legal have no choice whether to purchase insurance.

When it is not required by law, insurance is often required by contract. For example, most home purchases are financed by a mortgage, and the mortgagee inevitably requires insurance to protect its interest in the property—and its ability to recover the loan. Creditors also require insurance on business property of many types when it is used as collateral for a loan. Likewise, many business agreements require one or more parties to the agreement to purchase liability insurance. Insurance mandates may increase demand for insurance.

Attitude Toward Risk

Mandates aside, the demand for insurance is strongly influenced by the insurance buyer's attitude toward risk. Insurance premiums are an expense. However, because insurance decreases uncertainty, insurance can decrease the cost of risk. The net effect is that the cost of insurance is partly offset, because it reduces the measurable costs associated with the uncertainty. Insurers attempt to increase the demand for insurance by advertising and public education programs that make people aware of their risks that insurance can handle.

Financial Status

Survival is the most basic human or organizational risk management objective. Even a risk-averse person might not purchase insurance if he or she barely has enough money to buy food and other necessities essential to survival. Likewise, a business on the brink of bankruptcy might not buy insurance against the vague possibility of future loss but instead use the cash to pay bills that immediately threaten the firm's survival.

Only individuals or businesses whose income exceeds a certain minimum level are likely to purchase insurance. The higher an individual's income and asset level are, the more likely he or she is to purchase insurance, and the more protecting assets becomes important.

The demand for some forms of insurance diminishes for very wealthy individuals and for organizations with substantial assets. This phenomenon occurs when persons or organizations have financial resources sufficient to handle losses as current expenses, or use various forms of retention.

Price of Insurance

Another factor affecting demand for insurance is price. A given insurer's price is an important factor in selecting risk management alternatives when customers have a choice among several insurance companies—or, as is often the case with personal insurance, many competing insurance companies. Unless the customer sees some distinction other than price, he or she is likely to choose the company that offers the cheapest coverage. According to one recent survey, about six in ten Americans with cars do not shop for auto insurance.[2] Still, the company with high prices is likely to lose the customers that do shop.

One way insurers try to increase demand for their own products and overcome price concerns is to distinguish products from those of competitors, thereby reducing the perception that acceptable alternatives exist. Another way to increase demand, both for individual insurers' products and in the aggregate, is to introduce new insurance products, such as extended warranty products for autos, warranties for home buyers, and insurance against financial losses due to identity theft.

Overall, insurance price levels affect the aggregate demand for insurance. Despite the importance of insurance, individuals and organizations can handle risk in other ways. Risk control measures can reduce loss frequency and severity. Various funded or unfunded retention programs are also available. Recently, large commercial insurance buyers have increasingly turned to the alternative risk transfer market, discussed in Chapter 7.

Tax Incentives

Tax incentives affect demand by encouraging people to purchase certain types of insurance in which the premium is tax-deductible. For example, with employer-provided group life and health insurance, the cost of this insurance is not considered taxable income to an employee (subject to limitations), and it is a tax-deductible expense for employers. A tax deduction has the same effect as a discount because it lowers the net cost of insurance to purchasers, thereby increasing purchasers' demand for insurance. The difference between a tax deduction and a discount is that the deduction is provided by the government, not the insurance provider.

Tax considerations affecting the purchase of property-liability insurance are often more subtle. A few simple examples illustrate tax considerations:

- For an individual or a family, casualty losses (as defined by the tax code) can be income-tax-deductible in some cases, but property-liability insurance premiums are not tax-deductible. The tax deduction helps subsidize the cost of uninsured losses. Recognizing this, wealthy individuals in a high tax bracket might decide to forgo the purchase of property insurance or to purchase insurance with a high deductible.

- For a business, casualty losses (as defined by the tax code) are tax-deductible at the time they are paid, not during the year when they are incurred. A long delay often exists between the date of an occurrence and the date the loss is paid. Some losses, such as those involving a serious disability, are paid over a period of years. Alternatively, insurance premiums are tax-deductible as a business expense when they are paid. In many cases, the annual cost of insurance is much more consistent from year to year than the amounts that would otherwise be paid as retained losses. This is a powerful argument for insurance when earnings stability is a risk management objective.

Competition

Competition also affects the economics of the insurance business. The degree of competition in insurance is affected by the number of competing insurers, the extent to which insurance substitutes exist, and buyers' knowledge of the market.

Number of Competing Insurers

Competition in any industry is driven by the number of firms in that industry. Competition usually increases as the number of competitors increases, and vice versa. The public, as well as government agencies, sometimes becomes concerned when corporate mergers and acquisitions reduce the number of competing firms so that competition is limited.

Although the degree of competition varies by type of insurance, insurance is highly competitive. Several thousand different insurance companies write business in the United States, often through one of the many thousands of agents or brokers who serve as intermediaries.

One factor affecting the number of competitors is the ease with which competitors can enter the market. In recent years, entry into the insurance market seems easier. For example, passage of the Gramm-Leach-Bliley Act in 1999 has removed some of the barriers that previously kept banks or other financial services organizations from competing with traditional insurers. Also, the Internet that spawned many other "dot-com" businesses has also made it easy for insurance organizations to develop a widespread virtual presence without establishing a traditional marketing force.

Substitutes for Insurance

Competition in any industry, for any good or service, is affected by the availability of substitutes. Consider the airline industry. When only one airline provides service between cities, it might seem there are no alternatives. However, substitute transportation may be available. Often, getting a cheaper flight is possible by flying to or from a neighboring city. Trains, buses, rental cars, private cars, taxicabs, and sometimes boats, private airplanes, or helicopters might also be available. If air fares are high enough, and the demand exists, investors might seize the opportunity and capitalize a new startup airline to provide competing service.

At first, it might seem that insurance has no substitute. However, various loss-financing alternatives do exist, and the alternatives become increasingly appealing as the cost of insurance increases. Chapter 7 discusses some of those alternatives.

A simple substitute involves the financial resources of each person or business. Some families find that their insurance needs *decrease* over time as their wealth accumulates and they become better able to absorb a moderate loss without going bankrupt or otherwise jeopardizing their financial stability. Likewise, a business that is in good financial condition might choose to retain certain losses rather than buy high-priced insurance.

Knowledge of the Market

Another aspect of competition is consumer knowledge of the market. If a prospective insurance buyer *knows* that one insurance company will charge $500 for a particular policy while another company will charge only $400, the customer will probably patronize the company with the lower price, assuming that no substantial difference exists between the coverage or service provided by either insurer.

Competition generally depends on knowledge of the market, and perfect knowledge of the market usually does not exist. For example, a customer who wants to buy a new Hozdota 500 probably will compare prices at just a few dealers, not every Hozdota dealer in the region. This means that Local Hozdota's competition is limited; it does not need to beat every other Hozdota dealer in the country to get this customer's business.

Insurance companies have benefited, to some extent, from the fact that it was not practical or convenient for a typical insurance purchaser to make insurance shopping a major research project because of the cost in both time and effort to obtain information. Some personal insurance shoppers would contact a few producers, each of whom represents one insurance company, while others might shop at one or more independent agents, each of whom represents several insurers. A number of state insurance departments publish rate surveys that list many insurance companies' rates for a few typical situations, but prices vary depending on one's situation, and rates change frequently. Commercial insurance buyers' options for some types of insurance are often more limited, although they might obtain competing proposals from a few brokers.

The Internet dramatically changed the amount of price information available to insurance buyers and the speed with which that information can be obtained. The availability of this market information will inevitably make insurance marketing even more competitive. The Internet and other modern telecommunication facilities improve consumer access not only to pricing information but also to other information such as insurer financial ratings and consumer satisfaction surveys.

Internet access to insurers' price quotes is a fairly new concept. Although few firms are actively selling insurance policies over the Internet, consumers are using the Web to compare insurance quotes. Some observers expect Internet sales of insurance to grow substantially over the next several years.

Insurance Pricing

The law of supply and demand suggests that an insurance transaction (transfer of risk) will occur at a price that is satisfactory to both the insurer and the insurance buyer. Insurers supply insurance at a price that is higher than the expected value of the losses they cover, and buyers purchase insurance even when the cost of insurance is higher than the expected cost of losses that would otherwise be retained.

When selling insurance to a group of insurance buyers, an insurer generally intends to collect premiums that are adequate to generate an operating profit from the group. Losses are the largest component of the insurance premium dollar, so insurance must be priced at a level that is adequate to recoup the insurer's losses. This goal is accomplished when the insurance premium for each policy is set at a level that reflects the loss exposures covered by that policy, with an allowance for the insurer's expenses, profits, and contingencies—and, perhaps, an adjustment for investment income. Insurers refer to this as a premium that is *commensurate with the exposure*.

Insurance company actuaries use a combination of skills, experience, and sophisticated mathematical models in developing insurance rating systems for many different coverages that match premiums with exposures. Specific rating approaches are discussed in other CPCU courses. This chapter discusses only three general pricing issues: adverse selection, actuarial versus social equity, and timing.

Adverse Selection

Adverse selection

The process by which people with the greatest probability of loss are those most likely to purchase insurance.

Kenneth Abraham defines **adverse selection** as "the process by which low-risk insureds tend to purchase less coverage, and high-risk insureds tend to purchase more coverage than they would if prices were more accurate."[3]

Naturally, an insurance buyer is eager to transfer risks to an insurance company when the insurance premium seems relatively inexpensive. People (such as property owners in a flood plain) are eager to purchase insurance when they think the cost of insurance is less than the probable cost of losses they would retain if they did not purchase insurance. Of course, insurance companies do not want to intentionally sell insurance at a loss. However, an insurance company can be interested in selling insurance at a price much higher than its expected losses and expenses. Both the insurance company and the insurance buyer consider their own best interests in an insurance transaction.

Information is especially important in assessing the price in any transaction. The insurance buyer presumably knows its own risks better than any outsider, such as an insurance company. On the other hand, insurance companies are in the business of evaluating and insuring risk, and they might have more expertise in those matters than the individual or business seeking insurance. But in either case, evaluation of the risk depends on information. Information is important in both risk identification and risk analysis. Information does not reduce losses, but it leads to a better understanding of the risks one faces, which, in turn, improves one's ability to handle risks.

Appropriate insurance pricing requires that the insurer be able to gather the information necessary to assess and price a particular policy. Relevant information is generally available from the insurance buyer and from other sources.

Significant ethical, social, and legal issues exist with respect to the information insurers need to develop appropriate insurance prices. The explosion in computer networks and computer databases, and a rapidly increasing ability to access and analyze information, raise serious privacy issues, especially when they involve the sharing of customer information among related entities such as banks and insurance companies, or healthcare organizations and insurers. People and businesses are entitled to a degree of privacy. However, if too much information is kept private, the insurance buyer would know more than the insurance company about the risks involved in their transaction. Such a situation would discourage insurers from supplying insurance.

Actuarial Equity Versus Social Equity

Ideally, the premiums charged to policyholders should vary in direct proportion to the policyholders' insured loss exposures. Fair discrimination, which charges an equitable premium to each insured, is an essential element of insurance pricing. State insurance laws prohibit insurance rates that are *unfairly* discriminatory. Equity has a different meaning for different people, and opinions often vary as to whether insurance pricing should achieve actuarial equity or social equity.

Insurers generally want to achieve **actuarial equity**, in which each insured pays a premium directly related to the loss exposures that are transferred to the insurer. The concept of actuarial equity is founded in cost-based pricing. Cost-based pricing attempts to identify and control every variable that will significantly affect quantifying differences between otherwise identical risks. Actuarial equity has been the traditional test applied by regulatory authorities to distinguish between fair and unfair discrimination, but a trend in recent years has been to consider another test, social equity.

The states or courts have not specifically defined **social equity,** but it seems to involve two concepts. The first of those concepts is that insurers should relate the amount each person should pay for insurance to ability to pay rather than to the person's loss exposure or expense factor. The second concept is that insurers should not increase a person's insurance premium because of criteria that are beyond that individual's control. To help achieve social equity, legislators and the public have identified certain insurance rate variables that are socially unacceptable—including, in virtually every state, the use of race, religion, and national origin. Even if loss experience differs based on these variables, they cannot be reflected in rating plans, and this can affect underwriters' decisions. For example, in some jurisdictions, gender has been eliminated as a rating factor for auto insurance—although insurers have gathered historical loss information that detects that youthful male operators have more losses relative to youthful female operators. In those jurisdictions where gender has been eliminated as a rating factor, youthful males and youthful females pay the same rates, other things being equal.

Actuarial equity
The development of insurance rates based on the actuarially calculated costs associated with the loss exposures that will be transferred to the insurer.

Social equity
The development of insurance rates based on an insured's ability to pay; not allowing insurers to alter premiums because of factors outside an insured's control, e.g., gender.

When regulatory constraints distort actuarial equity, with the effect that some groups (youthful male operators) are undercharged for their insurance, insurers need to overcharge other groups (youthful female operators) to break even.

Timing

Another issue in insurance pricing is timing. For some kinds of losses, especially large losses arising from liability exposures, a substantial delay—often lasting for years—can occur among the date when an event occurs, the date when the loss is discovered, and the date when the loss is paid. During this period, the insurer invests the premium paid for the coverage and generates investment income. This investment income offsets the cost of the insurer's expected losses, and this is often reflected in insurer's pricing.

FINANCIAL VIEW OF INSURANCE

Insurance companies have a variety of publicly stated objectives. A few examples appear in Exhibit 5-1. Although some of these objectives are expressed in financial terms, many are not.

Insurers cannot meet their objectives unless they are financially successful. *A business is financially successful when its revenues over time exceed its expenses by a satisfactory margin.* Insurance companies face a special challenge because the largest portion of their expenses involves losses that are somewhat difficult to project.

After discussing the stakeholders who have an outcome in an insurance company's success, this chapter will take a close look at measuring insurance companies' financial performance.

Insurance Company Stakeholders

A successful insurer's revenues should exceed its expenses over time by a "satisfactory margin." Who should be satisfied, and what amount of profit, over what time period, will satisfy them? Stockholders and/or policyholders must be satisfied because they own and control the insurance company. However, financial success is also important to other stakeholders such as agents, employees, regulators, reinsurers, and the community where the insurer's offices are located.

The people who own the insurance company are among its most important stakeholders for at least two reasons:

1. They commit the capital that provides the cushion to pay unexpectedly high claim costs.
2. They have a right to excess funds when claim costs are low enough to generate a profit.

EXHIBIT 5-1

Insurers' Stated Objectives—A Sampling

Liberty Mutual Group is a diversified international financial services organization with a common mission of "helping people live safer, more secure lives."

World Wide Web: http://www.libertymutual.com/about/annual_report_2000/html/lm_at_a_glance.htm (25 July 2002).

State Farm's mission is to help people manage the risks of everyday life, recover from the unexpected and realize their dreams.

We are people who make it our business to be like a good neighbor; who built a premier company by selling and keeping promises through our marketing partnership; who bring diverse talents and experiences to our work of serving the State Farm customer.

Our success is built on a foundation of shared values—quality service and relationships, mutual trust, integrity and financial strength.

Our vision for the future is to be the customer's first and best choice in the products and services we provide. We will continue to be the leader in the insurance industry and we will become a leader in the financial services arena. Our customers' needs will determine our path. Our values will guide us.

World Wide Web: http://www.statefarm.com/about/mission.htm (25 July 2002).
©Copyright, State Farm Mutual Automobile Insurance Company, 2000. Used by permission.

Investor-Owned Insurance Companies

A **stock insurance company** issues shares of stock to the investors who provide the initial capital that meets regulatory requirements and provides the initial capacity to begin writing insurance. Additional capital is accumulated through earnings on insurance operations, investment earnings, and the sale of additional stock or bonds. Stockholders own the company and have the right to profits the insurer earns. The insurance company's board of directors might declare a dividend by which some dollar amount per share is distributed to shareholders. The stock's value also will rise—or fall—depending on the value of company ownership as perceived by other investors who are willing to purchase or sell the stock.

To many stockholders, including both individual and institutional investors, insurance company stock represents a portion of a diversified investment portfolio. Although stockholders face the risk of uncertain dividends, as well as the risk that their stock will increase or decrease in value, they are not otherwise exposed to the risks associated with operating an insurance company. Even if insured claims are much worse than expected and exceed the insurance company's assets, the stockholder might lose his or her investment but is otherwise isolated from liability.

Stock insurance company
An insurer owned by stockholders and formed as a corporation for the purpose of earning a profit for the stockholders.

Lloyd's of London
An association (not an insurance company) that provides the physical and procedural facilities for its members to write insurance.

Lloyd's of London is not an insurance company but rather a unique type of investor-owned insurance exchange or market. Lloyd's is an organization that provides a set of rules and procedures, as well as a location where insurance business is transacted. The owners of the insurance organizations, or syndicates, conducting business at Lloyd's are called *names*. Until the early 1990s, Lloyd's names were exclusively very wealthy individual investors who agreed to accept unlimited personal liability for the risks they accepted. Unlimited liability means that these individuals would be obligated to sell almost all of their personal assets to cover any shortfall in their syndicates' ability to pay claims. Large losses during the 1990s severely tested this structure and caused Lloyd's to reorganize. Currently, Lloyd's names include about 2,500 individual investors with unlimited liability, plus corporate names with limited liability. Such corporations supply about 80 percent of Lloyd's capital.[4] Contrary to popular myth, Lloyd's activity is not limited to unusual forms of insurance but includes a variety of commercial insurance, reinsurance, and auto insurance. Both individual and corporate investors intend to increase their wealth by collecting premiums that substantially exceed the losses they underwrite. However, they are exposed to risk.

Policyholder-Owned Insurance Companies

Mutual insurance company
An insurer owned by its policyholders and formed as a corporation for the purpose of providing insurance to its policyholder-owners.

Mutual insurance companies represent the most common form of policyholder ownership. As reflected in names like "Millers Mutual," "Jewelers Mutual," or "Florists' Mutual," many mutual insurance companies have been formed by people or businesses with a common need. Local farmers have founded a number of mutual insurance companies to provide property insurance on the farms in many counties around the United States.

A mutual insurance company sometimes obtains initial capital from would-be policyholders but usually obtains it by borrowing money from investors. If the company is successful, borrowed money is ultimately repaid from the insurer's operating profits. Additional operating profits may be retained to finance future growth and provide a cushion against future liabilities. Insurance company management can also decide to share profits with policyholders in the form of policyholder dividends.

Reciprocal insurance company
An insurer owned by its policyholders, formed as an unincorporated association for the purpose of providing insurance services to its members, and managed by an attorney-in-fact.

Mutual insurance company policyholders generally are not responsible for losses that exceed the insurance company's resources. However, some mutual insurers, known as *assessable mutuals*, preserve the right to assess policyholders to obtain additional funds if that becomes necessary for the insurer to meet its obligations. Such assessments typically are limited to one additional annual premium payment.

A **reciprocal insurance company** closely resembles a mutual insurance company, but they have technical differences. For example, while a mutual insurance company is incorporated, a reciprocal is managed by a management company, referred to as an attorney-in-fact.

Captive insurance company
An insurer, formed as a subsidiary of its parent company, organization, or group, that provides all or part of the insurance for its parent company or companies.

Some consider **captive insurance companies** a sophisticated form of self-insurance or retention, rather than classify them as insurance companies.

They are mentioned here because captives are owned by the organizations they insure. A **single-parent captive** is an insurance company organized solely to provide insurance to its "parent" company. A **group captive** or an **association captive** provides insurance to a group of corporations that also own the captive. A **risk retention group** is a special type of group captive or association captive formed under the Risk Retention Act of 1986 to provide liability insurance and subject to limited state regulation.

Hybrid Forms of Ownership

To obtain greater access to capital, which can be raised by selling stock, many mutual insurance companies have "demutualized" by converting to stock insurers. Others have established a hybrid structure in which mutual insurance companies remain policyholder-owned but also create special operating units that issue stock or create a mutual holding company structure to access capital through the sale of securities.

Insurance company stakeholders can understand and evaluate insurers' financial performance using various measures, such as balance sheets, income expenses, profitability, performance ratios, and pricing.

Balance Sheets

A **balance sheet**, sometimes called a statement of financial position, is a summary of any organization's assets, liabilities, and owners' equity at a particular point in time.[5] It is called a balance sheet because it is divided into two sections, (1) assets and (2) liabilities plus owners' equity, and the totals of both sections must be equal—that is, they must be in balance.

$$\text{Assets} = \text{Liabilities} + \text{Owners' equity}$$

Assets are property owned by an insurance company. The assets typically accumulated by an insurance company include money, stocks, and bonds; tangible property, such as buildings, office furniture, and equipment; and accounts receivable from agents, brokers, and reinsurers.

Liabilities are financial obligations, or debts, that a company owes to another entity. An insurance company's major liabilities are the loss reserve and the unearned premium reserve. The **loss reserve** is the insurer's best estimate of the final settlement amount on all claims that have occurred but have not yet been paid. The **unearned premium reserve** represents insurance premiums prepaid by policyholders for insurance coverage that the insurer will provide in the future. The insurer has not yet earned the right to keep this portion of the premiums it has collected. If the insurer would somehow cease to operate, the unearned premiums would have to be refunded to policyholders.

The relationship between assets and liabilities can easily be demonstrated by examining the situation of a typical homeowner who has a home worth

Single-parent captive
An insurer that is a subsidiary of only one parent company formed for the purpose of writing all or part of the insurance for its parent company.

Group captive or association captive
An insurer that is a subsidiary of its parent group of corporations formed for the purpose of writing all or part of the insurance for its parent companies.

Risk retention group
A group captive or an association captive that provides liability insurance subject to limited state regulation under the Risk Retention Act of 1986.

Balance sheet
A financial statement that indicates an organization's assets, liabilities, and owners' equity at a particular point in time.

Assets
The property (tangible and intangible) owned by an entity

Liabilities
The financial obligations, or debts, owed to another entity.

Loss reserve
A liability on an insurer's balance sheet that estimates the final settlement amount on all claims that have occurred but have not yet been paid.

Unearned premium reserve
The insurance premiums prepaid by policyholders for insurance coverage that the insurer will provide in the future.

$300,000 and an unpaid mortgage balance of $200,000. The home is an asset valued at $300,000. The mortgage is a liability valued at $200,000. The difference between the house's value and the amount owed on the mortgage is the owner's equity in the house, in this case $100,000. As the mortgage is paid off, the owner's equity in the house increases while the owner's liabilities decrease.

The owners' equity of an insurance company is generally referred to as **policyholders' surplus**. This term emphasizes the priority given to satisfying policyholder obligations. So, for an insurance company, the balance sheet formula could be stated as follows:

$$\text{Assets} = \text{Liabilities} + \text{Policyholders' surplus}$$

The policyholders' surplus of an insurance company is equal to the difference between its assets and its liabilities. When the insurer's assets increase without a corresponding increase in liabilities, surplus increases. As an insurer's surplus grows, it gains an increasingly large cushion that can absorb losses. Increasing the policyholders' surplus also increases an insurer's capacity to write new business.

Conversely, the policyholders' surplus of an insurance company decreases whenever its assets decrease without a corresponding decrease in liabilities. Such a decline will occur, for example, when the value of investments, such as stocks and bonds, decrease.

Revenue

Another financial aspect of the insurance business is how revenue is generated. Insurance companies receive revenue from two major sources:

1. *Premiums*—payments by policyholders to purchase insurance
2. *Investments*—interest, dividends, capital gains, and other earnings on funds held by the insurer

Comparably small amounts of revenue might also come from various other sources, such as selling loss control services or renting property to others.

Premiums

The first major source of revenue, premiums, can be characterized in two ways:

1. Written premium
2. Earned premium

An insurer's **written premium** for any given time period, such as a year, is the total premium on all policies "written," or put into effect, during that time period.

Earned premium represents the portion of written premium that is recognized as revenue only as time passes and as the insurance company provides the

---

Policyholders' surplus
The owners' equity of an insurance company calculated as assets minus liabilities.

Written premium
The total premium on all policies written, or put into effect, during a given period.

Earned premium
The amount of written premium recognized as revenue for the portion of the policy period that has already elapsed.

protection promised under its insurance policies. The portion of written premium that has not yet been earned is referred to as **unearned premium**. Unearned premium is a liability, not an asset.

Unearned premium
The amount of written premium for the portion of the policy period that has not yet elapsed.

Written Premiums Versus Earned Premiums

Two fundamental concepts of insurance ratemaking are written premiums and earned premiums. Written premiums for a period consist of all of the premiums for policies and endorsements recorded on the company's books during the period. Earned premiums for the period consist of the premiums used to pay for protection actually provided during the period. For example, assume that a company writes only one policy during the year, a one-year policy with an annual premium of $100 written on October 1. The written premium for the year would be $100, the entire premium for the policy. The earned premium for the year would be $25, because only three months of protection would be provided during the year. The remaining $75 of premium for the policy would be earned in the next year. The $75 not earned by December 31 would be shown on the company's year-end balance sheet as a liability called the unearned premium reserve.[6]

Investments

The second major source of revenue for an insurance company is investments. Insurers invest any money available that is not immediately being used to pay claims and other expenses. The insurer's resulting investment income can be quite substantial, especially during periods in which interest rates are high or the stock market is performing well. When stock or bond markets are performing poorly, an insurer can suffer investment losses.

Premiums provide a major source of funds that can be invested to increase an insurer's earnings. Premiums can be invested until they are needed to pay claims. The policyholders' surplus provides a second source of funds that can be invested to produce investment income.

Insurers' investment income indirectly serves to reduce insurance premiums. Because insurance is highly competitive, insurers base their premiums not only on expected losses and expenses but also on the investment income they expect to earn. Additionally, all funds from premiums are accompanied by underwriting risk. That is, losses and expenses might prove to be greater than the premiums or even greater than the premiums plus the investment income from those premiums.

Expenses

The next financial aspect of the insurance business is expenses. The major expenses incurred in operating an insurance company stem from delivering the insurance promise by paying claims and paying for handling those claims. An insurer also has expenses associated with selling, delivering, and servicing its insurance products, as well as expenses associated with investing available funds. See the following box.

> ## Six Types of Expenses
> 1. Losses
> 2. Loss adjustment expenses
> 3. Acquisition expenses
> 4. General expenses
> 5. Taxes and fees
> 6. Investment expenses

Losses

For property and liability insurers, losses often represent about 80 percent of their total expenses but may be much more or less. Losses are counted as they are *incurred*, which—because of the timing of insurance claims—is not the same as when they are paid. Claims resulting from an auto accident occurring during 2002 might not be paid until 2003. That is a short delay; many losses have a much longer lapse of time between occurrence and payment. For any given year, an insurance company knows with certainty only the amount of losses it has paid, but it does not know with certainty the amount it will ultimately have to pay for losses incurred that year.

Paid losses
The losses that have been paid to, or on behalf of, insureds during a specific period.

- **Paid losses** have been paid to, or on behalf of, insureds during a given period.

- *Loss reserves* are estimates of amounts that will be paid in the future for losses that have already occurred. In a given year, insurers will have reserves for claims that occurred that year plus reserves for losses that occurred in prior years but have not yet been paid. Also, because losses are not always reported immediately, an insurance company's loss reserves usually include an estimate for **incurred but not reported (IBNR) losses**.

Incurred but not reported (IBNR) losses
The losses that have occurred but have not yet been reported to the insurer.

Incurred losses
The losses that have occurred during a specific period, no matter when claims resulting from the losses are paid. Incurred losses for any given period are equal to paid losses plus or minus changes in loss reserves over that period.

- **Incurred losses** for any specific time period are equal to paid losses plus or minus changes in loss reserves over that time period.

Loss Adjustment Expenses

Loss adjustment expenses
The expenses the insurer incurs to investigate, defend, and settle claims.

In addition to the amounts that must be paid to policyholders or third-party claimants in satisfying a claim, insurers incur additional expenses, known as **loss adjustment expenses**, to investigate, defend, and settle claims. Substantial defense costs are associated with some liability claims, even in cases in which no payment for damages is made.

Acquisition Expenses

Insurers incur significant expenses in acquiring new business. These **acquisition expenses** include marketing, advertising, and underwriting expenses. Because most of the expenses of selling an insurance policy are paid upfront (for example, producers receive a commission when the policy is sold and delivered), the insurer is essentially spending some of the money it expects to earn during the policy period. Consequently, whenever the company writes a new policy, it creates a short-term loss that it hopes will be offset by earned premiums the insured will pay to the insurer during the policy period.

The timing of acquisition costs is one factor that limits insurance companies' capacity to write new business. When a policy is sold, acquisition expenses reduce the company's surplus, although the surplus is replenished as premiums are earned over time. However, insurance companies often do not have enough surplus to support unlimited growth. An insurance company that grows too rapidly might reduce its surplus to the point at which it becomes insolvent, even if the new business is properly underwritten and priced.

Acquisition expenses
The expenses the insurer incurs to acquire new business, including marketing, advertising, and underwriting expenses.

General Expenses

Like other businesses, insurance companies have various general expenses that do not relate directly to claims, marketing, and underwriting. General expenses include staffing and maintaining such insurance company departments as information systems, human resources, accounting, legal, research, product development, customer service, and building maintenance. Insurers must also provide office space, telephones, and other utility services, as well as the office equipment and supplies necessary to support other functions.

Taxes and Fees

Other expenses facing insurers are taxes and fees. Insurers pay income tax and a variety of additional government-imposed taxes and fees such as premium taxes. Insurance companies usually must pay for licenses in each state where they operate and participate in various state insurance programs such as guaranty funds[7] and automobile insurance plans.[8]

Investment Expenses

Insurance companies incur expenses to support the staff of professional investment managers who oversee the insurance company's investment program. Other investment expenses include brokerage, registration and transfer, and custodial fees.

Profitability

Like any business, an insurer generates income, or profits, when its revenue exceeds its expenses. The amount by which revenue exceeds expenses can be measured in the following two ways.

Net Underwriting Gain or Loss

Net underwriting gain or loss
The earned premiums, minus losses and expenses, for a specific period.

The first way to measure insurer profits is through net underwriting results. An insurer's **net underwriting gain or loss** is its earned premiums minus its incurred losses and underwriting expenses for a specific period, such as one year. Because this dollar figure ignores investment income (or investment losses), it accurately represents the extent of the insurer's profit or loss derived *strictly from the sale of insurance*.

Net underwriting gain *or* loss = Earned premiums − (Incurred losses + Underwriting expenses)

Overall Gain or Loss From Operations

The second way to measure profits is through overall results. When an insurer adds its net investment gain or loss results to its net underwriting gain or loss, the resulting figure is its **overall gain or loss from operations**. This overall figure gives a more complete picture of an insurance company's profitability because investment gains generally help to offset underwriting losses.

Overall gain or loss from operations
The net underwriting gain (loss) plus investment gain (loss).

Overall gain (loss) from operations = Net underwriting gain (loss) + Investment gain (loss)

After an insurance company has paid losses and reserved money to pay additional incurred losses, paid expenses, and paid income taxes, the remainder is net operating income, which belongs to the company owners. The owners (stockholders or policyholders) might receive a portion of this remainder as dividends. The amount that is left after dividends are paid is added to the surplus. The increase in policyholders' surplus enables the insurer to expand its operations in the future and provides a cushion against catastrophic losses.

Another element of profitability in insurance is float. Insurers' profits and losses are based not only on how much money they receive but also when they receive it—and what they do with it while they hold it. The key to success lies in the "float," as explained by Warren Buffett in Exhibit 5-2.

Performance Ratios

Several ratios are commonly used to evaluate aspects of an insurance company's financial performance. The key ratios discussed here include the loss ratio, expense ratio, combined ratio, investment income ratio, overall operating ratio, and capacity ratio. These ratios are often expressed as percentages.

Loss Ratio

Loss ratio
An insurer's incurred losses (including loss adjustment expenses) for a specific period divided by earned premiums for the same period.

The **loss ratio** compares an insurance company's incurred losses to its earned premiums for a specific time period. The figure for incurred losses includes loss adjustment expenses. The loss ratio is defined as follows:

$$\text{Loss ratio} = \frac{\text{Incurred losses (including loss adjustment expenses)}}{\text{Earned premiums}}$$

EXHIBIT 5-2

The Economics of Property-Casualty Insurance

Our main business—though we have others of great importance—is insurance. To understand Berkshire, therefore, it is necessary that you understand how to evaluate an insurance company. The key determinants are: (1) the amount of float that the business generates; (2) its cost; and (3) most critical of all, the long-term outlook for both of these factors.

To begin with, float is money we hold but don't own. In an insurance operation, float arises because premiums are received before losses are paid, an interval that sometimes extends over many years. During that time, the insurer invests the money. This pleasant activity typically carries with it a downside: The premiums that an insurer takes in usually do not cover the losses and expenses it eventually must pay. That leaves it running an "underwriting loss," which is the cost of float. An insurance business has value if its cost of float over time is less than the cost the company would otherwise incur to obtain funds. But the business is a lemon if its cost of float is higher than market rates for money.

A caution is appropriate here: Because loss costs must be estimated, insurers have enormous latitude in figuring their underwriting results, and that makes it very difficult for investors to calculate a company's true cost of float. Errors of estimation, usually innocent but sometimes not, can be huge. The consequences of these miscalculations flow directly into earnings. An experienced observer can usually detect large-scale errors in reserving, but the general public can typically do no more than accept what's presented, and at times I have been amazed by the numbers that big-name auditors have implicitly blessed. In 1999 a number of insurers announced reserve adjustments that made a mockery of the "earnings" that investors had relied on earlier when making their buy and sell decisions. At Berkshire, we strive to be conservative and consistent in our reserving. Even so, we warn you that an unpleasant surprise is always possible.

. . .

Growth of float is important—but its cost is what's vital. Over the years we have usually recorded only a small underwriting loss—which means our cost of float was correspondingly low—or actually had an underwriting profit, which means we were being *paid* for holding other people's money.

Warren E. Buffett
Chairman of the Board
Berkshire Hathaway Inc.
March 1, 2000

The loss ratio provides the percent of earned premiums used to fund and handle losses. This percentage helps insurers, regulators, investors, and others determine how closely actual loss experience compares to expected loss experience. For example, at the beginning of the year, management might have decided that a 75 percent loss ratio is the target for the coming year.

As each month progresses, the loss ratio is recalculated based on the company's experience to date to determine whether the insurer is meeting the targeted 75 percent ratio.

> ## Ratios To Measure Insurer Performance
> - Loss ratio
> - Expense ratio
> - Combined ratio
> - Investment income ratio
> - Overall operating ratio
> - Capacity ratio

Expense Ratio

Expense ratio
An insurer's incurred underwriting expenses for a specific period divided by written premiums for the same period.

The **expense ratio** compares the underwriting expenses that an insurer has incurred to its written premiums in a specific time period. The expense ratio is defined as follows:

$$\text{Expense ratio} = \frac{\text{Incurred underwriting expenses}}{\text{Written premiums}}$$

The expense ratio indicates what proportion of an insurer's written premiums is being used to pay acquisition costs, general expenses, and taxes. This ratio indicates the insurer's general cost of doing business as a proportion of the premiums it has written. (Investment income and investment expenses are not part of either the loss ratio or the expense ratio.) The expense ratio gives a general picture of how efficiently the insurer is operating. Insurers watch the expense ratio carefully over time and attempt to reduce it by managing cash flows and controlling expenses.

Combined Ratio

Combined ratio
An insurer's loss ratio plus its expense ratio; measures an insurer's underwriting performance, not its overall financial performance, because it does not include investments.

The **combined ratio** combines the loss ratio and the expense ratio to compare inflows and outflows from insurance operations. The combined ratio is defined as follows:

$$\text{Combined ratio} = \text{Loss ratio} + \text{Expense ratio}$$

In other words, the combined ratio is calculated as follows:

$$\text{Combined ratio} = \frac{\text{Incurred losses (including loss adjustment expenses)}}{\text{Earned premiums}} + \frac{\text{Incurred underwriting expenses}}{\text{Written premiums}}$$

Notice both the numerators (top numbers) and the denominators (bottom numbers) in the loss ratio and the expense ratio are different.

- The *loss ratio* compares the level of losses as they are incurred to the premiums earned during the same period. Both incurred losses and earned premiums reflect insurance coverage provided over time. These two measurements represent corresponding inflows and outflows on an accrual basis. They are measured—*not* on the basis of money *collected* or *paid* during the period—but rather on the basis of money that must ultimately be paid to cover losses occurring during the period, and money that the insurer is entitled to keep in exchange for providing coverage during the same period.

- The *expense ratio* recognizes that many of an insurance company's underwriting expenses involve acquisition expenses, such as agents' commissions. Because these expenses occur at the beginning of the policy period, the use of written premiums, which recognizes the entire premium as soon as it is written, is appropriate for comparing underwriting expenses to revenues.

The combined ratio is considered the accepted measure of an insurer's *underwriting* performance. A combined ratio under 100 percent would suggest that the insurer is earning an underwriting profit. However, this ratio does not reflect the insurer's investment income. Therefore, the combined ratio does not measure the insurer's overall financial performance that results from both underwriting and investment activities.

Investment Income Ratio

The **investment income ratio** compares the amount of net investment income (investment income minus investment expenses) with earned premiums over a specific period. It is defined as follows:

$$\text{Investment income ratio} = \frac{\text{Net investment income}}{\text{Earned premiums}}$$

The investment income ratio measures the insurance company's investment performance.

Investment income ratio
An insurer's net investment income (investment income minus investment expenses) divided by earned premiums for a specific period; measures an insurer's investment performance.

Overall Operating Ratio

The combined ratio (loss ratio plus expense ratio) minus the investment income ratio (net investment income divided by earned premiums) can be used to provide an overall measure of the insurance company's financial performance for a specific time period. The **overall operating ratio** is defined as follows:

Overall operating ratio = Combined ratio − Investment income ratio

The lower the overall operating ratio, the better. The investment income ratio must be *subtracted* from the combined ratio because investment income is used

Overall operating ratio
An insurer's combined ratio minus its investment income ratio; measures financial performance for a specific period.

to *offset* the insurer's losses and underwriting expenses. Of all the commonly used ratios, the overall operating ratio is the most complete measure of an insurance company's financial performance. To obtain a true picture of an insurer's profitability, one should analyze overall operating ratios for several years because any company might have a single bad year that is offset by a pattern of profitability over a longer period.

Most insurance companies tend to lose money on their underwriting activities (that is, the combined ratio is usually over 100 percent) but generate a profit on investments. Ideally, the investment profit is more than enough to offset the underwriting loss.

Return on Equity

Return on equity
The net income divided by average owners' equity for a specific period.

Investors invariably expect a return on their investments, and they compare the return on any given investment with potential returns that might instead have been earned by investing their money elsewhere. For organizations, the key calculation is called a **return on equity**, calculated by dividing the organization's net income by the average amount of owners' equity for the period in question. In general, the owners' equity is invested in operations to generate income for the organization. In an insurance company, owners' equity—policyholders' surplus—is invested in underwriting activities.

Capacity Ratio

Capacity ratio, or premium-to-surplus ratio
The written premiums divided by policyholders' surplus; used by insurance regulators to determine whether the insurer might experience financial difficulty.

An important concern for insurance company performance is an insurer's capacity to write new business and thus to grow. An insurer's capacity is limited by its **capacity ratio**, also known as its **premium-to-surplus ratio**, calculated as shown below:

$$\text{Capacity ratio} = \frac{\text{Written premiums}}{\text{Policyholders' surplus}}$$

The capacity ratio compares an insurance company's written premiums (which represent its exposure to potential claims) to its policyholders' surplus. The surplus represents the insurer's cushion for absorbing adverse results: If losses and expenses exceed written premiums, an insurer must draw on its surplus to meet its obligations. Therefore, an insurer's new written premiums should not become too large relative to its policyholders' surplus.

While it is not a magic figure, insurance regulators use the capacity ratio as a benchmark to determine whether an insurer might be headed toward financial difficulty. A premium-to-surplus ratio above 3-to-1 is often considered a sign of financial weakness. Although this ratio is important, it is not the only measure that should be used to evaluate an insurer's financial condition. More sophisticated measures recognize the lines of business written, the adequacy of the loss reserves, the quality of assets, the amount of reinsurance, and other factors.

FUNCTIONAL VIEW OF INSURANCE

The last two sections showed how insurance works from an economic stand-point and from a financial standpoint. This section completes the picture by outlining the functional view of insurance by looking at insurers' core functions of marketing, underwriting, and claims. Insurers perform these functions to facilitate risk transfer, promote efficiency, and meet financial and nonfinancial objectives.

Core Functions of Insurers

- Marketing
- Underwriting
- Claims

Marketing

An insurer's marketing department generates business by acquiring buyers for the insurer's goods and services. Potential buyers of insurance must be adequately informed of the company's products, including its policies, rating plans, loss adjustment services, loss control capabilities, and other services that make a complete insurance product. Communicating this information to potential customers and producers is primarily the function of the insurer's marketing personnel.

Many insurers sell through independent agents and brokers, who are independent business people representing several otherwise unrelated insurers. Some insurers market through exclusive agents, who represent only one insurer or a group of insurers under common ownership and management. Other insurers rely on their own employees' sales efforts. Some insurers advertise through the mail, on television, or in newspapers and magazines or use the Internet to market their services, with no direct face-to-face marketing contact with their customers. An increasing number of insurers use more than one marketing method to reach the widest possible audience.

Marketing is more than merely making sales calls. A successful marketing program is likely to include (1) market research to determine potential buyers' needs, (2) advertising and public relations programs to inform potential buyers about the company's products, (3) training programs to equip the company's employees and agents to meet the public's needs, (4) production goals and strategies, and (5) effective motivation and management of the producer network.

The marketing department's objectives must be balanced with other insurer goals. The insurer's capacity must also be taken into account because too much emphasis on marketing might result in premium growth at the expense of profitability.

Underwriting

Underwriting

The process of evaluating insurance risks, accepting or rejecting them, classifying accepted risks, and determining an appropriate insurance premium.

Another core function insurers perform is underwriting. **Underwriting** serves both insurance companies and insurance buyers—see Exhibit 5-3. The underwriting department decides the price as well as the terms and conditions under which the insurer will provide coverage and also decides which applicants will be offered insurance. The primary purpose of these functions is to ensure that the insurer writes a profitable and reasonably stable book of business.

EXHIBIT 5-3

Proper Underwriting Produces Best Insurance Product for Consumers:
Why being a good investment for an insurance company is good for you.

Insurance underwriting. It may not be the most in vogue topic around, but for consumers of insurance products, proper underwriting plays a crucial role in making insurance available and affordable, and in keeping insurers strong enough to pay claims when consumers suffer a loss.

Barron's Dictionary of Insurance Terms defines underwriting as: "the process of examining, accepting, or rejecting insurance risks, and classifying those selected, in order to charge the proper premium for each. The purpose of underwriting is to spread the risk among a pool of insureds in a manner that is equitable for the insureds and profitable for the insurer."

Underwriting relates to risk. To underwrite is to assume risk. When individuals call an insurance agent or visit an insurance Internet site and decide to purchase insurance, they are essentially asking the insurance company to accept them as a new risk. Each underwriting decision becomes the basis of what is known as an insurance company's "book of business." The underwriting decisions a company makes, and how those decisions are made, play a major role in determining how fiscally healthy and profitable an insurance company will be.

To properly underwrite, an insurer's underwriting policy must be competitive with other insurers, while still providing a level of profitability for the company. The company also must apply its underwriting capabilities as efficiently and effectively as possible. Changing technologies today—such as predictive scoring software, modeling programs, and automated risk evaluation systems—along with consumer credit information and state motor vehicle records, enable insurance companies to get better at underwriting.

Why should consumers care about insurance underwriting? What does it mean for them? Why is it in their best interests for insurance companies to underwrite?

Effective spreading of risk. Proper underwriting helps insurance companies effectively manage the risks that all of their consumers collectively represent.

Think of all of an insurance company's consumers as a group of investments, kind of like a 401(k) plan. To succeed in managing your own 401(k) fund, you have to know what kinds of risk each of your investments represent. That way, you can balance the risk level associated with one group of investments with those of your other groups of investments.

When one group of investments generates higher losses than average for a time, but another group brings in bigger returns during the same period, the risk to the overall fund is balanced and the stability to the fund is maintained. On the other hand, a third group of investments may provide smaller returns, but do so reliably over an extended period of time. This group of investments can help provide a reliable flow of cash while higher risk investments slump for a period of time. Then when the high-flying investments regain their momentum, their gains can provide a surplus that will cover losses somewhere else in the portfolio.

The same principles apply to your insurance. And just as each individual investor has his or her own investment strategy, so too does each insurance company have an underwriting strategy.

Some consumers, just like investment vehicles such as stocks or bonds, are riskier than others. For instance, teenage drivers, as a group, represent a higher risk to an insurance company than, say, middle-aged homeowners. Through proper underwriting, insurance companies know each of their individual risks as well as each group of risks, so they are able to balance these groups, otherwise known as their "books of business," more successfully than they otherwise could.

Increased availability and affordability. Sound underwriting also means there is more insurance for more consumers, at better prices, under more favorable terms.

The better you handle your investment fund, the more money you have to invest in the future. Similarly, the better a job an insurance company does of underwriting its risks—that is, balancing its investments in consumers—the more resources it will be able to invest in still more consumers going forward. That means more consumers will be protected with insurance coverage.

The fiscal strength that results from proper underwriting also means more competition for those consumers, so companies can offer better prices under more favorable terms.

Product innovation. Good underwriting also produces new kinds of insurance products for consumers to pick and choose from.

Just as a successful investor has the wherewithal to invest in new and exciting business opportunities—such as starting a home business or providing the seed capital for an Internet "dot com" start-up—successful underwriting gives insurance companies the flexibility to develop innovative insurance coverages that might not otherwise be developed.

Let's say ABC Insurance Company Inc. successfully manages its "portfolio" of consumer investments. It has a firm grasp of all of the risk potential it has on its books, sees there is a segment of the marketplace that isn't having its insurance needs met, and decides that, because it has such a strong underwriting base, it can afford to expand into a new kind of product. Or maybe the company has such a good understanding of its current customers, it decides it can offer them a new kind of coverage and provide it at a substantial discount, all because it knows its current customers have been such a good "investment."

Continued on next page.

Summary

Successful underwriting is not gouging the consumer over prices. It means knowing your customer (your investment) and intelligently running a business by generating more gains than losses and expenses combined. Like running a good 401(k) fund, sound underwriting gives an insurer the ability to spread its risk around (reducing every consumer's individual risk), look for new investment opportunities (provide more coverage to more people), and develop new products to better serve its market group.

So it may not be a topic that generates a lot of headlines right now, but solid underwriting helps protect the lives of each insurance consumer: it gives us the peace of mind that our homes, our cars and our families are protected and that financial loss will be compensated, should the need arise.

Rodger S. Lawson, Ph.D., President, Alliance of American Insurers

The underwriting department counterbalances the marketing department because restraints on underwriting policy can reduce the number of applicants that are accepted. However, the underwriting and marketing departments must coordinate their efforts. Over time, an unduly restrictive underwriting policy combined with an aggressive marketing department will drive up the insurer's expenses. The cost of investigating and rejecting applicants increases an insurer's expense ratio, and the restricted premium volume reduces the revenues available to pay for those expenses.

The underwriting department aids the marketing department in developing marketable policy forms and rating plans and trying to find ways to insure marginal risks by modifying the policy contract, the rating plan, or the risk.

Claims

Handling claims is another core function in insurance. An insurance contract is a promise to make a payment to, or on behalf of, the policyholder if some insured event occurs. The claim department's purpose is to fulfill the insurer's promise. The insurer's claim department is staffed by employees who are trained in the skills necessary to evaluate and settle claims and to negotiate or litigate the settlement of claims by or against policyholders.

The purpose of the loss adjustment process is to achieve a fair settlement in accordance with the applicable insurance policy provisions. Loss settlements that exceed the proper amount payable under the policy increase the cost of insurance for everybody. Settlements that are less than the proper amount deprive the policyholder of some benefits of the insurance contract. Consistently inadequate loss settlements can hamper the insurer's reputation and can lead to litigation and regulatory actions against the company for not operating in "good faith."

Other Functions

Apart from the core functions mentioned above, some other major functions include information systems, loss control, premium auditing, reinsurance, actuarial activities, and investments.

Information Systems

Like most other businesses, insurers use information technology systems to conduct their daily operations. Information systems are especially important to insurers because of the vast amounts of data associated with their operations.

Loss Control

An insurance company's loss control department provides information to the underwriting department to assist in the selection and rating of risks. It also works with commercial policyholders to help prevent losses and to minimize those that cannot be prevented.

Premium Auditing

Although the premium for many types of insurance is known and guaranteed in advance, for other types of insurance, the premium is variable and cannot be precisely calculated until after the policy period. For example, the premium for workers compensation insurance policies is influenced by wages paid during the policy period. Other commercial insurance policies might use another variable, such as sales or revenues. Premium auditors ensure equitable treatment of insureds by reviewing policyholder records to obtain accurate information on rating variables.

Reinsurance

When a primary insurer accepts a risk that is larger than it is willing or able to bear, it can transfer all or a part of that risk to other insurers around the world through reinsurance transactions. Many insurers have a separate reinsurance department that arranges facultative reinsurance on individual accounts and maintains treaty reinsurance agreements.

Actuarial

The actuarial department performs an insurer's mathematical functions, such as the calculation of rates, the development of rating plans, and the estimation of loss reserves. Actuaries might assist in corporate planning and be involved in establishing corporate goals and assessing the company's success in meeting those goals.

Investment

An insurer's investment operations enable it to earn investment income on the funds generated by its underwriting activities. The investment income, in turn, reduces the premium that the insurer must charge in exchange for the risks it assumes.

The relationship works in both directions, however. The kinds of insurance risks that an insurer assumes is one of the factors that determine the kinds of investments it acquires. For example, liability losses are paid out over a longer period than property losses, and these policies can therefore support more long-term investments—such as corporate bonds with a longer maturity period. An insurer that assumes only moderate underwriting risks might be able to assume greater investment risks, with their higher investment yield. An insurer that assumes very high underwriting risks might need to be more conservative in its investment strategy.

SUMMARY

This chapter explained *how* insurance works as a business by examining insurance from an economic perspective, a business perspective, and a functional perspective.

From an economic perspective, the chapter examined supply and demand. The supply of insurance is affected by the amount of risk involved and by the insurer's capacity. The demand for insurance depends on the size of the overall insurance market, mandatory insurance and other insurance mandates, attitude toward risk, the insurance buyer's financial status, the price of insurance, and tax incentives. Insurance is a competitive business, with many competing insurers, and an increasing number of substitutes for insurance. Competition is also affected by insurance buyers' knowledge of the alternatives available in a competitive market.

From a financial perspective, the chapter examined the distinction between investor-owned and policyholder-owned insurance companies and some hybrid forms of ownership. The chapter briefly examined insurance company balance sheets. Insurer income comes primarily from two sources: premium revenue and investment income. Insurers' expenses include losses, loss adjustment expenses, acquisition expenses, general expenses, taxes and fees, and investment expenses. Insurers make—or lose—money from underwriting activities, investment activities (taking advantage of the float), or both. Insurer performance can be evaluated by using a number of measures, including the loss ratio, expense ratio, combined ratio, investment income ratio, overall operating ratio, return on equity, and capacity ratio. Insurance pricing takes into account the challenges of competition, adverse selection, the conflicting goals of actuarial equity and social equity, and the timing of both premium collection and loss payments.

From a functional viewpoint, this chapter examined the core functions of marketing, underwriting, and claims and briefly examined other functions necessary to make insurance work.

Chapter 6 will explain what risks are privately insurable and how government insurance can handle some of the risks that cannot be handled by private insurers.

CHAPTER NOTES

1. Arthur Snyder, "Sailing on a Rising Tide," *Best's Review*, March 2000, pp. 43–44.

2. Insurance Research Council, *Public Attitude Monitor 2001, Issue 2* (Malvern, Pa.: Insurance Research Council, 2001).

3. Kenneth S. Abraham, *Insurance Law and Regulation: Cases and Materials (University Casebook Series)* (New York: Foundation Press, 2000), p. 15.

4. James R. Hagerty and Christopher Oster, "These Days, 'Names' at Lloyd's Find Investing Can Be Costly, Contentious," *The Wall Street Journal* (July 12, 2002), p. A1.

5. Much more detail on this point can be found in the following CPCU text: David H. Marshall, Wayne W. McManus, and Kenneth N. Scoles Jr., *Accounting and Finance for Insurance Professionals*, 2d ed. (Malvern, Pa.: American Institute for CPCU, 2001).

6. Bernard L. Webb, Connor M. Harrison, and James J. Markham, *Insurance Operations*, 3d ed., vol. 2 (Malvern, Pa.: American Institute for CPCU, 1997), p. 103.

7. A guaranty fund is a state fund providing a system to pay insolvent insurers' claims. The money in the guaranty fund comes from assessments collected from all insurers licensed in the state.

8. An automobile insurance plan, also known as an assigned risk plan, provides insurance to high-risk drivers who are unable to obtain insurance in the voluntary insurance market.

Chapter 6

Direct Your Learning

Insurable Risks

After learning the subject matter of this chapter, you should be able to:

- Identify the six characteristics of an ideally insurable loss exposure.

- Explain why each of the six characteristics of an ideally insurable loss exposure is important to the insurance mechanism.

- Describe the constraints or obstacles an insurer might face in insuring a loss exposure that is commercially insurable.

- Illustrate how the six characteristics of an ideally insurable loss exposure apply to various types of exposures.

- Explain the reasons for government insurance programs.

- Describe government insurance's three possible roles.

- Identify the three types of government insurance plans, and give examples of insurance offered under each type of plan.

Develop Your Perspective

What are the main topics covered in the chapter?

This chapter identifies certain characteristics that insurers look for when evaluating the insurability of a loss exposure. Other factors affecting insurability and reasons for government-sponsored insurance are also covered.

Analyze your organization's current insurance portfolio.

- For what types of loss exposure does your organization carry insurance?

Why is it important to know these topics?

Knowing about insurability will help you understand why insurers choose to insure some loss exposures over others; why insurers cannot always assume risks they might otherwise choose to insure; and why government insurance competes with, reinsures, or complements private insurance.

Examine your organization's insurance coverages again.

- How many different insurers provide the necessary coverages?
- Does any one insurer cover multiple loss exposures?
- Do any constraints prevent an insurer from covering multiple loss exposures?

How can you use this information?

Evaluate your organization's insurance needs that the government covers.

- What are some reasons why the government would provide this coverage?
- Why might a private insurer be unable or unwilling to provide this coverage?

Chapter 6

Insurable Risks

The risks that insurers assume and for which they provide coverage should consist of loss exposures that possess certain characteristics. No loss exposure completely possesses all of the ideal characteristics; however, many loss exposures are insured. Insurability becomes an issue when a particular loss exposure departs too far from the ideal. What is "too far" is subjective and viewed differently over time. Some loss exposures that are now routinely insured were once considered uninsurable, and vice versa. This chapter also deals with the constraints that restrict insurability.

What if a loss exposure is considered uninsurable? Stockholder-owned or policyholder-owned insurers provide insurance for loss exposures that are considered insurable. Sometimes the state and federal governments provide insurance because a loss exposure is not otherwise insurable. In other cases, the government competes with private insurers. This chapter's final section examines several forms of insurance available from state and federal governments.

INSURABLE RISKS FOR PRIVATELY OWNED INSURERS

Private insurance companies insure some, but not all, loss exposures. These commercially insurable loss exposures ideally have certain characteristics. Those loss exposures that do not possess enough of the ideal characteristics are not suitable for insurance by private insurers. However, the government might provide an insurance program for such loss exposures.

A commercially insurable loss exposure ideally possesses the following six characteristics:

1. Loss exposure involves pure, not speculative, risk.
2. Loss exposure is subject to accidental loss from the insured's standpoint.
3. Loss exposure is subject to losses that are definite in time and that are measurable.
4. Loss exposure is one of a large number of similar, but independent, exposures.
5. Loss exposure is not subject to a loss that would simultaneously affect many other similar loss exposures; loss would not be catastrophic.
6. Loss exposure is economically feasible to insure.

Note that these are *ideal* characteristics. The box below outlines each of the characteristics and explains why they are important to insurability. Most insured exposures do not completely meet all of these criteria.

Six Ideal Characteristics of a Commercially Insurable Loss Exposure

Loss exposure involves pure, not speculative, risk.	One purpose of insurance is to make the insured financially whole after a loss, that is, to restore the insured to the same financial position the insured had before the loss. A speculative risk offers the possibility of gain as well as loss. Therefore, if a loss exposure involved a speculative risk, and the insured gained as a result of that risk, this purpose of insurance would be defeated.
Loss exposure is subject to accidental loss from the insured's standpoint.	If the insured has some control over whether or when a loss will occur, the insurer is at a disadvantage because the insured might have an incentive to cause a loss. Also, if losses are not accidental, the insurer cannot calculate an appropriate premium because the chance of loss could increase as soon as the policy is issued. Private insurance is suitable for situations in which there is reasonable uncertainty about the probability or timing of a loss.
Loss exposure is subject to losses that are definite in time and that are measurable.	If the happening, time, and location of a loss cannot be definitely determined and if the amount of the loss cannot be definitely measured, writing an insurance policy that defines what claims to pay and how much to pay for them would be extremely difficult if not impossible. Also, insurers are able to establish premiums partially based on being able to project the losses for a type of loss exposure. If losses cannot be measured, they cannot be projected.
Loss exposure is one of a large number of similar, but independent, exposures.	The loss exposure must be common enough for the insurer to pool a large number of them. This large pool enables the insurer to accurately project losses and determine appropriate premiums because loss statistics can be maintained over time and because losses for similar exposures can be projected with a high degree of accuracy.
Loss exposure is not subject to a loss that would simultaneously affect many other similar loss exposures; loss would not be catastrophic.	Insurance operates economically because many insureds pay premiums that are small relative to the cost of the potential losses that they could each incur. The cost can stay relatively small because insurers project that they will incur far fewer losses than they have loss exposures. So, if it is expected that a large number of insureds, who are covered for the same type of loss, all incur losses at the same time, the insurance mechanism would not operate economically. Nonetheless, insurers do provide coverage for loss exposures subject to some catastrophes, like hurricanes. An insurer can manage such exposures by limiting the amount of exposures it insures within a geographic area and by purchasing reinsurance for such exposures.
Loss exposure is economically feasible to insure.	Loss exposures involving high frequency of occurrence and low severity of damage are not economically feasible to insure because the expense of providing the insurance probably exceeds the amount of potential loss. It also does not make economical sense to insure a loss exposure for a loss that is almost certain to occur, like auto wear and tear.

CONSTRAINTS ON INSURABILITY

Although a particular loss exposure has the characteristics of a commercially insurable loss exposure, an insurer still might be unable to write insurance for it because of externally or internally imposed constraints.

State laws regulate the kinds of insurance that can be written in each state. State laws also prescribe the minimum capital and surplus a domestic stock or mutual insurer must have to transact business. Some financial requirements are so high that an insurer might forgo writing a line of business it would otherwise prefer to include in its portfolio. State insurance departments regulate forms and rates for some types of coverage, which could involve substantial red tape, making it relatively unattractive for an insurer to offer those coverages. Regulatory approval is often a slow process that constrains insurers' ability to provide new products and services because various marketing practices are also regulated, and some activities are prohibited.

An insurer might face other internal and external obstacles to writing a certain type of insurance. See the following box.

Examples of Internal and External Obstacles to Insurability

- Personnel—The insurer might want to enter a certain line of business but conclude that its present staff is not capable of profitably writing and servicing this new line. Hiring personnel might not be feasible, or insufficient volume might not justify the cost.

- Reinsurance—The insurer's interest in writing a new line of business might depend on whether it can obtain reinsurance for large losses or catastrophes.

- Financing and capacity—To write more insurance at an acceptable premium-to-surplus ratio might require the insurer to seek more funds from its stockholders, issue surplus notes, or generate more surplus from operations, none of which it might be able or willing to do.

- Custom and tradition—Most insurers hesitate to pioneer in areas that other insurers have not successfully tested.

- New business—A new line of insurance, in which losses are indeterminable, might lead to variable underwriting results that are difficult to price and that might unnecessarily expose the insurer's assets to loss.

CHARACTERISTICS OF FIRE LOSSES AND INSURABILITY

This section identifies several fire loss exposures and evaluates each against the ideal criteria of a commercially insurable loss exposure. Examining such loss exposures against these criteria helps someone to understand why and when underwriters choose to write insurance for some exposures and decline it for others.

For more than 300 years, fire insurance on dwellings has been commercially available, so the exposure to the fire peril is obviously insurable. Reviewing how and why the exposure generally meets the criteria established for commercial insurability helps someone to understand why these policies are written. It also shows how this widely insured exposure does not meet the criteria of an "ideal" loss exposure.

Loss Exposure Involves Pure, Not Speculative, Risk

Fire loss to a dwelling generally involves only the possibility of loss but no possibility of gain. An exception might be an obsolete run-down building at a prime location. Sometimes the land is worth more without the building, and the building's destruction can actually increase the land's value. Therefore, a fire risk is almost always a pure risk, which makes it attractive for insuring.

Loss Exposure Is Subject to Accidental Loss From the Insured's Standpoint

Although a high degree of uncertainty exists about whether or when an *accidental* fire will occur, some fires are not accidents. Arson committed by the insured (also called arson-for-profit) must be distinguished from arson committed by others. The latter is considered accidental while the former is not.

An insurer can project aggregate accidental fire losses with reasonable confidence based on past experience. However, sometimes riots and civil commotion have resulted in catastrophic property losses in some cities. The possibility of riot or civil commotion remains a concern for property underwriters in some urban areas.

So while fires generally meet the criteria of being accidental, the fact that they can be deliberately set detracts from being considered an "ideal" risk.

Loss Exposure Is Subject to Losses That Are Definite in Time and That Are Measurable

Occasionally, pinpointing the time of an unobserved property fire is difficult, such as when the fire occurs over a weekend. Because fire insurance is usually written for a one-year policy period, loss timing becomes critical only if the loss occurs near the expiration date and a question exists about whether the loss occurred during the policy period. In some cases, continuous coverage exists (such as a renewal policy), but the question is which policy was in force at the time of the loss.

Knowing the value of a building or its contents is critical in measuring the amount of a fire loss, and such value can be measured in different ways. It is necessary to specify—before a loss occurs—whether the insured loss will be the amount of dollars necessary to repair or replace with like kind and quality, or whether the insured loss will be a depreciated actual cash value. Some insurance provides coverage for additional living expenses, fair rental value, or other financial losses resulting from a building that cannot be used. These losses are somewhat more difficult to measure because they depend on an estimate of "what might have been" if an insured event had not occurred.

Fire loss exposures, therefore, are usually "ideal" to insure because a fire's occurrence is typically obvious. However, uncertainty about the timing of a fire's occurrence may make insuring such a fire loss less than "ideal." Similarly, when the value of a building or its contents has been specified before a fire occurs, a fire loss to such property is ideally insurable. Fire losses to property of unknown value at the time of loss are not "ideal" to insure.

Loss Exposure Is One of a Large Number of Similar Exposures

Fire insurance can be written on many similar, but independent, dwellings. Although all homes are different, they can be grouped into classes facing essentially the same loss potential. Therefore, fire loss exposures are ideally suited to insurability because a large number of similar yet independent exposure units are available for pooling.

Loss Exposure Is Not Subject to a Loss That Would Simultaneously Affect Many Other Similar Loss Exposures; Loss Would Not Be Catastrophic

Unless they are close to one another, each insured dwelling presents an independent loss exposure to fire. An insurer writing fire insurance on several geographically separated buildings would generally have a good, diversified spread of risks. However, insuring a large number of properties exposed to a devastating fire would not be "ideal." To avoid exceeding their capacity, insurers must evaluate the amounts exposed to a single loss in the event of a major fire in a large multiple-occupancy building, a congested urban area, or even an uncongested rural area subject to forest and brush fires. Reinsurance can effectively mitigate such large-loss exposures.

Loss Exposure Is Economically Feasible To Insure

Dwelling fires tend to be low-frequency, high-severity (from the insured's perspective) events that insureds could not usually recover from financially without insurance. Although the frequency of fire loss to any one specific building is usually too small for insurers to project with confidence, aggregate fire losses generate credible statistical information on which fire insurance rates can be based. For these reasons, dwelling fire insurance can generally be priced at a marketable level that is very attractive to buyers wanting to protect their home investments.

Conclusions

Fire insurance on dwellings meets most of the ideal requirements of commercial insurability. Insurers still must identify buildings with higher-than-normal hazards, guard against arson-for-profit, avoid excessive concentration of loss exposure, ensure adequate diversification of exposures, and carefully establish the insurable value of property subject to loss. If insurance is not readily available through private insurers, then it might be available through a Fair Access to Insurance Requirements (FAIR) plan.

FAIR plan
An insurance pool, through which private insurers collectively address an unmet need for property insurance on urban properties, especially those susceptible to loss by riot or civil commotion.

A **FAIR** (Fair Access to Insurance Requirements) **plan** is an insurance pool, through which private insurers collectively address an unmet need for property insurance on urban properties, especially those susceptible to loss by riot or civil commotion. FAIR plans make basic property insurance available to property owners who are otherwise unable to obtain insurance because of their property's location or any other reason.

Currently, FAIR plans are available in more than half of the U.S. states. Each plan's specifics vary by state, and exploring the details is beyond the scope of this text. The goal of FAIR plans is to make at least basic property insurance available to all property owners in a way that is equitable for insurers writing that coverage in a state. The FAIR plans are not meant to replace normal channels of insurance.

CHARACTERISTICS OF WINDSTORM LOSSES AND INSURABILITY

Windstorm insurance is usually written in conjunction with fire insurance. However, the insurability characteristics of losses due to the wind peril differ from those due to fire.

Loss Exposure Involves Pure, Not Speculative, Risk

Except in unusual circumstances, windstorm damage to a building presents only the possibility of loss, but no possibility of gain. So, like fire, windstorm is almost always a pure risk and well suited for insurance.

Loss Exposure Is Subject to Accidental Loss From the Insured's Standpoint

Windstorm exposure clearly satisfies the requirement that losses be accidental from the standpoint of the insured. Insureds cannot create a windstorm. They can, however, fail to take proper preventive measures, claim that a windstorm caused a loss that it did not, or claim that damage was more extensive than it actually was.

Windstorm frequency cannot be controlled. However, loss severity from windstorm can be reduced through building design and other preventive measures.

When a hurricane or another windstorm is forecast, preventive measures such as securing storm doors and shutters, removing awnings, and securing outdoor furniture and umbrellas will mitigate loss severity.

Loss Exposure Is Subject to Losses That Are Definite in Time and That Are Measurable

When and where a windstorm loss has occurred are usually obvious. Even for unattended property, the date and time of a storm can be documented with weather reports. Sometimes, distinguishing between covered windstorm damage and not-covered flood damage is difficult because a storm may produce both perils.

Valuation of a windstorm can be complicated. When a windstorm does widespread damage in the same geographic area, the surge in demand for construction contractors, equipment, and supplies can substantially increase repair costs, presenting special challenges.

Loss Exposure Is One of a Large Number of Similar Exposures

Like fire, windstorm insurance can be written on many similar buildings. However, identical buildings at different locations can face substantially different windstorm exposures.

Generally, projecting losses is enhanced when many similar units are exposed to loss. For windstorm losses, however, forecasters have been most successful in projecting how many hurricane-force storms will strike nationally each year, not where they will strike. Projecting local tornado activity is even more problematic. Diversification requires a geographical spread of risks, as well as a large number of exposure units.

Loss Exposure Is Not Subject to a Loss That Would Simultaneously Affect Many Other Similar Loss Exposures; Loss Would Not Be Catastrophic

Different buildings in the same geographic area are not independently exposed to windstorm loss. Unlike fire, a single windstorm is likely to damage many buildings. Hurricanes generally affect a widespread geographic area. Although tornadoes are more concentrated, they can cause catastrophic damage on all property in a limited area, sometimes wiping out an entire community. As in the care of the fire peril, reinsurance can help mitigate an insurer's risk of large losses from windstorm.

Loss Exposure Is Economically Feasible To Insure

The catastrophic nature of some windstorms—notably hurricanes—makes windstorm insurance difficult to underwrite, especially for insurers with a high volume of business in a limited geographic area. Appropriate rating is complicated by the fact that premium and loss calculations are performed in one-year periods, while weather cycles are much longer.

Conclusions

Beach and windstorm plan
An insurance pool operated by property insurers in several Atlantic and Gulf Coast states to ensure that property insurance is available, in specified areas, for damage due to hurricanes and other windstorms.

Windstorm does not meet the ideal characteristics of an insurable loss exposure as effectively as does fire insurance on the same property. In coastal areas or other areas exposed to severe windstorm losses, private insurers are often unable to write windstorm insurance. Consequently, industry-sponsored FAIR plans or beach and windstorm plans operate to fill the gap. A **beach and windstorm plan** is an insurance pool operated by property insurers in several Atlantic and Gulf Coast states to ensure that property insurance is available, in specified areas, for damage due to hurricanes and other windstorms. Although these plans vary by state, in all cases property insurers are required to share in plan losses according to their share of state property insurance premiums. A disadvantage of these programs is that insurance availability tends to encourage construction in coastal areas.

CHARACTERISTICS OF FLOOD LOSSES AND INSURABILITY

Flood damage to property at fixed locations was traditionally considered uninsurable, even for property that was readily insured against fire and windstorm losses. On the other hand, flood insurance is readily available for autos and other personal property that can easily be moved out of harm's way.

Loss Exposure Involves Pure, Not Speculative, Risk

Except in unusual circumstances, flood damage presents only the possibility of loss, but no possibility of gain. Floods result from an excess of water, but an inadequate water supply can cause other problems, such as crop failure, dried-up wells, or inability to operate car washes. Although one can have too much or too little water, the flood exposure does involve pure risks of loss to flooded buildings. On this characteristic, flood is insurable.

Loss Exposure Is Subject to Accidental Loss From the Insured's Standpoint

Most floods are caused by unusually severe, random weather conditions that result in excessive rainfall. Timing might be seasonal but otherwise unpredictable.

However, some floods are caused by controllable factors. A major dam's construction usually results in intentional flooding of the area upstream. The bombing or bursting of a dam or dike, or an intentional water release, can cause downstream flooding. Sometimes, releasing water that floods one community has been necessary to prevent more serious flood damage in another area.

Although some uncertainty exists about whether a flood will occur at a particular location in a particular year, in many areas the long-term probability of flood can be forecast. Some property, located within a 10-year, 20-year, or 100-year flood plain, is almost certainly exposed to loss. Although that does not mean a flood occurs at specified intervals, on *average* a flood can be expected every so often. A 100-year flood could occur in two consecutive years.

Loss Exposure Is Subject to Losses That Are Definite in Time and That Are Measurable

Determining when and where a flood loss has occurred is usually straightforward. However, determining whether damage was caused by a windstorm, flood, or water driven by the wind may be necessary. The distinction can be very important when windstorm insurance and flood insurance are written under different policies or when, for example, windstorm damage is covered but flood damage is excluded.

Another issue arises when a given loss can be attributed to more than one occurrence of a particular peril, such as a fire in an already flooded area. How insurers address issues such as proximate cause, contributory causation, and ensuing loss issues is addressed in other chapters.

Loss Exposure Is One of a Large Number of Similar Exposures

Flood insurance can be written on many similar buildings. Buildings of similar construction at different locations can face substantially different exposures depending on their altitude and proximity to water.

Loss Exposure Is Not Subject to a Loss That Would Simultaneously Affect Many Other Similar Loss Exposures; Loss Would Not Be Catastrophic

Flood risks are not well diversified, and serious floods tend to affect all properties within a widespread area. Flood losses are often catastrophic, making the loss exposure less than ideal for insurance.

Loss Exposure Is Economically Feasible To Insure

The catastrophic nature of some floods, combined with the fact that an eventual flood is virtually certain at many locations, generally makes offering flood insurance difficult for private insurers. Adverse selection (when high-risk individuals or organizations are more likely to demand insurance than low-risk individuals or organizations) is present because property owners in flood zones are more likely to want flood insurance. Private insurers would need to conduct costly risk assessment programs or engineering studies to evaluate the probability of flooding for each applicant. Consequently, the insurer would need to charge a premium that most people would be unwilling to pay.

Conclusions

Buildings and most personal property in flood zones are difficult to insure privately because the exposures are not independent, which poses the risk of catastrophic loss. Premiums in flood zones would be too high for most insureds to pay without government assistance. Flood insurance is now readily available under a government insurance program, one of several government programs discussed in this chapter. The federal government has also devoted engineering resources to evaluating flood zones, and these evaluations have facilitated underwriting flood insurance by private insurers.

GOVERNMENT INSURANCE

Many loss exposures that are not commercially insurable, such as real property in high-crime areas, can be insured by the government. Some government insurance programs are available only from a government agency, but some government insurance competes with, reinsures, or complements private insurance plans. Government insurance programs include social programs, financial security programs, and certain types of otherwise unavailable property-liability insurance.

Reasons for Government Insurance Programs

The following reasons justify government participation in insurance:

- To fill insurance needs unmet by private insurers
- To compel people to buy a particular type of insurance
- To provide convenience to insurance buyers
- To obtain greater efficiency
- To achieve collateral social purposes[1]

Fill Unmet Needs

When private insurers are unable or unwilling to satisfy certain insurance needs, public insurers often step in to provide insurance to meet legitimate public demands. By doing this, the government provides protection against loss that would otherwise not be provided.

Compel Insurance Purchase

Most government programs are compulsory to best serve the public need. For example, some employers would not purchase workers compensation insurance if they were not required to. Similarly, without Social Security, many people might not save enough money for their retirement and medical needs. The government handles much of the compulsory insurance because government has the resources to handle the size, complexity, and adjustments necessary in these programs.

However, the government does not provide all compulsory insurance. Most workers compensation and auto insurance is written by private insurers, even when coverage is required by law.

Provide Convenience

Legislators often find it easier and faster to establish government insurance plans for particular purposes than to invite and analyze bids from private insurers, and then supervise and regulate the resulting plans.

When the National Flood Insurance Program (NFIP) was founded, the federal government was able to coordinate insurance, flood plain surveys, and land-use controls, and to integrate flood insurance benefits with disaster relief administered by the Federal Emergency Management Agency (FEMA).

Obtain Efficiency

Efficiency—saving taxpayers' money—appears to be a major, but often an unspoken, rationale for government participation in insurance. When insurance provided by the government is compulsory, spending money on marketing or paying sales commissions is unnecessary. Governments sometimes try to avoid sales costs by setting up their own distribution channels; at other times, they market through established insurance producers who also market other insurance.

Achieve Collateral Social Purpose

The government often participates in insurance to accomplish social goals. For example, Social Security provides a base layer of economic security, and workers compensation laws encourage injury prevention and injured workers' rehabilitation. Similarly, the National Flood Insurance Program provides strong incentives to amend and enforce building codes and otherwise reduce the loss exposure of new construction to floods.

The Roles of Government Insurers

The government can act as an exclusive insurer, a partner with private insurers, or a competitor of private insurers.

Exclusive Insurer

The government can be an exclusive insurer either because of law or because no private insurer offers a competing plan. Governmental insurers can function either as primary insurers or as reinsurers.

- *Primary insurer.* A federal or state government can function as a primary insurer by providing coverage and paying all claims and expenses with government funds.
- *Reinsurer.* The government can function as a reinsurer either by providing 100 percent reinsurance to private insurers writing a particular coverage, or by reinsuring part of the risk in excess of the private insurer's retention.

Partnership With Private Insurers

A government agency can offer an insurance plan as a partner with private insurers. The nature of the partnerships can vary considerably. One type of partnership exists when the government operates a reinsurance plan, providing reinsurance on specific loss exposures for which private insurers retain only part of the loss. In other cases, such as the National Flood Insurance Program, the federal government bears the risk of loss, but private insurers and insurance producers deliver the policies.

Competition With Private Insurers

Governments can operate an insurance plan in direct competition with private insurers. This happens when the government performs essentially the same marketing, underwriting, actuarial, and claim functions as a private insurer. Examples include the competitive workers compensation funds offered in some states.

Types of Government Insurance

Government insurance programs tend to fall into three broad categories:

1. Property-liability insurance plans
2. Social insurance plans
3. Financial security plans

This section provides only a few examples in each category to illustrate the nature of government insurance in the United States.

Property-Liability Insurance Plans

The government provides a number of property-liability insurance plans, including the National Flood Insurance Program, state workers compensation programs, and other types of insurance. See the following box for an outline of government property-liability insurance plans and social insurance plans.

Social Insurance Plans

Some government insurance plans are designed to solve social problems. In social insurance, the loss need not be accidental, and the plan must be established by law. Most social insurance plans have the following characteristics:

1. They provide benefits received as a matter of right, not charity.

Examples of Property-Liability Insurance Offered by the Government

Plan	Characteristics of Government Plan	Relationship to Private Insurance
National Flood Insurance Program	• Meets previously unmet needs for flood insurance • Serves the social purposes of amending and enforcing building codes; reducing new construction in flood zones	• Federal government can act as primary insurer. • Federal government can partner with private insurers; private insurers sell the insurance and pay claims; government reimburses insurers for losses not covered by premiums and investment income.
Workers Compensation Insurance	• Helps employers meet their obligations under state statutes to injured workers	• Private insurers provide most workers compensation insurance. • State government can operate as an exclusive monopoly, as a competitor to private insurers, or as a residual market.
Federal Crop Insurance	• Provides crop insurance at affordable rates to reduce losses that result from unavoidable crop failures • Cover most crops for perils such as drought, disease, insects, excess rain, and hail	• Federal government subsidizes and reinsures private insurers; private insurers sell and service the federal crop insurance. • Private insurers also independently offer crop insurance for certain perils.
Parcel Post and Registered Mail Insurance	• Provides coverage for property lost in transit by parcel post and registered mail	• Parcel post service offers this insurance. • Private insurers also offer this insurance.

Examples of Social Insurance Plans Offered by the Government

Plan	Characteristics of Government Plan	Relationship to Private Insurance
Social Security	• Provides coverage for the financial consequences of wage earners' premature death or disability, insufficient income during retirement, and sizeable medical expenses incurred by the aged and certain groups under age 65.	• Federal government is the primary insurer. • Private insurers play no role.
Unemployment Compensation Insurance	• Provides weekly cash benefits for a short period to covered workers who are involuntarily or temporarily unemployed • Helps unemployed workers find jobs • Helps stabilize the economy during a period of business recession	• State governments all act as primary insurers. • Private insurers play no role.

Federal Deposit Insurance Corporation (FDIC)
An independent federal agency that insures depositors against loss resulting from financial institutions' failure or insolvency.

Pension Benefit Guaranty Corporation (PBGC)
A federal corporation that provides plan termination insurance to qualified defined-benefit pension plans to protect plan participants against the loss of pension benefits if a plan terminates or if the employer goes bankrupt.

2. They provide benefits unrelated, or only loosely related, to premiums paid so that low-income recipients receive a larger benefit relative to premiums paid than do high-income recipients.

3. They provide an element of compulsion, including compulsory contributions by those who are not personally insured (for example, employers or the government).

One of the major differences between private and public insurance is the matter of equity versus adequacy. A major premise of private insurance is actuarial equity (that is, treating policyholders fairly by charging them premiums directly proportional to the loss exposure borne or the benefits paid). By contrast, a major goal of social insurance is social equity, providing benefits to the public in response to a far-reaching hazard.

Financial Security Plans

Another group of government insurance programs provides guarantees to lenders that their loans, investments, or deposits will be repaid. See the following box.

Examples of Financial Security Plans Offered by the Government		
Plan	**Characteristics of Government Plan**	**Relationship to Private Insurance**
Federal Deposit Insurance Corporation (FDIC)	• Provides coverage for depositors against loss due to a financial institution's failure or insolvency • Reduces potential economic insecurity that could result from widespread failure of economic institutions	• Federal government is the primary insurer. • Private insurers play no role.
Pension Benefit Guaranty Corporation (PBGC)	• Provides pension plan termination coverage to qualified defined-benefit plans • Protects plan participants against loss of pension benefits due to employer bankruptcy	• Federal government is the primary insurer. • Private insurers play no role.

SUMMARY

Private insurance works only for risks that come close to possessing the ideal characteristics of an insurable loss exposure. Government insurance sometimes insures exposures that are not privately insurable.

The ideal characteristics of a privately insurable loss exposure are as follows:

• Loss exposure is subject to pure, not speculative, risk.

- Loss exposure is subject to accidental losses from the insured's standpoint.
- Loss exposure is subject to losses that are definite in time and measurable in amount.
- Loss exposure is one of a large number of similar, but independent, exposures.
- Loss exposure is not subject to a loss that would simultaneously affect many other similar loss exposures; loss would not be catastrophic.
- Loss exposure is economically feasible to insure.

Few, if any, risks have all of these characteristics. Even those that do cannot necessarily be covered by private insurance because of regulatory constraints, capacity constraints, and other matters.

This chapter further examined the ideal characteristics of a commercially insurable loss exposure by applying them to examples involving fire, windstorm, and flood insurance for a dwelling. A fire loss exposure meets most of the characteristics, windstorm loss exposure meets many characteristics, and a flood loss exposure is difficult for private insurers to handle.

Reasons for government insurance include unmet needs, compulsion, convenience, efficiency, and collateral social purpose. Government can function as an exclusive insurer, in partnership with private insurers, or in competition with private insurers.

CHAPTER NOTE

1. Adapted from Mark R. Greene, "Government Insurers," *Issues in Insurance,* 4th ed., vol. 1 (Malvern, Pa.: American Institute for Property and Liability Underwriters, 1987), pp. 195–199.

Direct Your Learning

Risk Financing Alternatives

After learning the subject matter of this chapter, you should be able to:

- Compare the advantages and disadvantages of (a) self-insurance and (b) traditional insurance.
- Describe the ten alternative risk financing techniques.

Develop Your Perspective

What are the main topics covered in the chapter?

This chapter covers key objectives of risk financing, advantages and disadvantages of self-insurance (retention) and traditional insurance, alternative risk financing techniques, and ways to optimize retained risks.

Consider the risk financing alternatives other than retention and insurance.

- Under what conditions might an insurer choose a partial retention risk financing arrangement?

Why is it important to know these topics?

Knowing these topics will enable you to compare retention and insurance in specific situations.

Investigate your organization's portfolio of retained risks.

- Does your organization use alternative risk financing techniques?

- Why were those alternatives chosen?

How can you use this information?

Evaluate your organization's overall mix of retained risks.

- Using a risk and return analysis, how could your organization optimize its portfolio?

Chapter 7

Risk Financing Alternatives[1]

The preceding chapters introduced two fundamental forms of risk financing: retention and transfer. This chapter explores the objectives of risk financing, the advantages and disadvantages of self-insurance (a retention technique) and traditional insurance (a transfer technique), as well as some risk financing alternatives that are not, strictly speaking, either retention or traditional insurance.

OBJECTIVES OF RISK FINANCING

Risk management attempts to manage the cost of risk. *Risk financing* objectives are more narrowly focused on generating funds to pay for potential losses. An organization's specific risk financing objectives are likely to include the following:

- *Paying for losses*—having funds available when needed to respond to losses.

- *Maintaining an appropriate level of liquidity*—paying for retained losses with assets that can readily be converted to cash. The higher the level of an organization's risk retention, the greater the need for liquidity.

- *Managing uncertainty*—maintaining a tolerable level of uncertainty. The amount of uncertainty an organization can tolerate depends on factors such as the organization's size, its financial strength, and its risk tolerance and risk aversion. Most risks are not correlated, and an organization should assess the combined uncertainty arising from all sources of risk. For example, a newspaper must consider risks arising from fluctuations in the price of newsprint and the possibility of a libel suit, among others.

- *Managing the cost of risk*—minimizing the cost of pure risks and optimizing the risk/return balance of speculative risks.

- *Complying with legal and contractual requirements*—including mandatory insurance and other externally imposed requirements.

ADVANTAGES AND DISADVANTAGES OF SELF-INSURANCE

Compared with insurance and other risk transfer measures, retention or self-insurance programs have both advantages and disadvantages in achieving risk financing objectives. See the following box.

Advantages and Disadvantages of Self-Insurance

Advantages

- Control of claim handling
- Incentives for risk control
- Long-term cost savings
- Increased cash flow

Disadvantages

- Uncertainty about retained loss outcome
- Administrative functions
- Delayed tax benefits
- Difficult contractual compliance

Advantages of Self-Insurance

Self-insurance enhances control over claims, provides incentives for risk control, produces long-term cost savings, and presents cash flow advantages.

Control Over Claims

A self-insured organization can exercise direct control over how its claims are handled. The self-insured organization can select its own defense attorneys and set guidelines for handling its claims. One advantage of this control is that it allows the organization to determine the amount of effort put into defending rather than settling a given claim. For example, an organization faced with claims that could affect its reputation, such as claims alleging that the organization negligently manufactured a product, might want to strenuously defend against such claims to preserve its reputation. An insurer, however, might find reaching a settlement to be more cost-effective than incurring substantial defense costs. Compared with self-insureds, an insured party generally has less control over claim handling by an insurer that is also protecting its own interests.

Risk Control

Self-insurance encourages risk control. When an organization directly pays for its own losses, it has an incentive to prevent and reduce them. By preventing losses, an organization does not waste valuable resources on losses and eliminates the sometimes unexpected costs that accompany losses.

Long-Term Cost Savings

Another advantage is that self-insurance's long-term cost tends to be lower than traditional insurance's cost. A self-insured organization does not have to contribute to an insurer's marketing and underwriting costs, overhead costs, or profits, nor does it have to pay an insurance company's "risk charge." (*Risk charge* is a contingency fee that insurer rating plans charge in addition to a charge based on expected losses. This practice recognizes loss projection limitations and the possibility that actual losses might be higher than what was projected.) A self-insurance plan also avoids premium taxes and residual market loadings that insurers must pay. (*Residual market loadings* are mandatory fees that insurance companies pay to support auto assigned risk programs and other subsidized insurance programs.) However, a self-insurance program has its own overhead costs, and it can be subject to various other taxes, assessments, and fees, as mentioned later.

Cash Flow

Contrasted to an organization that pays insurance premiums, a self-insured organization is able to benefit from cash flow generated by retaining losses that are paid over a time period or are not paid until long after they are incurred rather than paying immediate insurance premiums. Money can be invested or used in operations until the loss payment is actually made.

Disadvantages of Self-Insurance

The obvious disadvantage of self-insurance is that all uncertainty—including the possible cost of serious losses—rests with the organization. Other disadvantages involve the service that is required to administer a self-insurance plan, tax-deductibility issues, and the difficulty of using self-insurance to meet contractual requirements.

Uncertainty of Retained Loss Outcomes

The uncertainty associated with retained losses can negatively affect an organization's earnings, net worth, and cash flow. The possibility always exists that uninsured losses might be more frequent or severe than what was considered likely. To mitigate this risk, organizations often supplement self-insurance programs with excess insurance.

Services Required

A self-insured organization must handle for itself many administrative matters that are normally provided by an insurance company. Claims must be recorded, adjusted, and reserved; litigation must be managed; regulatory filings must be made with the states (depending on the type of loss exposure); and taxes and fees must be paid (depending, again, on the type of exposure). The self-insured organization's own staff can provide these services, or they can be outsourced for a fee to insurance companies, third-party administrators, independent adjusters, or other service organizations.

Loss control services and other risk management services can be separately purchased from brokers, risk management consultants, or other service organizations.

Tax-Deductibility

The timing of tax deductions is an important risk financing issue. An organization enjoys a cash-flow benefit when it can take a tax deduction immediately rather than at some future time.

Insurance premiums are tax-deductible for the year in which they are paid, regardless of when losses are paid. In contrast, a self-insured organization may take a tax deduction for losses only in the year when losses are paid—not in the year when they are incurred. This means that the tax deduction is often delayed because some losses—especially large liability losses—are not paid until several years after the loss is incurred.

Contractual Requirements

Contracts often require one party to purchase insurance for another party's benefit, and using a self-insurance plan to satisfy "insurance" requirements is often difficult. For example, if an organization leases a building, it might be required to name the landlord as an additional insured under a general liability insurance policy covering liability arising from the building's occupancy. The landlord might not accept the tenant's self-insurance plan— even if the tenant is part of a major corporation— and might insist that the tenant purchase a general liability policy for this purpose.

ADVANTAGES AND DISADVANTAGES OF TRADITIONAL INSURANCE

Although insurance clearly presents some advantages over self-insurance, it is not without its disadvantages. See the following box.

Advantages and Disadvantages of Traditional Insurance

Advantages

- Reduction of uncertainty/risk
- Claim and risk management services provided by insurer
- Tax-deductibility of premiums
- Legal and contractual requirements

Disadvantages

- Reduced cash flow
- Higher long-term administrative costs
- Increased premium due to adverse selection
- Increased premium due to moral and attitudinal hazards

Advantages of Traditional Insurance

For an organization, the most obvious advantage of purchasing insurance is that the uncertainty and risk associated with losses are transferred to the insurer. Other advantages of purchasing insurance include the following: various services such as claim processing and risk management expertise that are provided by the insurer, tax-deductibility of premiums, and ease in meeting legal and contractual requirements.

Reduction of Uncertainty/Risk

Insurance is a formal device to transfer risk from the insured to the insurer, reducing uncertainty about the financial consequences of future losses. In exchange for the insured's payment of a specified premium, the insurer agrees to protect the insured against specified types of potential losses, subject to applicable limits. This agreement is stated in a legally enforceable contract, the insurance policy, in which the insurer agrees to make payments to or on behalf of the insured in the event of a covered loss. With liability insurance, the insurer also agrees to pay defense costs.

Services Provided

In addition to paying claims, insurers provide a number of related services. Sometimes these services are even more important than the actual payment of claims. Some of the more significant insurer-provided services include claim and risk management services.

Claim Services

Because they continuously handle many different policyholders' insured losses, insurers are skilled in handling claims. The insurer has an incentive to control claim costs because of its direct accountability for making loss payments.

Many claims, especially liability claims, require the attention of attorneys having special expertise. Insurers develop a network of legal resources, over a large geographic area, for the benefit of policyholders with widespread operations.

With liability insurance, an insurer's claim services interject an outside party between the claimant and the insured. As compared with self-insurance, this arm's-length relationship reduces stress on other relationships between parties that might need to continue to cooperate in other matters. A clear example involves workers compensation claims and the potential for conflict between worker and employer. The conflict may be buffered when the insurer, rather than the employer, negotiates some claim issues.

Risk Management Services

Insurers' broad experience in handling diverse losses also contributes to their expertise in recognizing and controlling loss exposures. This expertise is especially important for exposures to high-severity, low-frequency losses, which are the greatest concern of insurance buyers and also the most difficult to evaluate. Insurers help both in identifying loss exposures and in recommending ways by which these exposures might be financed or controlled.

For example, because insurers bear the immediate effect of loss, they have strong financial incentives to identify and implement loss control measures. Insurers' loss control services are often provided to businesses when insurance coverage is written. Insurers' loss control representatives sometimes work directly with policyholders in the mutual goal of controlling losses. An insurer provides these services not only to serve its insureds but also to benefit itself.

Tax-Deductibility of Premiums

Insurance premiums normally are tax-deductible business expenses when the premium is paid, whereas retained losses are tax-deductible only when the loss is paid. Although losses must eventually be paid and, therefore, are eventually deductible, losses can be uneven and unpredictable from year to year, while premium payments are usually more predictable and consistent. Consequently, long-term tax liabilities are expected to be lower and more predictable with insurance than with retention. This financial advantage can partially offset insurance costs.

Legal and Contractual Requirements

Sometimes insurance is the only way to provide protection against loss because it is legally mandated or required by contract.

Disadvantages of Traditional Insurance

Although insurance presents several advantages over retention or other loss financing methods, it is not without its problems or difficulties. Cash-flow issues, additional administrative costs, adverse selection, and moral and attitudinal hazards are disadvantages to traditional insurance.

Cash-Flow Issues

Insurance premiums must be paid in advance to cover losses that are incurred while the insurance is in force. A disadvantage of paying insurance premiums is that money that has been paid in premiums is no longer available to the insured for investment and cannot earn further income for the organization.

Higher Long-Term Administrative Costs

Another disadvantage of traditional insurance is higher administrative costs compared to retention. In addition to covering the costs of expected losses, an insurer charges an additional amount to cover its expenses of doing business. That additional charge reflects costs the insurer expects to incur in marketing insurance, administering claims, covering other expenses, and developing a fair return on equity (profit). A risk charge is also included. As these costs increase, buyers become increasingly reluctant to purchase insurance, and self-insurance or other risk financing alternatives might be used instead.

Adverse Selection

The phenomenon of adverse selection tends to increase the cost of insurance as a whole. Adverse selection results from each insurer's inability to measure with complete accuracy the loss exposures associated with each individual exposure. If an insurer charges a premium reflecting the average expected losses of the members of a group, those with higher-than-average risks of loss will have a greater tendency to purchase insurance than those with lower-than-average risks. Insurance that is priced according to the average risk seems like a bargain to those with high exposures, and it seems unduly expensive to those with low exposures.

Simply increasing premium levels to compensate for adverse selection does not always solve the problem. In fact, high premium levels can lead to even greater adverse selection: Those with lower-than-average risks might find other insurers who are willing to provide their insurance at a favorable cost, leaving only the higher-risk insurance buyers to purchase the high-priced insurance. Many of the problems associated with rate regulation arise because measuring the risks associated with each individual applicant is difficult.

Moral and Attitudinal Hazards

Another disadvantage of insurance is that uncontrolled moral and attitudinal (morale) hazards increase insurance premium levels. The existence of insurance can have a subtle effect on behavior. An insured might devote fewer resources to loss control because he or she does not directly bear the full financial effect of insured losses. Inattention to loss control tends to increase loss frequency and/or severity. Insurers monitor their policyholders' activities to ensure that exposures do not change once the premium has been paid, and they attempt to structure insurance contracts and prices to provide incentives for loss control.

ALTERNATIVE RISK FINANCING TECHNIQUES

Self-insurance and traditional insurance are not the only available risk financing alternatives. Alternatives range from simple deductible schemes to capital market products that have limited resemblance to either insurance or self-insurance. This section discusses ten alternative risk financing techniques: partial retention, experience-rated insurance plans, retrospectively rated insurance plans, layering, self-insurance pools, purchasing groups, captive insurers, risk retention groups, finite risk insurance plans, and capital market products for risk financing.

Ten Alternative Risk Financing Techniques

1. Partial retention

2. Experience-rated insurance plans

3. Retrospectively rated insurance plans

4. Layering

5. Self-insurance pools

6. Purchasing groups

7. Captive insurers

8. Risk retention groups

9. Finite risk insurance plans

10. Capital market products

Partial Retention

Partial retention is a hybrid risk financing technique that involves retaining part of a loss exposure and transferring the rest. This section briefly examines three forms of partial retention: small deductibles, large deductibles, and self-insured retentions (SIRs).

Small Deductibles

Deductible
A portion of a covered loss that is not paid by the insurer.

A **deductible** in an insurance policy is a specified portion of an insured loss that will be subtracted (deducted) from the amount the insurer would otherwise pay. Claims falling within the deductible—for example, a $300 claim under a policy with a $1,000 deductible—do not involve any payment by the insurer and often are not even reported to the insurer. Deductible provisions appear in relatively few liability insurance policies; property insurance policies usually contain a deductible provision.

Deductibles reduce attitudinal hazards and encourage loss control because the insured bears a part of any loss. By eliminating coverage for small losses, insurers reduce the number of covered losses, thereby reducing their loss costs and loss adjustment expenses. With small claims, an insurer's administrative expenses often exceed the cost of the claim itself. Small deductibles therefore help keep premiums down.

Large Deductibles

In the United States, the term **large deductible plan** is usually applied to an insurance plan for workers compensation, commercial auto liability, or general liability, in which the deductible is $100,000 or higher.

In a large deductible plan, the insurance company adjusts and pays all claims for loss, even those below the deductible level, and seeks reimbursement from the insured. The insured agrees to reimburse the insurer for all losses up to the deductible level, in exchange for a premium reduction. The insured retains losses under the deductible level, and transfers the portion of losses that exceed the deductible level, up to the policy limit.

A large deductible plan gives the insurer direct control over individual claims that start small but have the potential to exceed the deductible level. Because the insurer adjusts claims, the insurer guarantees the payment of all claims. The insured usually must provide the insurer with some form of financial security, such as a letter of credit, to guarantee reimbursement for losses falling within the deductible level.

Usually, an organization chooses a large deductible plan to reduce costs, as compared with a traditional insured plan with no deductible. The insurance premium for a large deductible plan can be much lower because the insurer pays only for losses that exceed the deductible. Even though the organization must pay for losses below the deductible, costs are still reduced because the insurer's premium taxes, residual market loadings, and overhead costs—usually a percentage of premiums—are reduced. A large deductible plan also allows the insured to benefit from the cash flow available on the reserves for retained losses, especially for losses paid over several years after they are incurred.

A large deductible plan does increase risks for the insured organization. Retained losses under the deductible might be higher than expected, lowering the organization's net income and cash flow. By keeping its deductibles at a prudent level, an organization can manage its uncertainty about the cost of its retained losses. The uncertainty level must be balanced against the total cost (retained losses plus premiums) of a large deductible plan, and alternative deductible levels often must be considered.

Self-Insured Retentions (SIRs)

A **self-insured retention (SIR)** is a risk financing technique in which the insured organization is responsible for adjusting and paying its own losses up to the self-insured retention level. An SIR is similar to a deductible. Because the insurer lacks control over individual self-insured claims, a policy with a self-insured retention usually requires strict reporting to the insurer of any claims that have the potential to exceed the self-insured retention level.

Large deductible plan
An insurance plan for workers compensation, commercial auto liability, or general liability, having a deductible of $100,000 or higher.

Self-insured retention (SIR)
A risk financing technique in which the insured organization adjusts and pays its own losses up to the self-insured retention level.

Partial retention can also be implemented in many ways not discussed here, including intentional underinsurance—buying limits of insurance insufficient to pay for a total loss—or insuring against only some causes of loss while retaining loss by other perils.

Experience-Rated Insurance Plans

Experience rating
A ratemaking technique that adjusts the insured's premium for the upcoming policy period based on the insured's experience for the current period.

Although **experience rating** is largely an insurance pricing technique rather than a risk financing technique, it is mentioned here because experience rating has the *effect* of limiting the amount of risk transferred. In experience rating plans, the insured's own *past* loss experience directly affects the premium charged for a *future* policy period. The insured retains some control over the cost of insurance because reducing losses, through loss control activities, will reduce future premiums. Experience rating is commonly available to medium- and large-sized organizations on coverages involving a large number of exposure units.

Retrospectively Rated Insurance Plans

Another alternative risk financing technique, retrospectively rated insurance plans ("retro plans"), are sometimes used for workers compensation, commercial auto liability, and general liability (including products liability) insurance, lines in which some loss frequency is expected for a larger organization. The insured pays a premium to the insurance company, which reimburses claimants for losses and pays other expenses such as loss adjustment costs and legal defense fees. The premium also covers the insurer's overhead and profit. On the surface, a retrospective rating plan appears the same as a guaranteed cost insurance plan. The difference is not in the coverage but in the premium calculation. A retro plan has an element of loss retention because the premium ultimately depends on a portion of the insured's actual losses *during the policy period*. The rating scheme itself is called **retrospective rating**.

Retrospective rating
A ratemaking technique that adjusts the insured's premium for the current policy period based on the insured's loss experience during the current period; paid losses or incurred losses may be used to determine loss experience.

Under a retro plan, the deposit premium is just that: a deposit. The final premium—determined after the policy period is completed—is based on a portion of the insured's actual losses during the policy period. The higher the insured's losses, the higher the retro plan premium, and vice versa—subject to a minimum premium and a maximum premium. See Exhibit 7-1.

The premium for a retrospective rating plan is not calculated solely on an insured's losses. A minimum premium is payable regardless of losses. The retrospective rating premium formula includes amounts for costs such as insurance company overhead and profits, residual market loadings, service bureau charges, premium taxes, and loss adjustment expenses. Another portion of the premium compensates the insurer for accepting the risk that losses exceed a specific limit. Up to the loss limit, an insured retains individual losses because they are used to raise or lower its retrospectively rated premium, subject to a maximum premium amount.

When total losses reach a specified level, the maximum premium level is reached, and the insured pays no additional premium regardless of how much higher losses become for that policy period. Losses above that level are transferred to the insurer, subject to any applicable policy limits.

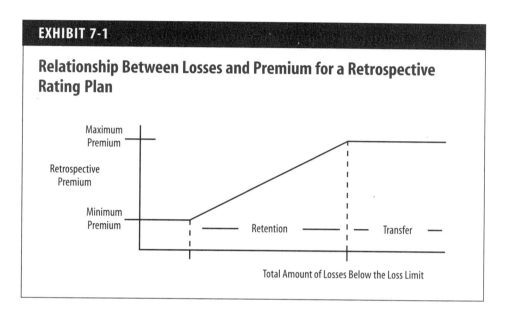

EXHIBIT 7-1

Relationship Between Losses and Premium for a Retrospective Rating Plan

A retro plan enables an insured to retain a substantial portion of its losses and can be suitable for retaining low-to-medium-severity losses. An insured that successfully controls its losses under a retro plan is able to lower its premium.

Retro plans might or might not provide cash-flow benefits on the reserved portion of retained losses.

- With a *paid-loss retrospective rating plan*, the insured pays a small deposit premium at the beginning of the policy period and reimburses the insurer for a portion of its losses as the insurer pays for them. Therefore, the insured benefits from the cash flow available on the loss reserves for the retained portion of its losses.

- With an *incurred-loss retrospective rating plan*, the insured pays a deposit premium based on its projected incurred losses for the policy period. Shortly after the end of the policy period, the insurer adjusts the premium, based on the insured's actual incurred losses, and pays a return premium or charges an additional premium. Because losses are recognized earlier, an incurred loss retro plan offers fewer cash-flow advantages than does a paid-loss retro plan.

Layering

Another alternative risk financing technique involves layering insurance policies. Liability insurance programs with high limits are usually arranged in layers. The primary (first) layer of a layered liability insurance program consists of one or more primary (underlying) policies, such as general liability, commercial auto liability, and employers liability, with per accident/occurrence limits typically ranging between $500,000 and $2 million. Large organizations might retain all or part of the primary layer. The primary layer is sometimes referred to as a **working layer** because it is the layer most often used to pay losses.

Working layer
The primary layer of insurance that is most often used to pay losses.

Most individuals, families, and small businesses have only one layer of liability insurance: the working, or primary, layer. Many organizations have only one layer in excess of the primary layer, typically, an umbrella policy. An organization might also have one or more separate excess liability policies providing a layer of coverage above other primary policies for exposures that the umbrella policy does not cover.

Buffer layer
A layer of excess insurance between a primary layer and an umbrella policy.

In some cases, an insured must purchase a **buffer layer** of excess insurance between the primary layer and the umbrella policy. This approach is used when the umbrella insurer will only provide coverage with underlying coverage limits that are higher than those that the primary insurer is willing to provide.

Insureds who want limits of liability higher than those offered by a primary policy and an umbrella policy usually purchase one or more additional layers of excess coverage. The number of layers depends on the limits desired by the insured and available from insurers. The premium per $1 million of coverage usually falls for each successively higher layer because there is a lower probability that losses will fall into each successively higher layer. Exhibit 7-2 shows an example of a multilayered liability insurance program.

EXHIBIT 7-2

Multilayered Liability Insurance Program That Includes a Buffer Layer

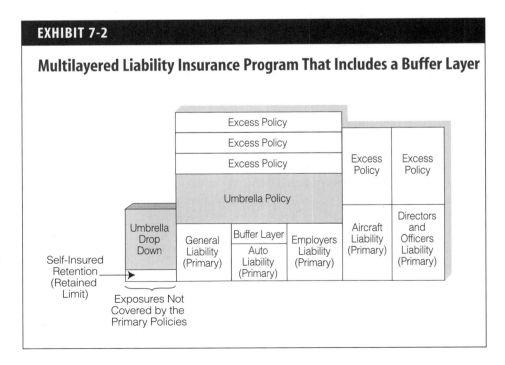

When an excess liability program is layered, each excess policy should follow as closely as possible the coverage provisions of the policy beneath it. Careful analysis and expertise are necessary to avoid significant coverage gaps that could result in unintentional retention of a major loss. Policy limits and "other insurance" provisions are discussed in later chapters.

Layering is not as common in property insurance, but it can sometimes be valuable as an alternative risk financing technique. In property insurance, two or more policies are arranged in levels of coverage, and the policies in the second or higher levels provide coverage only when a loss exceeds the coverage provided by the lower-level policy or policies. The level at which a given insurer's policy participates in the loss is called the **attachment point**. Generally, the first layer of property coverage covers high-frequency losses, and the upper layers cover catastrophe losses.

Attachment point
The level at which a given insurer's policy participates in the loss involving two or more layered policies.

Self-Insurance Pools

A **self-insurance pool** is an arrangement in which participating organizations agree to jointly finance their risks. Several hundred pools currently exist in the United States, and they have various forms. For example, twenty city governments might agree to pool member contributions to pay workers compensation or general liability claims from any member of the group, as well as administrative expenses.

Self-insurance pool
An arrangement in which participating organizations agree to jointly finance their risks.

Purchasing Groups

Purchasing groups include several—or many—insurance buyers who have banded together to purchase insurance as a group.[2] Presumably, working on a group basis results in better terms and lower rates because of economies of scale. Some purchasing groups include trade associations or other organizations for which the group purchase of insurance is not a primary activity. Purchasing groups and risk retention groups, discussed later, were enabled by the Liability Risk Retention Act, partly to overcome state laws that would otherwise prohibit an insurer from discrimination in favor of a group. A purchasing group must be registered with state regulators.

Purchasing group
Insurance buyers who obtain coverage as a group, presumably on favorable terms.

Captive Insurers

A captive insurance company is a subsidiary of its parent corporation, formed to insure the risks of its parent and affiliates. A captive is sometimes owned by and insures more than one parent. Because it is an insurance company, a captive performs many of the same functions of a typical insurance company.

Since the 1960s, thousands of captive insurance companies have been formed worldwide. The vast majority of large multinational organizations use one or more captive insurers to finance their loss exposures.

Like any other insurer, a captive collects premiums, issues policies, and pays covered losses. Most captive insurers purchase reinsurance, usually on an excess of loss basis, to transfer some of their risk of loss to another insurance company. Reinsurance provides a captive insurer with many benefits, including large-risk capacity and stability of underwriting results.

Because a captive is an insurance company, it requires an initial capital investment by its parent(s), as well as expenditures to manage the company, including accounting, auditing, legal, and underwriting expenses. For a captive to be economically feasible, its parent organization(s) should have loss exposures that generate a substantial premium revenue for the captive. One source places the minimum annual premium at $2.5 million for a viable single-parent captive.[3]

A single-parent captive is an alternative risk financing technique because, from its parent's point of view, a single-parent captive usually combines elements of retention and transfer. Because a single-parent captive covers its parent's losses and is part of the same economic family as its parent, losses retained by the captive are, in effect, retained by its parent. For the same reasons, losses transferred by the captive (for example, through reinsurance) are, in effect, transferred by its parent. Single-parent captive insurers that do not purchase reinsurance are categorized as retention plans.

In some group captives (or association captives), each insured member retains a portion of its own losses within the captive and pools the balance of its losses with other members. In others, each member pools all of its losses with other members, essentially a transfer plan only.

The advantages and disadvantages of a captive insurance plan depend on the plan's design—in particular, the amount of retention versus transfer built into the plan. Using a captive may include the usual advantages associated with retention, as well as the ability to obtain insurance when it is not otherwise available, direct access to reinsurers, centralized loss retention, and potential tax savings. Disadvantages can include capital and startup costs, the possible unavailability of reinsurance, and payment of premium taxes or residual market loadings levied on premiums paid to the captive.

Risk Retention Groups

A risk retention group is a group captive formed under the Liability Risk Retention Act of 1986. This is a United States federal law that allows the formation of risk retention groups (group captives) to insure any type of liability coverage except personal lines, employers liability, and workers compensation. To form a risk retention group, all owners must be from the same industry and must be insured by the risk retention group. Conversely, all owners must be insureds. A major advantage is that a risk retention group needs to be licensed in only one state to write liability coverage in all fifty states. This benefit saves the risk retention group the expense of complying with regulations in each of the fifty states.

Finite Risk Insurance Plans

As an alternative risk financing technique, the primary purpose of a **finite risk insurance plan** is to stabilize risk costs over time by distributing large losses over several accounting periods. Fluctuations in loss experience over accounting periods are smoothed by contractual transfers between the insurer and the insured, but over time, the insured pays its own losses.

A finite risk plan usually has the following characteristics:

Finite risk insurance plan
A risk financing plan in which a limited amount of risk is transferred to an insurer; usually includes a profit-sharing arrangement.

- It is used to provide coverage for high-severity and low-frequency exposures, such as coverage for environmental and earthquake loss exposures. It can be used to insure risks traditionally not covered by an insurance company.

- It usually requires the insurer to share a large percentage of its profit with the insured.

- It can be used to cover known losses as well as future losses that arise from loss exposures.

- It has a premium that is a very high percentage of the policy limits, which usually apply on an aggregate basis. For example, an insurer might provide an aggregate limit of $10 million for a $7 million premium. The insurer's risk is limited because the most the insurer would ever have to pay is $10 million, and it has the opportunity to earn investment income on the $7 million premium until losses are paid.

- It is sometimes written on an integrated-risk basis, meaning that it applies to more than one line of coverage, usually for more than one year.

Both the insured and insurer can benefit from finite risk insurance plans. For the insured organization, a finite risk plan has the effect of smoothing results across several years. For the insurer, coverage on more than one line for more than one year provides some diversification that substantially reduces its risks.

The value of a finite risk plan to an insured depends largely on favorable financial accounting and income tax treatments. At this time, much uncertainty exists regarding these matters.[4]

Capital Market Products for Risk Financing

A capital market is a financial market in which bonds and other financial assets having a maturity of more than one year are bought and sold. Recent innovative approaches to risk financing have used the capital market products described here—insurance-linked securities, insurance derivatives, and contingent capital arrangements—to provide alternatives to traditional insurance or reinsurance.

Because these new capital market products involve significant time and expense to implement, only a few large organizations, mainly insurers and reinsurers, have used them to finance risk. Capital market products have been used mainly for catastrophe risks, such as the risk of a large number of earthquake or hurricane losses. However, capital market products could be used to finance any type of insurable risk, and some predict that the use of capital market products will expand rapidly during the next decade.

Securitization

Securitization means to create a marketable investment security based on a financial transaction's expected cash flows. For example, a bank might securitize its mortgage receivables and sell them for cash to an intermediary known as a special purpose vehicle, or an SPV, which, in turn, sells securities to investors. These securities appeal to investors when they offer a sufficiently attractive return for the perceived risk. The bank exchanges one asset for another. It sells its accounts receivable, which are subject to the possibility of default and other risks, and it receives risk-free cash in exchange. Through the technique of securitization, the risk inherent in mortgage receivables is transferred from the bank to the investors. Many other examples are also possible.

Insurance securitization
The creation of a marketable insurance-linked security that is based on the cash flow arising from the transfer of insurable risks.

Insurance securitization is a unique form of securitization, defined as creating a marketable insurance-linked security based on the cash flows that arise from the transfer of insurable risks. These cash flows are similar to premium and loss payments under an insurance policy. For example, imagine that an investor purchases a bond from an SPV that provides a rate of interest higher than that provided by a United States Treasury bond of comparable maturity. In exchange for this relatively high rate of interest, the investor's return on the bond is linked to the risk that a hurricane might occur during the bond's term. If a hurricane does occur and causes total property losses that exceed a specified dollar threshold, the investor's return on the bond is reduced in direct proportion to the size of these losses. If total property losses are high enough to trigger a reduced return on the bond, the investor's (1) interest income or (2) interest income and principal repayments on the bond are lowered, depending on the terms of the bond and the extent of the losses. The SPV uses the savings in interest and principal repayments to pay cash to an insurance, or a noninsurance, organization, which uses the cash to offset its hurricane losses. Through the process of insurance securitization, the risk of loss due to a hurricane has been "securitized" by linking it with the returns provided to investors in a marketable security. See the following box for an actual example.

From the insurer's perspective, securitization offsets some risks, thereby reducing its overall risks. From the investor's perspective, insurance-linked securities help diversify the investor's portfolio because the insurable risk embedded in insurance-linked securities is not closely correlated with the risks normally involved in other investments.

United Services Automobile Association (USAA) Securitizes Its Hurricane Risks

In June 1997, the United Services Automobile Association (USAA) used an SPV to issue $477 million in insurance-linked securities to reinsure its Gulf Coast and East Coast hurricane risks. The securities were in the form of catastrophe bonds. The bond investors lose (1) interest or (2) interest and principal, depending on the bond series, if a Category 3, 4, or 5 hurricane causes insured losses to USAA of between $1 billion and $1.5 billion. USAA receives reimbursement for any catastrophe losses from the SPV. The bond offering was reported to be highly successful, with investors unable to purchase as much of the issue as they would have liked.[5]

Insurance Derivatives

The second category of capital market products used for alternative risk financing is insurance derivatives. A **derivative** is a financial contract that *derives* its value from the value of another asset, such as a commodity. A derivative can also derive its value from the yields on another asset or the level of an index of yields or values, such as the Standard and Poor's 500 stock index.

An **insurance derivative** is a financial contract that derives its value from the level of insurable losses—hurricane losses, for example—that occur in a specific area during a specific time period. Two major categories of insurance derivatives are swaps and options.

1. Swap—A **swap** is an agreement between two organizations to exchange their cash flows that result from movements in the value of an asset, yields on an asset, or an index of values or yields. The swap derives its value from the value of the underlying asset, yield, or index.

    An organization can use a swap to transfer its insurable risk, in which case the swap is an insurance derivative. For example, one insurance company could exchange a portion of the cash flows (premiums and losses) arising from its hurricane exposure in the Southeastern United States with a portion of the cash flows arising from another insurance company's tornado exposure in the Midwestern United States. A swap arrangement between two insurance companies is, in effect, a reinsurance agreement that enables both parties to hedge their risks.

2. Insurance options—An option gives the holder the right, but not the obligation, to buy or sell an asset at a specific price over a period of time. The buyer of an insurance option pays a premium and receives cash when the value of the insurable losses exceeds the specified deductible or self-insured retention level (the strike value) during the period of the option. The seller of the option is in the opposite position because he or she receives the premium and must pay cash if the insurable option's value exceeds the specified deductible, or strike value.

Derivative
A financial contract that derives its value from the value of another asset, such as a commodity.

Insurance derivative
A financial contract that derives its value from the level of insurable losses that occur over a specific period.

Swap
An agreement between two organizations to exchange their cash flows based on movements in the value of an asset, yields on an asset, or an index of values or yields.

Insurance option
A derivative that is valued based on insurable losses, either an organization's actual insurable losses or an index of losses covered by a group of insurance companies.

Like a swap, an **insurance option** is a derivative because it derives its value from insurable losses, either an organization's actual insurable losses or an insurance industry index of losses. The value of an insurance option increases as the value of the underlying insurable losses increases. Therefore, an organization can use a gain on an insurance option to offset its losses from insurable risk.

Advantages and Disadvantages of Insurance Derivatives

Insurance derivatives provide an alternative to traditional insurance and supplement existing risk-transfer capacity. Whether this is an important advantage depends on the cost and supply of traditional insurance and reinsurance.

A major disadvantage lies in the fact that the market for insurance derivatives is not well developed or understood, and an organization might not be able to purchase the amount of protection it requires. Also, a risk of nonperformance (so-called counterparty risk) is associated with any options that are not traded on an organized exchange. Finally, the value of the insurance derivative might not correspond exactly with losses. Insurance derivatives are valued based on indices such as industry-wide losses, and individual losses will not likely correspond exactly to industry-wide losses. Thus, the value of a derivative will not perfectly hedge individual losses due to this "basis" risk.

Contingent Capital Arrangements

Contingent capital arrangement
An agreement, entered into before any losses occur, that enables an organization to raise cash by selling stock or issuing debt at prearranged terms following a loss that exceeds a certain threshold.

Finally, contingent capital arrangements can be used as a risk financing technique. A **contingent capital arrangement** is an agreement, entered into before any losses occur, that enables an organization to raise cash by selling stock or issuing debt at prearranged terms following a loss that exceeds a certain threshold. The organization pays a capital commitment fee to the party that agrees in advance to purchase debt or equity following a loss.

With a contingent capital arrangement, the organization does not transfer its risk of loss to investors. Instead, after a loss occurs, it receives a capital injection in the form of debt or equity to help it pay for the loss. Because the terms are agreed to in advance, the organization generally receives more favorable terms than it would receive if it were to raise capital after a large loss, when it is likely to be in a weakened capital condition.

OPTIMIZING RETAINED RISKS

Every organization faces various pure and speculative risks, each of which can be managed with a variety of techniques. Ideally, risk management addresses the entire portfolio of risks and retains the amount of risk for which the organization receives a sufficient return. Enterprise-wide risk management is a goal toward which risk management should ideally strive, and one that is being addressed by some large organizations that are in a position to conduct a highly sophisticated analysis. See, for example, Citigroup's statement on

"Managing Global Risk," in Exhibit 7-3. This statement deals with the broad range of risks faced by Citigroup as a diversified holding company providing financial services, which are by no means limited to the risks it assumes as an insurer.

EXHIBIT 7-3

Managing Global Risk

Risk management is the cornerstone of Citigroup's business. Risks arise from lending, underwriting, trading, insurance and other activities routinely undertaken around the world. Outlined below is the process that management employs to provide oversight and direction of risk taking, followed by discussions of the credit and market risk management processes in place across the Company.

The Windows on Risk Committee is the most senior corporate forum for reviewing the corporation's risk tolerance and practices. It provides top-down examination and review of material corporate-wide risks. The Committee is chaired by Citigroup's Senior Risk Manager and includes the Chairmen of Citigroup and other senior officers in the Company.

The Windows on Risk process has three major components: an assessment of the global external environment, drawing on our own knowledge and frequently on the knowledge of outside experts; an assessment of the Company's exposures in terms of the various risk windows, with special focus on potentially material risks to Citigroup; and decisions on desired exposure levels and determination of follow-up actions required to adjust exposure.

The review of the external environment encompasses the outlook for major country and regional economies; significant consumer markets and global industries; potential near-term critical economic and political events; and the implications of potential unfavorable developments as they relate to specific businesses.

The review of the risk profile covers the following 18 windows:

- Risk ratings, including trends in client creditworthiness together with a comparison of risk against return;

- Industry concentrations, globally and within regions;

- Limits assigned to relationship concentrations and consumer programs;

- Product concentrations in consumer managed receivables, by product and by region;

- Global real estate limits and exposure, including commercial and consumer portfolios;

- Country risk, encompassing political and cross-border risk;

- Counterparty risk, evaluating presettlement risk on foreign exchange, derivative products, and securities trades;

- Dependency, linking and evaluating specific industry and consumer product exposure to external environmental factors;

- Distribution and underwriting risk, capturing the risk that arises when Citigroup commits to purchase an instrument from an issuer for subsequent sale;

Continued on next page.

- Audit and Risk Review, evaluating and measuring defects in our business processes;
- Price risk, evaluating the earnings risk resulting from changing levels and implied volatilities of interest rates, foreign exchange rates, and commodity and security prices;
- Liquidity risk, evaluating funding exposure;
- Commodities risk, evaluating earnings risk resulting from changing levels and volatilities of commodity prices;
- Life Insurance, evaluating the risks that result from the underwriting, sale, and reinsurance of life insurance policies;
- Property & Casualty, evaluating the risks that result from the underwriting, sale, and reinsurance of commercial, personal, and performance bonds insurance policies;
- Equity and subordinated debt investment risk, monitored against portfolio limits;
- Legal, evaluating vulnerability and business implications of legal issues; and
- Technology, assessing vulnerability to the electronic environment.

The review is intended to provide Citigroup with a view of the environment in which it operates and of the risk inherent in its businesses. Based on this review, the Windows on Risk Committee formulates recommendations and assigns responsibility for recommended actions.

Citigroup 1999 Annual Report and Form 10-K, p. 34, © Copyright, Citigroup, Inc., 2000.

To optimize retained risks, it is necessary to conduct a risk and return analysis. To conduct a risk and return analysis, an organization can construct many retained risk portfolios based on combinations of various types and sizes of risk, with each portfolio containing its own set of risk and return characteristics. For the organization to maximize the net present value of its cash flows, it must select a portfolio of retained risks that maximizes its return at a level of risk it can tolerate.

In constructing portfolios of retained risks, the organization is subject to a number of constraints. It might be required to transfer some risks (purchase insurance), and it might have no choice but to retain other risks that are not transferable.

SUMMARY

Insurance and retention are not the only tools for financing risks. This chapter evaluated self-insurance and traditional insurance along with a variety of other risk financing alternatives.

The chapter began by examining the advantages and disadvantages of self insurance, as compared with traditional insurance. The advantages of self-insurance include control over claims, incentive for risk control, long-term cost savings, and increased cash flow. Disadvantages include uncertainty about retained loss outcomes, administrative functions, delayed tax benefits, and the difficulty of using self-insurance to meet contractual insurance requirements. The advantages of traditional insurance include reduction of uncertainty or risk, claim and risk management services provided by insurers, tax-deductibility of traditional insurance premiums, and legal and contractual requirements. Disadvantages include reduced cash flow, higher long-term administrative costs, increased premium due to adverse selection, and increased premium due to moral and attitudinal hazards.

Alternative risk financing techniques include partial retention (small deductibles, large deductibles, and SIRs), experience-rated insurance plans, retrospectively rated insurance plans, layering, self-insurance pools, purchasing groups, captive insurers, risk retention groups, finite risk insurance plans, and capital market products (securitization, insurance derivatives, and contingent capital arrangements).

Every organization must optimize its overall mix of retained risks, ideally taking into account diverse pure and speculative risks from all sources. The Citigroup example illustrates the range of risks considered by one corporation in the financial services sector.

The next chapter examines some fundamental assumptions about insurance.

CHAPTER NOTES

1. Much of this chapter is based on Michael W. Elliott, *Risk Financing*, 1st ed. (Malvern, Pa.: Insurance Institute of America, 2000).

2. Purchasing groups are sometimes inaccurately referred to as "risk purchasing groups." This incorrect usage developed soon after the Products Liability Risk Retention Act of 1981 authorized the formation of "risk retention groups" and "purchasing groups." Many writers added the extra word "risk" for parallelism, and some still refer to "risk retention groups" and "risk purchasing groups." The label is a complete misnomer; purchasing groups purchase insurance—not risk.

3. International Risk Management Institute, *Risk Financing: A Guide to Insurance Cash Flow* (Dallas: International Risk Management Institute, Inc., 2000), 1st reprint, p. IV.K.5, March 1997.

4. The issues are discussed in Michael W. Elliott, *Risk Financing*, 1st ed. (Malvern, Pa.: Insurance Institute of America, 2000), pp. 10-14–10-20.

5. Rodd Zolkos, "Hurricane Bond Issue Takes Market by Storm," *Business Insurance*, June 23, 1997.

Chapter 8

Direct Your Learning

Fundamental Assumptions Underlying Insurance

After learning the subject matter of this chapter, you should be able to:

■ Identify and describe the nine fundamental assumptions underlying insurance.

■ Explain why the nine fundamental assumptions outlined in this chapter are important to understanding the business of insurance.

■ Identify and describe some examples of how the practice of insurance (or the business of insurance) sometimes does not operate according to the assumptions listed.

Develop Your Perspective

What are the main topics covered in the chapter?

This chapter covers nine fundamental assumptions (or principles) about insurance on which the practice of insurance is based.

Review the assumptions.

- What contradictions do you see between the fundamental assumptions and how insurance works in practice?

Why is it important to know these topics?

Knowing how these assumptions are supposed to work and the factors affecting them in practice will help you understand why gaps occur between the two and why insurers need to react to those gaps.

Examine the concept of overindemnification.

- Why does overindemnification present a "moral hazard," and how do insurers address the problem?

How can you use this information?

Consider the ways in which insurers can bridge the gap between theory and practice.

- Does regulation come to mind?
- How might regulation address the gaps?

Chapter 8

Fundamental Assumptions Underlying Insurance

This chapter describes nine fundamental assumptions about insurance, some of which have been called insurance principles because they form the theory behind the business of insurance. When one examines these assumptions and determines how well current insurance practices follow these ideal assumptions, the fact that the practice of insurance sometimes does not match the theory behind it becomes clear.

Many insurance practices discussed in future chapters are based on the assumptions outlined in this chapter.

Nine Fundamental Assumptions About Insurance

1. Insurance requires good faith.

2. The policy drafter should not receive an unfair advantage.

3. The goal of insurance is to indemnify.

4. Insurance should not overindemnify.

5. Insureds should not be indemnified more than once per loss.

6. Parties to be insured should face potential loss.

7. Insurance is intended for fortuitous future losses.

8. Insureds should not profit from their own wrongdoing.

9. Insurance should equitably distribute risk costs.

INSURANCE REQUIRES GOOD FAITH

The first of the nine fundamental assumptions is that insurance requires good faith. Generally, the insurance mechanism is highly vulnerable to abuses such as misrepresentation or opportunism. These abuses can be prevented if all parties exercise good faith in the insurance transaction.

Good faith requires that a person applying for insurance make a full and fair disclosure of the risk to the insurer and its agent. An insurance buyer who intentionally conceals material information from the insurer or who misrepresents material facts in an insurance application or a claim does not act in good faith. If an insured conceals or misrepresents a material fact or commits fraud, at any time, the insurance contract can be voided.

Similarly, the insured and the insurer have entered into an enforceable contract. The insurer must fulfill its promises as outlined in the contract. This **good faith** must also carry through to claim handling, in which insurers are obligated to investigate and pay claims promptly. Insurers who act in "bad faith" may face serious penalties under the law.

Good faith
The principle that imposes a standard of honesty on the parties to an insurance contract.

THE POLICY DRAFTER SHOULD NOT RECEIVE AN UNFAIR ADVANTAGE

The second fundamental assumption underlying insurance is that the insurer has a good-faith obligation to draft a contract that clearly expresses what it intends to cover. Any policy provision that can reasonably be interpreted more than one way can be considered ambiguous. What matters is the written contract's *actual wording*, not the *intentions* of the party who drafted it. If the courts rule that a provision is ambiguous, then it is ambiguous.

The insurance company or an insurance service organization develops most insurance policies. Standard contract forms are used to insure many different insureds. The insurance company chooses the exact wording in the policies it offers, and the insured generally has little choice but to take it or leave it. A basic insurance contract might be altered by endorsements, but the insurer also typically develops these endorsements. In short, a party who wants insurance usually has no choice but to accept and adhere to the contract drafted by the insurer.

Contract of adhesion
Any contract in which one party must either accept the agreement as written by the other party or reject it.

The typical insurance policy is, therefore, a contract of adhesion. A **contract of adhesion** is prepared by only one party, with the other party either accepting the agreement as written or rejecting it. Courts have ruled that any ambiguities or uncertainties in an insurance contract of adhesion are to be construed against the party who drafted the agreement. *If an insurance policy's interpretation creates any ambiguities or uncertainties, the policy will be interpreted in favor of the insured who played no role in drafting the policy, and against the insurer.* In such a situation, the insurer theoretically had an opportunity to express its intent clearly and unequivocally in the insurance contract, but did not.

In any case in which the *insured* actually drafts the contract and the *insurer* accepts it, the doctrine of adhesion might be applied to interpret any ambiguity in favor of the *insurer*. No matter who drafts the policy, that party should not receive an unfair advantage in setting the terms of the contract.

THE GOAL OF INSURANCE IS TO INDEMNIFY

The goal of insurance is to **indemnify** (make whole) those people who have suffered a loss. **Indemnity** is the compensation they receive to make them whole. Under a **contract of indemnity,** the insured is entitled to payment only if he or she has suffered a loss and then only up to the extent of the financial loss actually suffered. Insurance is a contract of indemnity when the amount the insurer pays is no more than the full amount of the insured's loss.

An insurance policy does not necessarily pay the *full* amount necessary to restore an insured who has suffered a covered loss. Most insurance policies contain a dollar limit, a deductible, or other provisions or limitations that indemnify the insured for less than the entire loss amount. Insurance sometimes does not indemnify for inconvenience, time, hassle, and other nonfinancial expenses involved in recovering from an insured loss.

Some insurance policies are **valued policies**, not contracts of indemnity. With a valued policy, the insurer agrees to pay a preestablished dollar amount in the event of an insured loss. For example, in a life insurance policy with a $100,000 face amount, the insurer agrees to pay $100,000 upon the insured's death.

A valued policy does not necessarily indemnify the insured—and it might even pay the insured more than he or she lost—because the amount payable by the insurer for a total loss is the policy limit, which is not necessarily related to the loss's financial value.

Valued policies are not contracts of indemnity, because they do not attempt to directly match the insurer's obligations with the loss's value. However, like contracts of indemnity, they still serve a basic goal of insurance, which is to indemnify people for losses.

Indemnify
The act of making someone, who has suffered a loss, whole.

Indemnity
The compensation an insured receives after a loss to make the insured whole.

Contract of indemnity
A contract under which the insured is entitled to payment only if he or she has suffered a covered loss and then only up to the extent of the financial loss actually suffered.

Valued policy
A policy that preestablishes a dollar amount the insurer will pay for an insured loss.

INSURANCE SHOULD NOT OVERINDEMNIFY

The fourth fundamental assumption underlying insurance is that insurance should not overindemnify people for losses. That is, insureds should be indemnified but not overcompensated, or "overindemnified," for a loss. The insured should be put back into approximately the same financial position as that before a loss.

The **principle of indemnity** is probably the most fundamental insurance principle. The principle of indemnity asserts that insurance contracts should confer a benefit no greater in value than the loss suffered by an insured.[1] The principle of indemnity simply means that a person should not profit from an insured loss.

The potential for overindemnification (insurers' paying more than the claim is worth) can create a moral hazard for some insureds. A moral hazard exists when an insured considers intentionally causing a loss or exaggerating a loss to benefit financially from the loss. For example, an insured, but run-down,

Principle of indemnity
The principle that insurance policies should provide a benefit no greater than the loss suffered by an insured.

building on a valuable piece of property might be a tempting arson target for an owner who could use the insurance money to build a better building on that site. Insurers can reduce moral hazards (and overindemnification) by clearly defining the extent of a covered loss in the policy provisions and by carefully setting policy limits.

INSUREDS SHOULD NOT BE INDEMNIFIED MORE THAN ONCE PER LOSS

The fifth fundamental assumption underlying insurance is that people should not be indemnified more than once per loss. Ideally, one insurance policy, or one portion of a policy, standing alone, should cover a given loss. Duplicate sources of recovery (receiving payment from many policies) could result in the insured's overindemnification.

However, sometimes duplicate recovery is not only available but also viewed as very fair. For example, prohibiting duplicate recovery for an insured could unfairly absolve the responsible parties from bearing the financial consequences of the loss.

People can be insureds under more than one policy when they carry multiple policies, such as auto and health insurance. Or, a person can receive payment from another source that is not necessarily insurance, also known as a collateral source. The **collateral source rule** is a rule of tort law that holds that the tortfeasor (defendant) is not allowed to deduct from the amount he or she would be held to pay to the tort's victim, any goods, services, or money received by the victim from other "collateral sources" (e.g., insurance benefits) as a result of the tort.[2]

Although only one source of recovery per loss has been identified as a fundamental principle of insurance, some strongly believe that duplicate recovery can be appropriate in some cases for the above reasons.

Collateral source rule
A tort law rule that prevents the tortfeasor (defendant) from deducting from the amount owed to the victim any goods, services, or money the victim received from other "collateral" sources (e.g., insurance benefits) as a result of the tort.

PARTIES TO BE INSURED SHOULD FACE POTENTIAL LOSS

The sixth fundamental assumption underlying insurance is that parties to be insured should face potential loss. That is, to have legally enforceable insurance coverage, a person must possess an **insurable interest** in the subject of the insurance and should face the possibility of financial harm resulting from the kinds of losses covered by the insurance. Whether a person legally has an insurable interest depends on the relationship between that person and the property, life, or event in question. If the relationship exposes the person to possible financial loss, and the relationship is not unduly remote, insurable interest usually exists.

Insurable interest
Any interest a person has in property that is the subject of insurance, such that damage to the property would cause the insured a financial loss or another tangible deprivation.

When applied to contracts of indemnity such as insurance, the principle of insurable interest supports the principle of indemnity by indemnifying only those people whose relationship to an insured event would cause them to suffer a financial loss, and then only to the extent of that loss.

For example, if a homeowner sold her house but did not cancel the homeowners policy, and the property suffered a loss, she could not present a claim because she no longer owns the property and lacks an insurable interest.

INSURANCE IS INTENDED FOR FORTUITOUS FUTURE LOSSES

The seventh fundamental assumption underlying insurance is that insurance is intended for *fortuitous* future losses. **Fortuitous losses** are losses that happen accidentally or unexpectedly, with reasonable uncertainty about the probability or timing of loss. To provide coverage for a loss, the courts generally require that losses be fortuitous.

Fortuitous loss
A loss that is accidental and unexpected.

However, many losses happen fortuitously but are *not covered* by an insurance policy. These include losses due to wear and tear or inherent vice, which is a characteristic of property that causes the property to destroy itself. For example, wine sours, and fruit rots.

According to the principle of adverse selection, if people know of a loss in advance, they will insure against it, thereby changing the loss distribution for everyone the insurer insures. To maintain an equitable loss distribution among insureds, underwriters must avoid adverse selection by precluding coverage for these types of losses. Insurers must carefully specify what is an insured event, what circumstances will "trigger" (apply) coverage, and when the policy goes into force and terminates (the policy period).

In some cases, an insurer might be willing to *apply coverage* to known losses or losses in progress. In the case of liability insurance, an insurer writing a "claims-made" policy might be willing to cover a claim that occurs outside the policy period, assuming that the loss occurred after a retroactive date was specified in the policy.

Therefore, while the fundamental assumption discussed here is that insurance is intended for fortuitous future losses, the actual practice of insurance makes many exceptions to that principle. See the following box.

MGM Grand Hotel and Timing Risk

Timing risk was virtually the only uncertainty that was insured with a controversial coverage known as "retroactive insurance" following the 1980 MGM Grand Hotel fire in Las Vegas, where eighty-seven people were killed and hundreds were injured. The insured event had already taken place, and the number of claims could be estimated

---

Continued on next page.

with reasonable accuracy. However, it was expected that these claims would be paid over an indeterminate period of years as lawsuits were handled. The hotel was able to purchase "retroactive liability insurance" with a single $40 million premium for $120 million in retroactive insurance, transferring to an insurance company the risks associated with the timing of actual claim payments. Counting on a long settlement process, the insurance company intended to earn investment income on the money it held until claims were actually paid. The hotel planned to take the premium cost as a tax deduction, which otherwise would have to be spread over a number of years as claims were paid.

In this case, things did not work out as the insurer had planned. The settlement came within five years, and the insurer ended up paying $87.5 million in claims.[3]

INSUREDS SHOULD NOT PROFIT FROM THEIR OWN WRONGDOING

The eighth fundamental assumption underlying insurance is that insureds should not profit from their own wrongdoing. It would be against public policy to permit an insurance contract to indemnify a person against loss caused by his or her own willful wrongdoing. Most insurance policies contain carefully worded provisions that exclude coverage for intentional injuries. But even without an intentional injuries exclusion, the courts permit an insurer to deny coverage that allows a party to profit by intentionally causing an insured loss.

An intentional act—even a very foolish one—can have unintended consequences. For example, an insured might intentionally light a candle in his or her house for decorative purposes but unthinkingly place it so that a pet could knock it down, causing a serious fire loss. Many insured losses are caused by negligence, a temporary lapse in judgment, or foolish behavior. In part, that is what insurance is for. On the other hand, insurance clearly ought *not* to protect a person who pours gasoline onto the carpets in his or her own home and then intentionally ignites it.

In most cases, understanding the reasons for the intentional loss exclusion is easy. Insureds should not be able to intentionally destroy their own property and collect insurance proceeds. Otherwise, many would have an incentive to dispose of obsolete or unsaleable property by "selling" it to the insurance company. Arson-for-profit on buildings, prearranged thefts of cars, and other fraudulent claims do occur, and when they are detected, coverage is denied. Detecting and proving fraud can be a challenge—one reason why underwriters generally prefer to avoid coverage presenting a moral hazard.

INSURANCE SHOULD EQUITABLY DISTRIBUTE RISK COSTS

The ninth and final assumption underlying insurance is that the cost of each insured's policy should be commensurate with the risks it presents to the insurer. The insurance mechanism as a whole works most effectively when the cost of risk is distributed equitably among insurance buyers. This generally means that each insured's insurance premiums are directly proportionate to that insured's expected losses on an actuarially sound basis. See the following box.

Equitable Distribution of Risk

Insurance achieves an equitable distribution of risk costs in various ways, including the following:

- Rating plans—Generally, actuaries develop complex rating systems that project expected loss costs and expenses for each insurance policy so that they can charge premiums commensurate with the insured's loss exposures, as well as with the insurer's projected expenses.

- Coinsurance and subrogation—Both help equitably spread the risk among insureds.

    1. Coinsurance in property insurance—The purpose of coinsurance is to provide an incentive for people to avoid a penalty by purchasing amounts of insurance that reflect their exposures to loss.

    2. Subrogation—Through subrogation, loss costs are ultimately allocated to the party most responsible for the loss.

However, other forces can affect the ability to achieve actuarial equity. These include the following:

- Insurance regulation—Most insurance regulators must approve many of the rates charged by insurance companies. Such rate approval can sometimes affect the free-market economic forces intended to match insurance premiums with insured exposures.

- Social equity—Social equity is a system to redistribute wealth. Under the concept of social equity, good drivers subsidize the cost of insurance for bad drivers; owners of "safe" property subsidize the owners of "high-hazard" property.

- No-fault insurance—With **no-fault laws**, the costs of auto-related injuries are assigned to the insurer of the party who is injured, not the at-fault party. Although this results in an inequitable distribution of loss costs, it can also eliminate the substantial expenses otherwise involved in determining which party was at fault in any given accident. The no-fault concept clearly violates the fundamental

No-fault laws
Laws that distribute the costs of auto-related injuries to the insurer of the party who is injured, rather than to the insurer of the party who causes the injury; usually do not apply to property damage.

Continued on next page.

assumption that losses should be charged against the party that causes them. Nevertheless, the no-fault approach is supported in a number of states because it serves other goals.

Therefore, while insurers generally strive for the equitable distribution of risk costs *in theory*, in practice certain forces work against it.

SUMMARY

This chapter examined nine fundamental assumptions about insurance that form the theory on which the practice of insurance is based.

The nine assumptions discussed were these:

1. Insurance requires good faith.
2. The policy drafter should not receive an unfair advantage.
3. The goal of insurance is to indemnify.
4. Insurance should not overindemnify.
5. Insureds should not be indemnified more than once per loss.
6. Parties to be insured should face potential loss.
7. Insurance is intended for fortuitous future losses.
8. Insureds should not profit from their own wrongdoing.
9. Insurance should equitably distribute risk costs.

This chapter also examined some of the ways in which the modern practice of insurance deviates from the principles upon which it is based.

CHAPTER NOTES

1. Robert E. Keeton and Alan I. Widiss, *Insurance Law* (St. Paul, Minn.: West Publishing Company, 1988), pp. 141–142.
2. *Duhaime's Law Dictionary*, World Wide Web: http://www.duhaime.org/ diction.htm.
3. Data are based on an article by Ed Koch and Mary Manning, "MGM Grand Fire Altered Safety Standards," *Las Vegas Sun*, November 19, 2000.

Chapter 9

Direct Your Learning

Forming an Insurance Contract

After learning the subject matter of this chapter, you should be able to:

- Describe each of the elements of a legally enforceable insurance contract.
- Given a case situation, determine whether the necessary elements of a legally enforceable insurance contract exist.
- Describe five situations in which genuine assent might be questionable.

Develop Your Perspective

What are the main topics covered in the chapter?

This chapter covers general contract law, the insurance contract, factors affecting the enforceability of a contract, and genuine assent as it relates to forming a contract.

Consider a contract's legal purpose.

- What type of agreement might constitute an illegal contract?

Why is it important to know these topics?

To determine whether or not coverage should be provided for a loss, you must first decide if the elements of an enforceable contract have been met, whether the policy (as a contract) is legally enforceable, and whether the party suffering the loss has an insurable interest in the loss.

Analyze "offer and acceptance" of a contract.

- How might fraud, duress, or other circumstances involving genuine assent affect the insurance contract?
- How does this affect possible coverage?

How can you use this information?

Examine an auto insurance policy.

- Is it a legally enforceable contract?
- Who has the insurable interest if a loss occurs?

Chapter 9

Forming an Insurance Contract

The first important question to determine whether insurance coverage is available is whether an enforceable contract exists between the insurer and the party claiming coverage. An insurance policy should be a contract that contains an enforceable legal agreement. An insurance buyer purchases an insurance policy intending to activate a *legally enforceable* obligation under which the insurer must provide financial protection to the insured. The obligation is enforceable through the courts by any insured party with an *insurable interest* (discussed in more detail in Chapter 10) in exposures covered by the insurance.

This chapter begins with general contract law, and the important distinctions between contracts that are legally enforceable and those that are not. The chapter also discusses what must transpire to create an enforceable insurance contract.

CONTRACTS

Contract law principles apply to both insurance contracts and other contracts. To understand how a legally enforceable *insurance* contract can be formed, one must first understand some basic principles of contract law.

Elements of Any Contract

A contract creates obligations that did not exist before the contract was formed. Any enforceable contract involves five elements:

1. Offer and acceptance
2. Consideration
3. Competent parties
4. Legal purpose
5. Legal form

Offer and Acceptance

The first element of a contract is offer and acceptance. *Agreement* is reached when one party makes a specific *offer* and the other party makes specific and genuine *acceptance* of the exact terms of that offer.

1. The offeror must express, by word or conduct, an intent to enter into a contract.

2. The terms of the proposed contract must be sufficiently definite.

3. The offer must be communicated to the offeree.

An offeree who receives an offer may exercise one of three alternatives:

1. Accept it
2. Reject it
3. Make a *counteroffer*

A counteroffer cancels the original offer and constitutes a new offer, originated by the party who was originally the offeree. The party who was originally the offeror may accept or reject the counteroffer—or make yet another counteroffer.

Acceptance occurs when a party to whom an offer has been made either agrees to the proposal or does what has been proposed. An acceptance must meet three requirements:

1. It must be made by the party to whom the offer was made.
2. It must be consistent with the offer. If the acceptance does not conform in substance with the exact terms of the offer, it is not an acceptance but a counteroffer.
3. It must be communicated to the offeror by appropriate word or act.

Consideration

The second element of any contract is consideration. The consideration necessary to enforce a promise (or make a contract legally enforceable) might be paying money, giving a promise in return, performing an act, or relinquishing a right to do what one is legally entitled to do. In other words, **consideration** is something of value given by each party to a contract.

Consideration
Something of value given by each party to a contract.

Competent Parties

The third element of a contract is competent parties. The parties to any contract must be considered legally capable of entering into an agreement for the contract to be legally enforceable. A contract may be voidable if any contracting party was not legally competent at the time of agreement. Some individuals by virtue of their age or mental ability are not legally competent. So, for example, minors cannot enter into legally enforceable contracts.

Legal Purpose

Legal purpose is the fourth element of a contract. To be enforceable, any contract must serve a legal purpose. A contract is illegal when forming the contract or performing the agreement constitutes a crime or a tort.

The courts consider contracts to be illegal if they are against the law or against public policy—as defined by the courts. The following are examples:

- *Illegal contracts*, such as a contract to murder a person

- *Agreement against public policy*, such as a contract to bribe a public official in exchange for a government job

Insurance policies are designed to include all of the elements of a legally enforceable contract.

Legal Form

The fifth element of a contract is legal form. Contracts generally need not be in writing in order to be valid. Only agreements that are within the so-called Statute of Frauds,[1] or other statutes requiring written form, fail to be enforceable unless in writing.

Enforcement of a Contract

The essence of a contract is that it is a *legally enforceable* promise or set of promises.[2] If a valid, enforceable contract is breached by any party to the contract, the other party(ies), if injured by the breach, may seek a remedy through the legal system. Here are two common legal remedies:

1. *Payment of damages*. A court might order a party to pay money damages for having breached the contract by failing to perform its duties as specified in the contract.

2. *Specific performance*. A court might order a party to perform its duties as specified in the contract.

However, some contracts are not legally enforceable. The courts will not require the parties to perform duties specified in an unenforceable contract, and courts will not require the payment of damages for breaching an unenforceable contract. A contract can be unenforceable if it is void, voidable, or canceled.

A **void contract** never had any legal existence, even though one or more parties might have considered it a contract, because some key element of a contract is missing. For example, lack of "consideration" by one party makes the contract void. *Either* party may choose to ignore a contract that is void, or *both* parties may also choose to treat a void contract as though it were a valid contract.

A **voidable contract** legally exists, but its existence is tenuous because it can legally be rejected (made void, "avoided") at the option of one or both of the parties to the contract.

A **canceled contract** is a legally enforceable contract that is no longer in effect. Many contracts include provisions detailing how and when either party may cancel the contract. To cancel a contract, a party to the contract must first acknowledge that it *is* a legally valid contract and then terminate it according to its own contractual terms.

Void contract
A contract that never had any legal existence because some key contractual element was missing.

Voidable contract
A contract that legally exists but can legally be rejected (made void, "avoided") at the option of one or both parties to the contract.

Canceled contract
A contract that is legally enforceable but that is no longer in effect because it has been terminated.

INSURANCE CONTRACTS

The first important question in evaluating coverage available to any party under any insurance policy is whether an enforceable contract exists between the insurer and the party claiming coverage. Generally, an insurance contract must have the same five elements as other contracts.

Elements of an Insurance Contract

1. Offer and acceptance = Agreement
2. Consideration
3. Competent parties
4. Legal purpose
5. Legal form

The next section describes how an insurance policy becomes a legally enforceable contract and factors that could affect the legality of a proposed insurance contract.

Offer and Acceptance in Insurance Contracts

As in other contracts, the first key element in the *insurance* contract is offer and acceptance.

An applicant who submits a completed application to the insurance company makes the actual offer, or is the offeror. If the insurance company (the offeree) issues a quote and the applicant pays the corresponding premium on the quote, a policy is issued. The policy issuance constitutes acceptance and thus consummates the agreement.

However, a policy is not an enforceable insurance contract until its acceptance has actually been communicated to the offeror or to the offeror's authorized agent.

When insurance transactions are handled by mail, the contract is considered communicated when the acceptance is mailed, not when it is received. For example, the insurer issues a quote (the offer), and it is accepted when the policyholder mails the premium in response to that offer.

If the insurance company (offeree) issues a policy that does not completely conform to the application (the initial offer from the offeror), then the policy is considered a counteroffer. This counteroffer changes the terms of the proposed insurance contract, which essentially restarts the offer and acceptance stage of contracting.

Consideration in Insurance Contracts

The second key element in an insurance contract is the consideration offered by both parties.

- The insurer's consideration is its promise to make payment upon an insured event's occurrence.
- The insured's consideration is its payment of the premium or its promise to pay the premium.

The insured need not pay the insurer immediately, at least with property or liability insurance. The courts will find a property or liability insurance contract to be valid without actual prepayment of the premium, as long as they can find a readily implied promise to pay the premium. Suppose the insured does not pay the premium before the policy's inception date and a claim materializes a few days after the inception date, before the initial premium is paid. Because the insured implicitly promised to pay the premium, the courts will not support an insurer who denies the claim based on a lack of consideration by the insured.

If the insured fails to make the initial premium payment when it is due, the insurer can cancel the policy for nonpayment of premium. This is considered a **flat cancellation**. A policy that is canceled flat because it lacked consideration was never in effect. However, there are exceptions.

Flat cancellation
A contract cancellation initiated by an insurer to void an insurance policy for which the insured has never paid any premium.

- In practice, it is generally not feasible to cancel a policy "flat" if an insured event has occurred. Assuming the amount of premium involved is less than the amount of the loss, the insured would almost always prefer to pay the overdue premium rather than retain an uninsured loss.
- Because policy issuance and billing do not always occur immediately, delayed payments are common. Permitting insurers to deny every claim arising before the insured has a chance to pay the initial premium would be against public policy.

Competent Parties in Insurance Contracts

The third key element in forming a legally enforceable insurance contract is the competency of the parties involved. Like other contracts, an insurance contract may be voidable by any contracting party who was not competent at the time of agreement. For example, people might be able to void policies if they can show that they were under the influence of medicine that clouded their judgment when the policy was purchased. The parties who must be competent as they form an insurance contract typically include the insurance company, the agent—if any, and the insured.

Insurance Companies

Competency for an insurance company concerns its legal authority to do business in a state. Insurance companies are licensed by the various states to sell insurance, and their activities are regulated by state insurance departments.

Insurance agents' competency to participate in forming a contract has seldom been an issue. Authority to act as an insurance agent is granted by the state, which also imposes some basic competency standards through pre-license exams and continuing education requirements.

An insured can be deemed incompetent to participate in forming a contract because of one insured's insanity, minority, or intoxication. As a practical matter, insureds who want to void an insurance contract rarely raise the issue of competency because the same effect can be accomplished simply by exercising a cancellation right or not paying premiums.

Legal Purpose in Insurance Contracts

After the key elements of acceptance, consideration, and competency have been satisfied, the contract must serve a legal purpose not contrary to the public interest. This legal purpose is the fourth element in forming a legally enforceable insurance contract. Courts refuse to enforce any insurance contract that tends to harm the public welfare or that is illegal. Issuing such contracts is against public policy. Contracts that tend to increase crime or encourage violations of the law may also be deemed invalid. Several examples below illustrate how certain insurance coverages for some types of losses could be against public policy.

Examples of Insurance Coverages That Could Be Against Public Policy

Liability insurance coverage for punitive damages—In a liability claim, courts sometimes award not only compensatory damages to make the plaintiff "whole," but also punitive damages, designed to punish the defendant for greater culpability than simple negligence. Some believe that liability coverage for these types of damages is against public policy because it is the insurer, not the defendant, who ends up paying the damages. Some states, citing these public policy issues, prohibit insurers from paying punitive damages on behalf of an insured.

Homeowners insurance coverage for child molestation and spousal abuse—In some cases, a convicted child molester has sought protection against civil suits under the liability portion of the homeowners policy. In response, many states have enacted laws (which insurers have reflected in policy exclusions) declaring that no coverage exists for such incidents because this coverage would shield molesters from the financial consequences of their wrongdoings.

Property insurance coverage on illegal goods—Property insurance coverage on illegally owned or possessed goods (such as illegal drugs) is unenforceable and against public policy because the public suffers the consequences of the illegal activity.

Property insurance coverage in the absence of an insurable interest—Without an insurable interest requirement, people could obtain insurance on other people's property, essentially wagering on insured events. An insured party with no insurable interest in the property would have nothing to lose but the premium, but everything to gain if a loss occurred. This is against the public interest because it creates a moral hazard.

Legal Form in Insurance Contracts

The fifth key element in forming a legally enforceable insurance contract is legal form. In the absence of statutory prohibitions, insurance contracts need not be in writing to be valid. Some insurance contracts are created orally, such as when two parties agree on the terms of the contract over the phone. Typically, these "oral contracts," known as **binders**, are documented after the call in the form of written contracts that clarify the terms of the agreement. The courts generally enforce oral contracts of insurance, provided that they are specific enough to show the parties' mutual assent on key matters such as the identities of the parties, the risks insured, and the policy limits. Statutes prescribing a standard form of insurance policy do not normally invalidate an oral contract of insurance; the oral agreement is merely subject to the standard policy provisions.

Binder
A temporary oral or written agreement to provide insurance coverage until a formal written policy is issued.

Unenforceable Insurance Contracts

An unenforceable insurance contract lacks one or more of the key elements of an enforceable contract. If an insurance agreement is unenforceable, then no legal remedies are available. The courts will not require the insurer to perform the duties specified in an unenforceable insurance contract, and they will not require the insurer to pay damages for breaching an unenforceable contract. See the following box on void, voidable, breached, and canceled insurance contracts.

Void, Voidable, Breached, and Canceled Contracts

Insurers have several possible methods for getting out of insurance contracts. The following example shows when an insurer may choose not to cover a policyholder and how the insurer can handle the coverage situation.

Scenario: Peggy owned a 100-year-old house. She submitted and signed a homeowners insurance application to XYZ Insurance Company and included a check for the first year's premium. In exchange, XYZ issued a homeowners insurance policy to Peggy.

XYZ later discovered that Peggy misrepresented the age of the house as only two years old. Because XYZ does not write insurance on homes over thirty years old, Peggy's misrepresentation of the house's age resulted in the insurer's assuming a risk (the old house) that the insurer would not otherwise choose to assume. XYZ wanted to get out of this insurance contract and identified the following options in doing so:

Option 1—XYZ Insurance Company could *void* the contract based on lack of consideration if Peggy's check bounced. The contract is not enforceable.

Option 2—XYZ Insurance Company could have the policy avoided based on Peggy's material misrepresentation in the insurance application. The policy is *voidable* by XYZ because the company's offer to Peggy was based on the information misrepresented by Peggy. In this case, the contract is not enforceable.

Option 3—XYZ Insurance Company could *enforce* the contract provisions by denying coverage to Peggy based on her *breach* of policy conditions. The policy conditions

---

Continued on next page.

state that no coverage applies in the event of policyholder misrepresentation. In this case, the insurer actually precludes coverage. It is not a question of whether or not the policy is enforceable.

Option 4—XYZ Insurance Company could have the house inspected. Upon learning its actual age, XYZ could send a notice to Peggy advising that her policy is being *canceled* because the house's age does not agree with the house's age identified in the insurance application. In this case, the contract is not enforceable.

GENUINE ASSENT

This next section emphasizes the law as it has been applied to insurance contracts, rather than the general principles of contract law. Most litigation regarding the enforceability of insurance contracts involves genuineness of assent. An insurance policy that appears valid might still be unenforceable if either party's consent was not genuinely given and it is therefore determined that the parties failed to reach the legally required agreement. An innocent party whose **genuine assent** was lacking may avoid the contract.

Genuine assent
The parties' intent to enter into a contract expressed by their actions and/or words.

Genuine assent can be found lacking under circumstances involving the following:

- Fraud
- Concealment or misrepresentation
- Mistake
- Duress
- Undue influence

Fraud

The first situation that can affect genuine assent is fraud. Fraud occurs when someone knowingly makes a false representation with the intent to deceive someone to enter into a contract. The innocent party must rely on the false representation, and the false representation must be material. That is, the false representation concerns contract terms to which the innocent party would not have agreed had that party known the truth. Courts consider six elements when evaluating allegations of fraud. The first five elements must be present to rescind a contract on the basis of fraud. The sixth element must also be necessary for a plaintiff to obtain damages.

The six elements of fraud are as follows:

1. *False representation*—Of a past or an existing fact.
2. *Knowingly made*—A party must know a fact to be false or must have made the representation in reckless indifference toward the truth or falsity of the statement made.

3. *Intent to influence or deceive*—One party must have intended to influence or deceive another party.

4. *Material fact*—The misrepresented fact influenced or induced the other party to enter the contract or affected the terms under which the other party would have been willing to contract.

5. *Reasonable reliance*—The innocent party must show justification in relying on the statement.

6. *Detriment*—In a suit for damages, the plaintiff must show injury or loss.

A person fraudulently induced to make or sign an insurance policy application may sue to cancel or rescind that policy. If an insurance agent fraudulently misrepresents the nature of the document the applicant is signing or the protection that is being purchased, the fraud victim may rescind the agreement and recover any premium paid. An insurer also is permitted to avoid a contract based on the applicant's fraud in procuring the policy.

Concealment or Misrepresentation

The second situation that could affect genuine assent in insurance contracts is concealment or misrepresentation by either party. Both parties rely on full disclosure for the correct assessment of risk and a mutual understanding of contract terms. **Concealment** and/or **misrepresentation** is inconsistent with mutual confidence and good faith.

Concealment and/or misrepresentation is determined by looking at material facts. A **material fact** affects whether an insurer would accept the insurance application or on what terms the insurer would accept it. Courts agree that any fact the insurer specifically asks about is material. Failure to disclose the answers to specific questions in the insurance application is strong evidence of concealment that may give the insurer adequate grounds for denying any obligation to make payment under the policy. Incorrect answers to questions in the application are strong evidence of misrepresentation.

Most courts would find that facts unrelated to the policy's coverage are not material. For example, an applicant's misstatement of a lienholder's address in an auto insurance application would not likely be misrepresentation. Likewise, an applicant's accidental omission of his or her telephone number would not likely be concealment.

Concealment
An intentional failure to disclose a material fact.

Misrepresentation
A false statement of a material fact.

Material fact
A fact that would have influenced whether the insurer would accept the insurance application or on what terms the insurer would accept it.

Mistake

Another situation that can affect genuine assent involves a mistake. A mistake is a perception that does not agree with the actual facts. Many different kinds of mistakes are possible, and the law does not treat them all identically. Mistakes can be made regarding the facts of the transaction or the law affecting the agreement. Mistakes can involve errors in data entry, arithmetic errors, or misstatements about the property's value. While some mistakes do not affect the rights of the parties to a contract, others make the agreement voidable or unenforceable.

When a mistake occurs in an insurance transaction, the courts sometimes interpret the policy to determine how or whether coverage applies. Sometimes courts may act to reform or change a formal contract so that it conforms to both parties' true intention.

Duress

Genuine assent can also be affected by whether or not undue pressure, coercion, or threats were involved in the contact negotiation. Under contract law, a party may seek to avoid or rescind a contract on the basis that the other party used wrongful force, or **duress**, to obtain assent to the agreement. To establish sufficient duress to escape liability under a con- tract, the plaintiff must show that the threat of violence or other harm actually restrained the victim's free choice. Economic pressure alone, even if significant, is not usually considered duress. The question for a fact-finder is whether this person was deprived of free will in entering the agreement. If so, the court may void the contract.

Duress
The wrongful force used to obtain assent to an agreement.

One of the major concerns of financial services modernization—blending insurance companies with banks and other financial institutions—involves the potential for abuse. A "bancassurance" company could exercise considerable pressure "encouraging" loan applicants to also apply for insurance through the bank, or "encouraging" insurance applicants to purchase other financial services that the organization offers. Other banks or insurance companies without a range of financial services would find themselves at a competitive disadvantage. Tie-in sales, *requiring* the purchase of one or more products or services in addition to the desired product or service, probably do not rise to the legal level of duress. Thus, legislating against them is important. Respond- ing to these concerns, the Gramm-Leach-Bliley Act includes certain "safe harbor" provisions listed in Exhibit 9-1 that permit states to adopt restrictions:

EXHIBIT 9-1

Gramm-Leach-Bliley Act and Duress

Section 104 of the Gramm-Leach-Bliley Act prohibits states from "preventing or signifi- cantly interfering with" the ability of a depository institute or an affiliate to engage in insurance sales, solicitation, and cross-marketing activities. However, the Act adopts thirteen "safe harbor" provisions that permit states to adopt rules targeted specifically at bank-insurance sales activities, including insurance sales conducted by bank affiliates. These safe harbors include restrictions:

1. Prohibiting the rejection of an insurance policy by a depository institution or an affiliate solely because the policy has been issued or underwritten by an unaffiliated entity.

2. Prohibiting a requirement that any debtor or unaffiliated insurer or agent pay a separate charge in connection with the handling of insurance required in connection with a loan, extension of credit, or other traditional bank product or service unless the same charge would be required of an affiliated insurer or agent.

3. Requiring depository institutions to provide customers with "free-choice" disclosures when loans are pending—i.e., notice that the customer's choice of insurance provider will not affect the loan decision process. The depository institution may, however, impose reasonable requirements concerning the insured's creditworthiness and the scope of the coverage chosen.

4. Requiring that when a customer obtains insurance (other than credit or flood insurance) and credit from a depository institution or an affiliate, the credit and insurance transactions be completed through separate documents.

Undue Influence

The final situation that could affect genuine assent occurs when one party influences another to make certain decisions. Most legal cases involving undue influence concern gifts, wills, or the selection of insurance beneficiaries.

Like duress, **undue influence** prevents a person from exercising his or her own free will in making a contract because another person in a dominating position unduly influences or controls the decision. Mere persuasion and argument are not of themselves undue influence. Likewise, a friend's or relative's nagging insistence usually is not undue influence. For undue influence to occur, the following situations must be present:

Undue influence
Any action preventing a person from exercising free will in making a contract because another person's dominating position unduly influences or controls the decision.

- A confidential relationship must exist between the parties.
- One party must exercise some control and influence over the other. For example, the relationships of parent and child, nurse and invalid, attorney and client, doctor and patient, guardian and ward, or agent and principal give one party a position of dominance over the other.
- An element of helplessness or dependence must be involved.

In contracts between such individuals, the law will assist a person who is a victim of undue influence. The dominating party must prove that he or she did *not* unduly influence a contract from which the dominated party obtains inadequate benefits.

Mental Infirmity

Mental infirmity may form the basis for a claim of undue influence. Even in the absence of a fiduciary relationship, in which a person has a mental infirmity that seriously impairs judgment, even though insufficient to constitute lack of legal capacity, a court may find undue influence. Thus, courts look carefully at contracts entered into by bereaved widows, widowers, and others who suffer from mental infirmity even temporarily. Undue influence may involve a party's taking advantage of the fiduciary relationship or mental infirmity.

The mentally infirm person might have known the contract's nature or subject matter, but the motive for entering into the contract might have resulted from seriously impaired judgment.

Proof

The law assumes undue influence whenever the dominated person receives inadequate benefit from a contract made with the person who is dominating.

SUMMARY

In evaluating how a given insurance policy applies to a loss, the first step is to determine whether an enforceable contract exists between the insurer and the party claiming coverage.

The elements of any contract are offer and acceptance, consideration, competent parties, legal purpose, and legal form. A legally enforceable contract may be enforced by the courts. A contract might be unenforceable because it is void, voidable, breached, or canceled.

Insurance contracts likewise require offer and acceptance. Consideration is necessary in the form of a premium and a promise to provide coverage. Insurance companies, agents, and insureds must qualify as competent parties, and the purpose of the insurance contract must not be contrary to the public interest. Insurance has sometimes been deemed contrary to the public interest when it covers punitive damages, child molestation or spousal abuse, illegal goods, or the absence of an insurable interest. Insurance contracts must have legal form.

To be legally enforceable, an insurance contract must not only exist but must also involve genuine assent. Assent might be absent in cases of fraud, concealment or misrepresentation, mistake, duress, or undue influence.

Even if a legally enforceable insurance contract exists, it is not effective unless the party claiming benefits has an insurable interest in the loss covered by insurance. Chapter 10 examines the issue of insurable interests.

CHAPTER NOTES

1. A Statute of Frauds is a law enacted by legislative bodies describing certain classes of contracts that must be in writing to be valid. Real estate contracts and suretyship agreements are examples of contracts that come under the Statute of Frauds and, therefore, must be in written form to be enforceable.

2. Jane P. Mallor, A. James Barnes, Thomas Bowers, Michael J. Phillips, and Arlen W. Langvardt, *The Legal Environment*, First CPCU Edition (Malvern, Pa.: American Institute for CPCU, 2000), p. 149.

Chapter 10

Direct Your Learning

Insurable Interests for Property Insurance

After learning the subject matter of this chapter, you should be able to:

■ Answer the five questions relating to insurable interests:

1. What is insurable interest?
2. When must the insurable interest exist?
3. Why require an insurable interest?
4. What factors affect the extent of an insurable interest?
5. What happens when insurable interests overlap?

■ Explain the legal bases on which a party might have an insurable interest in property.

■ Determine the insurable interest(s) of parties exposed to property loss.

Develop Your Perspective

What are the main topics covered in the chapter?

This chapter describes the basic concepts behind insurable interest and the legal bases courts use to determine the nature and extent of insurable interest in property claims.

Evaluate the reasons for the insurable interest requirement.

- How does this requirement enforce the principle of indemnity?

Why is it important to know these topics?

Knowing the basic concepts behind the insurable interest requirement will help you determine whether a specific party has a viable financial interest in a loss, and to what extent the party is entitled to recover for the loss.

Consider the notion of property rights.

- How might property rights determine who has an interest in a loss if, for instance, the loss involved an apartment building that burned down?

How can you use this information?

Imagine a loss exposure that your organization faces.

- For this exposure, who has an insurable interest?
- Does more than one party have an insurable interest?
- How might these overlapping interests be addressed?

Chapter 10

Insurable Interests for Property Insurance

The elements of a legally enforceable contract include an offer and an acceptance, consideration, competent parties, legal purpose, and legal form. One additional element required by a property insurance contract is an insurable interest. A property insurance contract can be enforced only by an insured party who has an insurable interest in the property insured. Depending on the circumstances, a party with an insurable interest might be one or more individuals, a corporation, or some other legal entity.

Both the nature and the extent of insurable interests vary with each situation. The *extent* of any party's insurable interest reflects the amount that the party could lose in the event of a loss.

This chapter examines the basic concepts behind insurable interests and then describes the various legal bases for insurable interests.

BASIC CONCEPTS

The basic concepts of insurable interests revolve around five questions.

> **Five Key Questions in Determining Insurable Interest**
> 1. What is insurable interest?
> 2. When must the insurable interest exist?
> 3. Why require an insurable interest?
> 4. What factors affect the extent of an insurable interest?
> 5. What happens when insurable interests overlap?

What Is Insurable Interest?

Insurable interest is an exposure to financial loss that a person must possess for the property insurance coverage to be legally enforceable. For example, the owner of a building has an insurable interest in the building if the building burns down because of fire.

However, someone with an insurable interest might or might not be insured by an insurance policy. Suppose the owner of the building mentioned above had a "silent partner" who had a financial interest in the building but was not listed on the policy as an insured. That person might have a financial interest in the property (and thus an insurable interest), but that person would not have insurance.

Insurable interest is a legal concept; the identity of the insured party(ies) is a contractual matter specified in the insurance contract's wording.

When Must the Insurable Interest Exist?

An insurable interest in the loss exposures covered by a property insurance policy must exist at the time of the loss for coverage to be provided. With property insurance, the insurable interest need not necessarily exist at the time insurance becomes effective. For example, Todd could purchase a collision insurance policy effective today, providing coverage on the car he will purchase later this week.

Why Require an Insurable Interest?

Insurable interest requirements prevent gambling, reduce intentional losses, and enforce the principle of indemnity.

Without an insurable interest, an insurance contract is a gambling contract, and gambling contracts cannot legally be enforced. Courts generally hold that private gambling contracts (except contracts with licensed gaming establishments and state lotteries) are contrary to public policy. For example, James could not buy property insurance on Mary's house, in which he has no insurable interest, betting (gambling) that the house will be destroyed by fire. If James could win this bet, he would receive a return that far exceeded the premium he otherwise would lose.

The insurable interest requirement reduces intentional losses by preventing an insured from profiting by intentionally causing a loss. For instance, after purchasing property insurance on Mary's house, James might deliberately start a fire to collect the insurance.

Finally, the principle of indemnity enforces the insurable interest requirement by dictating that a person should be made whole after an insured loss but not profit. If the insurer paid a claim for more than the amount representing the insured's insurable interest, the insured would profit from insurance, and the principle of indemnity would be violated. For example, James is the owner of his house, but he purchased the home with the help of a mortgage loan from his bank. Both James and the bank have an insurable interest in the house. The bank's insurable interest is limited to the amount outstanding on the loan, which represents the maximum amount the bank could lose if the house is destroyed.

What Factors Affect the Extent of an Insurable Interest?

The fourth key question in determining insurable interest is what factors affect the extent of an insurable interest. The extent of any party's insurable interest in property is based on two elements: portion of property rights and duration of property rights. See the following box.

Factors Affecting the Extent of a Party's Insurable Interest in Property

1. *Portion of property rights*—The full owner of property has outright and full ownership of property and a corresponding insurable interest equal to the intrinsic value plus use value. When two or more parties own or use the property, the extent of each party's insurable interest might be only a portion of the full intrinsic value and/or use value.

2. *Duration of property rights*—The full owner of property has an ownership interest that extends for an unlimited time. This interest can be sold or willed to others. Under some circumstances, a party might have a present interest that terminates at some future point or a party might have a future interest but no present interest.

What Happens When Insurable Interests Overlap?

Under some circumstances, the sum of all insurable interests exceeds the property's value. Examples include mortgaged property and property jointly owned by two or more parties. The following discussion focuses on the nature and extent of various insurable interests.

Mortgaged Property

Frequently, a mortgage company and an individual both have an insurable interest in an insured property. The mortgage company's interest is the extent of the unpaid loan, and the owner's interest is the property's full value. Combined (and if actually paid), the amount of these two interest could greatly exceed the property's value. Many insurance policies contain provisions that insure the property's full value but pay each party only the amount of the party's insurable interest and nothing more.

Jointly Owned Property

When more than one person owns the same property, the nature of the ownership affects the extent of each party's insurable interest.[1]

- In **joint tenancy,** each tenant has a right of survivorship, that is, an automatic right to the share of the joint tenant who passes away.

Joint tenancy
The ownership of property by two or more persons, called joint tenants.

Because any one tenant could become the property's sole owner, each tenant has an insurable interest to the extent of the property's full value.

Tenancy by the entireties
A type of joint tenancy available only to a husband and wife.

Tenancy in common
The ownership of property, in equal or unequal shares, by two or more joint tenants who lack survivorship rights.

Tenancy in partnership
The joint ownership of property by a partnership.

- In **tenancy by the entireties,** each spouse has an insurable interest to the full extent of the property and cannot sell a share without the other spouse's consent.

- In a **tenancy in common,** joint tenants who lack survivorship rights own the property. Each party's insurable interest is limited to that owner's share of the property and upon death, ownership share is passed to the person(s) named in the decedent's will.

- In a **tenancy in partnership,** both the partnership entity and the individual partners have an insurable interest in property used by the partnership.

Condominium Property

A condominium owner (1) owns a unit and (2) has a tenancy-in-common interest in the areas that serve the owners of all units. The unit is technically nothing more than a box of air in a specified space. Ownership in these two elements combined may be sold, mortgaged, inherited, or otherwise treated like individually owned property. Although specifics vary, each owner normally has an insurable interest equal to the unit's total value and the percentage interest in the common areas, as well as any alterations and additions to a building by the unit owner.

Property Being Sold

The process of selling property involves transferring the title, loss exposures, and insurable interest in the property from the seller (who owns it before the transaction) to the buyer (who owns it after the transaction). During the selling process, both the seller and the buyer may have insurable interests in the property.

Fee simple estate
A full ownership interest in property with the unconditional right to dispose of it.

Life estate
An interest in property that lasts for a specific person's lifetime, after which the property passes to somebody else.

Future interest
A right to take possession of property at some specified time.

Trust
A legal entity, created to hold property, that consists of three legal parties: a grantor, a trustee, and beneficiaries.

Present and Future Interest in Property

In a **fee simple estate**, the property owner has an insurable interest in the property's full intrinsic value plus its use value for unlimited durations. In a **life estate,** the property interest lasts for a specific person's lifetime, after which the property passes to another. The present owner, the next owner, and the last owner generally have an insurable interest in the property. When a party has a **future interest** in property, over time that interest "matures" to full ownership. The holder of the interest has a present right to future possession of one property.

Property Held in Trust[2]

A **trust** is a legal entity, created to hold property, that consists of three legal parties:

1. A *grantor* (or *donor, creator,* or *settlor*) who establishes the trust and places assets in it

2. A *trustee* who has legal title and manages the trust property

3. *Beneficiaries* who receive income, assets, use, or other consideration as stipulated in the trust agreement. Beneficiaries are said to have equitable title to the trust property.

By allowing the legal title and the equitable title to be held by different persons or entities, trusts can potentially increase the number of parties having an insurable interest in trust property.

Households increasingly use trusts to reduce taxes, pass property to their heirs, and keep personal assets off the public record. A trust allows property to be passed down to heirs more quickly and at less cost than through a will. Under a trust agreement, assets can pass immediately from the grantor to the beneficiaries without having to go through the cost and public disclosure of probate.

The five key questions outlined in this section explain how the insurable interest requirement operates for property insurance. For coverage to apply, the party must be subject to financial loss, and an insurable interest must exist when the loss occurred. This requirement exists for several reasons. The nature and extent of the insurable interest can vary according to ownership, and if ownership interests overlap, specific policy provisions outlining the terms of each party's insurable interests would apply.

If a party has an insurable interest, and all other legal elements of a valid contract exist, the party would have a legally enforceable insurance contract. The next section examines the legal bases for the insurable interest requirement.

BASES FOR INSURABLE INTERESTS

An insurable interest, for purposes of property insurance, has one or more legal bases.

Legal Bases for Insurable Interest Ownership

- Property rights
- Contractual rights
- Potential legal liability for damage to specific property
- Factual expectancy
- Representative status

In evaluating the nature and extent of insurable interests in any particular property, the courts traditionally examined whether the insurable interest was based on ownership or some other legal right to the property.

Property Ownership Rights

The rights a party possesses regarding owned property are legally protected. For example, property owners have a legal right to sell, give away, and put property to use. The extent of legal ownership justifies the extent of insurable interest in the property.

The term **property** is commonly applied to tangible objects. However, property also includes the property's bundle of rights that have economic value. These rights are guaranteed and protected by law. Some rights pertain to tangible property and others to intangible property, such as copyrights, patents, trademarks, intellectual property, and corporate stock certificates.

Real property differs from personal property. Real property is land and anything permanently attached to the land (for example, buildings); embedded in the land (for example, minerals); or growing on the land. Sometimes, by virtue of real property ownership, someone might also have a legal interest in the real property owned by another.

Personal property is all property that is not real property.

Property and its associated rights can be owned by one party, known as the **sole owner**. Property can also be owned by several parties, each with one or more rights.

Contractual Rights

A contract is an agreement between two or more parties who make a set of promises enforceable by law. Generally, contractual rights, and related insurable interests, can be classified into two major categories:

1. *Contractual rights regarding persons.* One party to a contract has a claim against a second party but no claim against any *specific* property belonging to the second party. For example, if Jerry does not pay his credit card debt, the credit card company does not have the right to repossess a television set purchased with the credit card. The credit card company is an unsecured creditor. Unsecured creditors do not have insurable interest in debtors' property.

2. *Contractual rights regarding property.* One party to a contract has a claim on specific property held by the second party. For instance, If Jerry purchases an auto subject to a secured loan, the lender may repossess the car if Jerry fails to make payments. A contractual right generally creates an insurable interest in that property. In the case of secured property, the creditor's insurable interest is equal to the debt's remaining balance.

Potential Legal Liability for Damage to Specific Property

Sometimes property is not owned by a party but that party has legal responsibility for or a financial interest in the property. Consequently, that party has an insurable interest that may be covered by property insurance.

Property
The real estate, buildings, objects or articles, intangible assets, or rights with exchangeable value for which someone may claim legal ownership.

Real property
Land and anything that is permanently attached to, embedded in, or growing on the land.

Personal property
All property that is not real property.

Sole owner
The person who possesses all rights to the property.

Some *property* insurance covers potential damage to specific property owned by others when the insured is legally responsible for such damage.

Note the following examples:

• A hotelkeeper has an insurable interest in guests' property.

• A tenant has an insurable interest in the portion of the premises the tenant occupies.

• A contractor has an insurable interest in a building under construction, according to the terms of most construction contracts.

In these cases, the responsible party has an insurable interest based on its potential legal liability. The extent of that insurable interest is the property's full value, including the owner's use value.

Some property insurance policies provide "single-interest coverage" and apply *only* when the insured is legally responsible for damage to another party's property. Other policies ("dual-interest coverage") apply to any loss by a covered peril, even if the insured is not legally responsible.

One might argue that single-interest contracts, which provide coverage only when the insured is legally liable for damage to specific property of others, are liability insurance rather than property insurance. They are a hybrid, falling somewhat between property insurance and liability insurance. However, nearly all single-interest contracts are written on property insurance forms, are underwritten as property insurance, and are technically classified as property insurance.[3]

Factual Expectancy

Factual expectancy exists when a party experiences an economic advantage if the insured event does not occur or, conversely, economic harm if the event does occur.

A majority of states have accepted factual expectancy as a valid basis for an insurable interest. In these states, the insured does not have to establish a specific property right, a contractual right, or potential legal liability to prove insurable interest. The person only has to show potential financial harm resulting from the event to be insured. The focus is on the insured's economic position rather than on a legal interest.

As an example of factual expectancy without a legal property right, consider the situation in which a driver purchases a car, buys physical damage insurance on the car, has an accident resulting in damage to the car, and then discovers that the car had previously been stolen from somebody else. Because one person cannot legally obtain title to property owned by another, the driver could not legally own the car; therefore, the driver could have no insurable interest based on ownership rights. The great majority of courts dealing with such situations have held that the insured still has an insurable interest in the car based on factual expectancy of loss if the car is damaged or stolen.[4]

Factual expectancy
A situation in which a party experiences an economic advantage if the insured event does not occur or, conversely, economic harm if the event does occur.

Representative Status

One person who represents someone else may have an insurable interest by virtue of the representative status. For example,

- An agent may insure property in his or her name for the principal's benefit.
- A trustee may insure property in his or her name for the trust's benefit.
- A bailee may insure property in his or her name for the bailor's benefit.

In those situations, the party obtaining the insurance is not required to have an independent insurable interest in the property. The party derives its interest from its relationship with the party whom it represents. Although not essential, the insured's representative status is sometimes shown by inserting, after the name of the insured, phrases such as "for the benefit of _____," or "for whom it may concern."

SUMMARY

A party without an insurable interest at the time of the loss has no right to claim coverage under a property insurance policy. Insurable interest must exist at the time of the loss. Insurable interests are required by property insurance policies to prevent gambling, reduce intentional losses, and enforce the principle of indemnity. The extent of an insurable interest is affected both by the portion of property rights held by the insured and the length of time for which those rights exist. Overlapping insurable interests can also exist, sometimes adding up to more than the value of the property itself. This happens with mortgaged property, jointly owned property, condominium property, property being sold, property subject to present and future interests, and property held in trust.

The legal bases for insurable interests include property rights, contractual rights, potential legal liability, factual expectancy, and representative status.

To determine whether a given insurance policy applies to a given loss, one must first determine whether an enforceable insurance contract is in effect covering a party with an insurable interest. Then the insurance policy must be read to determine whether the loss itself is covered. Reading an insurance policy is the topic of Chapter 11.

CHAPTER NOTES

1. Property law is examined in more detail in another CPCU textbook.
2. This discussion contains excerpts from the following booklet: Joseph S. Harrington, CPCU, ARP, *Insuring the Personal Trust* (Wheaton, Ill.: American Association of Insurance Services, December 1999).
3. Many are inland marine forms, but others can be classified as crime insurance, auto physical damage insurance, or commercial property insurance.
4. John F. Dobbyn, *Insurance Law* (St. Paul, Minn.: West Publishing Company, 1996), p. 92.

Chapter 11

Direct Your Learning

Reading an Insurance Policy

After learning the subject matter of this chapter, you should be able to:

- Identify and describe the types of insurance policies.

- Identify the six parts of a property-liability insurance policy, and describe the purpose of each section.

- Explain the seven reasons why policies contain exclusions.

- Given a policy excerpt, identify which part of the policy (declarations, definitions, insuring agreements, exclusions, conditions, or miscellaneous provisions), the text might fall under.

- Identify the six questions that must be answered to pay a loss after it has occurred, and describe why each question must be answered before paying the claim.

Develop Your Perspective

What are the main topics covered in the chapter?

This chapter describes an insurance policy's physical structure; a policy's parts, provisions, and exclusions; and how to interpret a policy using the information in these sections.

Consider how the organization of these policy provisions differs between a self-contained policy and a modular policy.

- Why are these differences present?

Why is it important to know these topics?

Knowing how to read and interpret an insurance policy will enable you to determine whether a particular loss would be covered under the terms of the contract.

Review an auto insurance policy.

- What types of losses are covered?
- Where did you find this information?

How can you use this information?

Imagine that you are a claim representative assigned to an auto accident claim.

- How would you begin your coverage investigation?
- What questions would help you determine whether the loss was covered under the policy?

Chapter 11

Reading an Insurance Policy

An insurance policy is the complete written contract of insurance and communicates the details of an agreement between the insurer and the insured. Every risk management or insurance professional must be able to interpret the complex legal documents found in an insurance policy. Many different types of insurance policies exist, and each has its own distinct advantages in providing coverage. By carefully examining the structure of the property-liability insurance policy, one can understand how the policy provisions grant, clarify, qualify, or eliminate coverage.

> One way that this text illustrates property-liability insurance concepts is by providing excerpts from various insurance policies along with interpretations and explanations of the concepts. These excerpts are meant to acquaint readers with the precise language that policies use to convey their meanings. Because many different excerpts could similarly illustrate the concepts presented, the excerpts are not meant to be memorized.

PHYSICAL CONSTRUCTION OF INSURANCE CONTRACTS

Insurance policies are assembled in several ways. This section discusses an insurance policy's arrangement as a physical document, explaining each of the written components that is likely to be found in, attached to, or incorporated by reference into, any insurance policy.

Numerous terms may be used to describe an insurance policy's components. Sometimes, such terms are not consistently used by insurance practitioners, but the following box lists the definitions of frequently used terms.

Insurance Policy Terms

- *Insurance contract*, or *contract*—generally, means policy. The term "contract" emphasizes the insurance agreement's legal nature .
- *Line of insurance*—the term "line" is loosely used to refer simply to different types of insurance.

Continued on next page.

- *Monoline policy*—policy that covers a single line of insurance or part of a single line.
- *Package policy*—policy that covers more than one line of insurance, such as the homeowners policy that contains property and liability insurance.
- *Form*—one of the major documents within an insurance policy. In some cases, one form constitutes the entire policy, except for a declarations page (discussed later).
- *Endorsement*—document that modifies one or more policy forms. In life and health insurance, the term "rider" is used instead of endorsement.
- *Coverage part*—one or more forms that, together, provide coverage for a line of insurance. In some policies, a section of the policy form that provides a particular coverage is also referred to as a part. For example, the liability section of the Personal Auto Policy is captioned Part A—Liability Coverage.

Self-Contained Versus Modular Policies

Self-contained policy
A policy that uses a single document to indicate the agreements between the applicant and the insurer.

A **self-contained policy** is a single, complete-by-itself document containing all the agreements between the applicant and the insurer. The policy identifies the insurer and the insured, "the subject matter of the insurance," and the amounts, terms, and conditions of coverage. Endorsements are occasionally used to add optional coverages.

A self-contained policy is appropriate for insuring loss exposures that are similar among insureds. For example, private passenger auto insurance typically is provided in a self-contained policy that is used to insure all of an insurer's individual auto policyholders throughout a state—and maybe even in several different states. When needed, a towing and labor costs coverage endorsement or a customizing equipment coverage endorsement, for example, might be added.

Modular policy
A policy that combines several documents to indicate the agreements between the applicant and insurer; designed around one basic document (such as a policy jacket or common conditions form).

A **modular policy** is a mix-and-match set of components, designed around one basic policy component (such as a "policy jacket"). This policy jacket—includes conditions, definitions, or other provisions that apply to, or match, all other documents used with it. The policy jacket is sometimes referred to as a "common conditions form."

The modular approach is commonly used in commercial insurance. Exhibit 11-1 illustrates the structure of an Insurance Services Office (ISO) commercial package policy. Every policy contains (1) common policy conditions and (2) common declarations. If one type of insurance is covered, the policy is completed by adding the necessary forms to make up that *coverage part*. For example, if commercial property insurance is provided, the *commercial property coverage part* includes a commercial property declarations page, the necessary commercial property coverage forms, and a commercial property conditions form. This combination of documents would be a *monoline policy*, which is a complete policy covering one type of insurance: commercial property.

EXHIBIT 11-1

Components of the ISO Commercial Package Policy (CPP)
(Example of a modular policy)

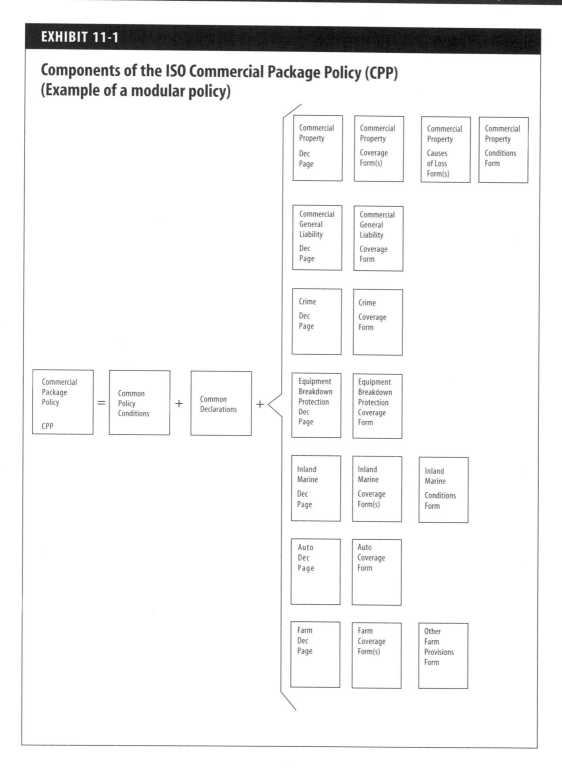

An advantage of the modular approach is that a single policy can include several types of insurance. The resulting combination is not a monoline policy but a *commercial package policy*.

The various coverages are not *required* to be combined in a commercial package policy. Similar coverage could be provided with separate self-contained commercial property policies, commercial general liability policies, crime policies, and so forth. However, as compared with self-contained policies, the modular approach to policy construction has the following advantages:

1. Carefully designed and coordinated provisions in the various forms minimize the possibility of gaps and overlaps that might exist when several monoline policies are used.
2. Consistent terminology, definitions, and policy language make coverage interpretation easier.
3. Fewer forms are required to meet a wide range of needs.
4. Underwriting is simplified because much of the same basic information that must be analyzed applies to all lines of insurance.
5. Adverse selection problems can be reduced when the same insurer provides several types of insurance for the same insured.
6. Insurers often give a package discount when several coverages are included in the same policy.

Preprinted Policies

Most insurance policies are assembled from one or more preprinted forms and endorsements. Preprinted policies are ready-made, off-the-shelf policies, developed for use with many different insureds.

When insurers write a policy using preprinted forms, they send the insured the preprinted policy and a declarations page that indicates the form number or numbers and edition dates of the company's form or forms that apply to this policy.

When an insurer uses preprinted forms, the insurance company and its producer generally do not need to keep in their files a complete duplicate of each policyholder's entire policy. All that is filed is the declarations page, and what is actually filed may be an electronic file rather than a sheet of paper. Details of applicable coverage can be obtained, whenever necessary, by examining copies of the preprinted forms referenced in the declarations. Of course, the policyholder receives a complete written contract.

Standard Versus Nonstandard Policies

An insurer might adopt standard policies, also used by other insurers, or develop its own nonstandard policies. A nonstandard policy drafted or adapted by one insurer is sometimes referred to as a *company-specific form*.

Insurance service and advisory organizations, such as ISO and the American Association of Insurance Services (AAIS), have developed **standard insurance forms** that are available for use by individual insurance companies. These standard forms are usually accompanied by a portfolio of coordinated endorsements that reflect necessary state variations or customize coverage. Because they are widely used, standard forms provide benchmarks ("the standard approach") against which nonstandard forms can be evaluated. Much of the material in this text describes the standard forms' coverage provisions.

Standard insurance form
A preprinted insurance form that an insurance service or advisory organization has developed.

Many insurance companies have developed their own company-specific preprinted contracts, especially for high-volume types of insurance (such as auto or homeowners) or for coverages in which an insurer specializes (such as recreational vehicle insurance). These are **nonstandard insurance forms** because policy wording and content can vary from the provisions used by other insurers or from those developed by insurance advisory organizations. Many nonstandard policies contain coverage enhancements not found in standard policies.

Nonstandard insurance form
A preprinted form that includes wording and/or provisions that vary from what is used in a standard form.

The wording of preprinted forms and endorsements is carefully chosen by the insurer (or it is developed by a service organization and then adopted by the insurer). Applying the doctrine of adhesion, courts of law tend to interpret any ambiguities in policy language in favor of the insured who did not have an opportunity to choose the policy wording.

Manuscript Policies

In contrast to preprinted policies, manuscript policies are custom contracts developed for one specific insured—or for a small group of insureds with common unique coverage needs. A **manuscript policy** can be specifically drafted or selected for a particular need, such as products liability coverage for a manufacturer of cardiac pacemakers. Usually, most manuscript policy provisions are not individually composed as in nonstandard policies but are adapted from wording previously developed and used in standard contracts or other insurance contracts. As a whole, a manuscript policy is a one-of-a-kind document being used for one or more insureds in some cases. For example, a manuscript policy might be developed to meet the specific needs of a particular association or group of businesses.

Manuscript policy
A policy that is developed to meet a unique coverage need; generally a one-of-a-kind policy.

A manuscript policy's wording is generally developed through negotiation between the insurer and the insured. When the parties develop contract language together, they are equally accountable if the court must step in to interpret contract ambiguity.

Related Documents

The preceding paragraphs have described insurance policies' basic formats. Several other documents can become part of the policy, either by being physically attached or by being referred to within the policy. Examples include the completed application for insurance, endorsements, the insurer's bylaws, the terms of relevant statutes, and other miscellaneous documents.

An insurance application is the documented request for coverage, whether given orally, in writing, or over the Internet. The application contains information about the insured and the loss exposures presented to the insurer. Underwriters and raters use the application to price the policy. The insurer will usually keep the completed application to preserve the representations made by the insured, which sometimes prove to be misleading or false at some future date. In some jurisdictions, some statutes explicitly require that any written application be made part of the policy for some types of insurance.

Other documents that are sometimes part of a policy are the endorsements. An endorsement is a provision that adds to, deletes, replaces, or modifies another document in an insurance policy. Terms that might be used instead of endorsement include "policy change," "addition," "amendment," and "codicil." Alternatively, an endorsement might have only a descriptive title, such as "Loss Payable Clause."

An endorsement may be a preprinted, computer-printed, typewritten, or handwritten line, sentence, paragraph, or set of paragraphs on a separate sheet of paper attached to other documents forming the policy. An endorsement may take the form of a handwritten note in the margin of a basic policy, form, or coverage part, dated and initialed by an insured and the insurer's authorized representative.

Endorsements often are intended to modify a more basic policy form. This means that the provisions in an endorsement often differ from the provisions in the basic policy to which it is attached—which can raise questions about interpreting an insurance policy. Two general rules of interpretation apply:

1. An endorsement takes precedence over any conflicting terms in the policy to which it is attached.
2. A handwritten endorsement supersedes a computer-printed or typewritten one.

Agreements between insurer and insured—especially handwritten alterations—tend to reflect true intent more accurately than do other, preprinted policy terms.

In certain circumstances, the insurer's bylaws or the provisions of pertinent statutes are incorporated into an insurance contract. For example, the policyholders of mutual and reciprocal insurers typically have some rights and duties associated with managing the insurer's operations, and these rights and duties are specified in the policy.

Policies providing workers compensation insurance or auto no-fault insurance are among those that typically provide benefits specified by state statute. The relevant statutes usually are not printed in the insurance policy; rather, they are incorporated by reference. For example, the standard workers compensation policy includes the following provisions:

We Will Pay

We will pay promptly when due the benefits required of you by the workers compensation law.

Workers Compensation Law

Workers Compensation Law means the workers or workmen's compensation law and occupational disease law of each state or territory named in item 3. A. of the Information Page. It includes any amendments to that law which are in effect during the policy period. It does not include any federal workers or workmen's compensation law, any federal occupational disease law or the provisions of any law that provide nonoccupational disability benefits.[1]

"Information Page" refers to the declarations page of this particular policy.

Insurance policies sometimes incorporate the insurer's rating manual (or the insurer's rules and rates, whether found in the manual or elsewhere) not by including the entire manual but by referring to it in the policy language. For example, the ISO Commercial General Liability Coverage Form contains the following provision:

Premium Audit

We will compute all premiums for this Coverage Part in accordance with our rules and rates.[2]

Although the rules and rates themselves do not appear in the policy, they become, in this way, part of the contract. The applicable rules and rates often have been approved by an insurance regulator.

Subject to statutory or regulatory constraints, insurance policies may incorporate virtually any documents. Some frequently used miscellaneous documents include premium notes (promissory notes, accepted by the insurer in lieu of a cash premium payment), inspection reports, and specification sheets or operating manuals relating to safety equipment or procedures.

In some situations, an insurer and an applicant might agree that the coverage provided by a particular property or liability insurance policy is conditioned on the use of certain procedures or safety equipment. For example, a set of operating instructions or a manual of specifications can be incorporated into the policy by reference and used to define precisely and conveniently the agreed-upon procedures or equipment.

States are increasingly requiring insurance companies to provide a "notice to policyholders," informing them of significant changes when an insurance policy is revised. In other cases, insurers are required to furnish policyholders with documents summarizing the coverage options available to insureds and choices that must be made. These informational documents generally are not part of the policy contract as such.

INSURANCE POLICY CONTENT

This section of the chapter examines the types of provisions contained in an insurance policy. Every property-liability insurance policy provision can be placed into the following six categories, depending on the purpose it serves:

Six Parts of the Property-Liability Insurance Policy

1. Declarations
2. Definitions
3. Insuring agreements
4. Exclusions
5. Conditions
6. Miscellaneous provisions

Policies usually contain several "Sections," or "Coverages," and often a variety of headings and subheadings.

The following discussion is not intended to describe the labeled sections of an insurance policy, but rather the *characteristics* of individual policy provisions regardless of the policy section or heading under which any specific provision is located.

Declarations

Declarations refers to the portion of the policy containing information that was "declared" by the insured on the insurance application, along with the insurance company's "declaration" about what coverage it provides. Insurance policy declarations typically contain not only information that has been "declared" but also information unique to a particular policy.

The declarations (sometimes called the "Information Page") typically appear as the first page(s) in an insurance policy, and contain the following information:

- Policy number
- Policy inception and expiration dates
- Name of the insurance company
- Name of the insurance agent
- Name of the insured(s)
- Mailing address of the insured
- Physical address and description of the covered property or operations
- Numbers and edition dates of all attached forms and endorsements

- Dollar amounts of applicable policy limits
- Dollar amounts of applicable deductibles
- Names of persons or organizations whose additional interests are covered (for example, a mortgagee, a loss payee, or an additional insured)
- Premium

Sometimes policy forms or endorsements also contain information that qualifies as declarations. This information is sometimes called a schedule. For example, an endorsement providing glass coverage might contain either a narrative description or a diagram of the covered glass.

Definitions

Another part of a property-liability insurance policy is the "Definitions." Many policies or forms contain a section titled "Definitions," which generally defines terms used throughout the entire policy or form. Sometimes a Definitions section appears near the beginning of the policy, sometimes within the text, and sometimes as a glossary. Policies typically use **boldface** type or "quotation marks" to distinguish words and phrases that are defined elsewhere in the policy.

Many modern policies refer to the insurer as "we" and the named insured as "you," and such personal pronouns are used extensively throughout these policies. "You" and "we," together with related pronouns such as "us," "our," and "your," often are defined in an untitled preamble to the policy rather than in a Definitions section.

Words and phrases defined within a policy have a special meaning when they are used within that particular insurance contract. Undefined words and phrases are interpreted according to the following rules of contract interpretation:

- Everyday words are given their ordinary meaning.
- Technical words are given their technical meaning.
- Words with an established legal meaning are given their legal meaning.
- Consideration is also given to the local, cultural, and trade-usage meanings of words, if applicable.

Insuring Agreements

An **insuring agreement** is any insurance policy statement indicating, under some circumstances, that the insurer will make a loss payment or provide a service. Following the declarations, and possibly preceded by a section containing definitions, the body of most insurance policies begins with an "Insuring Agreement."

A policy can have more than one insuring agreement. Some policies provide more than one "coverage," each coverage based on an insuring agreement. Examples include the Personal Auto Policy, which typically provides

Insuring agreement
An insurance policy statement indicating, under specific circumstances, that the insurer will make a loss payment or provide a service.

"liability," "medical payments," "uninsured motorists," and "damage to your auto" coverages; and the homeowners policy, which typically provides coverages for "dwelling," "other structures," "personal property," "loss of use," "personal liability," and "medical payments to others."

The term "insuring agreement" most often is applied to statements that introduce a coverage section of the policy. However, "insuring agreement" is also an entirely appropriate label for statements introducing coverage extensions, additional coverages, supplementary payments, and so forth. Even relatively obscure unlabeled statements within declarations, definitions, exclusions, or conditions can serve as insuring agreements.

Introductory Insuring Agreement

The insuring agreements that introduce a coverage section of a policy (introductory insuring agreements) *broadly* state what the insurer agrees to do under the contract, subject to clarification elsewhere in the policy. Insuring agreements usually contain one or more defined terms. Someone cannot fully understand an insuring agreement without examining any defined terms it uses because those definitions might further define the insuring agreement. For example, a workers compensation provision might state that the insurer will pay benefits required by the workers compensation law. Therefore, this law will affect the policy terms.

Whether long or short, introductory insuring agreements merely state the insurer's obligations in relatively broad terms. The full scope of coverage cannot be determined without examining the rest of the policy, because the insurer's obligations are invariably clarified or modified by other policy provisions.

Comprehensive Versus Limited in Scope

Insuring agreements can be divided into two broad categories.

Named-perils, specified-perils, or specified-causes-of-loss coverage
Coverage in a property insurance policy restricted to the perils (causes of loss) identified in the policy.

1. *Comprehensive, all-purpose insuring agreements* describe extremely broad, unrestricted coverage that applies to virtually all causes of loss or to virtually all situations. This broad coverage is both clarified and narrowed by exclusions, definitions, and other policy provisions.

2. *Limited or single-purpose insuring agreements* restrict coverage to certain causes of loss or to certain situations. Exclusions, definitions, and other policy provisions serve to clarify, narrow, and sometimes broaden the coverage.

For *property insurance*, insuring agreements fall into two categories:

Basic-form coverage
Property insurance coverage against a list of named perils.

Broad-form coverage
Property insurance coverage against the named perils in the Basic Form and additional named perils.

1. **Named-perils, specified-perils,** or **specified-causes-of-loss coverage**
   a. **Basic-form coverage**—provides protection against a list of named causes of loss
   b. **Broad-form coverage**—provides protection against the named causes of loss in the basic form and additional named causes of loss

2. **Special-form coverage**—provides protection against causes of loss that the form does not specifically exclude. This comprehensive approach invariably covers broad-form causes of loss as well as additional causes of loss that are not otherwise listed in the broad or basic forms.

Special-form coverage
Property insurance coverage against perils that the form does not specifically exclude.

As evidenced by their names, these categories are determined by how the *covered causes of loss* (perils) are described. For example, the federal Standard Flood Insurance Policy illustrates a single-purpose named-peril insuring agreement. If a policy says the insurer will pay for "direct physical loss by or from flood," then coverage applies for loss to covered property only if this listed peril (a flood) caused the loss. Sometimes, a homeowners insurance policy insuring agreement for insured property restricts coverage to only losses arising from a limited number of named perils, a basic-form coverage. A broad form might expand this coverage by also covering damage from additional named perils that are not covered under the basic form. A special-form policy might cover all damage related to the covered property, except damage specifically excluded.

For *liability* insurance, like property insurance, coverage is also limited or broad. In a single-purpose insurance agreement (which uses specific policy language to define the policy terms), coverage applies to a limited number of incidents. On the other hand, comprehensive liability insurance agreements are much broader and do not limit coverage to a particular location, to some specified operation, or to any particular activity. Additional policy provisions, such as exclusions, limit the coverage on these policies.

Insuring Agreements for Extended, Additional, Supplemental Coverages

Many insurance policies include supplemental, more-or-less secondary, coverages, along with the main coverage in the insuring agreement. These coverages are labeled by various headings such as "coverage extensions," "additional coverages," or "supplementary payments."

Generally, a "coverage extension" *extends* a portion of a basic policy coverage to apply to a type of property or loss that would not otherwise be covered. "Additional coverage" *adds* a type of coverage not otherwise provided. "Supplementary payments" *clarify* the extent of coverage for certain expenses in liability insurance. All of these policy areas are considered insuring agreements. However, these labels can vary from policy to policy.

For example, one policy's additional coverages might cover debris removal following a covered loss. This additional coverage applies for only a limited dollar amount or a limited amount of time, and it covers loss consequences that might not otherwise be within the scope of other insuring agreements.

Other Provisions Functioning as Insuring Agreements

Other policy provisions that grant or restore coverage otherwise excluded, and therefore serve as insuring agreements, might appear within a definition, as an exception to an exclusion, or elsewhere in the policy.

Definition

For example, the insuring agreement of the ISO Commercial General Liability (CGL) policy provides broad liability coverage, but this broad coverage is restricted by an auto exclusion, which reads in part as follows:

> [This insurance does not apply to] "Bodily injury" or "property damage" arising out of the ownership, maintenance, use or entrustment to others of any . . . "auto" . . . owned or operated by or rented or loaned to any insured. Use includes operation and "loading or unloading".[3]

The definition of "auto" reads as follows:

> "Auto" means a land motor vehicle, trailer or semitrailer designed for travel on public roads, including any attached machinery or equipment. But "auto" does not include "mobile equipment".[4]

The CGL insuring agreement is broad enough to include claims involving liability for motor vehicle accidents. The exclusion removes coverage for autos, but the definition of "auto" states that mobile equipment is not an auto. The *effect* of the last sentence in the definition, therefore, is to grant coverage (actually, to restore coverage otherwise excluded) for liability arising out of mobile equipment (subject to other policy provisions). ("Mobile equipment" has its own long definition, which includes such things as bulldozers and farm tractors.) An insurance practitioner might refer to the "mobile equipment coverage" of the CGL, even though the most specific grant of coverage appears within a definition. For these reasons, the final sentence of the above definition technically qualifies as an insuring agreement, although it is not often referred to that way in practice.

Exception to an Exclusion

Exceptions to exlusions can further define the terms of the insurance contract. For example, the CGL also grants liquor liability coverage for most businesses through an exception to the liquor liability exclusion. The entire exclusion, which concludes with the exception, reads as follows:

> [This insurance does not apply to:] "Bodily injury" or "property damage" for which any insured may be held liable by reason of:
>
> (1) Causing or contributing to the intoxication of any person;
>
> (2) The furnishing of alcoholic beverages to a person under the legal drinking age or under the influence of alcohol; or
>
> (3) Any statute, ordinance or regulation relating to the sale, gift, distribution or use of alcoholic beverages.
>
> This exclusion applies only if you are in the business of manufacturing, distributing, selling, serving or furnishing alcoholic beverages.[5]

Because of the exception in the final sentence of this exclusion, coverage applies to office parties and other liquor-related situations for businesses that are not *in the alcoholic beverage business*. This provision is frequently referred to as "host liquor liability coverage," and it is, in effect, an insuring agreement.

Exclusions

Another part of the property-liability insurance policy is the exclusions. Exclusions have been defined as "policy provisions that state what the insurer does not *intend* to cover." The word "intend" is important: The primary function of exclusions is to *clarify* the coverages granted by the insurer, not to take away coverage from the insured. Specifying what the insurer does *not* intend to cover is a proven way of clarifying what aspects the insurer *does* intend to cover. Any exclusion may serve more than one purpose and help keep premiums at a reasonable level. See the following box.

Seven Purposes of Exclusions

1. *Eliminate coverage for uninsurable loss exposures*

    Some exposures (such as intentional acts) possess few if any of the ideal character-istics of an insurable loss exposure. Exclusions allow insurers to preclude coverage for these exposures.

2. *Assist in managing moral hazards*

    Moral hazards are defects or weaknesses in human character that lead some people to exaggerate losses or intentionally cause them to collect insurance proceeds. Exclusions help insurers minimize these types of exposures.

3. *Assist in managing attitudinal (morale) hazards*

    Attitudinal hazards, also called morale hazards, exist when the likelihood or severity of a loss is increased because a person is not as careful as he or she should be. Some exclusions assist in managing morale hazards by making the insureds themselves bear the losses that result from their own carelessness.

4. *Reduce likelihood of coverage duplications*

    In some cases, two insurance policies provide coverage for the same loss. Exclusions ensure that two policies work together to provide complementary, not duplicate, coverage and that insureds are not paying duplicate premiums.

5. *Eliminate coverages not needed by the typical insured*

    Exclusions sometimes allow insurers to exclude coverage for exposures not faced by the typical insured. This means that all insureds would not have to share the costs of covering the substantial exposures of relatively few insureds.

6. *Eliminate coverages requiring special treatment*

    Exclusions eliminate the coverages that require rating, underwriting, loss control, or reinsurance treatment substantially different from what is normally applied to the insurance contract.

7. *Assist in keeping premiums reasonable*

    Exclusions allow insurers to preclude risks that would otherwise drive up costs. By keeping costs down, insurers can offer premiums that a sufficiently large number of insurance buyers will consider reasonable.

Eliminate Coverage for Uninsurable Loss Exposures

The first purpose of exclusions is to eliminate coverage for exposures that are considered uninsurable by private insurers. Nearly all property and liability insurance policies exclude losses arising out of war. (The main exception is the "war risks coverage" often available in ocean marine insurance policies covering vessels or cargoes, even those that might pass through war zones, but at appropriately higher rates.)

Other common exclusions of uninsurable exposures involve losses due to intentional acts of the insured or other nonaccidental events, nuclear radiation, earthquake, flood damage to fixed-location property, normal wear and tear, and "inherent vice." (*Inherent vice* is a quality inherent in an object that tends to destroy it, as when iron rusts, wood rots, or rubber deteriorates.)

Each of those excluded exposures fails to sufficiently possess at least one of the ideal characteristics of an insurable loss exposure. War and nuclear losses involve an incalculable catastrophe potential. Inherent vice and similar perils are not accidental or fortuitous in nature but are predictable, expected, and, in varying degrees, controllable by the insured.

Assist in Managing Moral Hazards

Exclusions can help manage moral hazards to the extent that they eliminate coverage for the insured's intentional acts that are essentially uninsurable. One such example is found in the liability section of the ISO Homeowners Policy:

> **Coverage E—Personal Liability and Coverage F—Medical Payments to Others**... do not apply to... "bodily injury" or "property damage" which is expected or intended by an "insured".... [6]

This exclusion eliminates coverage for blatantly intentional harmful results. Other conditions and miscellaneous provisions make it difficult to exaggerate losses successfully.

Assist in Managing Attitudinal Hazards

Some exclusions assist in managing attitudinal, or morale, hazards by making insureds themselves bear the losses that result from their own carelessness. A good example is the following exclusion, which appears not under the "Exclusions" heading, but within the "freezing" peril of the ISO Homeowners Policy:

> [We cover direct physical loss to...property...caused by...] freezing of a plumbing, heating, air conditioning or automatic fire protective sprinkler system or of a household appliance but only if you have used reasonable care to:
> (1) Maintain heat in the building; or
> (2) Shut off the power supply and drain all systems and appliances of water.
>
> However, if the building is protected by an automatic fire protective sprinkler system, you must use reasonable care to continue the water supply and maintain heat in the building for coverage to apply. [7]

Reduce Likelihood of Coverage Duplications

It usually is unnecessary and wasteful if two insurance policies provide coverage for the same loss. It is unnecessary because coverage under one policy is all that is needed to indemnify the insured (unless policy restrictions or limits of insurance preclude full recovery). It is wasteful because, at least in theory, each policy providing coverage for certain types of losses includes a related premium charge (which is admittedly negligible in some cases).

Consider these examples:

• Personal liability policies usually exclude losses arising from business activities.

• "Commercial property" insurance policies typically exclude autos from the description of covered property because auto physical damage insurance is readily available and widely purchased.

Eliminate Coverages Not Needed by the Typical Insured

A fifth purpose of exclusions is to eliminate coverages that are not needed by the typical purchaser of that type of insurance. For example, the typical individual does not own or operate private aircraft, use the family auto as a taxicab for hire, or rent portions of the family home for storage of others' business property—and coverage for such exposures is excluded by typical auto and homeowners policies.

People who do have these exposures may be able to obtain coverage separately, usually by paying additional premiums. Requiring all insureds to share the costs of covering the substantial exposures of relatively few insureds would be inequitable. However, that is exactly what would happen if, for example, their personal auto policies were to automatically provide coverage whenever a covered auto is used as a taxicab.

Insurers are not always permitted to exclude coverage for exposures not faced by the typical purchaser. For example, insurers might like to exclude auto liability coverage for drivers who have accidents while driving under the influence of alcohol or narcotics, but state insurance regulators would be very unlikely to approve such a policy exclusion because it would tend to eliminate a source of recovery for the innocent victims of drunken drivers. The effect is that auto policyholders who never drink and drive are required, in effect, to share the costs of accidents caused by those who do.

Eliminate Coverages Requiring Special Treatment

A sixth purpose of exclusions is to eliminate coverages requiring special rating, underwriting, loss control, or reinsurance treatment substantially different from what is normally applied to the contract containing the exclusion. These are examples:

• Many standard policies covering valuable personal property exclude coverage for losses occurring while the property is on exhibition at a convention or trade fair. Paintings, stamps, coins, and other collectors' items sometimes are displayed in exhibits open to the public, and property on exhibit is especially vulnerable to loss by theft and other perils. When the exposure exists, an underwriter may agree to provide coverage for an additional premium.

- General liability policies usually exclude the professional liability exposure. Physicians, attorneys, and other professionals may purchase professional liability insurance to cover losses arising out of errors or omissions in their professional activities.

Assist in Keeping Premiums Reasonable

A seventh purpose of exclusions is to assist in keeping premiums at a level that a sufficiently large number of insurance buyers will consider reasonable. This goal is shared by insurers, rate regulators, and consumers alike.

All exclusions serve this purpose to some extent. However, it is the primary reason for some exclusions, and it is the only reason for others. For example, consider the following exclusions from the "damage to your auto" section of the Personal Auto Policy:

[We will not pay for damage due and confined to]: . . .

c. Mechanical or electrical breakdown or failure; or

d. Road damage to tires.[8]

The excluded losses are not exactly uninsurable. Auto dealers, tire shops, and various other organizations offer insurance-like service warranties covering just such losses. However, few people would be willing to pay the premiums necessary to include in their auto insurance policies coverage for such predictable losses. An insurance policy could probably be priced to reflect the expected costs of mechanical breakdowns or tire losses, but the insured would end up paying the projected costs of maintenance plus the insurer's expenses in administering insurance to cover the maintenance costs.

Conditions

Another part of the property-liability policy is the conditions. A policy **condition** is any provision that qualifies an otherwise enforceable promise of the insurer. Some policy conditions are found in a section of the policy titled "Conditions," while others may be found in the forms, endorsements, or other documents that together constitute the entire insurance contract.

In a policy's insuring agreement, the insurer promises to pay to the insured, to pay on behalf of the insured, to defend the insured, and/or to provide various additional services. However, those are not unconditional promises. The insurer promises to pay, furnish a defense, or provide other services that are enforceable *only if* an insured event occurs *and if* the insured has fulfilled its contractual duties as specified in the policy conditions.

Condition
A policy provision that qualifies an otherwise enforceable promise of the insurer.

Examples of common policy conditions include the insured's obligation to pay premiums, report losses promptly, provide appropriate documentation for losses, cooperate with the insurer in any legal proceedings, and refrain from jeopardizing an insurer's rights to recover from responsible third parties (under subrogation actions). If the insured does not do these things, then the insurer may be released from any obligation to perform some or all of its otherwise enforceable promises.

Miscellaneous Provisions

Insurance policies often contain provisions that do not strictly qualify as declarations, definitions, insuring agreements, exclusions, or conditions. They may deal with the relationship between the insured and the insurer, or they may help to establish working procedures for implementing the policy, but they do not have the force of conditions. Consequently, if the insured does not follow the procedures specified in the miscellaneous provisions, normally the insurer must still fulfill its contractual promises.

One example of a miscellaneous provision is a valuation provision that sets standards for measuring losses under the policy. Some miscellaneous provisions are unique to particular types of insurers, as in the following examples:

- A policy issued by a mutual insurance company is likely to describe each insured's right to vote in the election of the board of directors.

- A policy issued by a reciprocal insurer is likely to specify the attorney-in-fact's authority to carry out its powers on the insured's behalf.

ANALYZING AN INSURANCE POLICY

A common goal in analyzing an insurance policy is determining the answers to these two important questions:

1. *Before a loss:* What losses would be covered?
2. *After a loss:* Was the loss covered?

Ideally, every policyholder should read his or her policy as soon as he or she receives it to have a basic understanding of what losses would be covered. (However, most insureds do not read their insurance policies until after a loss—if then. At that time, the policy often is scrutinized in an attempt to find coverage for the loss.)

Insurers' claim representatives ask similar questions in applying coverage to a known loss. Insurance agents and brokers may follow the same approach in answering "What if?" questions raised by an insured (and underwriters may do so when dealing with producers' questions or evaluating an application).

Before-Loss Policy Analysis

Determining whether and how much coverage applies to a loss can be a formidable task. Analyzing a policy is much more difficult when no particular loss has occurred. Before-loss policy analysis requires a wide range of skills, including the following:

- Understanding the alternative ways in which insurance policies customarily describe coverage in addressing loss exposures
- Identifying and evaluating insurance policy provisions that depart from the customary approach
- Understanding the exposure—to which the policy will apply

The most effective after-loss policy analysis requires an understanding of how insurance policies are constructed and interpreted. The remainder of this chapter describes a basic approach to after-loss policy analysis.

After-Loss Policy Analysis

After a loss that might be covered has occurred, someone can analyze a policy by answering the following six questions:

1. Does an enforceable insurance contract exist?
2. Did the loss occur to an insured party who has an insurable interest?
3. Do policy conditions affect coverage?
4. Has an insured event occurred?
5. What dollar amount, if any, is payable?
6. Do any external factors affect the claim?

Before deciding *how much* should be paid, determine *whether* the claim is covered. The two major questions to answer are the following: "Is it covered?" And, if so, "For how much?" "Evaluating dollar amounts payable is usually pointless until it is determined whether the claim is covered at all. This elementary point seems obvious, yet it is sometimes overlooked. In one such case, the insured's business tools were stolen from his auto, which was covered under an auto insurance policy. The insured presented the claim to a claim representative who agreed to pay only $200 of the loss because the policy in question included $200 coverage for "personal effects." Only later did the claim representative realize that business tools do not qualify as personal effects.

However, when it is clear that the amount payable would be zero *if* the loss is covered—perhaps because the policy's deductible is larger than the amount of the loss, then there is no need to determine whether coverage applies.

Question 1: Does an Enforceable Insurance Contract Exist?

Because most insurance claims involve an enforceable insurance contract, it can be too easy to overlook this important question. In some cases, a contract was never formed, perhaps because one of the elements of a contract was lacking (for example, consideration did not exist because the policyholder did not pay the premium when due). The contract might be void or voidable by either party, or it might have been canceled. The contract might be unenforceable because it serves a purpose contrary to the public interest. Genuine assent to the contract might be lacking because of fraud, mistake, duress, or undue influence.

Question 2: Did The Loss Occur to an Insured Party Who Has an Insurable Interest?

Only a party with an insurable interest can enforce a property insurance contract. The insurable interest must exist at the time of the loss, and the extent of any party's insurable interest might be limited to some portion of the property's full value.

The next chapter discusses various ways of identifying the parties insured in a policy.

Question 3: Do Any Policy Conditions Affect Coverage?

Many policy conditions outline the duties of the insurer and the insured. Policy conditions should be taken very seriously because violating a policy condition might change the coverage on an otherwise-covered claim.

Policy conditions clarify important points. For example,

- One group of policy conditions, such as "payment of premium" provisions, deals contractually with one of the key elements necessary to create an enforceable contract.

- A second group of policy conditions identifies insured parties. Various other issues might also be addressed, such as how coverage applies to one insured party when another insured party breaches a policy condition.

- A third group of policy conditions stipulates when and where the loss must occur. Coverage triggers and provisions affecting coverage for losses occurring outside the normal coverage territory are also detailed.

- A fourth group of policy conditions identifies with maintenance issues: the insurer's right to inspect covered premises and audit the insured's books, the rights of either or both parties to cancel the contract (and how any unearned premium is handled), coverage modifications and how they are made, and increases in hazard.

- A fifth and sixth group of policy conditions deal with the post-loss duties of both parties to the contract: the insured and the insurer.

- A seventh group of policy conditions involves claim disputes and how they can be resolved.

- An eighth group of policy conditions addresses the post-loss matters of subrogation and salvage.

These provisions that may seem unimportant can critically affect the coverage available for any claim, and they must always be considered.

Question 4: Has an Insured Event Occurred?

Coverage does not apply unless an insured event occurs. For property insurance, an insured event requires the following elements:

- Covered property
- Covered cause of loss
- No exclusion applies
- Covered consequences
- Covered location
- Covered time period

For liability insurance, an insured event requires the following elements:

- Covered activity
- Alleged responsibility to pay covered damages
- No exclusion applies
- Covered consequences
- Covered location
- Covered time period

Question 5: What Dollar Amount—if Any—Is Payable?

After determining that the loss is covered, the next question is, "How much is payable?" For property insurance, the amount payable is affected by several issues. First, the valuation provision in the policy indicates whether property is valued on the basis of its replacement cost, its depreciated actual cash value, or some other basis. The amount payable might be affected by applicable policy limits and can be limited by a coinsurance provision or other insurance-to-value provisions. Also, a deductible might be subtracted from the amount otherwise payable. All of these might simultaneously affect the amount payable for a covered property loss.

For liability insurance, the valuation of a covered loss is set by the courts or, more commonly, by a negotiated settlement. The amount payable under a given insurance policy might be affected not only by the value of the loss but also by policy limits and deductibles or self-insured retentions.

The amounts payable for both property and liability insurance claims can also be affected by other insurance or noninsurance sources of recovery.

Question 6: Do Any External Factors Affect the Claim?

Most of the information necessary to determine whether a particular insurance policy covers a given claim, and for how much, can be found in the policy itself. However, the coverage can be affected by a wide range of external factors.

Answering the six questions just discussed provides a sound approach to determining whether and to what extent coverage applies to either an illustrative or actual loss. This systematic approach can be used by producers, claim representatives, and insureds alike. It serves all parties to the insurance contract well by ensuring that the coverage intended to be provided by the insurance policy is actually delivered as promised.

Other CPCU courses are designed to develop the policy-analysis skills discussed in this chapter, building on the concepts that this text introduces.

SUMMARY

Insurance policies are complex legal documents. A policy can be self-contained or modular. Most are preprinted policies, but some are manuscript policies; preprinted policies can be either standard or nonstandard. With preprinted policies, ambiguities are usually interpreted in the insured's favor, but the burden of proof might shift if the insured was involved in drafting a manuscript policy. Various labels apply to policy parts and the nature of related documents, such as the application, endorsements, and other documents that might be referenced by the policy.

Every policy provision in a property-liability insurance contract can be categorized as declarations, definitions, insuring agreement, exclusions, conditions, or miscellaneous provisions. However, some policies are not neatly divided into those categories, and a provision that serves one function might appear under an unrelated heading. Both property and liability insuring agreements can be either comprehensive or limited in their scope.

Insurance policy exclusions have seven purposes. Exclusions are intended to do the following:

1. Eliminate coverage for uninsurable loss exposures
2. Assist in managing moral hazards
3. Assist in managing attitudinal (morale) hazards
4. Reduce likelihood of coverage duplications
5. Eliminate coverages not needed by the typical insured
6. Eliminate coverages requiring special treatment
7. Assist in keeping premiums reasonable

Two important reasons for analyzing an insurance policy are the following: (1) to determine what losses would be covered and (2) to determine whether a given loss was covered.

After-loss policy analysis requires answering six questions:

1. Does an enforceable insurance contract exist?
2. Did the loss occur to an insured party who has an insurable interest?

3. Do any policy conditions affect coverage?
4. Has an insured event occurred?
5. What dollar amount, if any, will be paid?
6. Did any external factors affect the claim?

The bases for the first two questions have been examined, at least in part, in earlier chapters. The remaining chapters examine the rest of the questions in greater detail, beginning with Chapter 12, which examines common insurance policy conditions.

APPENDIX—BACKGROUND ON INSURANCE POLICIES

The word *policy* is derived from the Italian *polizza*, a written contract that furnishes evidence of, or creates, a legal obligation. Although the Italians did not use *polizza* only for insurance contracts, the term "policy" has been carried into the English language as a name for the insurance contract. Partly because of this origin, some scholars have speculated that written insurance contracts had their origin in Italy.[9]

Early U.S. insurance policies were simple contracts written by insurers who knew their insureds well. Most insurers confined their operations to a relatively small geographical area and to insureds with whom the underwriters were familiar. Insurance was sold primarily through home-office employees, without agents' or brokers' assistance. A typical fire insurance policy was extremely brief, including little more than the description of the property, the coverage amount, the coverage period, and a premium citation. Insurance operations were characterized by individual underwriting and mutual understanding between insured and insurer. The importance of the insurance was not so much in the written policy's wording as in the understanding between the parties as to what they sought to achieve.

Complexity

As insurance grew into a large business, simple contracts and marketing methods began to bow to complexity. The prosperity experienced by commercial fire insurance, for example, increased competition and led to creative marketing systems. The result was decentralization of underwriting activities, lessening of firsthand knowledge in the underwriting selection process, and marketing through producers who often were significantly detached from the insurer's home office.

Selling and servicing policies in expanded geographical areas added further challenges because the insured property or the damage caused by each loss was not readily available for examination. Insurance companies recruited agents in various communities to sell and service insurance policies on their behalf. While local agents alleviated some of the difficulties that distance had created, they also created some new problems. An insurance company could not supervise the agents' honesty or determine whether the out-of-state insurance applications contained accurate information. Moreover, the insured's physical separation from the insurer left insurers more subject to moral and attitudinal hazards. To address these problems, insurers issued policies filled with provisions designed to protect insurance companies from unwittingly accepting undesirable business and paying unjust claims.

Unfortunately, many policies were filled with restrictions, exclusions, exceptions, small type, confusing sentences, and undefined terms. Insureds often found they could not collect on their policies because of unseen exclusions buried deep in the fine print. Insurers found negotiating claim settlements to be difficult because their policy conditions had become nullified, or otherwise modified, by widely differing court decisions.

As early fire insurance developed in the mid- to late-1800s and early 1900s, each insurer generally created its own independent fire insurance contract. Insurers' lack of cooperation to develop a common form or even guidelines toward a generally acceptable agreement led to a hodgepodge of insurance contracts with resultant consumer confusion. Not surprisingly, the insurance industry was increasingly viewed with suspicion.

Standardization

Because insurers developed their own contracts without reference to any common wording, fire insurance contracts were often ambiguous. Problems often developed in interpreting coverage, in litigating, and in settling losses involving dual coverage. The need for uniform fire policies that were both simpler and shorter became increasingly apparent. A long series of slow developments reached their climax with the introduction of the 1943 New York Standard Fire Policy that, for almost four decades, was used in nearly all states in all policies providing fire insurance on buildings and contents. Despite its name, the 165-line standard fire policy was not a complete insurance contract that could stand on its own. It was a foundation form supporting other attached documents that specifically described covered property, additional covered perils, and other relevant conditions.

The 1943 Standard Fire Policy was a major milestone for policy standardization, and its widespread use led to consistent and predictable legal interpretation. However, like other policies of its day, it is not a paragon of clarity when compared with today's standards of written communication. For example, the first sentence of the policy itself reads as follows:

> **IN CONSIDERATION OF THE PROVISIONS AND STIPULA-TIONS HEREIN OR ADDED HERETO** AND OF the premium above specified, this Company, for the term of years specified above from inception date shown above At Noon (Standard Time) to expiration date shown above At Noon (Standard Time) at location of property involved, to an amount not exceeding the amount(s) above specified, does insure the insured named above and legal representatives, to the extent of the actual cash value of the property at the time of loss, but not exceeding the

amount which it would cost to repair or replace the property with material of like kind and quality within a reasonable time after such loss, without allowance for any increased cost of repair or reconstruction by reason of any ordinance or law regulating construction or repair, and without compensation for loss resulting from interruption of business or manufacture, nor in any event for more than the interest of the insured, against all **DIRECT LOSS BY FIRE, LIGHTNING AND BY REMOVAL FROM PREMISES ENDANGERED BY THE PERILS INSURED AGAINST IN THIS POLICY, EXCEPT AS HEREINAFTER PROVIDED**, to the property described herein while located or contained as described in this policy, or pro rata for five days at each proper place to which any of the property shall necessarily be removed for preservation from the perils insured against in this policy, but not elsewhere.

The degree of standardization among insurers depended on several factors. Policy language was based on the writing style of other legal documents. Insurers were reluctant to discard existing wording that courts had interpreted over time. A legitimate concern was that neither the insurer nor the insured could be certain of the meaning of innovative policy language that was untested in the courts. Although coverage modifications were periodically made, sometimes in response to adverse court interpretations of existing language, insurers were reluctant to replace tested policy language—even if it was not easy to understand.

Simplification

The situation began to change during the 1970s for various reasons. As coverage evolved, provisions in the attached standard forms increasingly superseded many of the Standard Fire Policy provisions. Seeming contradictions between the Standard Fire Policy and the attached forms made the complete insurance contract increasingly difficult for both consumers and practitioners to read and interpret. Moreover, standards for written English shifted as the language evolved. Society became more interested in concise, pointed expression than complex, precisely crafted verbiage. Of legitimate concern was that consumer documents communicate clearly to people with limited English language skills. And courts were increasingly interpreting policies based on a policyholder's "reasonable expectations" to understand the policy. Also, the consumer movement began to place more demands on organizations providing consumer services.

Insurers have responded to these changing demands by developing insurance policies that are somewhat easier to read. Nevertheless, claims based on earlier policy editions will be litigated for many years to come.

Today's insurance practitioner encounters insurance policies in numerous forms. Many ocean marine insurance policies continue to use language several hundred years old. At the opposite extreme are some "user-friendly" insurance policies that become almost chatty. Many policies present a compromise, using simple sentences to present complex concepts.

Insurance regulations in many states require that personal insurance policies meet specified readability requirements. A National Association of Insurance Commissioners (NAIC) model regulation for personal insurance specifies a minimum score of 40 on the Flesch Reading Ease Test, described in the following box. The Flesch Reading Ease Test, often called the Flesch Test, is a method for scoring written text's readability. A similar model regulation, not widely adopted, exists for commercial insurance policies, although it provides that Flesch scores lower than 40 may be accepted by the insurance commissioner.

The Flesch Reading Ease Test[10]

A National Association of Insurance Commissioners (NAIC) model regulation for personal insurance specifies a minimum score of 40 on the Flesch Reading Ease Test,

1. For a policy containing 10,000 words or less* of text, the entire policy shall be analyzed. For a policy containing more than 10,000 words, the readability of two 100 word samples per page may be analyzed instead. The samples shall be separated by at least 20 printed lines.

2. The total number of words in the text or sample shall be divided by the total number of sentences. The figure obtained shall be multiplied by 1.015.

3. The total number of syllables in the text or sample shall be divided by the total number of words. The figure obtained shall be multiplied by 84.6.

4. The sum of the figures computed under (2) and (3) subtracted from 206.835 equals the Flesch Reading Ease Test score.

5. For purposes of this Section, the following procedures shall be used:

   a. A contraction, hyphenated word, numbers, and letters, when separated by spaces shall be counted as one word;

   b. A unit of text ending with a period, semicolon, or colon shall be counted as a sentence;

   c. A syllable means a unit of spoken language consisting of one or more letters of a word as divided by an accepted dictionary. Where the dictionary shows two or more equally acceptable pronunciations of a word, the pronunciation containing fewer syllables may be used;

   d. At the option of the insurer, any form made a part of the policy may be scored separately or as part of the policy.

In addition, the policy must not be in less than ten-point type and "shall be written in every day*, conversational language, consistent with its standing as a contract. . . . Short sentences and a personal style shall be used wherever possible. . . . Technical terms and words with special meaning shall be avoided wherever possible."

[* "Fewer" should properly be substituted for "less," and, according to the dictionary, "everyday" is a single word when used as an adjective. These two word choices in the model regulation illustrate the word contortions sometimes found in insurance policies attempting to conform to a readability index.]

Policy simplification has greatly improved modern insurance policies' clarity. Insurance students are among those who benefit from the results. A disadvantage is that many policies now contain phrases untested by the courts. The ultimate interpretation of some policy provisions is therefore uncertain.

CHAPTER NOTES

1. Workers Compensation and Employers Liability Policy, Copyright, National Council on Compensation Insurance, 1987.
2. Form CG 00 01 07 98, Copyright, Insurance Services Office, Inc., 1997.
3. Form CG 00 01 07 98, Copyright, Insurance Services Office, Inc., 1997.
4. Form CG 00 01 07 98, Copyright, Insurance Services Office, Inc., 1997.
5. Form CG 00 01 07 98, Copyright, Insurance Services Office, Inc., 1997.
6. Form HO 00 03 10 00, Copyright, Insurance Services Office, Inc., 1999.
7. Form HO 00 03 10 00, Copyright, Insurance Services Office, Inc., 1999.
8. Form PP 00 01 06 98, Copyright, Insurance Services Office, Inc., 1997.
9. John H. Magee, *General Insurance*, 3d ed. (Homewood, Ill.: Richard D. Irwin, 1952), p. 8.
10. Personal Lines Property and Casualty Insurance Policy Simplification Model Regulation, Copyright, National Association of Insurance Commissioners, 1986.

Chapter 12

Direct Your Learning

Common Insurance Policy Provisions

After learning the subject matter in this chapter, you should be able to:

- ■ Describe each of the eight categories of common policy provisions.
- ■ Identify and explain the common provisions found in each of these categories.
- ■ Explain why each of the provisions found in these categories is commonly found in an insurance policy.
- ■ Given a claim situation, explain how common policy provisions could affect the actions taken by the insured or insurer.

Develop Your Perspective

What are the main topics covered in the chapter?

This chapter identifies insurance policy provisions, where provisions are commonly found in an insurance policy, and how provisions affect coverage.

Consider how the policy provisions define the terms and scope of the agreement between the insurer and the insured.

- How do they clarify the promises between the insurer and the policyholder?

Why is it important to know these topics?

Understanding how policy provisions affect coverage will help you interpret an insurance policy. Consulting the provisions is just one step in determining whether a given loss is covered under the policy.

Imagine that you have presented a claim to your insurance company and that a dispute exists about the amount to be paid or the applicability of coverage.

- How would you review the policy provisions at this point?

How can you use this information?

Examine your auto insurance policy.

- Who is an insured under the policy, and who is a named insured?
- How might distinctions like these affect coverage?
- If there is no coverage, can a claim representative pay the claim?

Chapter 12

Common Insurance Policy Provisions

This chapter examines the ready-made or all-purpose language common to many policies—the policy provisions. The policy provisions create a context that establishes how the rest of the contract functions. Many of the provisions discussed in this chapter are typically found in a "Conditions" section near the end of a self-contained policy or in a "common conditions" type form within a modular policy. In some cases, these conditions have a significant bearing on how or whether coverage applies.

For this discussion, the common policy provisions are grouped into eight categories relating to a policy's life cycle. This makes it easier to examine the technical terminology contained in the provisions and makes it easier to understand how the terminology can affect coverage in each category. These categories include the following:

1. Creating an enforceable contract
2. Insured parties
3. Policy period and territory
4. Maintaining coverage
5. Insured's duties in the event of loss
6. Insurer's duties in the event of loss
7. Resolving disputed claims
8. Subrogation and salvage

For each type of condition or provision examined, this chapter generally describes the need or issue that is addressed, cites typical provisions, and explains their implications. It also examines some variations among similar conditions and exceptions to the usual approach. The variations and exceptions illustrate why policy conditions cannot always be taken for granted.

Once they are familiar with the common policy conditions discussed here, insurance practitioners often scan insurance policies, assuming that they understand the contents just by reading the headings. However, it can be dangerous to assume that any specific provision of a given type is identical to the one cited here, or even that it is identical to comparable provisions in a similar policy. Readers are also warned not to *assume* that any particular policy contains all the provisions discussed here. Sometimes it is most important to notice that a particular provision, commonly found in other policies, is absent. Insurance professionals should be familiar with common policy provisions to better read and interpret commonly used policies.

Provision, Condition, Clause

Strictly speaking,

- A *provision* is any statement in an insurance policy.

- A *condition* is an insurance policy provision that qualifies an otherwise enforceable promise of the insurer or the insured.

- A *clause* is a particular article, stipulation, or provision in a formal document.

In practice, and in this chapter, the terms *provision*, *condition*, and *clause* are somewhat interchangeable. Usage sometimes depends on custom rather than on any precise meaning assigned to these words.

CREATING AN ENFORCEABLE CONTRACT

The first policy provision that is common among most policies involves how an enforceable contract is created. Enforceable contracts have five key elements: offer and acceptance, consideration, competent parties, legal purpose, and legal form. Provisions in nearly all insurance policies reinforce two of those elements:

1. The insured's consideration is reinforced by payment of premium provisions.
2. Genuine assent to the offer and acceptance is reinforced by concealment, misrepresentation, or fraud provisions.

Payment of Premium Provision

Payment of premium provision
A policy provision that indicates the insurer's agreement to provide insurance coverage in exchange for the insured's payment of premium.

A legally enforceable contract requires "consideration" by both parties. In an insurance contract, the "consideration" of the insured is the payment of premium—or the promise to pay the premium. Many policies and endorsements include a **payment of premium provision**, words to the effect that coverage is granted in consideration of the premium. For example, the standard workers compensation and employers liability insurance policy begins with this statement:

> In return for the payment of the premium and subject to all terms of this policy, we agree with you as follows:[1]

Some policies include additional provisions relating to premium calculation—for example, how premiums are determined and whether they may be changed while the policy is in force. Some provisions might indicate who is responsible for handling premiums and renewal options.

Concealment, Misrepresentation, or Fraud Provision

Even without a specific contractual provision, the insured's concealment, misrepresentation, or fraud can provide sufficient grounds for the insurer to avoid an insurance contract. Many insurance policies contain a **concealment, misrepresentation, or fraud provision** that explicitly reinforces this important point. Such a provision appears in the AAIS Homeowners Policy:

> **Misrepresentation, Concealment, or Fraud**—This policy is void as to "you" and any other "insured" if before or after a loss:
>
> a. "you" or any "insured" has willfully concealed or misrepresented:
>
> 1) a material fact or circumstance that relates to this insurance or the subject thereof; or
>
> 2) an "insured's" interest herein; or
>
> b. there has been fraud or false swearing by "you" or any other "insured" with regard to a matter that relates to this insurance or the subject thereof.[2]

Concealment, misrepresentation, or fraud provision
A policy provision that voids coverage if the insured is guilty of concealment, misrepresentation, or fraud.

INSURED PARTIES

The second category of common policy provisions is insured parties. Insurance policies provide protection only to persons or organizations that not only have an insurable interest but also qualify as insured parties.

An **insured party** is any of the various persons, corporations, partnerships, or other entities contractually entitled to a loss payment or other benefits according to the insurance policy's terms. Insured parties—especially those who qualify as named insureds—have a wide variety of valuable contractual rights under the terms of a typical insurance policy.

All insured parties have rights in an insurance contract, but some have more rights than others. This is why knowing how the policy provisions affect the rights of the parties is important.

Insured party
Person, corporation, partnership, or other entity contractually entitled to a loss payment or other benefits according to the insurance policy's terms.

Types of Insured Party Provisions

- Insured parties identified by name
- Insured parties identified by relationship
- Additional insureds
- Multiple insured parties or covered locations
- Parties not insured

Insured Parties Identified by Name

An insurance policy's declarations can specifically name (1) named insureds and (2) loss payees or mortgagees—who, typically, are secured creditors.

Distinguishing between named insureds and other insureds is very important because some policy provisions apply to all insureds while others apply only to named insureds.

Named insured—A **named insured** is the person, corporation, partnership, or other entity named as such in a policy's declarations page. One, several, or many parties may be named insureds. Throughout the policy, "you" means the named insured.

First named insureds—Although all named insureds receive protection under the policy, the order in which named insureds are listed in the policy declarations can be important. The first named insured is typically responsible for premium payment and is the only insured who can cancel the policy, receive notice of cancellation, make policy changes with the insurer's consent, receive claims and occurrence data from the insurer, and receive returned premiums.

Loss payee—A **loss payee** might be entitled to some payment for losses covered by the policy. However, a loss payee is neither an insured nor a named insured—even though its name appears in the policy declarations. Loss payees can include secured creditors, and their interests in personal property can be protected by a **loss payable clause**.

The typical loss payable clause promises only to make sure the loss payee participates in claims proceeds. That basic clause gives a creditor no greater rights than the debtor/insured has under the policy, and it does not create a separate contract with the loss payee.

Some loss payable clauses extend additional rights to the loss payee. For example, the loss payee might be entitled to receive the same advance notice of cancellation as the named insured, or the loss payee's rights might be protected even when the loss results from the named insured's fraudulent acts or omissions.

Mortgagee—The rights of a **mortgagee**, who has an interest in real property, are somewhat stronger than those of a typical loss payee with an interest in personal property. Property insurance policies commonly contain a **mortgage clause** that protects the creditor's (mortgagee's) interest in real property that has been pledged as collateral for a loan. Unlike a typical loss payable clause, the standard mortgage clause is viewed as a separate contract between the insurer and the mortgagee.

The mortgagee's rights under the policy cannot be impaired by an act or omission of the debtor (mortgagor). Although the typical loss payable clause is only a single sentence or a simple endorsement, the standard mortgage clause consists of several long paragraphs. The mortgage clause of an ISO Homeowners Policy, for example, clarifies that the mortgagee can still protect its interests, even if the insured violates policy conditions through the following:

- Failing to report important changes

Named insured
A person, corporation, partnership, or other entity named as such in an insurance policy's declarations page.

Loss payee
A secured creditor, identified by name as a loss payee, to whom the debtor has pledged specific personal property as collateral for a loan.

Loss payable clause
A policy clause that protects the creditor's interest in personal property pledged as collateral for a loan.

Mortgagee, or **mortgageholder**
A secured creditor—usually a bank or another financial institution—that made a mortgage loan to a borrower (called the mortgagor) to enable the borrower to purchase real property.

Mortgage clause, or **mortgageholder clause**
A policy clause that protects the creditor's (mortgagee's) interest in real property pledged as collateral for a mortgage loan.

- Failing to pay premiums when due
- Failing to submit a proof of loss as required by the policy

The mortgagee is also entitled to receive advance notice of cancellation or nonrenewal.

"You" and "an Insured": Are They Different?

When someone reads a typical insurance policy, he or she must understand the distinction between (1) "you" (the named insured) and (2) "an insured" (which includes, but is not limited to, the named insured).

- "You" means the named insured shown in the declarations and any other person or organization qualifying as a named insured or meeting the policy's definition of "you." Personal insurance policies typically include the named insured's spouse within the definition of "you," with the effect that the spouse is a named insured even if his or her name does not appear in the policy declarations.

- "An insured," "the insured," or "any insured" includes not only the named insured but also any other person or organization that qualifies as an "insured" under the policy. Under the Commercial General Liability (CGL) Coverage Form, for example, the named insured's employees are insureds even though they are not individually named.

The distinction can be crucial. For example, a liability insurance policy exclusion of damage to property in the custody of "the insured" would apply to property in the custody of the person or organization qualifying as "the insured" and against whom a claim is made. In contrast, an exclusion of damage to property in "your" custody would apply only to property in the *named* insured's custody.

Insured Parties Identified by Relationship

Most property and liability policies cover as an "insured" one or more parties identified only by their relationship to the named insured or to another insured party. Some insured parties are members of a class, while others receive protection as legal substitutes for the named insured.

Members of a Class

The most obvious class is "spouse." In a homeowners or personal auto policy, the definition of "you" encompasses both the named insured and his or her spouse if residing in the same household—even if the spouse is not named in the policy, under the most typical circumstances. Apart from situations involving a marital split, the pronouns "you" and "your" throughout these policies refer collectively to the named insured and his or her spouse, and the spouse therefore possesses the same rights and privileges as the named insured whose name appears in the declarations. For example, Laura marries her fiancé, Jon, who has no insurance, and he moves into her house. As Laura's new husband, Jon automatically becomes a named insured under both Laura's auto policy and her homeowners policy, even though Jon is not specifically named in either contract.

Various parties may qualify for status as an "insured" because they belong to some class such as the following:

- Family members
- Household residents
- Employees
- Officers and directors
- Other classifications stated in the policy based on personal or business relationships with the named insured.

The following excerpts from ISO's Personal Auto Policy illustrate several classes of insureds, as well as variations within a single policy.

Part A—Liability Coverage includes this very broad definition:

> **B.** "Insured" as used in this Part means:
>
> 1. You or any "family member" for the ownership, maintenance or use of any auto or "trailer".
> 2. Any person using "your covered auto".
> 3. For "your covered auto", any person or organization but only with respect to legal responsibility for acts or omissions of a person for whom coverage is afforded under this Part.
> 4. For any auto or "trailer" other than "your covered auto", any other person or organization but only with respect to legal responsibility for acts or omissions of you or any "family member" for whom coverage is afforded under this Part. This Provision **(B.4.)** applies only if the person or organization does not own or hire the auto or "trailer".[3]

This provision, sometimes referred to as the "omnibus"[4] clause, potentially includes a broad range of people or organizations as insureds. For example, Manuel's employer is an insured if any claim or suit is brought against the employer because Manuel has an accident while using his own car on business. Manuel's church would be an insured if the car Manuel is driving is used in connection with a church activity. In both cases, Manuel's own car would not have to be involved. (See paragraphs 3 and 4.)

In general, because of some relationship to the named insured, people or organizations in a wide range of categories might automatically qualify as insureds under any given policy.

Legal Substitutes for the Named Insured

A legal substitute for the named insured can also become an insured under the named insured's policy. A number of property and liability insurance policies define an insured to include one or more of the following parties:

- *Legal representatives*—such as an executor or administrator of a deceased insured's estate, or a receiver in a bankruptcy proceeding
- *Personal representatives*—such as a son who has been granted power of attorney to conduct his aging mother's business affairs
- *Heirs and assigns*—parties who will inherit the named insured's property either by a will or by applicable state law

These representatives do not literally qualify as separate insureds. Rather, they are acceptable legal substitutes for the named insured and are legally empowered to act on behalf of the named insured or his or her estate. Because legal substitutes have only the legal rights possessed by the named insured, they can collect only for the named insured's covered losses, not for their own.

Additional Insureds

A party can have the status of an insured by being a named insured, by being a member of some class defined as insureds, or by serving as the named insured's legal representative. A final way to acquire insured status is to be added as an *additional insured* to the named insured's policy.

An **additional insured endorsement** can be used to add coverage for one or more persons or organizations to the named insured's policy. Numerous standard and nonstandard endorsements have been used to address a wide variety of situations. The following examples illustrate the range of options available:

> **Additional insured endorsement**
> An endorsement that adds coverage for one or more persons or organizations to the named insured's policy.

- *Additional Insured—Club Members*: Members of a golf club or some other club are added to the club's general liability policy for liability arising out of club activities or activities performed on behalf of the club.
- *Additional Insured—Engineers, Architects, or Surveyors*: Any architect, engineer, or surveyor engaged by the named insured is included as an insured for liability arising out of the named insured's premises or operations. Professional liability is specifically excluded.
- *Additional Insured—Owners, Lessees or Contractors—Scheduled Person or Organization*: This form is used for owners or lessees on policies covering contractors, or for contractors on policies covering subcontractors. The person or organization named in the endorsement is included as an insured under the named insured's policy to which it is attached, but coverage applies only to liability for operations performed for the named insured.

Multiple Insured Parties or Covered Locations

Many insurance policies insure more than one party. Many cover property or operations at more than one location. Insurance policies therefore must address the inevitable questions as to how actions by one insured might affect coverage for other insureds, or how conditions at one location might affect coverage at another location.

Separation of Interests

When several parties are insured in the same insurance policy, questions like these could arise:

- What happens if one insured intentionally causes property damage that results in a financial loss for all insureds? Does the intentional damage exclusion in a property insurance policy preclude coverage for one insured or for all?

- If each insured has separate coverage, how do the policy limits apply?

- If one insured breaches a policy condition in a property or liability insurance policy, do the other insureds still have coverage?

- What happens if one insured in a liability insurance policy sues another insured for a loss the policy might cover?

Separation of interests provision

A policy provision that clarifies the extent to which coverage might apply separately to more than one insured party.

A **separation of interests provision** clarifies the extent to which coverage might apply separately to more than one insured party.

Many insurance policies contain a miscellaneous provision that addresses issues like these. For example, the liability conditions of an ISO Homeowners Policy include this provision:

> **Severability of Insurance.** This insurance applies separately to each "insured." This condition will not increase our limit of liability for any one "occurrence."[5]

This provision indicates that coverage applies as follows:

- With respect to this condition, coverage applies to one insured even if another insured causes an intentional loss or breaches a policy condition; however, violation of the concealment or fraud clause, discussed later, might still preclude coverage.

- Although coverage applies to each insured separately when a claim is brought against two or more insureds, the insurer's total liability under the policy is not multiplied.

- This particular provision would not bar coverage when one insured makes a liability claim against another insured; however, separate exclusions in the homeowners policy—for property damage to property of an insured or bodily injury to an insured—would preclude coverage for such suits.

Concealment, Misrepresentation, or Fraud by Only One Insured

Questions also arise when only one of several insureds is guilty of concealment, misrepresentation, or fraud. If the entire policy is voided, does one insured's fraud nullify coverage for all insureds, or only for the one who committed the fraud? Although many policies contain various conditions relating to concealment, misrepresentation, and/or fraud, their treatment of these issues is not consistent, and examining the coverage forms that apply to the situation is necessary.

Actions of Parties Beyond the Insured's Control

Coverage may be voided if a named insured's actions breach policy conditions. But what happens if the actions of another party, not acting under the named insured's direction, lead to a breach of policy conditions?

The relevant provision in the ISO Commercial Property Conditions Form is a typical example:

> CONTROL OF PROPERTY
>
> Any act or neglect of any person other than you beyond your direction or control will not affect this insurance....[6]

In short, coverage is not affected by actions of people whom the named insured cannot control. For example, Cameron operates a retail photo shop protected by a burglar alarm. Cameron's special-form property insurance policy includes a protective safeguards endorsement, in which he agrees to maintain the alarm system. After a burglary, Cameron discovers that workers hired by his landlord, and not controlled by Cameron, had disconnected the alarm without his knowledge or approval. This act of the landlord's workers will not affect Cameron's rights to collect from his insurer.

Breach of Condition at Only One Location

Multiple locations present a similar situation. The relevant question is this: If a policy condition is breached at one location, is coverage at other locations affected? For example, if a warehouse's sprinkler system is not operational, does the breach affect coverage for a fire in the firm's separate office building that the same policy covers?

One could logically argue that an entire policy should become voidable, at the insurer's option, if the insured breaches a condition at any covered location. But the issue is not that simple. The two exposures in the example, the warehouse and the office, were covered by the same policy, but they could have been covered under two different policies with little or no difference in premium. If different policies had been used, a breach of one policy's condition would not affect the other separate contract. One could argue that insureds should not weaken their protection by covering more than one exposure in the same policy. The Control of Property provision of the ISO Commercial Property Conditions Form resolves this dilemma:

> The breach of any condition of this Coverage Part at any one or more locations will not affect coverage at any location where, at the time of loss or damage, the breach of condition does not exist.[7]

Clearly, the breach of a policy condition at one location does not affect coverage for a loss at another location. That is how most insurance policies resolve this issue.

Parties Not Insured

Other policy provisions address parties not insured. Although a typical insurance policy extends coverage to many different named and unnamed parties, most insurance policies explicitly preclude coverage for bailees or assignees. Some also explicitly address the situation in which a consolidation or merger changes the identity of parties having an insurable interest in covered property or activities.

No Benefit to Bailee Provision

Bailee
A party having possession of another's personal property and a duty either to return it to the owner or to deliver or dispose of it as agreed. A bailee who is compensated for the bailment is a **bailee for hire.** The bailment is a **gratuitous bailment** when no compensation is involved, and the bailee owes a somewhat lesser degree of care.

Insurance deals with many types of property that can, at times, be in the custody of someone other than the property owner. A **bailee** is a party having possession of another's personal property and a duty either to return it to the owner or to deliver or dispose of it as agreed. When compensation is involved, the bailee is a **bailee for hire.** When no compensation is involved, the bailment is a **gratuitous bailment,** and the bailee owes a somewhat lesser degree of care. Under the terms of a **no benefit to bailee provision** found in many property insurance policies, the insurer provides protection for the insured property owner only, not for the bailee.

A bailee for hire is not legally responsible for all damage to property in its custody, but only for damage caused by the bailee's negligence. Suppose Bill's car is in the custody of an auto repair shop when a tornado blows the car from the shop's raised hoist. The shop owner did not cause the tornado, so it would hardly be appropriate to charge the shop owner for the destruction of Bill's car. A tornado might as readily have damaged the vehicle when it was parked in front of Bill's house.

No benefit to bailee provision
A property insurance policy provision that indicates that the insured is protected when its property is in the bailee's custody; does not protect the bailee.

Suppose, instead, Bill's car slipped off the hoist because a mechanic was careless. Assuming Bill has auto physical damage insurance, Bill's auto insurance company would pay Bill's claim. If possible, the auto insurer would then attempt to recover its payment from the bailee (the repair shop) through the process of subrogation. Bill, the property owner, is protected by his insurance, but Bill's insurance is not intended to provide a windfall that protects the bailee from its own negligence. The bailee might have its own insurance, but that is not the issue here; the focus is on the perspective of Bill and Bill's auto insurer.

The *no benefit to bailee* provision of many property insurance policies succinctly states that the insurer provides coverage for the property owner but not the bailee. One example is this provision in the ISO Personal Auto Policy:

> **NO BENEFIT TO BAILEE**
>
> This insurance shall not directly or indirectly benefit any carrier or other bailee for hire.[8]

This provision relates specifically to bailees for hire—such as the auto mechanic; it does not preclude coverage for another driver to whom an insured gratuitously lends the car.

Policy language varies, reflecting different types of property exposures. However, the effect of a *no benefit to bailee* provision, whatever its label, is generally the same:

- Subject to other policy terms, an insured does have protection for loss to property in the custody of a bailee for hire.
- The bailee—and the bailee's own insurer, if any—cannot benefit from this coverage. The property owner's insurance does not relieve the bailee of its legal responsibility to safeguard the property, thus preserving the insurer's subrogation rights.

Assignment Provision

Generally, contract law permits anyone who possesses a contract right to assign that right to another party. The procedure of transferring property is called **assignment**. However, it is usually not possible to transfer (assign) insurance coverage from one named insured to another party (the assignee) who would presumably become the new named insured without insurer approval.

Insurance policies are personal contracts. To guard against moral hazard, attitudinal hazard, and other problems, every insurer wants a chance to decide whom it will or will not insure. Most property and liability insurance policies therefore contain an **assignment provision** that, in effect, prohibits a policyholder who was approved by the insurer from transferring (assigning) the policy—and its protection—to another party (an "assignee") who might not meet the insurer's approval.

The assignment provision in an ISO Homeowners Policy is typical:

> **Assignment.** Assignment of this policy will not be valid unless we give our written consent.[9]

This means that if François sells his chateau to Michelle, he cannot include his homeowners insurance policy in the deal—unless the insurance company agrees in writing. That is not an absolute prohibition, because it allows for assignment with the insurer's permission. In practice, however, insurance policies are hardly ever assigned. Most likely, François would cancel his homeowners policy, and Michelle would purchase a new homeowners policy.

If François and Michelle attempted to assign François' homeowners policy without the insurer's permission, neither party would receive coverage. François would no longer have an insurable interest in the chateau he has sold, and Michelle would have no enforceable insurance in the home she now owns.

Many insurance policies do not use the "assignment" label but instead use a phrase such as "Transfer of Your Rights and Duties Under This Policy."

Although most insurance policies prohibit assignment, there are exceptions. Insurance on oceangoing cargo usually is written so that the cargo

Assignment
A transfer of a contract right from one party (the assignor) to another (the assignee).

Assignment provision
A policy provision that prohibits one insured from transferring ownership of an insurance policy to another party without the insurer's consent.

insurance policy can be assigned to other parties having an interest in the cargo as their interests develop. The cargo's ownership can change several times during the weeks when it is in transit from one port to another. Yet risks associated with the property do not change, and the property is normally outside any owner's control, so moral hazard is not an issue. For similar reasons, other property insurance policies occasionally are written to cover the interests of "for whom it may concern," or "the named insured or its assignees." (For example, a trustee may insure property in his or her name for the trust's benefit.) Either approach is broad enough to include an assignee as an insured.

Consolidation-Merger Provision

Consolidation-merger provision
A provision that clarifies whether, or to what extent, coverage automatically applies to employees or property acquired through a business consolidation, merger, or acquisition.

Assignment involves transferring an insurance policy to another party other than the original named insured. A somewhat comparable situation results from business mergers or consolidations when the organization itself changes into a somewhat different entity that involves different people, possibly at additional locations. Assignment is, generally, prohibited because insurance is a personal contract, and the insurer wants the right to decide which persons it will insure. This right is especially important when it involves crime coverages, particularly employee theft or employee dishonesty. A **consolidation-merger provision** clarifies whether, or to what extent, coverage automatically applies to employees or property acquired through a business consolidation, merger, or acquisition.

POLICY PERIOD AND TERRITORY

The third category of provisions relates to the policy period and territory. An insurance policy must specify *when* something must happen to trigger coverage, as well as *what* must happen and *where*. The *when* is addressed in part by provisions relating to the policy period, the *where* by provisions relating to the policy territory.

Policy Period Provisions

Most property-liability insurance coverage applies for a particular time period. The dates of the policy period, or at least the inception date, are usually entered in the policy declarations, and they naturally vary from one policy to the next. Other printed provisions state, in one way or another, that coverage applies only during the policy period.

Policy period
The time frame, beginning with the inception date, during which insurance coverage applies.

An insurance policy's coverage usually begins on a specified date (the inception date) and applies during a specified period of time (the **policy period**). Although one-year policies are typical with property-liability insurance, other time periods are also common.

Some property insurance policies depart from the general rule just described and terminate coverage when the exposure ceases to exist. For example, a builders risk policy (covering a building under construction) terminates before the stated expiration date under certain circumstances indicating construction is completed. Similarly, coverage under a crop-hail insurance policy ends when the crop is actually harvested, if the harvest precedes the policy expiration date.

To clarify whether coverage is effective on the first or last day of a policy, the precise time when coverage begins and ends must also be specified.

Today, many package policies provide both property and liability coverage, and it is desirable that the entire policy begin at the same time. Most—but certainly not all—property, liability, and other policies now begin and expire at 12:01 A.M. of the stated dates, one minute after midnight. That odd minute eliminates any ambiguity as to whether 12:00 A.M. might mean noon or midnight, or whether "midnight" means the instant at which the specified date begins or the one at which it ends.

Policy period provisions also address when something must happen to trigger coverage. A property insurance policy necessarily contains one or more provisions clarifying the coverage trigger. A typical example appears in the ISO Commercial Property Conditions:

> Under this Coverage Part:
>
> 1. We cover loss or damage commencing:
>
>   a. During the policy period shown in the Declarations....[10]

Generally, property insurance applies to losses that begin during the policy period. The single word "commencing" can be important when a loss occurs close to the time when the policy begins or expires. Suppose a fire begins at 11 P.M. and continues to burn until 1 A.M., and that Policy A expires at 12:01 A.M., when Policy B becomes effective. Which policy applies? In this case, the entire loss is covered by Policy A because it "commenced" during A's policy period.

The property policy in effect when the fire commences provides all the coverage. This provision is especially significant for business interruption claims and other time element losses that may, by definition, extend for a long time after they "commence." An insurer could be obligated to pay business income losses for many months after a business income policy expires, as long as the loss-producing event began during the policy period.

Liability insurance triggers can vary. Many liability policies refer to bodily injury or property damage that occurs during the policy period, but others trigger coverage when a claim is first made, regardless of the time of the occurrence that gave rise to the claim. In some cases, coverage has been found under a series of policies, for events that were considered to occur throughout the terms of several consecutive policies. Chapter 13 explores liability coverage triggers in more detail.

Territory Provisions

Before a loss occurs, an insurance policy must specify whether coverage will apply wherever the named insured has loss exposures. After a loss, it is necessary to determine if the insured event took place in a covered location.

In any given policy, the coverage territory provisions help identify broad geographical borders beyond which coverage does not apply. Other policy provisions can be much more restrictive. For example, real property might be covered only at the address specified in the policy declarations, and long-haul trucking exposures might be covered only within a described radius of operations.

A typical policy provision appears in the ISO Commercial Property Conditions Form:

> The coverage territory is:
>
> a. The United States of America (including its territories and possessions);
>
> b. Puerto Rico; and
>
> c. Canada.[11]

Only rarely would this provision become an issue, as commercial property coverage applies almost entirely to property at fixed locations described in the declarations.

Many insureds are based in one state but face loss exposures in other states, where laws may vary. State variation is especially important with workers compensation insurance—which provides funding for statutory benefits specified in state law, and auto insurance—which, in many cases, is subject to a state's mandatory insurance laws, no-fault laws, and minimum insurance requirements. Policies likely to be affected by state variations often contain a provision stating that the policy provides whatever coverage is required by the law of the state where the accident occurs.

An insurance policy provision is not enforceable if it conflicts with the applicable law of the state. Some policies contain an explicit **conformity with statute provision** addressing that point, such as this provision from the AAIS Contractors Equipment Coverage Form:

Conformity with statute provision
A provision that indicates that if a conflict exists between a state statute and the insurance policy, the statute applies.

> **Conformity With Statute**—When a condition of this coverage is in conflict with an applicable law, that condition is amended to conform to that law.[12]

Many insureds face loss exposures in states other than their home state, where laws may vary. Anticipating this problem, a policy might contain a provision stating, in effect, that the policy provides the coverage required by the law of the state where the accident occurs.

MAINTAINING COVERAGE

This section examines several typical policy provisions that address maintaining insurance coverage. See the following box.

Provisions That Address Maintaining Coverage

- Inspections and audit provisions
- Cancellation provisions
- Policy modifications provisions
- Increase in hazard provisions

Inspection and Audit Provisions

To properly handle some types of insurance, the insurer must be able to inspect the insured's premises and operations and to audit its financial records. Inspections and surveys provisions, and books and records provisions, explicitly give the insurer a right to perform these activities.

Inspections and Surveys Provision

An **inspections and surveys provision** clarifies the *insured's* duty to permit a representative of the *insurer* to enter the insured's premises and make loss control inspections and surveys.

Many insurance companies employ loss control representatives who may inspect the premises and operations of businesses that apply for insurance. Once a policy is in force, loss control representatives may also inspect the premises and operations, give reports to the insured and the insurer, and make safety recommendations. However, the inspections and surveys provision states that these are not safety inspections, that the insurance company does not take on the responsibility of protecting workers or the public from injury, and that the insurance company does not warrant that the business it in-spected is safe or healthful or complies with applicable laws. This disclaimer is used because some courts have held insurers liable for losses supposedly related to their inadequate inspections.

For example, the inspections and surveys condition in the ISO Common Policy Conditions Form reads as follows:

> **INSPECTIONS AND SURVEYS**
>
> We have the right but are not obligated to:
>
> 1. Make inspections and surveys at any time;
> 2. Give you reports on the conditions we find; and
> 3. Recommend changes.
>
> Any inspections, surveys, reports or recommendations relate only to insurability and the premiums to be charged. We do not make safety inspections. We do not undertake to perform the duty of any person or organization to provide for the health or safety of workers or the public. And we do not warrant that conditions:
>
> 1. Are safe or healthful; or
> 2. Comply with laws, regulations, codes or standards.

Inspections and surveys provision
A provision that indicates that an insured has a duty to permit an insurer's representative to enter the insured's premises and make loss control inspections and surveys.

This condition applies not only to us, but also to any rating, advisory, rate service or similar organization which makes insurance inspections, surveys, reports or recommendations.[13]

The final sentence extends inspection rights not only to the insurer but also to various rating and advisory organizations such as ISO, as well as other organizations that provide loss control services to insurers for a fee.

Inspection and survey conditions are common in commercial insurance policies but uncommon in personal insurance policies.

Examination of Books and Records Provision

Examination of books and records provision

A provision that indicates the insured's duty to permit a premium auditor, representing the insurer, to conduct the audits necessary to determine the final premium when the premium is based on an auditable exposure.

An **examination of books and records provision** clarifies the insured's duty to permit a premium auditor to conduct necessary audits. Insurance companies employ these premium auditors to audit insureds' financial records to determine the proper premium to charge for commercial insurance policies in which the final premium is based on the dollar amount of the insureds' actual (not projected) annual payroll, annual sales, or inventory on hand during the policy term. A typical provision appears in the ISO Common Policy Conditions:

EXAMINATION OF YOUR BOOKS AND RECORDS

We may examine and audit your books and records as they relate to this policy at any time during the policy period and up to three years afterward.[14]

Premium audit

A methodical examination of an insured's operations, records, and books of account to determine the actual insurance exposure for the coverages provided.

An insurance **premium audit** is a methodical examination of an insured's operations, records, and books of account. It determines the actual insurance exposure for the coverages provided and concludes with a report of the findings. Audit provisions simply ensure that the insurer has access to the information needed to fulfill its role under the insurance contract.

These two provisions ensure the insurer's access to information necessary to compute a premium. Other provisions in many policies deal with records that should be made available at the time of a loss. Audit provisions relate only to policies for which the premium is based on an auditable exposure. Personal auto policies and homeowners policies, for example, do not contain an audit provision.

Cancellation Provisions

Cancellation

An action by the insurer or the insured to terminate coverage during the policy period (before the policy's expiration date).

Another provision that addresses how coverage is maintained is the cancellation provision. **Cancellation** is an action, taken by either the insurer or the insured, to terminate coverage that otherwise would continue until the policy expiration. Cancellation must be distinguished from several closely related terms:

Expiration

The termination of coverage at the end of the policy term and upon nonrenewal.

- **Expiration**—the end of the policy term, at which time the policy simply reaches the end of its natural life, or *expires*, unless action has been taken to *renew* it (extend coverage for another term).

- **Nonrenewal**—an action by the insurance company to terminate coverage on the policy's expiration date. Sometimes the term is also used to refer to an insured's decision not to continue coverage with the insurer for an additional policy period.

- **Termination**—ending policy coverage by cancellation, expiration, or nonrenewal.

A policy typically expires, is renewed, or is nonrenewed on its **anniversary date**, which is the specific day and month that the policy initially became effective. The anniversary date is yearless (for example, July 30), while inception and expiration dates (July 30, 2005) change with each renewal.

It is customary to keep a property-liability insurance policy in force until it expires and, when changing insurers, to change only on an expiration date, commonly known as an "x-date." A policyholder can usually discontinue future coverage simply by not paying a renewal premium. Generally, an insurer can avoid future coverage by choosing not to renew the policy; advance written nonrenewal notice to the insured may be required by law or by contract.

Even though people usually change insurers or drop policies or coverages at a policy's anniversary, canceling a policy midterm is possible. Therefore, insurance policies must include provisions indicating whether, when, or under what circumstances the policy may be canceled, who has the right to initiate the cancellation, how much advance notice is required, what procedures must be followed, and how any necessary premium charges or refunds will be determined. These matters are generally addressed in a **cancellation provision**.

The ISO Common Policy Conditions is one example of the various issues involved in a cancellation provision.

CANCELLATION

1. The first Named Insured shown in the Declarations may cancel this policy by mailing or delivering to us advance written notice of cancellation.

2. We may cancel this policy by mailing or delivering to the first Named Insured written notice of cancellation at least:

   a. 10 days before the effective date of cancellation if we cancel for nonpayment of premium; or

   b. 30 days before the effective date of cancellation if we cancel for any other reason.

3. We will mail or deliver our notice to the first Named Insured's last mailing address known to us.

4. Notice of cancellation will state the effective date of cancellation. The policy period will end on that date.

5. If this policy is cancelled, we will send the first Named Insured any premium refund due. If we cancel, the refund will be pro rata. If the first Named Insured cancels, the refund may be less than pro rata. The

Nonrenewal
An action by the insurance company to terminate coverage on the policy's expiration date.

Termination
Ending policy coverage by cancellation, expiration, or nonrenewal.

Anniversary date
The specific day and month that the policy initially became effective; year not indicated.

Cancellation provision
A provision that typically indicates under what circumstances the policy may be canceled, who has the right to initiate the cancellation, how much advance notice is required, what procedures must be followed, and how any necessary premium charges or refunds will be determined.

cancellation will be effective even if we have not made or offered a refund.

6. If notice is mailed, proof of mailing will be sufficient proof of notice.[15]

Policy Modification Provisions

This section examines the rights of either the insured or the insurance company to modify an insurance contract once it is in force. The *changes provision* addresses the issue of modification to an existing contract. The *liberalization clause* explains what happens when the insurer makes changes to similar policies now being sold to other policyholders.

Changes provision
A provision that typically states that the entire policy is contained in the written agreement and that the policy terms can be changed at the named insured's request, but only by a written endorsement.

Many insurance policies contain a **changes provision**. Its most significant feature is not that it authorizes policy changes but that policy changes are limited. For example, the changes provision of the ISO Common Policy Conditions reads as follows:

CHANGES

This policy contains all the agreements between you and us concerning the insurance afforded. The first Named Insured shown in the declarations is authorized to make changes in the terms of this policy with our consent. This policy's terms can be amended or waived only by endorsement issued by us and made a part of the policy.[16]

The insured (specifically, the first named insured) may request a policy change. If the insurer agrees, a change will be made. But no change is effective unless it is indicated in an endorsement to the policy. In other words, oral agreements to modify coverage are not permitted.

In practice, court decisions have held that the insurer can waive such "entire contract" provisions either orally or in writing, and it is accepted practice for insurance agents to orally bind expansions of coverage in the same way as coverage may be bound under an additional policy.

Liberalization clause
A clause that automatically extends an existing policy to include any broadened coverage the insurer has added to the same policy and is now selling at no additional charge.

The **liberalization clause** explains what happens when an insurer introduces a revised policy that is broader than the insured's policy. Some policies include a liberalization clause within the changes provision. Others contain a separate liberalization clause, such as the following clause in the ISO Commercial Property Conditions:

LIBERALIZATION

If we adopt any revision that would broaden the coverage under this Coverage Part without additional premium within 45 days prior to or during the policy period, the broadened coverage will immediately apply to this Coverage Part.[17]

The insured automatically receives the benefit of such broadened coverage.

The liberalization provision gives existing insureds the same broadened coverage the company offers to new insureds. Automatically providing the new coverage to existing insureds is practical and eliminates administrative hassle. If insurance policies did not automatically provide broadened coverage, insurers would be swamped with requests that outstanding policies be endorsed or replaced whenever existing policyholders hear that an insurer has improved its coverage. However, liberalization does present ethical challenges (see the following box).

Liberalization and Ethics

The liberalization clause challenges insurance professionals, particularly claim professionals, to remain aware of policy changes that sometimes mean the insured has the right to benefit from coverage that is not written in the insured's insurance contract.

For example, the first edition of ISO's Building and Personal Property Coverage Form inadvertently eliminated coverage that would otherwise have applied to insureds' forklift trucks used to move stock in a warehouse. A revision to the form restored the coverage. As soon as any insurer adopted the revised form, insureds with an earlier version of the form also had forklift coverage because of the liberalization clause, even though their written contracts would preclude coverage.

An insurance professional handling a claim for damage to a forklift under the first edition of the policy faces the combined ethical challenge of (1) knowing coverage has changed in a way that activates the liberalization clause and (2) providing coverage to which the insured is entitled because of the liberalization clause, even if coverage is otherwise precluded.

Some liberalization clauses distinguish between policy revisions and revised policy editions and indicate that the liberalization clause does not apply to new editions. Typically, a new policy edition includes some provisions that broaden coverage and others that restrict it. Restrictions of coverage could not be enforced unless restrictive language is added to the insured's policy. Insurers consider it unfair to give policyholders the best of both worlds—their choice of the broader provisions of either the existing policy or the replacement policy, but only the restrictions of the old policy.

Increase in Hazard Provisions

Insurance policies typically do not exclude coverage for most situations involving an increase in hazard. However, some policies do contain **increase in hazard provisions** that do the following, in the face of a specified increase in hazard:

- Automatically suspend coverage against losses related to the hazard
- Automatically suspend all coverage
- Permit the insurer to suspend coverage immediately
- Automatically limit or reduce coverage

A policy whose coverage is suspended is not canceled, but all or part of the coverage is temporarily interrupted *while* (but not after) a particular hazard exists. When the hazard no longer exists, coverage may be restored.

Increase in hazard provision
A provision that suspends or reduces some or all coverage in a property insurance policy when a hazard increases by any means the insured can control.

Conditions Automatically Suspending Coverage

Some exclusions automatically suspend coverage for related losses while a certain hazard is present. One such exclusion is located within the freezing peril of the ISO Homeowners Policy:

> We insure for direct physical loss...caused by...**Freezing** of a plumbing, heating, air conditioning or automatic fire protective sprinkler system or of a household appliance, but only if you have used reasonable care to:
>
> **a.** Maintain heat in the building; or
>
> **b.** Shut off the water supply and drain all systems and appliances of water;
>
> However, if the building is protected by an automatic fire protective sprinkler system, you must use reasonable care to continue the water supply and maintain heat in the building for coverage to apply.[18]

The idea is to preclude coverage for losses within the insured's control. During any period in which the insured has not taken reasonable measures to prevent freezing, loss by freezing is not covered. Coverage against loss by another peril—fire, for example—would not be affected.

To illustrate, a loss by freezing would not be covered if the insured had gone on a skiing vacation and turned off all heat in the house, even though freezing weather was forecast. However, coverage for freezing damage would not be excluded if the damage instead resulted from some unexpected breakdown in the home heating system while the insured was on vacation.

Loss control measures, such as fire extinguishing systems or alarm systems, often earn a premium reduction. Sometimes these measures reduce the hazard enough that an insurer is willing to cover an otherwise unacceptable exposure. Either way, the insurer contemplates these loss control measures' continued use. The hazard would be increased without the protective safeguard.

Protective safeguards endorsement
An endorsement that suspends coverage when a protective device is not in operation.

Insurers commonly add a **protective safeguards endorsement** that suspends coverage when a protective device is not functioning. A protective safeguards provision is also included within the standard language of some policies covering exposures that frequently involve safeguards. A typical example appears in the AAIS Camera and Musical Instrument Dealers Coverage Form, where it is labeled *premises protection*:

> **Premises Protection** — "You" must maintain in proper working order the protective devices that were in operation at the premises described on the "declarations" on the effective date of this policy.
>
> If "you" fail to keep the protective devices:
>
> a. in working condition at the premises described on the "declarations"; or
>
> b. in operation when "you" are closed to business,
>
> coverage for property at such locations is automatically suspended. This suspension will stay in effect until equipment or services are back in operation.[19]

Whenever automatic sprinkler systems, burglar and fire alarms, and other protective devices are in use, an insurance professional should search the insurance contract for a protective safeguards provision—which might be in an endorsement—and evaluate its effect. Determining which protective devices are relevant can be important, whether coverage is suspended at one or all locations when a safeguard is inoperative, whether the suspension applies to loss by any peril, and whether coverage is automatically reinstated when the safeguard is restored. Some protective safeguards provisions allow for a protective system's temporary outages or maintenance.

Conditions Permitting the Insurer To Suspend Coverage

Some policy conditions permit the insurer to suspend coverage. A clear example is found in the ISO Equipment Breakdown Coverage Form:

> **Suspension**
>
> Whenever "Covered Equipment" is found to be in, or exposed to, a dangerous condition, any of our representatives may immediately suspend the insurance against loss from a "Breakdown" to that "Covered Equipment." This can be done by delivering or mailing a written notice of suspension to:
>
> (1) Your last known address; or
>
> (2) The address where the "Covered Equipment" is located.
>
> Once suspended in this way, your insurance can be reinstated only by an endorsement for that "Covered Equipment".
>
> If we suspend your insurance, you will get a pro rata refund of premium for that "Covered Equipment". But the suspension will be effective even if we have not yet made or offered a refund.[20]

Equipment breakdown insurance's success depends heavily on the insurer's ability to prevent losses through periodic inspections of the equipment. In rare cases in which an inspector discovers a very hazardous condition, he or she will request that the equipment be shut down until the condition is corrected. Most insureds are grateful for the opportunity to avoid a serious loss. But if the insured is not willing to shut down hazardous equipment, the insurance company representative has the right to immediately suspend insurance coverage. Just the threat of suspension usually convinces the insured to take immediate action. But if action is not taken, the inspector has a contractual right to suspend coverage immediately, as long as the action is documented in writing. By mentioning a pro rata premium refund, the provision suggests that suspensions are normally final. The suspension can be lifted, but it requires a written endorsement. Insurers are likely to think twice about reinstating coverage for an insured who has not been willing to address a serious hazard.

Conditions Automatically Reducing Coverage

Some policy provisions do not suspend coverage altogether but reduce it in some way—for example, by limiting the amount payable—under certain conditions involving an increase in hazard. An interesting example appears in the vacancy condition of the Building and Personal Property Coverage Form, which *suspends* coverage for certain perils and *reduces* coverage for others.

Even though no business operations occur in a vacant building, the vacancy itself is an increase in hazard: Vacant buildings are attractive to vandals and thieves, they are susceptible to undetected water damage or water damage relating to deterioration, and damage by any peril might not be detected and addressed if nobody is in the building to see it. After defining "vacancy" in paragraph **a.**, the provision continues:

> **b. Vacancy Provisions**
>
> If the building where loss or damage occurs has been vacant for more than 60 consecutive days before that loss or damage occurs:
>
> **(1)** We will not pay for any loss or damage caused by any of the following even if they are Covered Causes of Loss:
>
>> **(a)** Vandalism;
>>
>> **(b)** Sprinkler leakage, unless you have protected the system against freezing;
>>
>> **(c)** Building glass breakage;
>>
>> **(d)** Water damage;
>>
>> **(e)** Theft; or
>>
>> **(f)** Attempted theft.
>
> **(2)** With respect to Covered Causes of Loss other than those listed in b.(1)(a) through b.(1)(f) above, we will reduce the amount we would otherwise pay for the loss or damage by 15%.[21]

Paragraph (1) describes a suspension in coverage, while paragraph (2) is a reduction in coverage.

INSURED'S DUTIES IN THE EVENT OF LOSS

After any claim or loss occurs, the insured must tell the insurer. (Some liability policies even require the insured to report occurrences that might conceivably lead to a claim.) The insured also has other post-loss responsibilities. Usually, both property and liability insurance contracts impose on the insured a duty to do the following:

- Expeditiously report the loss to the insurance company
- Prevent further loss or damage
- Cooperate with the insurance company in evaluating and settling the claim
- Provide proof of loss
- Submit to examination under oath
- Comply with "abandonment" provisions

A technical error in meeting these duties does not necessarily preclude coverage. The courts sometimes hesitate to interfere, based on a technicality, with an insured's basic rights of recovery. Still, to avoid disputes over procedural matters, insureds should do their best to fulfill all their post-loss duties. Many insurance policies expressly state that the insurer is not obligated to pay benefits unless the insured has complied with the policy's notice and claims provisions. Most policies state that the insured cannot sue the insurer unless the insured has fully complied with the duties stated in the policy.

Property Insurance

When a property loss occurs, the insured has several duties, typically specified in a separate set of policy provisions. Generally, the insured must notify the insurer of the loss and might have to notify the police if a law has been broken. Provisions sometimes require that notification be "prompt."

According to the Building and Personal Property Coverage Form, the insured must do the following:

(2) Give us prompt notice of the loss or damage. Include a description of the property involved.

(3) As soon as possible, give us a description of how, when and where the loss or damage occurred.[22]

Prompt notification enables the insurer to investigate the claim and estimate its liabilities. Delay prevents prompt investigation and can therefore be prejudicial to the insurer. For example, it can be difficult, after a period of time, to determine the cause of a loss and, therefore, to determine whether a covered peril caused the loss.

Provisions might also require that the insured protect damaged property from further loss. The mitigation-of-loss provision in a typical property insurance policy reinforces the insured's obligation to use common sense in protecting damaged property against further damage. Again, quoting from the Building and Personal Property Coverage Form,

[You must]

(4) Take all reasonable steps to protect the Covered Property from further damage, and keep a record of your expenses necessary to protect the Covered Property, for consideration in the settlement of the claim. This will not increase the Limit of Insurance. However, we will not pay for any subsequent loss or damage resulting from a cause of loss that is not a Covered Cause of Loss. Also, if feasible, set the damaged property aside and in the best possible order for examination.[23]

Provisions might also require that the insured cooperate with an insurer after a loss. Once the immediate crisis is over and the insurer has been notified of the loss, the insured cannot simply await payment. The insured has a duty to work with the insurer to assess the nature and extent of the loss. These provisions might also require proof of loss. The Building and Personal Property Coverage Form imposes these duties:

> [You must]
>
> (5) At our request, give us complete inventories of the damaged and undamaged property. Include quantities, costs, values and amount of loss claimed.
>
> (6) As often as may be reasonably required, permit us to inspect the property proving the loss or damage and examine your books and records.
>
> Also permit us to take samples of damaged and undamaged property for inspection, testing and analysis, and permit us to make copies from your books and records.
>
> (7) Send us a signed, sworn proof of loss containing the information we request to investigate the claim. You must do this within 60 days after our request. We will supply you with the necessary forms.
>
> (8) Cooperate with us in the investigation or settlement of the claim.[24]

Most property insurance policies prescribe similar duties, subject to variations in the specific duties and their time frame depending in part on the nature of the covered property.

The insurer has the right to obtain an insured's sworn testimony. This right, which is occasionally invoked, can be important to insurers in cases of suspected arson or fraud, or when the adjuster has otherwise been unable to obtain information. Examination under oath also provides a way to support or refute information in the written records provided by the person being examined.

The right to examination under oath is expressed in this provision of the ISO Building and Personal Property Coverage Form:

> We may examine any insured under oath, while not in the presence of any other insured and at such times as may be reasonably required about any matter relating to this insurance or the claim, including an insured's books and records. In the event of an examination, the insured's answers must be signed.[25]

This provision treats examination under oath as a right, not a request. The insurer has a clear right to examine any insured under oath; some policies might limit this right to examining the named insured. Of course, the insurer can always *request* an insured or, for that matter, any other party to submit to examination under oath. If it is not a contractual "duty," an insured also has a right—to deny the request.

Abandonment provision
A provision that indicates that the insured has no contractual right to abandon damaged property and turn it over to the insurer.

An **abandonment provision** might also impose a post-loss duty *not to* abandon damaged property to the insurer. Many insurance policies state that the *insurance company* has the option of paying for damaged property and taking over its ownership. An abandonment provision indicates that the *insured* has no right to elect this option.

In some situations, abandonment would provide an attractive alternative for the policyholder. People would often like to convert a seriously damaged car to a total loss by turning it over to the insurance company in exchange for cash payment of the pre-loss value. However, many property insurance policies make it clear that the insured cannot simply drop the property and take the money. Insurance companies are in the insurance business, not the property-repair-and-resale business. Also, ownership of damaged property can present a considerable liability in some situations, especially if the property is toxic, radioactive, or otherwise contaminated.

Liability Insurance

As with property insurance, liability insurance policies require the insured to notify the insurer and cooperate with the insurer in resolving claims. However, liability insurance differs from property insurance because liability situations always involve a third party who might or might not present a claim.

Some common policy provisions require a prompt report of an occurrence or offense that might result in a claim, as well as an actual claim or suit. (An offense is an event of the kind covered by that policy's personal and advertising injury coverage.) The courts are especially likely to enforce the notice requirement under liability contracts because lack of prompt investigation could prejudice an insurer's ability to defend the insured against a third party. As time passes, obtaining evidence and witnesses becomes increasingly difficult, and minor injuries might become magnified. Prompt notice of one loss also helps prevent and minimize future losses, which is in the interest of the insured, the insurer, and the general public. Timely notice enables the insurer to take control of a claim, promotes favorable settlements, and reduces litigation expenses.

Along with the provisions requiring prompt notice are provisions that require insureds not to admit responsibility or otherwise prejudice the insurer's opportunity to defend a claim. The ISO Commercial General Liability Coverage Form includes this final duty:

> No insured will, except at the insured's own cost, voluntarily make a payment, assume any obligation, or incur any expense, other than for first aid, without our consent.[26]

By agreeing to assume responsibility, an insured might appear to admit he or she is liable for the loss, seriously weakening the insurer's ability to defend against the claim.

An exception within this provision specifically authorizes insureds to incur first-aid expenses without jeopardizing their insurance coverage. When someone is seriously injured, an insured may call an ambulance or hire a taxicab to take an injured person to a hospital.

INSURER'S DUTIES IN THE EVENT OF LOSS

The sixth category of common policy provisions relates to an insurer's duty in the event of a loss, essentially the "procedural items" that take place after report of a claim or a loss.

Property Insurance

The insurer provisions found in most property insurance policies offer several options in settling a property insurance claim, and they do not all include paying money. The property insurer has the option to pay the value of the lost or damaged property or the amount spent to repair or replace it, whichever is less. The insurer also has other options. For example, the Building and Personal Property Coverage Form expresses them this way:

> **Loss Payment**
>
> **a.** In the event of loss or damage covered by this Coverage Form, at our option, we will either:
>
> > **(1)** Pay the value of lost or damaged property;
> >
> > **(2)** Pay the cost of repairing or replacing the lost or damaged property...
> >
> > **(3)** Take all or any part of the property at an agreed or appraised value; or
> >
> > **(4)** Repair, rebuild or replace the property with other property of like kind and quality...
>
> We will determine the value of lost or damaged property, or the cost of its repair or replacement, in accordance with the applicable terms of the Valuation Provision in this Coverage Form...
>
> **c.** We will give notice of our intentions within 30 days after we receive the sworn proof of loss....[27]

The insurance company has thirty days after receiving the sworn statement of loss to announce whether it intends to pay the value of destroyed property, pay the cost of repairs, pay the full value of damaged property and take title to the property, or perform the repair or replacement service. Other policies may specify different time periods.

Another clause in the loss payment provision limits payment to the extent of the insured's insurable interests in the property:

> **d.** We will not pay you more than your financial interest in the Covered Property.[28]

Note that this provision does not say the insurer will not pay an amount greater than the insurable interest of the named insured ("you"), only that the insurer will not pay more *to the named insured*. An additional amount might be payable to a mortgagee.

Other Owners of Covered Property

Many property insurance policies include some coverage for property of customers, employees, guests, or others on the insured's premises or in the insured's care. If the property's value is disputed, the insured could be caught in the middle between the insurance company and the property owner. Because the insurance contract is between the insurance company and the insured, others have no contractual rights against the insurance company. For example, this dilemma is addressed in the Building and Personal Property Coverage Form with the following provision:

> e. We may adjust losses with the owners of lost or damaged property if other than you. If we pay the owners, such payments will satisfy your claims against us for the owners' property. We will not pay the owners more than their financial interest in the Covered Property.
>
> f. We may elect to defend you against suits arising from claims of owners of property. We will do this at our expense.[29]

The insurance company has contractual permission to settle claims directly with bailors, whose property is in the custody of an insured bailee, or with other property owners. If the property owner is not satisfied with the settlement and sues the insured, the insurance company may choose to defend the insured at the insurer's own expense.

Some policies explicitly state that the insurer is obligated to pay a claim within a specified period after receiving adequate information. For example, the Building and Personal Property Coverage Form contains this provision:

> We will pay for covered loss or damage within 30 days after we receive the sworn proof of loss, if you have complied with all of the terms of this Coverage Part and:
>
> (1) We have reached agreement with you on the amount of loss; or
>
> (2) An appraisal award has been made.[30]

Claims for *covered* loss or damage should be paid promptly, and within a realistic time limit. But this, too, is not as simple as it looks. The thirty-day period is triggered only after reaching an agreement on the amount of the loss or upon an appraisal award.

A time-consuming investigation might be necessary to determine the actual cause of loss or some other factor critical to knowing whether a claim is covered. An insurer that delays a claim payment, waiting for proof that a claim was not covered, might rightfully be accused of breaching the contract. By including these provisions, insurers let policyholders know that claims will be handled promptly, but with adequate information.

Liability Insurance

Unlike property insurance, relatively few liability insurance policy *conditions* relate specifically to the insurer's *procedural* post-loss duties. However, the bankruptcy provision is relevant after a loss. The **bankruptcy provision**

Bankruptcy provision
A provision that indicates the insurer's obligation to pay claims on behalf of an insured who has become bankrupt and who cannot pay the claim with its own resources.

indicates that the insurer is, in fact, obligated to pay claims on behalf of an insured who is bankrupt. For example, the condition in the ISO Commercial General Liability Form states the following:

Bankruptcy

Bankruptcy or insolvency of the insured or of the insured's estate will not relieve us of our obligations under this coverage part.[31]

Bankruptcy provisions generally are not necessary with property insurance, because claims are paid *to* the insured—whether or not the insured is bankrupt, not on behalf of the insured.

RESOLVING DISPUTED CLAIMS

The seventh category of common provisions relates to the resolution of disputed claims. The parties to a loss often disagree regarding the amount to be paid or the applicability of coverage. The policy provisions that address these two issues are appraisal (a property concept) and arbitration (a liability concept).

Appraisal

Appraisal clause
In a property insurance policy, prescribes a method for resolving a claim dispute regarding the value of property or the amount of a property loss.

Many property policies include an **appraisal clause**. The appraisal clause is useful when the insurer and the insured agree that a given property loss is covered but cannot agree on the value of the property or the amount of the loss. The appraisal condition also applies when the insured thinks the claim is worth more than the insurer is willing to pay.

Such disagreements usually do not involve bad faith by either party. Many factors affect property's value or repair cost, and reasonable parties can differ dramatically in their evaluations. Negotiation usually resolves the disagreement, but sometimes agreement is impossible. The *appraisal clause* clarifies how an impasse can be resolved. Indirectly, the appraisal clause also encourages the parties to negotiate between themselves to avoid hiring appraisers who will do the same thing.

The appraisal clause in the Building and Personal Property Coverage Form is typical:

Appraisal

If you and we disagree on the value of the property or the amount of loss, either may make written demand for an appraisal of the loss. In this event, each party will select a competent and impartial appraiser. The two appraisers will select an umpire. If they cannot agree, either may request that selection be made by a judge of a court having jurisdiction. The appraisers will state separately the value of the property and amount of loss. If they fail to agree, they will submit their differences to the umpire. A decision agreed to by any two will be binding. Each party will:

a. Pay its chosen appraiser; and

b. Bear the other expenses of the appraisal and umpire equally.

If there is an appraisal, we will still retain our right to deny the claim.[32]

The appraisal provisions in some policies also specify when the appraisal process must occur.

Some insurance claims end up in court, especially when large amounts are at stake and the insurer and the insured interpret the policy differently. The court system is the ultimate authority on the insurance contract's meaning and enforceability. However, an insured's right to sue the insurer and ask the courts to enforce the contract is limited by a common provision, traditionally called a *suit provision*, specifying that the insured must comply with other policy provisions before bringing a lawsuit against the insurer. A lawsuit should not be used as a shortcut to circumvent the contract or to address issues that the insurance contract adequately handles. Many policies also state a time limit within which any suit must be brought. Suit on the claim cannot be started after this time has passed.

For example, the suit provision in the ISO Common Property Conditions reads as follows:

> **LEGAL ACTION AGAINST US**
>
> No one may bring a legal action against us under this Coverage Part unless:
>
> **1.** There has been full compliance with all of the terms of this coverage Part; and
>
> **2.** The action is brought within 2 years after the date on which the direct physical loss or damage occurred.[33]

Under a liability insurance contract, the insured can also sue an insurance company to force it to perform. Before resorting to a lawsuit, the insured must first comply with its other obligations under the policy.

Arbitration

Unlike the appraisal process, which deals only with the amount of the loss, the arbitration process outlines a process for resolving disagreements of *two* types:

1. Disagreements on whether the insured is *legally entitled* to recover damages
2. Disagreements regarding the *amount* of damages.

Whether coverage applies is a question for the courts and may not be settled through arbitration.

Otherwise, the arbitration process closely resembles the appraisal process outlined in property insurance policies. Here, for example, is the arbitration clause from the uninsured motorists coverage part of the ISO Personal Auto Policy:

> **ARBITRATION**
>
> **A.** If we and an "insured" do not agree:
>
> > **1.** Whether that "insured" is legally entitled to recover damages; or

2. As to the amount of damages which are recoverable by that "insured" from the owner or operator of an "uninsured motor vehicle", then the matter may be arbitrated. However, disputes concerning coverage under this Part may not be arbitrated.

Both parties must agree to arbitration. If so agreed, each party will select an arbitrator. The two arbitrators will select a third. If they cannot agree within 30 days, either may request that selection be made by a judge of a court having jurisdiction.

B. Each party will:

1. Pay the expenses it incurs; and

2. Bear the expenses of the third arbitrator equally.

C. Unless both parties agree otherwise, arbitration will take place in the county in which the "insured" lives. Local rules of law as to procedure and evidence will apply. A decision agreed to by two of the arbitrators will be binding as to:

1. Whether the "insured" is legally entitled to recover damages; and

2. The amount of damages....[34]

SUBROGATION AND SALVAGE

The final category of common policy provisions deals with subrogation and salvage. After an insurer has paid a property loss to an insured, or has paid a liability loss on an insured's behalf, the insurer sometimes may recover all or part of its payment through the processes of **subrogation** and **salvage**. Policy provisions outline how these processes work under the policy.

Subrogation and salvage activities within the claim department enable insurers to recover a portion of the money paid out in satisfying claims. By reducing the insurer's overall loss ratio, subrogation and salvage activities reduce the premiums the insurer needs to charge. Closely related to the issue of salvage is a common policy provision dealing with recovered property.

Subrogation
The process by which an insurer recovers payment from a negligent third party who caused a property or liability loss that the insurer has paid to, or on behalf of, an insured.

Salvage
The process through which an insurer takes possession of damaged property, for which it has paid a total loss, and recovers a portion of the loss payment by selling the damaged property. Damaged property itself can also be called salvage.

Subrogation

Whenever somebody's property is damaged through another person's fault, the property owner has a legal right to recover from the responsible party. The property owner also has a right to recover from his or her property insurer. However, the insured should not receive a double recovery. The subrogation provisions in insurance policies clarify how these situations will be handled. In short, the insured may recover for the loss under its own property insurance. The property insurer then takes over any rights of recovery against a responsible third party. The property insurer now has the right, if it wishes, to make a claim against the responsible party that caused the property damage, seeking to recover whatever money it has paid to the insured.

Liability losses are handled in a similar way. After paying a third-party claim, the insurer takes over any rights of recovery previously possessed by the insured and may seek to recover damages from another responsible party.

The responsible party might turn the claim over to his or her liability insurance company, which will ultimately pay the claim.

Property and liability insurance policies contain a variety of **subrogation provisions** reflecting the policies' own varied nature. Sometimes a subrogation provision is not titled "subrogation" but rather bears a caption such as "Transfer of Your Rights of Recovery." The ISO Homeowners Policy includes the "subrogation" label in its policy condition that applies to both the policy's property and liability coverages:

Subrogation provision
A provision that transfers to the insurer who has paid a loss any of the insured's rights of recovery for that loss.

> Subrogation
>
> An "insured" may waive in writing before a loss all rights of recovery against any person. If not waived, we may require an assignment of rights of recovery for a loss to the extent that payment is made by us.
>
> If an assignment is sought, an "insured" must sign and deliver all related papers and cooperate with us.
>
> Subrogation does not apply under Section II to Medical Payments to Others or Damage to Property of Others.[35]

Assignment and Subrogation Combined

The following concepts all involve some form of assignment:

- The *assignment provision* prohibits assignment of policy ownership without the insurer's consent.

- The *subrogation provision* provides that an insured may waive its rights of recovery before a loss occurs.

- After a loss occurs, the insured may legally assign its rights of recovery, including its rights to collect from the insurer, to any other party.

- After an insurer has paid a loss for the insured, the *subrogation provision* requires that the insured must assign rights of recovery to the insurer.

Salvage

Suppose a camera was covered for theft under a special-form property insurance policy, the camera was stolen, the insurer has paid the claim after subtracting a deductible, and then the camera is recovered by the insurance company or by the insured. What happens? Does the insurer automatically get to keep the recovered property? A **recovered property provision** clarifies how the insurer and the insured will handle property that is recovered after a claim for its loss has been paid.

Recovered property provision
A provision that indicates how the insurer and the insured will handle property that is recovered after a claim for its loss has been paid.

The provision in the ISO Homeowners Policy is typical:

> Recovered Property
>
> If you or we recover any property for which we have made payment under this policy, you or we will notify the other of the recovery. At your

option, the property will be returned to or retained by you or it will become our property. If the recovered property is returned to or retained by you, the loss payment will be adjusted based on the amount you received for the covered property.[36]

The *insured* determines whether to take back recovered property, but the insured does not keep both the property and the claim money. Because of this provision, the insured can consider the case closed once a property claim has been paid, and the insured can proceed to purchase replacement property without worrying that the case will be reopened because property has been recovered. At the same time, the insured will be given the opportunity to take back any recovered property.

SUMMARY

This chapter examined the insurance policy common provisions. The usual insurance policy conditions provide an important framework for other policy provisions unique to a particular coverage, and they can be extremely important in determining whether a given claim will be paid.

This chapter examined the various conditions in eight categories:

1. Under the heading "Creating an Enforceable Contract," the *payment of premium condition* reinforces the fact that consideration is essential to the contract formation and that the *concealment, misrepresentation, or fraud provision* addresses situations in which genuine assent might be lacking or the contract might otherwise be unenforceable.

2. In connection with "Insured Parties Provisions," the chapter examined the corollary of insurable interests: Coverage applies to a party with an insurable interest, provided that party is also an insured party. There are many ways to identify insured parties. A named party might be a named insured, a first named insured, a loss payee, or a mortgagee. Other insureds might be members of a class or legal substitutes for the named insured. Additional insureds might be added to a policy by endorsement, and many different endorsements are available for that purpose. Also examined were the implications of a situation in which one of several insureds fails to comply with policy conditions. Finally, the *no benefit to bailee provision, assignment provision,* and *consolidation-merger provision* indicate that some parties are not insured parties.

3. In most insurance contracts, coverage applies only during a specified time period and applies to losses within a certain geographical territory. Policy period and territory provisions were discussed.

4. Under the heading of "Provisions Maintaining Coverage," the chapter examined *inspection and audit provisions, cancellation provisions,* and two types of provisions dealing with policy modifications: the *changes provision* and the *liberalization clause.* Also examined were conditions that might suspend or reduce coverage due to an increase in hazards.

5. The chapter examined the duties typically required of the insured following a loss.

6. It examined the insurer's duties in the event of a loss.

7. The chapter discussed various methods for resolving disputed claims as expressed in an *appraisal clause*, a *suit clause*, or an *arbitration provision*.

8. The chapter examined subrogation and salvage issues.

To determine whether an insurance policy provides coverage for a known loss, one must determine whether an enforceable contract exists involving an insured party with an insurable interest and whether any policy conditions affect the claim. If the claim passes these tests, the next step is to determine whether an insured event has occurred, discussed in Chapter 13.

CHAPTER NOTES

1. Form WC 00 00 00 A, Copyright, National Council on Compensation Insurance, 1991.

2. Form 3 Ed 2.0, Copyright, American Association of Insurance Services, 1995.

3. Form PP 00 01 06 98, Copyright, Insurance Services Office, Inc., 1997.

4. Defined by funkandwagnalls.com as pertaining to, including, or dealing with numerous objects or items at once.

5. Form HO 00 03 10 00, Copyright, Insurance Services Office, Inc., 1999.

6. Form CG 00 90 07 88, Copyright, Insurance Services Office, Inc., 1987.

7. Form CG 00 90 07 88, Copyright, Insurance Services Office, Inc., 1987.

8. Form PP 00 01 06 98, Copyright, Insurance Services Office, Inc., 1997.

9. Form HO 00 03 10 00, Copyright, Insurance Services Office, Inc., 1999.

10. Form CP 00 90 07 88, Copyright, ISO Commercial Risk Services, Inc., 1983, 1987.

11. Form CP 00 90 07 88, Copyright, ISO Commercial Risk Services, Inc., 1983, 1987.

12. Form IM 7002 08 99, Copyright, American Association of Insurance Services, 1999.

13. Form IL 00 17 11 85, Copyright, Insurance Services Office, Inc., 1982, 1983.

14. Form IL 00 17 11 85, Copyright, Insurance Services Office, Inc., 1982, 1983.

15. Form IL 00 17 11 85, Copyright, Insurance Services Office, Inc., 1982, 1983.

16. Form IL 00 17 11 85, Copyright, Insurance Services Office, Inc., 1982, 1983.

17. Form CP 00 90 07 88, Copyright, ISO Commercial Risk Services, Inc., 1983, 1987.

18. Form HO 00 03 10 00, Copyright, Insurance Services Office, Inc., 1999.

19. Form IM 1050 05 00, Copyright, American Association of Insurance Services, 2000.

20. Form BM 00 20 07 01, Copyright, ISO Properties, Inc., 2000.

21. Form CP 00 10 10 00, Copyright, Insurance Services Office, Inc., 1999.

22. Form CP 00 10 10 00, Copyright, Insurance Services Office, Inc., 1999.

23. Form CP 00 10 10 00, Copyright, Insurance Services Office, Inc., 1999.

24. Form CP 00 10 10 00, Copyright, Insurance Services Office, Inc., 1999.

25. Form CP 00 10 10 00, Copyright, Insurance Services Office, Inc., 1999.

26. Form CP 00 10 10 00, Copyright, Insurance Services Office, Inc., 1999.

27. Form CP 00 10 10 00, Copyright, Insurance Services Office, Inc., 1999.

28. Form CP 00 10 10 00, Copyright, Insurance Services Office, Inc., 1999.

29. Form CP 00 10 10 00, Copyright, Insurance Services Office, Inc., 1999.

30. Form CP 00 10 10 00, Copyright, Insurance Services Office, Inc., 1999.

31. Form CP 00 10 10 00, Copyright, Insurance Services Office, Inc., 1999.

32. Form CP 00 10 10 00, Copyright, Insurance Services Office, Inc., 1999.

33. Form CP 00 90 07 88, Copyright, ISO Commercial Risk Services, Inc., 1983, 1987.

34. Form PP 00 01 06 98, Copyright, Insurance Services Office, Inc., 1997.

35. Form HO 00 03 10 00, Copyright, Insurance Services Office, Inc., 1999.

36. Form HO 00 03 10 00, Copyright, Insurance Services Office, Inc., 1999.

Chapter 13

Direct Your Learning

Insured Events

After learning the subject matter of this chapter, you should be able to:

- Explain why determining whether an insured event occurred is important.

- Identify and explain the six elements of an insured event under property insurance.

- Identify and describe three common approaches to describing covered causes of loss in policy forms.

- Describe four major categories of covered consequences under property insurance.

- Identify and explain the six elements of an insured event under liability insurance.

- Explain the difference between occurrence-based coverage and claims-made coverage.

- Given a case and a property or liability insurance policy excerpt, explain which elements of an insured event are present.

Develop Your Perspective

What are the main topics covered in the chapter?

This chapter describes the different elements of an insured event for both property and liability insurance.

Assume that you were being sued for a mistake you made while rendering professional services.

- What factors would you look for to determine whether this was an insured event?

Why is it important to know these topics?

Knowing the characteristics of an insured event will enable you to determine whether a specific loss qualifies as an insured event and whether the loss will be covered under the policy.

Examine the differences between the elements of an insured event under property insurance and an insured event under liability insurance.

- Why do insurers make these distinctions?
- Can you think of a possible loss situation fitting the elements of an insured event under property insurance?

How can you use this information?

Consider a loss your organization might face.

- Based on your review of the elements of an insured event, would coverage apply to the loss?

Chapter 13

Insured Events

As previous chapters have discussed, an insurer *might* be contractually obligated to make a payment

- Under an enforceable contract of insurance;
- To, or on behalf of, a party with an insurable interest;
- Who qualifies as an insured;
- Subject to policy conditions.

The insurer's obligations are not triggered unless an *insured event* occurs. This chapter shows that an event is insured only if *it meets all six elements in the definition of "insured event."* The elements differ somewhat between property and liability insurance, as shown in the box below:

Elements of an Insured Event

Property Insurance	Liability Insurance
1. Covered property	1. Covered activity
2. Covered cause of loss	2. Alleged legal responsibility to pay covered damages
3. No exclusion applies	3. No exclusion applies
4. Covered consequences	4. Covered consequences
5. Covered location	5. Covered location
6. Covered time period	6. Covered time period

This chapter identifies and explains the elements of an insured event under both property and liability insurance.

INSURED EVENTS UNDER PROPERTY INSURANCE

Property insurance is coverage for real or personal property lost or damaged by a covered cause of loss and, sometimes, is also coverage for consequential financial losses resulting from property damage.

The six elements of an insured event under property insurance are as follows: covered property, covered cause of loss, no exclusion applies, covered consequences, covered location, and covered time period.

Covered Property

In analyzing an insurance contract to determine whether an insured event has occurred, one must understand covered property. *Covered property may be subject to an insured event, while property not covered under the policy (or excluded from coverage) cannot be subject to an insured event.*

Property is legally defined as a bundle of rights that have economic value legally guaranteed and protected. *Real property* refers to rights in land, including rights to water, minerals, things permanently attached to the land (such as buildings), and things growing on the land (such as trees). It also includes rights closely related to land, such as the right to have access to or use of the land belonging to another. *Personal property* refers to all other property rights—in other words, to all property that is not real property.

Most property insurance policies, including commercial building and personal property coverage forms as well as homeowners forms, share a similar format:

- An insuring agreement describing broad classes of covered property. (Some limited or single-purpose insurance policies cover only items specifically described in a list, or **schedule**.)

Schedule
A list that identifies specific items, usually with values attached, that are covered by a property insurance policy.

- An exclusionary section describing narrower subclasses of property that *are not covered.*
- Other provisions within the policy form, or in endorsements to the form, that may *add* or *exclude* specific types of property, or *exclude* damage for certain causes of loss.

Most policies begin with a broad generic description of the types of property that are covered. Exclusions then further define the coverage by removing coverage that would not be provided under specific circumstances or for specific reasons. What remains of the original covered property is what is then covered under the policy.

For example, in ISO's Building and Personal Property Coverage Form, property is divided into three categories: (1) Building, (2) Personal Property of the Insured, and (3) Personal Property of Others. Generally, the "Building" definition provides coverage for real property. The "Personal Property of the Insured" definition complements the "Building" coverage with a description of covered personal property of the insured, sometimes known as "contents coverage." The "Personal Property of Others" definition covers insureds whose "contents" include some personal property owned by others but which the insured might choose to insure. Newly acquired property, or property at new locations, can also be insured.

Generally, when someone decides what property is and is not covered by the policy, determining the following is necessary:

- The category of the property (i.e., real property, etc.), by reading the insuring agreement;

- Whether the property is actually covered or excluded, by reading the exclusions section; and

- Whether any other policy provisions either add or exclude specific types of property or exclude damage for certain causes of loss.

After determining that the property is covered, the next step is to find out whether the second element of a property loss insured event is present: a covered cause of loss.

Covered Cause of Loss

Under a property insurance policy, an insured event must involve damage to covered property by a *covered cause of loss, or peril*. More precisely, a covered peril must be the **proximate cause** of the loss to covered property. The concept of proximate cause is illustrated in the following box.

Proximate cause
The cause that initiates an unbroken chain of events leading to the loss.

Example of a Covered Cause of Loss

A fire ignited an electrical tower on the insured's premises some distance from the building in which covered machinery was located. The fire caused an electrical short circuit which, in turn, caused a sudden increase in the pressure on a belt driving a flywheel. The flywheel disintegrated, and its flying fragments damaged the covered machinery. The court ruled that damage to the machinery was proximately caused by fire. Because the insurance policy covered direct damage by fire (a covered peril), the insurer had to pay for the damaged machinery, even though "collision with flywheel fragments" or anything comparable was not a covered peril. The fire unleashed an unbroken chain of events that resulted in the machinery damage.[1]

The **proximate cause doctrine** generally holds that coverage for a loss is provided under a property insurance policy only if a covered cause of loss is the proximate cause of a covered consequence.

Proximate cause doctrine
A legal doctrine that generally holds that coverage for a loss is provided under a property insurance policy only if a covered peril is the proximate cause of a covered consequence.

Insurers use the following three common approaches to describe covered causes of loss in policy forms:

1. Basic-form
2. Broad-form
3. Special-form

The additional specified perils approach typically adds flood or earthquake coverage to any of those forms.

The basic and broad forms use the specified-perils or named-perils approach, meaning that they specifically name the perils that are insured against. To enforce coverage, the insured has the burden of proof to show that a covered peril was the proximate cause of covered loss consequences.

The special-form coverage, however, provides very broad coverage and names certain hazards and causes of loss that are excluded. To successfully deny coverage, the insurer must be able to prove that the loss resulted from a peril or hazard excluded in the policy.

Ensuing loss
A loss attributable to a covered peril that results from loss by an excluded peril.

Most property policies provide some coverage for **ensuing losses**, losses attributable to a covered peril that result from loss by an excluded peril. For example, the Water (flood) exclusion of the ISO Causes of Loss—Special Form exclusion ends with these words:

> But if Water, as described…results in fire, explosion, or sprinkler leakage, we will pay for the loss or damage caused by that fire, explosion or sprinkler leakage.[2]

Some policies contain an exception to an exclusion that has the effect of an insuring agreement, as discussed in Chapter 11. This exception to an exclusion (or insuring agreement) was particularly important to many businessowners in Grand Forks, North Dakota, in April 1997, when a major fire broke out in a flooded downtown area.

The ensuing losses covered, and against what perils they are covered, vary among policies and even within a single policy.

No Exclusion Applies

The third element of an insured event is that no exclusion applies. *Even if covered property is damaged or destroyed by a covered cause of loss, the loss is not considered an insured event if even one policy exclusion applies to the loss.* That is so unless the event is insured elsewhere within the policy.

However, sometimes one policy portion excludes coverage for a type of loss that the same policy covers in another part of the policy. For example, the ordinance or law hazard might be excluded, but an "additional coverage" within the policy or a policy endorsement might provide coverage under a separate insuring agreement.

Concurrent Causation

An issue regarding exclusions is the doctrine of *concurrent causation*, which applies to special-form coverages. This doctrine holds that if loss to covered property can be attributed to two or more causes of loss, one excluded and the other covered, then the policy covers the loss. In short, the doctrine seems to say that none of a special-form policy's exclusions has any effect if another, nonexcluded, cause of loss is involved in the loss event.[3]

The effect of the concurrent causation doctrine was to require an insurer providing special-form property coverage to pay for a property loss unless *all* causes of the loss are specifically excluded. Most property policies now incorporate wording to negate these court decisions that gave coverage where it presumably was not intended.

Covered Consequences

The fourth element of an insured event under property insurance is covered consequences. When a cause of loss damages or destroys property, some of the damage or adverse effects are covered by property insurance policies; others are not. The phrase "covered consequences" refers to the damage or adverse effects that *are covered* under the policy.

Covered consequences fall into four major categories: reduction in value, increased cost to replace, loss of revenue, and extra expense. See the following box.

Four Major Categories of Covered Consequences

1. *Reduction in value*—Reduction in property value because of damage by cause of loss is sometimes referred to as a direct loss. A policy usually contains provisions that determine how the value of such items can be determined.

2. *Increased cost to replace or repair*—Often, replacing damaged or destroyed property costs more than the property's worth before the damage. Consequently, replacement cost coverage, which provides sufficient coverage to replace the item if it is damaged, is often available for real property and many types of personal property.

3. *Loss of revenue*—Damage to property can cause a business slowdown or shutdown, cutting off the profits and the stream of income that normally pays operating expenses. The income loss resulting from damage to property is a covered consequence under many property insurance policies.

4. *Extra expense*—A business or family can incur extra expense during a period when it cannot use damaged or destroyed property that has not yet been repaired or replaced. Both business and family extra expenses are loss consequences that property insurance can cover.

Covered Location

To qualify as an insured event, the event must not only involve covered property, a covered cause of loss, a covered consequence, and no exclusions; it must also involve a covered location. A covered location is both of the following:

- Within the "coverage territory," as defined in the policy.
- A place where coverage applies within the coverage territory.

Location is not usually an issue in property insurance claims, in that some property never changes locations. Commercial and residential buildings are almost always at a permanent location. By definition, "contents" also have a permanent location—the building that contains them. But not all personal property is or remains as contents. Many personal property items are portable.

Different policies have different "covered locations" for personal property. Under a homeowners policy, coverage extends anywhere in the world. Specialized inland marine floaters can also provide worldwide coverage for business personal property. However, most commercial property forms only cover business personal property in or within 100 feet of the described premises. Likewise, most crime coverages are restricted to property inside the described premises—or even inside of a safe or vault on the premises.

A growing number of businesses have exposures outside the United States. Whenever property exposures exist, even if they are temporary, property insurance policies should be scrutinized to ensure that otherwise insured events also involve a covered location. The covered location should be investigated and confirmed when claims for personal property off-premises or out of the country are involved.

Covered Time Period

Finally, to be covered by property insurance as an insured event, an event must fall within the covered time period. The covered time period during which the insured has an enforceable agreement with the insurer is not always the same as the policy period written in the declarations of a policy. For example:

- The policy period might begin before a written policy is issued.[4] Sometimes an insurance agent binds coverage, orally or in writing, as soon as the insured agrees to buy it, but several weeks pass before a written policy is issued. Once issued, the written policy would normally have the same effective date as the binder (the temporary agreement to provide insurance coverage until a formal written policy is issued).

- After a policy is issued, coverage may be terminated by cancellation before the end of the policy period when it would otherwise expire.

- A policy could be renewed for many successive years, as shown in an endorsement that does not replace the original declarations page.

When does a covered cause fall within the critical time period necessary to make it an insured event? Generally, only the *onset or beginning* of the loss causation must lie within that period. As long as the loss-producing event from a covered cause commences during the policy period, the covered consequences need not fall entirely within the policy period. For example:

- If a fire starts to damage covered property ten minutes before policy inception, the loss would *not* be an insured event, even if the fire continues to burn well into the policy period.

- If a fire starts to damage covered property ten minutes before the policy expires, the loss *is* an insured event, even if most of the damage occurs after the time coverage expires.

In summary, when an insurer considers paying a property loss claim, one of the items it must evaluate is whether an insured event occurred. An insurer can determine this by examining *all* of the six elements of an insured event (on a property insurance policy). The next section discusses insured events under *liability insurance*.

INSURED EVENTS UNDER LIABILITY INSURANCE

An insured event under liability insurance is different from an insured event under property insurance. The following box reflects the six elements of an insured event under liability insurance: covered activity, alleged legal responsibility to pay covered damages, no exclusion applies, covered consequences, covered location, and covered time period.

Elements of an Insured Event Under Liability Insurance

1. Covered activity

2. Alleged legal responsibility to pay covered damages

3. No exclusion applies

4. Covered consequences

5. Covered location

6. Covered time period

Covered Activity

The first element of an insured event under liability insurance is a *covered activity*. The broadest personal and commercial liability policies have a comprehensive insuring agreement including protection for a wide range of activities. These liability policies do not specify what types of activities are covered, but they apply to all activities *not excluded*. Therefore, they could be loosely compared to special-form property coverage that applies to nonexcluded perils and hazards. Other liability policies—auto policies, for example—have limited or single-purpose insuring agreements that provide coverage for only one or a few types of activities.

The name of a policy or coverage often indicates what activities it covers. For example, a *commercial general liability* coverage form and the *personal liability* coverage of homeowners policies provide broad, comprehensive protection against a range of common business or personal activities, whereas the coverage of a *business auto* policy or a *personal auto* policy is limited to auto-related activities. While the policy name provides an important clue, the full range of activities covered under a particular liability policy can be understood clearly only by reading the entire contract, including all endorsements.

Unlike with property insurance, new activities or locations usually are not an issue with comprehensive liability insurance. Nothing in the commercial general liability contract, for example, limits liability coverage to activities or locations listed in the policy declarations. If the insured becomes involved in new activities during the policy period, premium auditors will add an additional rating category at audit and charge an appropriate premium.

Liability policies covering more specific exposures vary in their treatment of new activities or locations. When analyzing these policies, one must determine whether coverage automatically applies for new activities and determine any limitations on the automatic coverage.

Alleged Legal Responsibility To Pay Covered Damages

A liability loss is caused—linking a covered activity with a covered consequence—whenever something happens through which an insured allegedly becomes legally obligated to pay damages to a third-party claimant because of injury or damage covered by the policy. The liability insurer's obligation extends beyond the obligation to pay damages.

The insurer must defend the insured against any claim or suit alleging an insured event, using counsel of the insurer's choice, and to pay all costs of the defense provided. The insurer has these obligations even for claims that are clearly groundless, false, or fraudulent. Insurers are also obligated to defend insureds in any claim that includes at least one allegation that the policy covers. For example, the insurer would be obligated to defend a homeowners liability claim alleging damages for both bodily injury (which is covered) and slander (which is not covered by most unendorsed homeowners policies). Theoretically, at least, this is an unlimited obligation; defense costs usually are not subject to any dollar limit. In practice, limitations usually exist on how much an insurer will spend defending a claim before agreeing to a settlement.

Most liability insurance policies agree to pay for damages that the insured is legally obligated to pay. The legal obligation (becoming liable by law) to which various liability policies refer can stem from the following:

- *Negligence or other tort liability*—failure to fulfill a duty imposed by tort law
- *Statutory liability*—failure to meet a duty imposed by statute
- *Contractual liability*—failure to meet an obligation assumed under another contract, that is, the voluntary assumption of a liability one would not otherwise have under the law

Therefore, when one examines the activities covered under the policy and the liability conditions under which these activities are covered, a determination about whether the first and second elements of an insured event have occurred can be made.

No Exclusion Applies

Just as in property insurance, when a covered activity involves an incident alleging covered injury or damage resulting in a covered consequence, it is not an insured event if *even one* exclusion in the policy applies. Even when an exclusion applies, it is important to examine the rest of the policy for anything that might cancel out the exclusion. Sometimes one portion of a policy excludes coverage for a type of loss that is covered elsewhere in the policy or in an endorsement. At other times, an exception to an exclusion carves out coverage for losses that otherwise would be excluded.

Covered Consequences

The fourth element of a liability insured event is covered consequences. As previously suggested, liability insurance policies typically cover consequences in two broad categories:

1. *Defense costs* incurred to defend against a third-party claim for covered injury or damage brought against the insured, including miscellaneous expenses
2. *Damages* for which the insured is legally liable to a third party

Insurers rarely pay *damages* unless the wrong allegedly committed by the insured both arises from a covered activity and alleges injury or damage that would be covered by the policy. However, most liability policies obligate the insurer to *defend* the insured even when a claim seems to be false or fraudulent, as long as at least one of the claim's allegations is potentially within the coverage provided by the policy.

Covered Injury or Damage

An insurer is obligated to pay damages under a liability insurance policy only when the nature of the injury, damage, offense, wrongful act, and so forth is covered by that policy. Liability policies commonly cover bodily injury, personal injury, advertising injury, property damage, professional liability, and wrongful acts.

Bodily Injury

Many liability policies define **bodily injury** as follows:

> "Bodily injury" means bodily injury, sickness or disease sustained by a person, including death resulting from any of these at any time.[5]

Bodily injury (BI)
Bodily harm/injury, sickness, disease, and death.

The references to sickness, disease, and death demonstrate that the insurance-policy meaning of "bodily injury" includes some elements not normally characterized as bodily injuries. Some courts have held that emotional distress is bodily injury even when it does not involve physical harm. Other states have refused to stretch "bodily injury" that far without a broader policy definition.

Personal Injury

Personal injury
Intentional torts (offenses), specifically listed in the policy, such as libel, slander, defamation, wrongful entry or eviction, false arrest, wrongful detention, and malicious prosecution.

The term **personal injury**, as used in insurance policies, usually refers to a loosely related group of specific listed "offenses," typically including libel, slander, defamation, wrongful entry or eviction, false arrest, wrongful detention, and malicious prosecution. These offenses fall into the broad legal category of "intentional torts," but only the intentional torts (offenses) listed in the policy are covered.

Personal Injury

As used in liability insurance policies, "personal injury" means a loosely related group of listed offenses such as libel and slander as defined in the policy. Sometimes the term is defined to include bodily injury, along with other offenses.

As used in no-fault insurance, "personal injury protection" provides first-party coverage against injuries received in an auto accident.

As used by attorneys, "personal injury" often has the same meaning as "bodily injury."

Advertising Injury

Although it has no universal definition, advertising injury has been defined in some general liability policies to encompass liability stemming from libel or slander; publishing material that constitutes an invasion of privacy; misappropriation of advertising ideas; and infringement of copyright, title, or slogan. As broadly defined, advertising injury generally overlaps with personal injury, but other policy provisions preclude duplicate payment for the same loss.

Personal and Advertising Injury

Personal and advertising injury
Personal injury offenses and offenses relating to publication or advertising.

The 1998 edition of ISO's Commercial General Liability Coverage Form simplified matters—and eliminated the need for extensive wording in the policy—by combining **personal and advertising injury** into a single offense. This beginning of the insuring agreement and the definition illustrate the wide-ranging scope of this coverage:

COVERAGE B PERSONAL AND ADVERTISING INJURY
LIABILITY

1. **Insuring Agreement**

   a. We will pay those sums that the insured becomes legally obligated to pay as damages because of "personal and advertising injury" to which this insurance applies...

SECTION V — DEFINITIONS

…

14. "Personal and advertising injury" means injury, including consequential "bodily injury", arising out of one or more of the following offenses.

a. False arrest, detention or imprisonment;

b. Malicious prosecution;

c. The wrongful eviction from, wrongful entry into, or invasion of the right of private occupancy of a room, dwelling, or premises that a person occupies, committed by or on behalf of its owner, landlord or lessor;

d. Oral or written publication of material that slanders or libels a person or organization or disparages a person's or organization's goods, products or services;

e. Oral or written publication of material that violates a person's right of privacy;

f. The use of another's advertising idea in your "advertisement"; or

g. Infringing upon another's copyright, trade dress or slogan in your "advertisement".[6]

Property Damage

"Property damage" is typically defined in insurance policies as follows:

Property damage means:

a. Physical injury to tangible property, including all resulting loss of use of that property. All such loss of use shall be deemed to occur at the time of the physical injury that caused it; or

b. Loss of use of tangible property that is not physically injured. All such loss of use shall be deemed to occur at the time of the "occurrence" that caused it.[7]

According to this definition, **property damage** includes not only physical damage to tangible property but also the *resulting* loss of use, as well as loss of use of tangible property that has not been physically injured. This definition does not encompass loss of use of intangible property (goodwill, copyrights, and so forth).

The second part of this definition acts to provide coverage for certain claims or suits in which liability can result from loss of use of tangible property without physical loss or damage to that property. For example, suppose a tenant's negligence causes a major fire in a high-rise building. The entire area is roped off for safety reasons, and would-be customers are denied access to a nearby store that has not been damaged. The store owner makes a property damage liability claim against the tenant who caused the fire on the basis that the undamaged store's loss of income was the result of the tenant's negligence. The store's loss of income would qualify as "property damage" under this definition. The store owner suffered an economic

Property damage
Loss of use, destruction, or damage to a person's tangible property.

loss because the store could not be used, even though the store had sustained no physical damage.

Professional Liability; Errors and Omissions

Professional liability
Liability for damages that result from the improper rendering of professional services, errors in judgment, or omissions.

Professional liability involves claims for damages that result from the improper rendering of professional services, errors in judgment, or omissions. For example, a physician's professional liability policy would generally provide coverage for claims alleging inappropriate medical treatment. The damages that result from professional liability might involve bodily injury or property damage for certain professionals.

Wrongful Acts

Wrongful act
A harmful act or omission, allegedly committed or attempted by an insured.

The insuring agreements of directors and officers liability policies are worded so that the claim must be for a **wrongful act**. "Wrongful act" is defined broadly and ordinarily includes a wide range of acts or omissions, such as "any error, misstatement, misleading statement, act, omission, neglect, or breach of duty committed, attempted, or allegedly committed or attempted by an insured...." However, the definition is typically restricted to acts or omissions in the insured's capacity as a director or an officer for the corporation.

Damages

Whether the allegation involves bodily injury, property *damage*, or some other offense, an insured event does not occur unless the covered consequences involve a claim for *damages* that are covered under the policy. *Damages* usually means money that the law requires one person to pay to another because of loss or injury suffered by the other party. (In contrast, *damage* means loss or harm resulting from injury to a person, to property, or to someone's reputation.) A typical liability insuring agreement refers to "sums that the insured becomes legally obligated to pay as damages," and insurers usually do not define "damages." The common, plain meaning of the term would obligate the insurer to pay both compensatory damages and punitive damages (see Exhibit 13-1).

Compensatory Damages

Compensatory damages
Payment to indemnify or compensate a claimant for injury or damage; includes both economic (special) and noneconomic (general) damages.

Economic damages, or **special damages**
Payment to compensate for monetary loss.

Compensatory damages are money payments that indemnify or compensate claimants for their injury or damage. Compensatory damages can include both economic and noneconomic damages. **Economic damages**, also referred to as **special damages**, provide compensation for monetary loss and might include the following:

- Reasonable medical expenses
- Cost to repair or replace damaged property
- Loss of a property's use value
- Lost wages during a period of recovery or in the future
- Economic value of services lost in the present or the future

EXHIBIT 13-1

Damages in Liability Claims

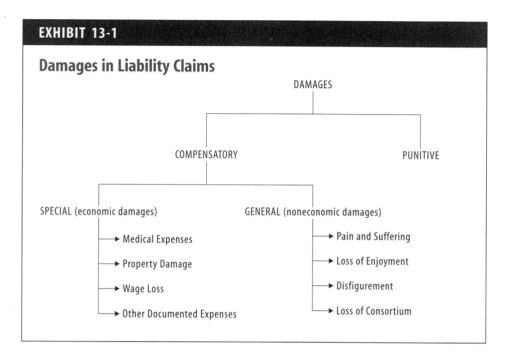

Noneconomic damages, also called general damages, are an amount of money awarded by the court to compensate for a loss that cannot readily be measured in dollars, including intangibles such as pain and suffering, bereavement, or loss of consortium.

Punitive Damages

Punitive damages are intended to punish a wrongdoer for having injured the claimant or damaged the claimant's property through acts of a greater culpability than simple negligence. Punitive damages awarded by the court in any given case might have no direct relationship to the actual monetary damage suffered by the claimant. Large punitive damages awards have been made in cases in which compensatory damages were negligible.

Punitive damages are not necessarily covered by insurance. Some insurance policies explicitly exclude payment of punitive damages; others, which are silent on the issue, would presumably provide coverage. However, a number of states, citing public policy issues, prohibit insurers from paying punitive damages on behalf of insureds even if they are covered by insurance, and even if punitive damages are awarded in a case that also involves covered compensatory damages. These states take the view that the insured does not receive much "punishment" when the cost of that punishment is paid for by an insurer. The majority viewpoint holds that punitive damages are, in reality, as much a source of unexpected financial loss as compensatory damages; people should be entitled to purchase insurance protecting them against punitive damages awards; and the exposure meets the requirements of a commercially insurable exposure.

Whenever policy language conflicts with prevailing law, the law controls. So if the law prohibits insurers from paying punitive damages, the insurer is not obligated to pay punitive damages even if the policy otherwise provides the coverage.

Noneconomic damages, or general damages
Payment awarded by the court to compensate for a loss that cannot readily be monetarily measured, including intangibles such as pain and suffering, bereavement, or loss of consortium.

Punitive damages
Payment, awarded by the court, intended to punish a wrongdoer for having injured the claimant or damaged the claimant's property through acts of a greater culpability than simple negligence.

Other Damages

Liability insurance is sometimes required to pay more than compensatory and punitive damages. Directors and officers liability policies, some professional liability policies, and other insurance contracts covering economic damages resulting from an insured's wrongful acts often are broad enough to encompass the **treble (triple) damage**s that can be assessed when certain federal laws are violated.

Actions in Equity

Rather than seek a monetary award, claimants sometimes seek "injunctive relief," asking the court to order some act to be performed—or, in some cases, to prohibit some act. Generally, if a lawsuit seeks only an injunction and not money damages, insurance would not apply. However, insurance might be triggered if an injunction were to require an insured to spend money. For example, a court might require a landowner to fence his property to prevent his cattle from wandering onto adjoining property. Erecting a fence does not involve paying monetary damages to the claimant, but the litigation—and the fence—still involve substantial costs. To prevent problems, some insurers insert exclusions to clarify their intention to limit coverage to money damages. Even such an exclusion will not relieve the insurer of its obligations in an action that seeks both compensatory damages and equitable relief. As previously mentioned, the insurer's duty to defend is broader than its duty to pay damages. If part of the allegations are covered and part are excluded, the insurer has the obligation to defend the entire action, but the insurer is obligated to pay only those damages that are covered.

Defense Costs and Other Claim Expenses

Primary liability insurance policies invariably cover defense costs, as well as a range of additional expenses generally referred to as **supplementary payments**.

The typical liability insuring agreement does *not* impose a dollar limit on an insurer's defense costs. Only the payment of a judgment or settlement exhausts the insurer's obligation to defend. If the insurer offers to pay the full policy limits to the claimant, and the claimant rejects this offer, the insurer is obligated to continue a defense until a settlement is reached or a judgment is awarded by the courts.

Liability insurance policies typically provide *supplementary payments* coverage, such as the following in the ISO Personal Auto Policy:

1. Up to $250 for the cost of bail bonds required because of an accident, including related traffic law violations. The accident must result in "bodily injury" or "property damage" covered under this policy.
2. Premiums on appeal bonds and bonds to release attachments in any suit we defend.
3. Interest accruing after a judgment is entered in any suit we defend. Our duty to pay interest ends when we offer to pay that part of the judgment which does not exceed our limit of liability for this coverage.

Treble (triple) damages (three times compensatory damages)
Payment assessed against a wrongdoer when certain federal laws are violated.

Supplementary payments
Payment for a range of additional claim-related expenses as specified in a liability policy.

4. Up to $200 a day for loss of earnings, but not other income, because of attendance at hearings or trials at our request.

5. Other reasonable expenses incurred at our request.[8]

Covered Location

The fifth element of an insured event under liability insurance is covered location. With liability insurance, two distinct locations can be relevant: the location of the incident and the location of a suit brought by a claimant against an insured.

Most liability insurance policies provide protection at any location within a broadly defined policy territory. In auto insurance, for example, the policy territory is usually defined as the United States of America; its territories or possessions; Puerto Rico; or Canada. Accidents involving a covered auto while being transported between their ports are also covered by these policies.

The broadest definitions of covered locations can be found in liability policies that apply "anywhere in the world." Others apply "anywhere" or do not specify their territorial scope.

An insurance policy providing defense coverage sometimes places a territorial restriction on *suits*. For example, the Commercial General Liability Coverage Form provides coverage for personal and advertising injury offenses that occur through the Internet, provided that the insured's responsibility to pay damages is determined in a suit in the United States of America, including its territories and possessions; Puerto Rico; or Canada.

Covered Time Period

The last element of an insured event under liability insurance is a covered time period. The important question is, "*What* must happen, and when must *that particular thing* happen, to trigger liability coverage?" It is essential to know whether coverage is triggered when an adverse event occurs, when the insured becomes aware that it happened, when a claim is made for damages arising out of that event, or at some other point in time.

Like property insurance policies, liability policies usually have a one-year term, but three-or six-month personal auto policies are common, and three-year policies also exist.

Any discussion of time periods covered by insurance policies eventually includes the term, "tail," a term that does not appear in insurance policies. Most claims—and nearly all property claims—involve a relatively short period of time, or tail, between the event, the discovery, the claim, and the settlement. Others, referred to as long-tail claims, may involve years from the date of the injury or damage, the date it is discovered, the date a claim is made, the date a claim is settled, and the date of final claim payment.

Claims involving long-tail exposures raise challenging questions about the point in time at which a covered event occurs. What must happen during the covered time period to "trigger" a claim under any given policy?

Occurrence-basis coverage
Coverage triggered by the actual happening of injury or damage during the policy period.

Claims-made coverage
Coverage triggered by a claim alleging injury or damage that is made during the policy period, even if the claim arises from an event that happened before policy inception.

The standard, traditional approach to liability insurance uses an occurrence-basis policy. Some liability coverages, however, are written on a claims-made basis. The difference between the two approaches lies in their coverage triggers. **Occurrence-basis coverage** is triggered by the actual happening of injury or damage during the policy period. A **claims-made coverage** is triggered by a claim alleging injury or damage that is made during the policy period, even if the claim arises from an event that happened before policy inception.

In theory, the claims-made approach is ideal. Over time, the insured buys a series of claims-made policies that cannot be stacked, each policy taking over when the previous policy expires. Unless coverage lapses, the insured should never be without current coverage that has appropriate policy limits.

In practice, it is not that simple. Many claims-made policies are subject to a *retroactive date*; claims for injury or damage that occurred before that date are not covered. Ideally, a retroactive date is designated on the insured's first claims-made policy, and that date remains fixed even when the initial policy is renewed or replaced. That does not always happen. A replacement claims-made policy with a different retroactive date would create a potential time gap. An insured who replaces a claims-made policy with an occurrence policy might also face a time gap in coverage.

The insuring agreement in the claims-made version of the Commercial General Liability Coverage Form expresses the trigger in these words:

> This insurance applies to "bodily injury" and "property damage" only if:...
>
> (2) The "bodily injury" or "property damage" did not occur before the Retroactive Date, if any, shown in the Declarations or after the end of the policy period; and
>
> (3) A claim for damages because of "bodily injury" or "property damage" is first made against any insured, in accordance with paragraph **c.** below, during the policy period or any Extended Reporting Period we provide under Section **V** — Extended Reporting Periods.[9]

Like many other claims-made policies, the claims-made Commercial General Liability Policy offers one or more extended coverage periods, sometimes referred to as "tail coverage." Usually, no additional *coverage* is provided,[10] but the "tail" does provide more *time* in which to report a covered claim. The specifics vary by policy, but "tail" coverage typically extends coverage to claims first made after the policy expires for injury or damage that occurred before the policy terminated but after its retroactive date. The right to tail coverage, the cost of the coverage, and the length of the "tail" are not always guaranteed.

Tail coverage applies to claims reported after the policy has expired. As suggested, another coverage gap could develop when an unforeseen claim results from an event that happened before the policy's retroactive date. Insurers writing claims-made coverage are sometimes willing to provide retroactive coverage for a period long enough to cover any claims that previously were incurred but unknown and unreported.

SUMMARY

No loss is covered unless an insured event occurs. An enforceable contract involving an insured party with an insurable interest must be in force, with no policy conditions nullifying coverage.

The elements of an insured event vary depending on whether property insurance or liability insurance is involved. For property insurance, the six elements of an insured event are the following:

1. Covered property
2. Covered cause of loss
3. No exclusion applies
4. Covered consequences
5. Covered location
6. Covered time period

For liability insurance, the six elements of an insured event are as follows:

1. Covered activity
2. Alleged legal responsibility to pay covered damages
3. No exclusion applies
4. Covered consequences
5. Covered location
6. Covered time period

After an insured event has occurred and all other checkpoints indicate a loss is covered, the next step in coverage analysis is to determine how much to pay. Chapter 14 addresses that issue in relation to property insurance; Chapter 15 deals similarly with liability insurance.

CHAPTER NOTES

1. Lynn Gas & Electric Co. v. Meriden Fire Insurance Co., 158 Mass. 570, 33 N.E. 690 (1893).
2. Form CP 10 30 10 00, Copyright, Insurance Services Office, Inc., 1999.
3. Eric A. Wiening, "An End to All-Risks Insurance?" *The Risk Report*, vol. VI, No. 6, February 1984.
4. This was reportedly the situation with billions of dollars of property coverage when the World Trade Center was destroyed on September 11, 2001.
5. Form CG 00 01 07 98, Copyright, Insurance Services Office, Inc., 1997.
6. Form CG 00 01 07 98, Copyright, Insurance Services Office, Inc., 1997.
7. Form CG 00 01 07 98, Copyright, Insurance Services Office, Inc., 1997.
8. Form PP 00 01 06 98, Copyright, Insurance Services Office, Inc., 1997
9. Form CG 00 02 10 01, Copyright, Insurance Services Office Properties, Inc., 2000.
10. Sometimes an aggregate limit is restored.

Chapter 14

Direct Your Learning

Amounts Payable: Property Insurance

After learning the subject matter of this chapter, you should be able to:

- Explain why insurance to value is important in property insurance.

- Explain the various approaches used in property insurance policies to value property.

- Identify, describe, contrast, and distinguish among the various types of policy limits used in property insurance.

- Explain the reasons for policy limits and loss valuation provisions.

- Given a property insurance policy or policy excerpt, identify and evaluate that policy's limits and loss valuation provisions.

- Explain the purpose of coinsurance.

- Explain why an 80 percent coinsurance requirement is the most common approach.

- State the coinsurance formula and explain its components.

- Compare coinsurance and insurance-to-value provisions.

- Identify the problems associated with maintaining insurance to value and explain what can be done to minimize these problems.

- Describe the alternatives to coinsurance.

- Explain the reasons for using deductibles.

- Describe the types of deductibles.

- Explain why some policies contain no deductibles.

- Given a property insurance claim situation, apply policy limits, valuation provisions, insurance-to-value provisions, and deductibles, separately or in combination, to determine the amount payable.

- Given relevant exposure and coverage information, explain what insurance-to-value and deductible provisions would be appropriate.

Develop Your Perspective

What are the main topics covered in the chapter?

The amount that should be paid under a property insurance policy depends on the policy's valuation provision, limits, coinsurance and other insurance-to-value provisions, and deductibles.

Review a property insurance policy.

- Identify the policy limits listed.

- Consider the property loss exposures that would fall under each of those limits.

Why is it important to know these topics?

Knowing this information will help you understand how to interpret a policy to determine the available coverage and the process for evaluating losses and amounts payable.

Explain how coinsurance and other insurance-to-value provisions encourage insureds to insure to value.

- Why is coinsurance alternately referred to as a punishment and a reward?

How can you use this information?

Consider a property loss exposure your organization might face. Investigate the coverage that applies to the loss.

- Do the policy limits provide adequate coverage for the possible loss exposures?

- How might you determine the amount that would be paid for the loss?

Chapter 14

Amounts Payable: Property Insurance

Every insurance policy must indicate how an insurer determines the amount payable for a covered loss. Under any property insurance policy, the amount payable depends on the policy's valuation provision, policy limits, coinsurance and other insurance-to-value provisions, and deductibles. This chapter examines these property insurance policy features that determine amounts payable.

When property is insured to its full insurable value, adequate limits of insurance are available to indemnify those who suffer a loss.

INSURANCE TO VALUE

Insurance to value, for property insurance, is a limit of insurance that approximates the maximum potential loss. A building with an insurable value of $100,000 that is covered by $100,000 of insurance is insured to value. By insuring to value, an insured will have sufficient funds available in the event of a total loss.

Insurance to value
A limit in property insurance that approximates the maximum potential loss.

People do not always buy enough property insurance to fully cover their property. Consider the following:

- Property insurance is normally priced at some rate per $100 of insurance. If the rate is $1.00, then $10,000 of insurance would cost $100, and $100,000 of insurance would cost $1,000.

- Most property losses involve only a small portion of the value of insured property. Approximately 2 percent of all property losses are total losses.[1]

Using these two pieces of information, a property owner might choose to buy less than the full value of insurance. For example, because most property losses are relatively small, the owner of Building A with an insurable value of $100,000 and a $1.00 rate could insure against most losses for a cost of, say, $250, buying a policy with a $25,000 limit. Meanwhile, the owner of Building B, also worth $100,000, could pay $1,000 for a $100,000 policy covering all losses. Insurance would cover most losses incurred by either building owner, but one has paid four times as much premium as the other. This situation is undesirable for two reasons:

- The owner of Building A faces a financial disaster in the event of an unlikely, but possible, total loss.
- The insurer collects four times as much premium from Owner B as from Owner A. Yet the insurer can expect to pay almost the same amount in claims to either owner. This appears unfair both to the insurer and to the insured who paid the higher premium.

Insurance buyers and sellers usually attempt to ensure that a close match exists between the insurable value of property and amount of insurance covering that property. The insurable value of property is partly determined by the valuation provision in the applicable insurance policy and the insurance amount depends on the applicable policy limits.

VALUATION PROVISIONS

Valuation provision
A provision that indicates how the insurer and the insured should determine lost or damaged property's value.

When covered property is lost or damaged, the amount payable under a property insurance policy depends on the property's value. Every property policy states *how* the insurer and the insured determine that value. Most property policies use replacement cost (RC), actual cash value (ACV), actual loss sustained, or another **valuation provision**. See the following box.

Types of Valuation Provisions

- Replacement cost (RC)
- Actual cash value (ACV)
- Actual loss sustained
- Other valuation provisions

Replacement Cost

Replacement cost is commonly used in insurance policies covering buildings, and in many policies covering personal property. When property insurance is written on a replacement-cost basis, the covered property's insurable value is the current cost, at the time of the loss, of repairing or replacing the damaged or stolen property with new property of like kind and quality.

The following is a typical replacement cost valuation provision:

> **9. Replacement Cost**—When replacement cost is shown on the **declarations** for covered property, the value is based on replacement cost without any deduction for depreciation.

This replacement cost provision does not apply to objects of art, rarity, or antiquity; property of others; or paragraphs 3. through 8. above. [*Paragraphs 3 through 8 relate to the valuation of glass, merchandise sold, valuable papers and records, tenant's improvements, pairs or sets, and loss to parts.*]

The replacement cost is limited to the cost of repair or replacement with similar materials on the same site and used for the same purpose. The payment shall not exceed the amount **you** spend to repair or replace the damaged or destroyed property.

Except as provided under Limited Replacement Cost, replacement cost valuation does not apply until the damaged or destroyed property is repaired or replaced. **You** may make a claim for actual cash value before repair or replacement takes place, and later for the replacement cost if **you** notify **us** of **your** intent within 180 days after the loss.[2]

At the time of loss, if property covered on a replacement-cost basis is damaged or destroyed, the insured is entitled to the current cost of repairing damaged property or of buying or building new property of like kind and quality, even if the destroyed property is several years old, and even if its replacement cost exceeds the original purchase price. If the cost of new property has decreased, as often happens with computer equipment or other electronic items, replacement cost coverage pays the current lower cost.

Often a particular model or style of electronic equipment is no longer made. Although the item is technically irreplaceable, one can still determine the replacement cost for property of comparable material and quality. For example, a manufacturer might have discontinued a particular style of armchair. However, something comparable exists, often from the same manufacturer. The insured is usually willing to settle a claim based on the existing model's cost, as long as the replacement item is not inferior.

Policies vary. Often replacement cost coverage does not apply to certain types of property such as antiques. Replacement cost valuation obviously is not suitable for objects that are valuable primarily because they are old.

Technically, replacement cost coverage violates the principle of indemnity. An insured who sustains a loss to old, used property and receives insurance payment for new property has profited from the loss. To reduce the moral hazard, most replacement cost policies pay on a replacement-cost basis only after the insured has actually replaced the damaged or destroyed property or, in some cases, when the loss is small. Some policies also require the insured to rebuild a building with one of identical construction, in the same location, or for the same purpose; otherwise, depreciation is deducted.

Policy limits on property covered on a replacement-cost basis should be based on the property's replacement cost value. For buildings, the replacement cost value is usually higher than the property's depreciated actual cash value. Property insurance rates per $100 of insurance are usually the same whether the property is insured for RC or ACV. However, replacement cost insurance is more costly because higher limits are required to insure to value.

Actual Cash Value

Actual cash value is another way of determining amounts payable for a property loss and is one of the most important terms in property insurance.

The ISO Personal Auto Policy uses the term as follows:

LIMIT OF LIABILITY

A. Our limit of liability for loss will be the lesser of the
1. Actual cash value of the stolen or damaged property; or
2. Amount necessary to repair or replace the property…
B. An adjustment for depreciation and physical condition will be made in determining actual cash value in the event of a total loss.[3]

Most policies do not define actual cash value, but courts have defined it as one of the following:

- Replacement cost minus depreciation

- Market value

- Broad evidence rule

Definitions vary by jurisdiction and depend partly on the property covered.

Policy limits on property covered on an ACV basis should be based on the property's actual cash value, which is usually lower than the property's replacement cost value.

Replacement Cost Minus Depreciation

Most property has its highest value when new. However, property depreciates at a fairly steady rate due to age and use. Depreciation reflects the value of the use the insured has already received from the property. **Depreciation** represents a loss of value; numerous factors affect the depreciation rate and amount.

Depreciation usually reflects at least three key factors:

1. Physical wear and tear

2. Age

3. Obsolescence

Although related, these factors are separate causes of depreciation. Physical wear and tear corresponds with age, but age alone can cause depreciation. Also, obsolescence caused by fashion, technological changes, or other factors can occur rapidly and suddenly.

Straight line depreciation
A method of determining the loss in value of an asset by depreciating the asset by the same amount each year over the asset's useful life.

Straight line depreciation is a commonly used, simple method of calculating gradual depreciation. If a carpet is expected to last eight years, it would lose one-eighth of its value every year. If two-year-old carpeting is destroyed by a covered peril, the amount of depreciation would be two-eighths or one-fourth of its current replacement cost. Suppose the carpeting had been purchased for $1,300 two years ago, but replacement carpeting would cost $1,600. The amount of depreciation would be one-fourth of $1,600, or $400. The carpet's actual cash value using this method would be $1,200 ($1,600 − $400 = $1,200). Depreciation is subtracted from the replacement cost, not the original cost.

Another term describing depreciation in insurance policies is "betterment." When property is insured on an ACV basis, the loss settlement amount is reduced by the "betterment" that *would* exist if replacement cost values were used instead.

Generally, actual cash value insurance restores the insured to its pre-loss condition. Some policies include a statement to this effect, like this one in the ISO Personal Auto Policy:

> If a repair or replacement results in better than like kind or quality, we will not pay for the amount of the betterment.[4]

The *concept* of depreciation is simple. However, disagreements regularly develop regarding the appropriate *amount* of depreciation.

Market Value

> Everything is worth what its purchaser will pay for it.
>
> Publilius Syrus, *Moral Sayings* (1st C. B.C.), 847, Darius Lyman, trans.

Another method of calculating actual cash value is by looking at the market value. Many courts have ruled that actual cash value means fair market value. The **market value** of property is the amount for which a knowledgeable buyer, under no unusual pressure, would buy and for which a knowledgeable seller, under no unusual pressure, would sell.

Market value
The amount for which a knowledgeable buyer, under no unusual pressure, would buy and for which a knowledgeable seller, under no unusual pressure, would sell.

The actual cash value of autos, for example, is usually based on fair market value. Fair market value is easily established for autos, personal computers, and other items having many buyers and sellers and having information about recent sales. However, the market for some property is too irregular to determine fair market value.

Market valuation is also useful when objects of like kind and quality are unavailable for purchase, such as antiques, works of art, and other collectibles. Market valuation can also be the most accurate way to determine the "worth" of some older or historic buildings built with obsolete construction methods and materials. Consequently, market value would reflect the price for which similar items have recently sold.

The market value of real property reflects the value of the land and its location, as well as the value of any buildings or structures on the land. Because most insurance policies cover buildings and structures but not land, the land's value must be eliminated in establishing insurable values.

The land's value usually excludes the value of any building or structure on it, so any damage to the building does not affect the land's value. However, there are exceptions. Sometimes zoning restrictions prohibit reconstruction of a building at its current location, and the land will actually lose value if the building is destroyed. Alternatively, a rundown structure on a prime piece of real estate can detract from the land's value, because any developer would have to tear down the building before a new one could be constructed. In this situation, destruction of the building, by any cause, is likely to increase the land's value.

Diminution in Value

Diminution in value
The decrease in market value that repaired property incurs as compared to the market value of property that has never been damaged.

Direct damage property insurance usually pays repair costs but does not reimburse the insured for any **diminution in value** that might result if repaired property has a lower market value than property that has never been damaged. Recently, a number of motorists have requested additional payment under their collision coverage for diminution in value. To clarify insurers' intentions, many auto policies now include an endorsement noting that coverage for diminution in value is specifically excluded.

Broad Evidence Rule

Broad evidence rule
A court ruling explicitly requiring that all relevant factors be considered in determining actual cash value.

Many states have adopted the broad evidence rule, which explicitly requires the consideration of all relevant factors in determining actual cash value. Exhibit 14-1 lists twenty-one elements that courts have used in applying the **broad evidence rule** to determine a building's actual cash value.

EXHIBIT 14-1

Factors Considered in Determining a Building's ACV

1. Reproduction cost less depreciation
2. Capitalization of income
3. Comparison sales of similar property
4. Market value based on 1., 2., and 3.
5. Opinion of qualified appraiser based on additional factors
6. Prior sales of the subject property, assuming they were bona fide, arm's-length transactions
7. Pre-loss contract to sell the subject property
8. Attempts to sell the subject property, including "listed" price with brokers and bona fide offers received
9. Insured's purchase price plus cost of capital improvements
10. Assessed values for real estate tax purposes
11. Insured's statements regarding value in official proceedings for tax relief, income tax returns, or the insured's own accounting records
12. The building's age and construction; prior unrepaired damage; depreciation
13. Obsolescence

14. Building's present use and its profitability

15. Alternate building uses

16. Present neighborhood characteristics; long-range community plans for the area where the building is located; urban renewal prospects; new roadway plans

17. Insured's intention to demolish building

18. Vacancy; abandonment

19. Excessive tax arrears

20. Original cost of construction

21. Inflationary or deflationary trends

Based on National Committee on Property Insurance, *ACV Guidelines,* 1982, pp. 12–13.

Court decisions regarding *personal property* can generally be summarized as follows:

- *Residential personal property* is valued at its replacement cost new at the time of loss, less depreciation. Its value in the secondhand market (used furniture and clothing stores) is not the test of its value.

- *Business personal property in use* (furniture, fixtures, and machinery) is generally valued at its replacement cost new at the time of loss, less depreciation. This class of property has a used market. For secondhand property, the market value of similar property in the same condition is its actual cash value.

- *Stocks of merchandise*, a special class of personal property, are valued at the cost of replacing the property rather than at the property owner's selling price. Freight and other transportation charges are added. However, active merchandise that cannot be replaced within a reasonable time is worth its selling price. Depreciation (which includes obsolescence) is generally deducted.

- *Personal property in the hands of a manufacturer* is valued, by most courts, at the cost of materials, plus transportation costs to get those materials to the manufacturer, plus the cost of labor and other expenses, unless this valuation standard is inconsistent with policy provisions.

Actual Loss Sustained

Another valuation provision in property insurance is **actual loss sustained.** Business income coverage is provided on the basis of actual loss sustained. The ISO Business Income Coverage Forms (*with emphasis added*), states the concept as follows:

> We will pay for the *actual loss* of Business Income you *sustain* due to the necessary "suspension" of your "operations" during the "period of restoration".[5]

The effect of actual loss sustained is comparable to the actual cash value concept that applies to direct property losses, because the intent is to

Actual loss sustained
A valuation method in business income policies that makes the insured whole.

support the principle of indemnity by making the insured whole but not creating an opportunity for enrichment.

Other Valuation Approaches

Insurers usually settle losses by paying the replacement cost (RC) or actual cash value (ACV) of lost or damaged property, depending on the applicable valuation provision. Ten other valuation provisions that are used for special classes of property, sometimes within policies that value most property on an RC or ACV basis, are discussed below.

1. *Repair or replace option.*   Many property insurance policies permit the insurer to repair or replace damaged property, rather than make a cash settlement. Although most claims are paid in cash, insurers sometimes exercise this option when it minimizes the claim payments or when it eliminates an insured's ability to profit from the claim.

2. *Settlement under valued policy laws.*   Valued policy laws dictate how much money the insured can expect from a claim. These laws require insurers to pay the policy's face amount for a total loss, even if the building is overinsured at the time of loss.

3. *Agreed value approach.*   Some property insurance policies are valued policies, not contracts of indemnity. These policies typically cover antiques, paintings, and other objects whose value can be difficult to determine. The valuation provision in these policies uses an **agreed value approach**. The insurer and the insured agree on the insured object's value and specify that value in the policy's schedule. For total loss of the insured object, the insurer pays the value amount specified in the policy. Partial losses are paid based on actual cash value, repair cost, replacement cost, or whatever other valuation standard the policy contains. The agreed value approach to valuation should not be confused with the agreed value coverage, an arrangement for suspending the coinsurance clause discussed later in this chapter.

4. *Stated amount approach.*   The *agreed value* approach ensures that the insured will receive a certain amount if the property is lost or stolen, even if the agreed amount exceeds the property's ACV. In contrast, the *stated amount* approach limits the insured's recovery. This approach is an underwriting tool that limits the insurer's liability on property that might increase in value. See Exhibit 14-2.

   The **stated amount approach** is used in auto insurance policies covering unusual vehicles, such as fire engines and antique autos that otherwise might be covered on an ACV basis. The stated amount approach resembles the agreed value approach because both are based on a schedule of values, but there are significant differences.

   When the stated amount approach is used, the insurer's liability is the least of the following:

   • The ACV of damaged or stolen property as of the time of loss

---

Agreed value approach
A valuation method in which the insurer and the insured agree on the insured object's value and then specify that value in a policy schedule.

Stated amount approach
A valuation method that limits the insured's recovery after a loss to no more than the stated amount for each insured object in the policy's schedule.

- The cost to repair or replace damaged or stolen property with other property of like kind and quality
- The amount of insurance specified in the schedule for the covered property

If the stated amount is less than the ACV or the repair cost, the insurer will pay the stated amount. But if the stated amount is greater than the ACV or the repair or replacement cost, the insured will collect less than the stated amount, even if the property has been stolen or is completely destroyed.

EXHIBIT 14-2

Agreed Value Approach Versus Stated Amount Approach

An antique fire truck kept in a museum is insured for $50,000 under an insurance policy using the agreed value approach. If the museum burns to the ground and the truck is destroyed, the insurer will pay the agreed value of $50,000.

An old fire truck, driven in parades and special events, is owned by a retired fireman who has insured it for $50,000 under a policy using the stated amount approach. If the fire truck is damaged in an auto accident, the insurer will pay the *least* of these amounts:

- The $50,000 stated amount
- The actual cash value of the fire truck
- The cost of repairing the fire truck

---

5. *Functional valuation.* **Functional valuation** is sometimes used when replacing buildings or personal property with property of like kind and quality is not practical and the actual cash value approach also does not match insurance needs. This approach is available by an endorsement to a commercial property policy. It is also used for residential buildings covered by the Homeowners Modified Coverage Form, sometimes called Form HO-8.

When applied to personal property, the functional valuation approach requires the insurer to pay no more than the cost to replace with equivalent but less expensive property. The insurer might also pay the actual repair cost or the applicable limit of insurance, if either is less than the cost of functionally equivalent property.

When applied to real property, the functional valuation approach would permit the insurer to use common construction methods and materials. For example, a three-coat plaster wall might be replaced with wallboard, restoring its function but not using the same material.

Functional valuation approach
A valuation method in which the insurer is required to pay no more than the cost to repair or to replace the damaged or destroyed property with property that is its functional equivalent.

6. *Selling price clauses.* ACV is the default valuation approach for personal property. Selling price clauses sometimes increase the value of a particular class of property:

- The ACV of a merchant's current stock is generally the same as its replacement cost, because most stock has little or no opportunity to depreciate. (Some merchandise can depreciate through obsolescence caused by age or technological advances.) A **selling price clause**, automatically included in some forms covering business personal property, provides that stock that has been sold, but has not yet been delivered, is valued at its selling price less discounts and expenses. The value of the property therefore includes the profit made on the sale. This selling price clause applies to property that is *sold but not delivered*.

- A **manufacturer's selling price endorsement** states that finished goods manufactured by the insured will be valued at their selling price, even if not yet sold. This optional valuation approach is important to many manufacturers, because it ensures that they will be compensated for the profit they would have made on these goods if the loss had not occurred. This selling price clause applies to property that is *manufactured but not sold*.

7. *Cost of reproduction.* The cost of researching, reproducing, or transcribing is a commonly used valuation basis for valuable papers and records. The value of these items lies in the value of the information on these papers and records. The **cost of reproduction** is essentially the cost of restoring the information.

Cost of reproduction is not a suitable valuation approach for papers and records that could never be restored. An example would be a dentist's file recording a patient's dental history over time. Unless duplicate records exist, it simply is not possible to recreate historical records showing the patient's dental X-rays, treatment, or other data collected several years ago. Sometimes it is more appropriate to insure irreplaceable items like these on an agreed value basis that would provide some compensation for the loss of goodwill and/or the expense of repeating the process that created the original records to the extent it is feasible.

8. *Pair or set clauses.* Replacement cost, actual cash value, or the other valuation approaches do not specify how to handle the loss of part of a matched pair or set, including a pair of earrings, a set of silverware, or a set of crystal chandeliers in a hotel ballroom. Loss of one item affects the value of the remaining item.

Many business and personal policies address this valuation issue through a **pair or set clause**, like the following from an ISO Homeowners Policy:

Loss to a Pair or Set. In case of loss to a pair or set we may elect to:

a. Repair or replace any part to restore the pair or set to its value before the loss; or

b. Pay the difference between actual cash value of the property before and after the loss.[6]

The differential actual cash value *of the entire pair or set* is used for valuation. This provision explicitly acknowledges the insurer's right to repair or replace any part of a pair or set to restore its pre-loss value. Indirectly, the provision also tells the insured that loss of half the pair does not constitute a total loss—unless the remaining part(s) have become completely and absolutely worthless.

9. *Use value of improvements and betterments.*   Tenants often modify a landlord's building. These "improvements" become a permanent part of the building. Because property that is part of the building belongs to the landlord, a tenant's insurable interest in this property is based not on property ownership but on a "use interest:" The tenant has an enforceable legal right to use the property until the lease expires.

   The ISO Building and Personal Property Coverage Form specifies three different approaches to determine the tenant's recovery when the tenant's improvements and betterments are damaged or destroyed by a covered peril:

   • When the building owner (or the owner's insurer) replaces the improvements without charge to the tenant, the tenant's insurer pays nothing.

   • When the tenant makes prompt repairs, the tenant's improvements and betterments coverage pays based on the actual cash value of the improvements, just as though the tenant owned them.

   • When the improvements are not replaced, payment to the tenant is based on the unamortized original cost. For example, if the improvement were installed exactly nine years before the loss and exactly one year remains on the ten-year lease, the insured tenant would recover one-tenth of the improvement's original cost. The tenant has already received nine out of the expected ten years of use from the original investment.

10. *Money and securities valuation.*   Because crime insurance policies cover money and securities, they must address the valuation issue. The following approaches are generally used:

    • When a loss involves money, the insurer will pay no more than its face value. Loss to money issued by countries other than the United States will be paid at either (a) the face value in the currency issued by the applicable country in question or (b) the United States dollar equivalent, determined by the exchange rate on the day the loss was discovered. The insurer chooses which option to exercise.

    • When a loss involves securities, the insurer will pay no more than the value of the securities at the close of business on the day the loss was discovered. The insurer has the option of paying the value of the securities or replacing them in kind.

POLICY LIMITS

Another important consideration in amounts payable is the policy limits. Policy limits state the maximum amount payable for most claims covered by the policy. These limits might apply to the policy as a whole or to a specific policy coverage. Most policy limits are expressed in dollars. Some policies use nonmonetary limits, such as time (number of hours or days); a few policies or coverages contain no explicit policy limit.

Policy limits are often called *limits of liability*. This term can create confusion because liability refers to the insurer's responsibility to pay damages rather than limits applying only to liability insurance. To avoid confusion, many policies use the term *limits of insurance*.

Reasons for Policy Limits

Most policies have policy limits for one of four reasons:

1. *Limit the insurer's obligations.* Without policy limits, occasional losses under some policies could be extremely large, making it difficult for insurers to project losses and charge appropriate premiums. Limits also put a ceiling on the insurer's obligations to pay for a "priceless" art item or a catastrophe loss that defies accurate measurement.

2. *Accommodate consumer preferences.* Consumers are able to select a limit of insurance that balances their coverage needs with their ability to pay a premium.

3. *Reflect insurer capacity.* Every insurer has a limited financial capacity to absorb losses. Policy limits enable an insurer to remain within its capacity.

4. *Substitute for exclusions.* Insurers sometimes use policy limits as a substitute, of sorts, for an exclusion. Instead of excluding problematic exposures, insurers sometimes find it more effective to provide explicit coverage subject to a modest limit. For example, insurers have found it difficult to develop liability policy language that excludes pollution losses that are not readily insured and that courts will uphold. In property insurance, insurers instead provide explicit coverage for pollution cleanup costs, subject to a nominal $10,000 aggregate limit.

Types of Policy Limits

There are many types of policy limits that affect amounts payable in property insurance. While these labels may not explicitly be used in insurance policies, these terms are used by insurance practitioners. See the following box.

Types of Policy Limits

- Scheduled property limits
- Unscheduled property limits
- Specific limits
- Blanket limits

- Sublimits
- Per item limits
- Per occurrence limits
- Limits in additions and extensions of coverage
- Variable limits
- Non-dollar limits

Scheduled Versus Unscheduled Property Limits

Property is said to be "scheduled" when the policy covers a list, or "schedule" of particular property items. Each scheduled item is listed and precisely identified with descriptions, serial numbers, or other identifying marks or characteristics. Each item of scheduled property typically is subject to a limit that reflects the amount of insurance applying only to that property. For example, a scheduled personal property endorsement to a homeowners policy might describe a specific diamond ring and state the ring's limit of insurance.

Most property insurance policies do not individually list, or schedule, personal property items, and the policy limits apply to all unscheduled items of covered property as a group. For example, the personal property coverage of a homeowners policy applies a single limit to all of the insured's personal property without listing individual items.

Some policies cover both scheduled and unscheduled items. For example, a stamp collector might purchase a stamp floater that covers specific prized stamps on a scheduled basis, with a separate amount of insurance listed for each specifically described stamp. The same policy might also provide a limit of unscheduled coverage, sometimes referred to as "blanket" coverage in this context, on several books of less-valuable stamps. A construction contractor might purchase scheduled insurance on a bulldozer and on other specific pieces of earthmoving equipment, and purchase a separate limit of unscheduled (blanket) insurance on other tools and equipment.

Specific Limits

A **specific limit** is the maximum dollar amount the insurer will pay, per item or per occurrence, for each loss of a particular item or class of property. Specific limits can apply to either a single item of property (such as a building) or a class of property (such as personal property).

One property insurance policy might have several specific limits, which are considered **separate limits**. Separate limits might apply to each of several items or classes of property. For example, a Building and Personal Property Coverage Form might include these limits:

- $240,000 on the building at 114 Main Street
- $160,000 on business personal property at 114 Main Street

Specific limit
The maximum dollar amount the insurer will pay, per item or per occurrence, for each of a particular item or class of property.

Separate limits
Limits for the maximum dollar amounts the insurer will pay; apply individually to several items or classes of property.

- $280,000 on the building at 312 South Street
- $120,000 on business personal property at 312 South Street

Each of these specific limits is indeed a separate limit. The limit on one building cannot be applied to another building. The limit on a building cannot be applied to personal property, or vice versa.[7]

Blanket Limits

Blanket limit
A limit that applies to two or more items or classes of property at one or more locations.

A **blanket limit** applies to two or more items or classes of property at one or more locations. Suppose an insured owns buildings and personal property at the following two locations with these values:

- $240,000 on a building at 114 Main Street
- $160,000 on business personal property at 114 Main Street
- $280,000 on a building at 312 South Street
- $120,000 on business personal property at 312 South Street

The owner could purchase specific insurance with separate limits on each of these four items. Or, with blanket insurance, the owner could instead purchase $800,000 coverage applying to loss to any or all of these items.[8]

A blanket limit is especially helpful when the total value of a firm's movable property is fairly constant, but the values might shift among covered locations. In the example above, *specific* insurance in the amounts shown would not be adequate if at the time of the loss the insured had, say, $180,000 of business personal property at 312 South Street and $80,000 at 114 Main Street. One location would be overinsured (a waste of premium dollars) while the other would be underinsured. *Blanket* insurance would provide sound protection for loss at either location.

Blanket insurance is less important for buildings than for personal property because their values usually do not shift or change rapidly. In practice, blanket insurance is often used for buildings as a hedge against inaccurate valuation. By purchasing a blanket limit of insurance for all locations rather than a specific limit for each location, the insured reduces the likelihood of a penalty, following a loss at one location, for underestimating that property's value and underinsuring it.

Regarding coverage, blanket insurance appears simpler than specific insurance. However, it can make underwriting, rating, and claim adjusting more complicated.

Sublimits

Sublimit
A limit within an upper limit that imposes a smaller limit for particular kinds of property or types of insurance.

The policy limits previously examined are usually shown in the policy declarations and represent upper limits on the amounts of recovery. Within these upper limits, many property insurance policies contain one or more sublimits. A **sublimit** is a limit within an upper limit that imposes a smaller limit for some particular kinds of property or types of insurance.

For example, the ISO Homeowners Policy contains this sublimit for personal property usually located at an insured's secondary residence:

> Our limit of liability for personal property usually located at an "insured's" residence, other than the "residence premises," is 10% of the limit of liability for Coverage C, or $1000, whichever is greater. However, this limitation does not apply to personal property:

> Moved from the "residence premises" because it is being repaired, renovated or rebuilt and is not fit to live in or store property in; or

> In a newly acquired principal residence for 30 days from the time you begin to move the property there.[9]

In this example the sublimit is followed by two exceptions. Sublimits can have exceptions, just as exclusions can.

Per Item Versus Per Occurrence Limits

A property insurance policy limit can apply to each loss event (occurrence), or it can apply to a specific item. The application of per item and per occurrence limits leads to an important question: What happens if the policy limits are reached to pay a claim on covered property?

If coverage is on an occurrence basis, covered property lost or damaged in each occurrence is covered up to a certain limit. The original policy's dollar limit remains in effect for each new occurrence. For example, a homeowners policy provides $75,000 coverage on unscheduled personal property. A covered peril destroys an item worth $10,000, and the insurer pays a claim for $10,000. The insured still has $75,000 in coverage against losses resulting from future occurrences.

If a scheduled item is destroyed, nothing remains to insure, and no insurance limit is needed unless the item is replaced with another scheduled item. What happens to the policy limit after a scheduled item has been destroyed? At least two approaches are possible.

1. Some policies explicitly state that limits are restored after a loss or that payment of a loss shall not reduce the policy limits.
2. Other policies state that limits are not reduced by a *partial* loss. After paying a *total* loss, however, the insurer usually refunds the unearned premium for that item's coverage.

Some policies providing per item coverage contain a **restoration of limits provision** that clarifies the situation. Here is an example from the AAIS Contractors Equipment Coverage Form:

> **Restoration of Limits**—A loss "we" pay under this coverage does not reduce the applicable "limit" unless it is a total loss to a scheduled item. In the event of a total loss to a scheduled item, "we" refund the unearned premium on that item.[10]

Restoration of limits provision
A provision that clarifies whether policy limits are restored after the insurer pays a loss for property that is subject to a per item limit.

Limits in Additions and Extensions of Coverage

Many policies automatically include "additional coverages" or "extensions of coverage," with no identifiable premium charge. Coverage additions or extensions are subject to limits as follows:

• Some additions or extensions provide coverage with separate limits that apply *in addition to* other policy limits.

• Others provide coverage subject to sublimits that *do not increase* the policy limits.

For example, the ISO Building and Personal Property Coverage Form includes six "coverage extensions" and five "additional coverages," summarized in Exhibit 14-3. The distinction between additional coverages and coverage extensions in this form is subtle. The additional coverages define or place practical limitations on some incidental losses that might otherwise be deemed to be covered without special limitations. In contrast, the coverage extensions provide additional amounts of insurance to cover loss exposures that clearly are not otherwise covered.

Variable Limits

Other limits that affect amounts payable are variable limits. Changing property values raise serious questions about the adequacy of property insurance limits expressed in fixed dollar amounts. Barely adequate amounts of insurance can easily become inadequate before the end of a policy period. The alternative, buying insurance that exceeds current values, involves paying for more insurance than is needed.

Underwriting Practices

During periods of economic inflation, some insurers automatically increase property insurance limits and premiums at each renewal unless the insured rejects the increase. The increase is usually based on a relevant price level index. For example, a construction cost index might be applied to building replacement cost values. While this approach is obviously sound, its shortcomings are the following:

• A policyholder who is underinsured at policy inception will still be underinsured at renewal, because this approach adjusts only established policy limits.

• Coverage that was adequate at the beginning of a policy period might become inadequate, because limits are increased only on renewal dates.

When values change, automatically changing limits during the policy period might be the best approach, which is the idea behind inflation guard.

Inflation Guard

Inflation guard
A method of protecting against inflation by increasing the applicable limit for covered property by a specified percentage over the policy year, with increases determined daily.

Inflation guard protects policyholders against economic inflation. Under this endorsement, the limit applicable for covered property increases by a specified

EXHIBIT 14-3

Example of Additional Coverages and Coverage Extensions in the ISO Building and Personal Property Coverage Form

TYPE OF PROVISION	LIMIT	IS IT AN ADDITIONAL LIMIT OR A SUBLIMIT?
Coverage Extensions		
Newly acquired or constructed property	• Buildings—$250,000 limit at each building	Additional limit
	• The Named Insured's Business Personal Property — $100,000 limit at each building	
Personal effects and property of others	$2,500 limit at each described premises	Additional limit
Valuable papers and records—cost of research	$2,500 limit at each described premises	Additional limit
Property off-premises	$10,000 limit	Additional limit
Outdoor property	$1,000 limit but not more than $250 for any one tree, shrub, or plant	Additional limit
Non-owned detached trailers	$5,000 limit	Additional limit
Additional coverages		
Debris removal	Limit of 25% of the amount paid for direct physical loss or damage plus the deductible, plus an additional $10,000	Sublimit plus up to $10,000 additional insurance
Preservation of property	No stated limit	Does not increase applicable limit of insurance
Fire department service charge	$1,000 limit; no deductible	Additional limit
Pollutant cleanup and removal	$10,000	Additional limit
Increased cost of construction	$10,000 or 5% of the limit of insurance applicable to that building, whichever is less	Additional limit

percentage over the policy year. Increases are determined daily. See the example in Exhibit 14-4.

EXHIBIT 14-4

Inflation Guard Example

Assume a building is covered by a property insurance policy with a $365,000 limit and a 10 percent inflation guard. Coverage will be increased by 10 percent of $365,000, which comes to $36,500, during a one-year policy period. One hundred dollars of that increase (1/365 of $36,500) applies each day. If a loss occurs after the policy has been in force 100 days, the applicable policy limit is not the policy limit in the declarations—$365,000, but $375,000, that is, the $365,000 limit plus $100 per day for 100 days ($10,000).

Although the inflation guard automatically increases coverage on a daily basis, it has its shortcomings, including the following:

- If the property is not adequately insured at the outset, the endorsement does not correct the basic coverage inadequacy.

- The selected percentage (10 percent in the preceding example) might bear little or no relationship to actual inflation rates.

The solution to the latter problem lies in indexed limits.

Indexed Limits

Some insurers offer policy limits linked to a price level index, such as the United States Department of Commerce Construction Cost Index. Indexes can be more accurate than an inflation guard percentage, but the indexed limit approach also has one major shortcoming: Government price indexes (typically used because they are readily available) measure *aggregate* price level changes not increases in *local* labor or material costs at the time and location of a loss. Despite this shortcoming, indexing can help maintain limits that reflect current values.

New Policy Editions

Underwriting practices, inflation guards, and indexing attempt to increase overall policy limits to reflect inflation, but they have no effect on policy sublimits. Insurers periodically introduce new editions of existing policies, and these new editions often include an increase in sublimits. Although periodic policy upgrades help keep sublimits reasonable, these changes are not automatic, and they are not within the insured's control.

Peak Season Endorsements

For some businesses, keeping policy limits in line with inflation is problematic due to seasonal fluctuation. For example, the inventory in a toy shop gradually increases during the calendar year but plummets when orders are filled in late

December. Inventory gradually builds again during the coming year. Other businesses have their own seasonal patterns.

A **peak season endorsement** adjusts policy limits according to a specified time schedule. Regardless of policy inception and expiration dates, a toy store owner might use a peak season endorsement to establish one limit of insurance for January, a higher limit for February, and so forth, during the calendar year. Other businesses might structure their coverage based on other seasonal patterns, possibly reflecting two or more peak seasons during the year.

A peak season endorsement is a relatively simple approach that does not require either the insured or the insurer to do anything during the policy term. Its major shortcomings are that it depends on an advance estimate of the pattern in which values will vary during a future policy period, and it does not respond to any unprojected changes.

Peak season endorsement
An endorsement that adjusts policy limits according to a specified time schedule.

Reporting Form

Reporting form policies address the same problem of changing property values as variable limits, but they do so without varying limits. In a reporting form, policy *limits* remain constant, but the *premium* adjusts to reflect changes in the covered property's value. A reporting form is typically used to cover a merchant's or a manufacturer's stock.

A **reporting form** tracks actual values rather than tries to project them. Generally, a limit of insurance is set higher than the greatest values expected during the year. The insured pays an initial premium and makes periodic (typically monthly) reports to the insurer about current property values. At the policy year's end, the insurer calculates the average value of monthly reports to calculate a final premium. If, for example, the policy limit is $1 million and the average reported value is $800,000, then the final premium is based on $800,000. The premium is also based on the 100 percent coinsurance rate, which is lower than the 80 percent rate more likely to be used without a reporting form.

Reporting form
A form to periodically report fluctuating property values to an insurer.

A reporting form with an adequate limit provides insurance to value without charging an excessive premium for periods of low value. If limits are inadequate, that is, if reported values exceed the policy limit, the insurer is still not obligated to pay more than the limit. As long as the insured reports values on time and accurately, the insurer will pay the full amount of any loss that does not exceed the policy limit.

The biggest shortcoming of the reporting form approach is its complexity. The insured must submit periodic reports to the insurer, and they must be accurate and timely. Otherwise, the insured could be penalized at the time of the loss. Therefore, reporting form policies are suitable only for insureds who maintain accurate and up-to-date records and make accurate and timely periodic reports. Many insureds find it simpler and more reliable to insure to a fixed limit even if it involves overinsuring for part of the year, especially when property insurance rates are low.

Non-Dollar Limits

Property insurance policies do not always contain dollar limits. However, policies without dollar limits generally presume that some other factor limits the insurer's dollar obligations. Two coverages illustrate this concept: auto physical damage coverage and the business income coverage found in businessowners policies. See the following box.

Examples of Non-Dollar Limits

Auto Physical Damage Coverage

No dollar value is stated in a typical Personal Auto Policy.[11] The limit of insurance for auto physical damage coverage usually is the actual cash value of the stolen or damaged property or the amount to repair or replace the property, whichever is less.

Business Income Coverage in Businessowners Policies

Many businessowners policies include coverage for loss of business income that is incurred within twelve consecutive months after the date of direct physical loss or damage. Although twelve months is a *time* limit, this additional coverage is not subject to any *dollar* limits.

COINSURANCE AND OTHER INSURANCE-TO-VALUE PROVISIONS

Another consideration in amounts payable is coinsurance and other insurance-to-value provisions. The amount payable under a property policy might be reduced—but not increased—through the effect of a coinsurance clause or another provision designed to provide an incentive for insuring to value.

Coinsurance

Coinsurance clauses serve a dual purpose, both rewarding those who have insured to value and penalizing those who have not. Coinsurance involves an equitable relationship between coinsurance requirements and property insurance rates. Briefly stated, insurers charge a lower rate per $100 of insurance to those who agree to meet an 80 percent coinsurance requirement. This rate is reduced by another 5 percent for those who purchase 90 percent coinsurance, and still another 5 percent for those who opt for 100 percent coinsurance.

In other words, those who agree to buy more insurance—or, more precisely, insurance more closely approximating the full insurable value of covered property—pay a lower rate for each dollar of insurance than those who do not. They buy more insurance, but each unit of insurance costs less.

What Is Coinsurance?[12]

Most often, agents explain coinsurance as a penalty the company imposes on the insured for not buying enough insurance....

A more accurate explanation defines coinsurance as a requirement in most property policies that makes the insured responsible for part of a loss if the property is underinsured below some specified percentage of the property's value. While this definition is more positive and places the emphasis on *under*-insurance, not *over*-insurance, it is still too complex for most insureds, and it fails to explain why this subject is important.

An even better explanation would characterize coinsurance as a reward for good behavior. Coinsurance in property insurance is similar to a coinsurance participation in a health program: the insured shares in the loss. However, if the insured insures his property to full value, the company agrees to waive the participation of the insured, except, of course, to the extent of the deductible.

This explanation communicates to insureds that responsible insurance buying is rewarded and that full insurance benefits the buyer as well as the seller.

Coinsurance "Requirement"

A coinsurance clause in a property insurance policy "requires" the insured to carry an amount of insurance equal to or greater than the stated *coinsurance percentage* of the *insurable value* of the covered property.

- The most common *coinsurance percentages* for buildings and personal property are 80, 90, and 100 percent.
- The *insurable value* is the actual cash value (ACV), the replacement cost (RC) value, or whatever other valuation method is specified in the policy's valuation clause.

Insurance practitioners usually refer to this as a "coinsurance *requirement*" although it is not literally required. Failure to meet a coinsurance requirement does not void coverage. If the requirement is not met, the policy remains in effect, but the insured will receive only a partial recovery when a covered loss occurs.

Coinsurance in Property Insurance Versus Coinsurance in Health Insurance

The property insurance meaning of coinsurance should not be confused with the health insurance meaning of coinsurance.

- A coinsurance clause in a property insurance policy provides that the insurer pays losses in full (subject to other policy provisions) for any insured who carries an amount of insurance that equals or exceeds some stated percentage of the covered

Continued on next page.

property's insurable value. For example, in a property policy with an 80% coinsurance clause, an insured who carries $80,000 or more of property insurance on a building with an insurable value of $100,000 will recover in full for a covered loss (subject to any applicable deductible or the $80,000 policy limit). Only a policyholder who does not insure to value shares the loss with the insurer, thereby becoming a co-insurer.

- A coinsurance clause in a health insurance policy is, in effect, a percentage deductible in which the insured and the insurer each agree to pay a stated percentage of covered losses. For example, in a health insurance policy with an 80% coinsurance clause, the insurer will pay 80% of every covered claim, and the insured will pay 20%. In a claim for $1,000 of covered medical expenses, the insurer would pay $800 and the insured would pay $200 (subject to other applicable policy provisions). Every policyholder shares the loss with the insurer and is therefore a co-insurer.

One might think most property insurance buyers would choose a 100 percent coinsurance clause and insure to full value; this approach essentially provides full coverage at the lowest rate per $100 of insurance. Some use that approach. In practice, however, 80 percent coinsurance is probably most common, for several reasons including the following:

- Tradition. For many years, 80 percent coinsurance has been viewed as the standard approach.

- Very few property losses are total losses. Insurance to 80 percent of the full insurable value provides adequate insurance limits to cover the vast majority of claims.

- Eighty percent coinsurance allows some margin for error in predicting the full insurable value of property at the time of the loss.

- The total premium for insurance to 80 percent of value with an 80 percent coinsurance clause would be less than the total premium for insurance to 100 percent of value with a 100 percent coinsurance clause. When property insurance rates are low, this is not a significant factor.

Some property insurance buyers use a conservative approach, insuring to approximately 100 percent of the estimated full insurable value, subject to an 80 percent coinsurance clause. If the estimated value is accurate, this approach provides insurance limits adequate to provide indemnity for a total loss. It also provides a margin of error that usually prevents a coinsurance penalty if the property turns out to be underinsured at the time of the loss. Coinsurance penalties can also be avoided by using the agreed value approach, discussed later.

Coinsurance Clause

For example, the ISO Building and Personal Property Coverage Form uses the following coinsurance clause:

> If a Coinsurance percentage is shown in the Declarations, the following condition applies.
>
> **a.** We will not pay the full amount of any loss if the value of Covered Property at the time of loss times the Coinsurance percentage shown for it in the Declarations is greater than the Limit of Insurance for the property.
>
> Instead, we will determine the most we will pay using the following steps:
>
> **(1)** Multiply the value of Covered Property at the time of loss by the Coinsurance percentage;
> **(2)** Divide the Limit of Insurance of the property by the figure determined in Step **(1)**;
> **(3)** Multiply the total amount of loss, before the application of any deductible, by the figure determined in Step **(2)**; and
> **(4)** Subtract the deductible from the figure determined in Step **(3)**.
>
> We will pay the amount determined in Step **(4)** or the limit of insurance, whichever is less. For the remainder, you will either have to rely on other insurance or absorb the loss yourself. [13]

Note that step (4) deals with the deductible. This chapter discusses deductibles later, concluding with some examples that combine coinsurance and deductibles.

Coinsurance Formula

The coinsurance formula explains how the amount payable is determined if the coinsurance requirement has not been met:

$$\text{Most that will be paid by insurance} = \left(\frac{\text{Limit of insurance}}{\text{Value of covered property} \times \text{Coinsurance percentage}} \times \text{Total amount of covered loss} \right)$$

Insurance students often condense this formula to "Did over should times loss" or, in formula form:

$$\left(\frac{\text{Did}}{\text{Should}} \times \text{Loss} \right)$$

- "Did" is the amount of insurance carried.
- "Should" is the minimum amount that should have been carried to meet the coinsurance requirement based on the insurable value (ACV, RC, or other) *at the time of the loss.*

An example using the coinsurance formula appears in Exhibit 14-5.

EXHIBIT 14-5

Coinsurance Example

Susan Smith owns a store building with a replacement cost value of $300,000. She insures the building for $200,000 under a policy providing replacement cost coverage subject to a 100 percent coinsurance clause. A covered peril causes $60,000 worth of damage to the building. Making the necessary substitutions in the coinsurance formula yields this result:

$$\text{Insurer payment} = \left(\frac{\$200,000}{100\% \times \$300,000} \times \$60,000 \right)$$

$$= \left(\frac{\$200,000}{\$300,000} \times \$60,000 \right)$$

$$= \left(\frac{2}{3} \times \$60,000 \right)$$

$$= \$40,000$$

If Susan's policy instead had an 80 percent coinsurance clause, the result would have been different:

$$\text{Insurer payment} = \left(\frac{\$200,000}{80\% \times \$300,000} \times \$60,000 \right)$$

$$= \left(\frac{\$200,000}{\$240,000} \times \$60,000 \right)$$

$$= \left(\frac{5}{6} \times \$60,000 \right)$$

$$= \$50,000$$

Three key points are crucial in applying the coinsurance formula:

1. *Coinsurance* calculations *are necessary only when the coinsurance requirement is not met because the limit of insurance is less than the insurable value times the coinsurance percentage*. In other words, coinsurance applies only when the "did" is less than the "should." If the coinsurance requirement is met (Did ≥ Should), the amount payable is the full amount of the loss, subject to the deductible, applicable policy limits, and other relevant policy provisions.

2. *The insurer never pays more than the amount of the loss*. If the amount of insurance carried is greater than the minimum limit of insurance required

(Did > Should), the coinsurance formula itself would indicate that the insurer should pay more than the amount of the loss.

3. *The insurer never pays more than the applicable limit of insurance.* If the amount of the loss is greater than the minimum limit of insurance required by the coinsurance clause (Loss > Should), the formula might indicate that the insurer would pay more than the limit of insurance. However, the insurer's obligation will not exceed the applicable limit of insurance.

Coinsurance can be critical in the event of a major loss and substantial underinsurance. To impose a coinsurance penalty, an insurer must accurately appraise the full insurable value of all covered property subject to the applicable insurance limit. This process alone can be time-consuming and costly. It can lead to disputes over the appraisal estimate's accuracy. A coinsurance penalty can also annoy the insured and lead to challenges and litigation. For these and other practical reasons, the vast majority of property claims are settled without any attempt to determine precisely whether a coinsurance requirement has been met. Coinsurance calculations usually are invoked only when both clear evidence of substantial underinsurance and a sizable claim exist.

Coinsurance clauses apply in policies covering direct damage to buildings and personal property. The coinsurance requirement in these policies is based on the building's full insurable value, normally the ACV or RC.

Coinsurance clauses are also used in business income policies, in which the coinsurance formula requires an amount of insurance *based on* net income and operating expenses that, if no loss had occurred, would have been earned or incurred during the current twelve-month policy period.

Insurance-to-Value Provisions in Homeowners and Businessowners Policies

Despite some similarities, the insurance-to-value provisions in homeowners and businessowners policies are different from coinsurance. In these provisions, the amount payable by the insurer will not be less than the ACV (subject to policy limits). Under the insurance-to-value provisions of current ISO homeowners; dwelling; and businessowners policies; the amount payable by the insurer may be one of the following:

*   The replacement cost value of the loss—a "reward" for those insured to at least 80 percent of the replacement cost value

*   The actual cash value of the loss—a "punishment" for those not insured to at least 80 percent of replacement cost value

*   An amount somewhere between the replacement cost value and the actual cash value of the loss—a penalty for those who are underinsured but only slightly

The worst penalty or punishment for underinsurance is loss payment on a depreciated ACV basis, rather than on an RC basis. This penalty usually is not as severe as a coinsurance computation would be on an RC policy.

These provisions are found within a "loss payment" or "loss settlement" condition that resembles the coinsurance provision just discussed—with a very important difference: Even if the property is substantially underinsured, the insurer will not pay less than the actual cash value of the loss, as long as that amount is within policy limits. Also, no option to choose a percentage other than 80 percent is available.

Under these policies:

- When the insurance amount at the time of the loss equals at least 80 percent of the property's full replacement cost value immediately before the loss, full replacement cost coverage applies—subject, of course, to policy limits and the applicable deductible. The situation would be the same on a replacement-cost policy with a coinsurance clause.

- If the insurance amount is less than 80 percent of the full replacement cost, the insurer will pay the *greater* of the following two amounts—but, of course, never more than the limit of insurance:

  - The actual cash value (ACV) of the lost or damaged property.

  - A proportion of the cost to repair or replace, without a deduction for depreciation. The proportion is the applicable limit of insurance divided by 80 percent of the property's replacement cost. The formula for this calculation resembles the familiar coinsurance formula: "Did over should times the loss."

Unlike coinsurance, the insurer will never pay less than the ACV—subject to policy limits.

Maintaining Insurance to Value

Maintaining insurance to value is important in order to avoid coinsurance penalties and other insurance-to-value penalties that might reduce the amount payable in the event of a loss. Underinsurance penalties are not a concern for those who maintain property insurance limits that meet or exceed coinsurance requirements or the 80 percent insurance-to-value requirement. Unfortunately, maintaining such limits is easier said than done, for at least the following four reasons:

1. The amount of insurance necessary to meet coinsurance requirements is based on the insured property's value at the time of the loss, but the limit of insurance is selected when the policy is purchased.

2. When selecting insurance limits, an insurance buyer typically estimates property values based on an informed guess—at best—rather than exact science.

3. The true insurable value at the time of the loss often cannot be precisely measured until the property is actually rebuilt or replaced.

4. Values change over time.

Property insurance buyers can take the following steps to address the valuation challenge:

- Hire a qualified appraiser to establish the current replacement cost value of the building or other covered property. (The major appraisal companies offer this service at relatively nominal cost.) Adjust the appraisal using indexes and/or a record of additions and deletions each year, and reappraise the property every few years.

- Purchase an inflation guard coverage option.

- Purchase a peak season endorsement, if a business's personal property values change in a cyclical and predictable pattern.

- Review and revise limits periodically.

Alternatives to Coinsurance

Maintaining insurance to value is only one way of avoiding coinsurance penalties and other insurance-to-value penalties. Several techniques and forms are available that avoid insurance-to-value problems by eliminating the penalties. See the following box.

Alternatives to Coinsurance

- Flat policies
- Agreed value
- Monthly limit of indemnity
- Maximum period of indemnity

Flat Policies

A **flat policy** is a policy without a coinsurance clause. Some insurers are willing to remove the coinsurance clause for a substantial additional charge—such as a 300 percent increase in the rate per $100 of insurance. Usually this option is prohibitively expensive, and it is more attractive to spend premium dollars on higher limits of insurance.

Some coverages are usually written on a flat (no-coinsurance) basis. A good example is unscheduled personal property coverage on a tenant's homeowners policy. It is usually difficult to determine the actual cash value of a typical residential tenant's personal property, and values constantly change as specific items are acquired, worn or used, discarded, or eaten.

Flat policy
A property insurance policy without a coinsurance clause.

Agreed Value

Agreed value applies to two different concepts:

1. The *agreed value approach to valuation*, discussed earlier, applies to objects whose value is difficult to determine after a loss. The insurer and the insured agree on the insured object's value and specify that value in a schedule in the policy. For a total loss to the insured object, the insurer pays the policy's valued amount.

2. The *agreed value approach that avoids coinsurance penalties* also requires that the insurer and the insured agree on an amount. In this case, however, what is agreed on is the amount that meets the requirement of the coinsurance formula. If the insured carries an amount of insurance at least equal to that agreed value, the insurer will not impose a coinsurance penalty at the time of loss. The amount payable is the ACV, RC, or other amount specified in the policy's valuation clause.

The agreed value approach—the approach preferred by many experienced insureds, producers, and risk managers—addresses one major challenge of insurance-to-value provisions: the difficulty of establishing values in advance of a loss. This approach is so popular that it is preprinted as an option in the Building and Personal Property Coverage Form. It works as follows:

- The insurer and the insured agree to what amount of insurance is sufficient to meet the "should" requirement of the coinsurance clause.

- If the insured carries an amount of insurance at least equal to that agreed value, the insurer will not impose a coinsurance penalty at the time of the loss.

- A premium increase, typically 5 percent, is applied.

The agreed value is based on a statement of values, submitted by the insured and acceptable to the insurer, stating the full ACV or RC of the covered property. The policy's coinsurance percentage is applied to the full ACV or RC to produce the "agreed value." The coinsurance clause is suspended if the limit of insurance equals or exceeds the agreed value. Except in unusual circumstances, the insured purchases insurance at least equal to the agreed value, thereby ensuring that no coinsurance penalty will apply.

The agreed value clause eliminates the only risk of a coinsurance penalty. If the limit of insurance equals the agreed value but the agreed value is only 80 percent of the full property value, the coinsurance penalty would be suspended, but the insured would still retain 20 percent of a total loss. Likewise, an agreed value clause does *not* convert the policy to a valued policy. The policy's loss valuation provision continues to apply, and the insurer is still obligated to pay only the insurable value of the loss or the policy limit, whichever is less.

Monthly Limit of Indemnity

Another alternative is the stipulation of a monthly limit of indemnity. The **monthly limit of indemnity** provides a popular alternative to coinsurance for business income policies—so popular that it is preprinted as an option in the standard ISO business income forms and activated by an entry on the policy's declarations page. The monthly limit of indemnity approach focuses less on the total dollar amount exposed to loss and more on the time period during which a loss of business income may occur. Rather than require an insurance limit that equals a specified percentage of the insurable value, as coinsurance does, this approach limits the total amount of insurance that can be collected for a loss incurred during a thirty-day period. No limit is set on the overall length of an interruption during which loss payments may be made.

The monthly limit of indemnity option is explained in these words:

> If shown as applicable in the Declarations, the following Optional Coverages apply separately to each item...
>
> **2. Monthly Limit of Indemnity**
>
>   **a.** The Additional Condition, Coinsurance, does not apply to this Coverage Form at the described premises to which this Optional Coverage applies.
>
>   **b.** The most we will pay for loss of Business Income in any period of 30 consecutive days after the beginning of the "period of restoration" is:
>
>   (1) The Limit of Insurance, multiplied by
>
>   (2) The fraction shown in the Declarations for this Optional Coverage.[14]

See Exhibit 14-6 for an example of a monthly limit of indemnity.

> **Monthly limit of indemnity**
> A limit in business income policies on the amount of insurance that can be collected during any thirty-day period, subject to the limit of insurance.

EXHIBIT 14-6

Monthly Limit of Indemnity Example

Mike's Phone Store has business income coverage on a *monthly limit of indemnity* basis with a policy limit of $40,000 and a fraction of one-fourth shown in the policy declarations. During any thirty-day period following a covered business income loss, Mike could recover either the amount of business income loss actually sustained or $10,000 (that is, one-fourth of the $40,000 limit), whichever is less. If the interruption continues for more than four months, Mike will continue to recover *up to* $10,000 per month until the $40,000 limit has been consumed.

Business income coverage on a coinsurance basis requires an accurate estimate of future insurable values. Sound estimates can be difficult for some businesses, especially smaller start-up operations. The monthly limit of indemnity approach presents an attractive, simpler option, because the firm need estimate only what it will need to recover in any thirty-day period for a worst-case period of interruption.

Maximum Period of Indemnity

Maximum period of indemnity
A limit in business income policies in which the insurer agrees to pay the amount of covered losses and expenses sustained during a 120-day period, up to the limit of insurance.

The **maximum period of indemnity** provides another popular alternative to coinsurance for business income policies. It, too, is preprinted as an option in the standard ISO business income forms. When this option is activated by an entry in the declarations, the coinsurance condition does not apply, and the insurer agrees to pay the amount of covered loss and expenses sustained during a 120-day period, up to the limit of insurance. There is no per-month limitation. See Exhibit 14-7.

EXHIBIT 14-7

Maximum Period of Indemnity Example

Suppose Mike's Phone Store has business income coverage on a *maximum period of indemnity* basis with a policy limit of $40,000. During the period of restoration following a covered business income loss, Mike could recover either the amount of business income loss actually sustained or $40,000, whichever is less. However, if the interruption continues for more than 120 days (approximately four months), Mike will recover no more than the amount of covered loss and expense sustained during the first 120 days.

DEDUCTIBLES

Amounts payable under property insurance are also affected by deductibles. Most property insurance policies contain one or more deductible provisions that can affect the amount payable under that policy. A deductible is a portion of a covered loss that is not paid by the insurer. In a property insurance policy, the deductible is subtracted from the amount of loss or the amount the insurer would otherwise be obligated to pay to the insured. The clause or policy provision describing a deductible is usually just referred to as a "deductible." More often than not, a dollar figure is stated; a provision describing a deductible amount of $1,000 would be referred to as a "$1,000 deductible."

Reasons for Deductibles

By requiring the insured to share in the loss, deductibles accomplish the following:

1. Reduce attitudinal (morale) hazards and encourage loss control
2. Eliminate the need for the insurer to process small losses, thereby reducing the insurer's loss costs and loss adjustment expenses
3. Reduce the premium cost to the insured

Reduce Attitudinal Hazards and Encourage Loss Control

Deductibles require the insured to retain (self-insure) a portion of every loss. Having some of the insured's own funds at stake theoretically gives the insured an incentive to prevent losses. A deductible serves this purpose most effectively when it is large enough to have a noticeable financial impact on any insured who suffers a loss that could have been prevented.

Deductibles are not particularly effective when used with large property exposures, especially those that are not likely to face a partial loss. Satellite launch insurance provides an example. With hundreds of millions of dollars at stake, even a $100,000 deductible would neither encourage loss control nor substantially reduce the insurer's costs.

Reduce Insurer's Costs

A typical property deductible removes the insurer's involvement in small losses. Insurance is not efficient in handling small claims because the insurer's loss adjustment expenses often exceed the amount of indemnity payable to the insured.

The expensive and inefficient process of insuring small claims is sometimes referred to as **dollar trading**: The insured pays money to the insurer who, in turn, pays the same money back to the insured—after subtracting its expenses.

Dollar trading
A situation in which the insured pays the insurer premiums for small claims and the insurer pays the same dollars back to the insured, after subtracting expenses.

Property insurance deductibles help to eliminate dollar trading. Instead of inefficiently swapping money with the insurer, the insured handles small—often foreseeable—losses as normal, out-of-pocket expenses. Rather than paying maintenance expenses, insurance is used to protect against major, unpredictable property losses.

Deductibles are effective in reducing insurers' expenses for coverages such as auto collision, in which small, partial losses are common.

Reduce Premiums

Because deductibles reduce insurers' overall loss costs and loss adjustment expenses, they also reduce the premiums insurers must charge. The premium reduction is not directly proportional to the size of the deductible. Because small losses are more frequent than large losses, the premium reduction is on a sliding scale, as illustrated in Exhibit 14-8.

The premium credit increases much more slowly than the size of the deductible. Shifting from a $1,000 deductible to a $2,500 deductible reduces premiums by $300 while increasing retained exposures by $1,500. The premium reduction for shifting from a $50,000 deductible to a $75,000 deductible is also $300, but retained losses are increased by $25,000. A basic risk management adage states, "Don't risk a lot to save a little." Given these figures, shifting from a $1,000 deductible to a $2,500 deductible would be attractive in many cases. But even if their firm could absorb a $25,000 loss, and the

EXHIBIT 14-8

Premium Credits for Various Deductibles

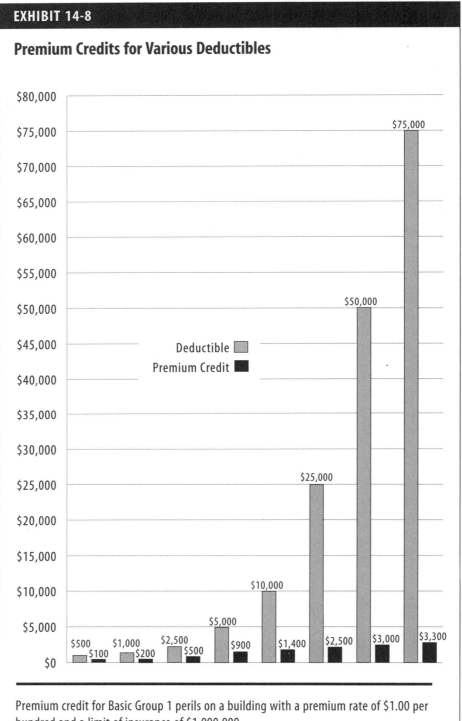

Premium credit for Basic Group 1 perils on a building with a premium rate of $1.00 per hundred and a limit of insurance of $1,000,000.

Based on *Commercial Lines Manual,* Copyright, ISO Commercial Risk Services, Inc., 1983, 1989, 2d ed., 10-90, p. CF-95-97.

pricing is actuarially sound, few risk managers would choose to retain an extra $25,000 in property losses to save $300 in premium unless other factors were involved. For example, some insurers offer much broader coverage when a high deductible applies.

When premium costs are considered, deductibles tend to encourage the use of medium-sized deductibles that eliminate dollar trading for small losses but provide a reliable source of recovery for larger losses. What constitutes "medium-sized" varies substantially among both families and businesses.

Types of Deductibles

Deductibles can be placed in two broad categories:

- A **per event deductible** applies to each item, each location, each claim, or each occurrence. Per event deductibles can be variously expressed as dollar amounts, percentages of some value or amount, or time periods.
- An **aggregate deductible** is a deductible that applies collectively to all losses occurring during a specific time period, typically a policy year. An aggregate deductible can be combined with a per event deductible.

Per event deductible
A deductible that applies to each item, each location, each claim, or each occurrence.

Aggregate deductible
A deductible that applies collectively to all losses occurring during a specific time period, typically a policy year.

Types of Deductibles

- Straight deductible
- Percentage deductible
- Time deductible
- Aggregate deductible
- No deductible

Straight Deductibles

A **straight deductible** is a dollar amount that the insured must pay toward a covered loss. In personal insurance, deductibles are small, typically under $1,000. In commercial insurance, deductibles range from $1,000 to over $1 million.

Straight deductible
A dollar amount that the insured must pay toward a covered loss.

Not all $1,000 deductibles are alike. Variations exist in what the $1,000 is subtracted from and how often it may be applied.

Usually, the deductible is subtracted from the amount of the loss. The property insurer pays nothing unless the covered loss exceeds the deductible amount. For losses greater than the deductible amount, the insurer pays the loss after subtracting the deductible. If the insured has a $100,000 policy, a $10,000 covered loss, and a $1,000 deductible, the insurer will pay $9,000. ($10,000 – $1,000 = $9,000, which is less than the policy limit of $100,000.)

Some insurance policies do not specify whether the deductible is subtracted from policy limits for losses exceeding limits. Alternatively, the ISO Building and Personal Property Coverage Form specifies that the insurer can, under some circumstances, pay the full policy limit:

> **Deductible**
>
> In any one occurrence of loss or damage (hereinafter referred to as loss), we will first reduce the amount of loss if required by the Coinsurance Condition or the Agreed Value Optional Coverage. If the adjusted amount of loss is less than or equal to the Deductible, we will not pay for that loss. If the adjusted amount of loss exceeds the Deductible, we will then subtract the Deductible from the adjusted amount of loss, and will pay the resulting amount or the Limit of Insurance, whichever is less....[15]

As it appears in the policy, this provision includes two examples to illustrate how the deductible should be computed when no coinsurance penalty applies. Other examples, within the coinsurance provision, illustrate the computations when a coinsurance penalty is involved.

The insured can collect the full policy limit if the loss is large enough. For example, assume an insured suffers a $110,000 loss under a policy with a $100,000 limit of insurance and a $5,000 straight deductible. Also assume coinsurance requirements have been met. The insurer will pay the policy limit of $100,000. This is an example of absorbing a deductible. To absorb a deductible means to apply the deductible to the actual loss before applying any coverage limits. If a property loss exceeds the coverage limit by at least the amount of the deductible, then the insured can collect the full coverage limit without further application of a deductible. The $5,000 deductible in this example is subtracted from the amount of the loss ($110,000 − $5,000 = $105,000), but it has been absorbed, and the insurer will pay the *full* policy limit ($100,000).

The deductible in a property insurance policy may be applied separately to each item or location, or it may apply to each occurrence. Depending on which of these approaches is used, the same dollar deductible can produce dramatically different results. See Exhibit 14-9.

EXHIBIT 14-9

Per Item Versus Per Location Versus Per Occurrence Deductibles

Suppose a commercial bakery owns twenty trucks that are parked on two lots several blocks apart when a severe hailstorm causes at least $500 in damage to each truck. The trucks have physical damage coverage for the peril of hail. With a $500 deductible, the bakery's retained loss could be either $10,000, $1,000, or $500:

- If the $500 deductible applies per vehicle, the bakery will retain $500 for each of the twenty vehicles, for a total of $10,000.

- If the $500 deductible applies per location, the bakery will retain $500 for each of the two locations, for a total of $1,000.

- If the $500 deductible applies per occurrence, the bakery will retain only $500.

Insurance policies occasionally use a **split deductible** in which the policy, for example, provides one deductible for most causes of loss but a different, higher deductible, for other specified causes of loss. For example, a higher theft deductible could be used to give the insured a greater incentive to guard against theft. And a higher windstorm deductible might be used to reflect the high probability of windstorm damage to property at some locations.

Split deductibles are common in auto insurance, which often contain one deductible for the peril of collision and another, often smaller, deductible for "other-than-collision" losses.

Percentage Deductibles

Not all deductibles are expressed in dollar amounts. **Percentage deductibles** are expressed as a percentage of some other amount, such as the following:

- The amount of insurance
- The value of the covered property
- The amount of the loss

Obviously, the dollar amount of these percentage deductibles is not a fixed dollar amount, but increases as the insurance amount, the property value, or the loss amount increases.

When property is insured to 100 percent of its insurable value, the dollar amount of a deductible based on the amount of insurance is the same as the dollar amount of a deductible based on insurable value. The difference in these approaches is relevant only when policy limits and insurable values differ. Sometimes such a difference results from insuring to, say, 80 percent of value either to barely meet coinsurance requirements or because a total loss is not considered likely.

Earthquake insurance presents a good example, because most earthquake losses are partial losses. Assume the Book Company purchases $100,000 of earthquake coverage on a building valued at $500,000. The earthquake coverage is subject to a 10 percent deductible. Book will retain the following:

- $10,000 of each insured loss if the 10 percent deductible applies to the amount of insurance.
- $50,000 of each insured loss if the 10 percent deductible applies to the value of covered property.

Percentage deductibles are normally based on the amount of insurance. However, this approach tends to *discourage* insurance to value, because insureds who purchase *less* insurance are *rewarded* with a lower dollar deductible. (Consider what would happen to the Book Company if it had purchased $200,000, or $500,000 of earthquake coverage with a deductible applying to the amount of insurance.) For this reason, insurers sometimes base a percentage deductible on property values.

Split deductible
A deductible that applies one deductible for most causes of loss but a different, higher deductible, for other specified causes of loss.

Percentage deductible
A deductible expressed as a percentage of some other amount, such as the amount of insurance, the covered property's value , or the amount of the loss.

A percentage deductible can also apply to the amount of the loss. This approach is common with health insurance and is called a "coinsurance clause." With an 80 percent coinsurance clause in a health insurance policy, the insurer pays 80 percent of every covered loss, and the insured retains a percentage deductible of 20 percent of the loss—all subject to other policy conditions. Such percentage deductibles are also used in some professional liability insurance policies.

Property insurance deductibles can also be stated as a percentage of the amount of the loss. This approach is used, for example, with a windstorm or hail percentage deductible when blanket limits apply and coverage is written on a reporting form basis.

A percentage deductible can apply to various values. When analyzing coverage with a percentage deductible, insurance and risk management practitioners must ask *"Percentage of what?"* and they must be able to understand, evaluate, and apply the answer.

Time Deductibles (Waiting Periods)

Some property coverages commonly state a deductible in time rather than dollars. Although it serves the same effect as other deductibles, a **time deductible** or **waiting period** usually is not captioned as a deductible.

Time deductible, or waiting period
A deductible expressed in time rather than dollars.

One example of a time deductible appears in the Personal Auto Policy, which provides coverage up to a specified dollar sublimit (currently $20) per day with a $600 maximum for transportation expenses (such as renting a substitute auto) if a covered auto has been stolen. However, the payment does not begin until forty-eight hours after the theft. Many stolen cars are recovered within two days. Even though it is not titled as a deductible, this forty-eight-hour period constitutes a two-day waiting period deductible.

Aggregate Deductibles

Per item, location, or occurrence deductibles can leave the insured exposed to substantial retained losses if many items, locations, or occurrences suffer losses within a short time span.[16] An aggregate deductible minimizes retained losses resulting from a high frequency of small losses. Under an aggregate deductible, all losses that occur during a specified time period, typically a policy year, are accumulated to satisfy the aggregate deductible. After the insured has retained losses in the amount of the aggregate, the insurer begins to pay subsequent losses.

Although aggregate deductibles are more common with liability insurance, they are sometimes used in property insurance policies, along with a straight or percentage per event deductible.

The ideal deductible, from a risk management perspective, would be a single aggregate deductible applicable to all property and liability insurance coverages. An individual or a business should be more concerned with the collective impact of all deductibles during a year than with the details of specific policies. Broad, enterprise-wide aggregate deductibles are not common, but they may sometimes be arranged for very large insurance buyers.

No Deductible

Despite the value of property insurance deductibles, some property policies do *not* have a deductible for sound reasons.

Scheduled personal property endorsements to a homeowners policy cover specific listed items of personal property. Many such items, jewelry, for example, are compact and valuable; the most common losses are total theft losses rather than partial damage losses. The amounts of insurance involved with other items commonly insured, such as musical instruments or cameras, are small enough that a deductible would eliminate most coverage for loss of that item. It would make no sense to insure a camera for $250 subject to a $500 deductible.

Plate glass insurance covers a property exposure for which partial losses are almost impossible.[17] A pane of glass is either broken or unbroken. As a result, any deductible designed to eliminate coverage for partial losses would only reduce the insured's amount of recovery for a total loss.

Many time element coverages have no deductible at all. Usually coverage for business income and extra expense, or for additional living expense losses in a homeowners policy, applies only after property has sustained direct damage, and that damage is usually subject to a deductible. Even though the insured does not face a deductible for the time element coverage, the insured usually faces another deductible resulting from the same event.

EXAMPLES COMBINING VALUATION, LIMITS, COINSURANCE, AND DEDUCTIBLES

For a given loss, the amount payable under a property insurance policy depends on the interaction between its loss valuation provisions, policy limits, coinsurance or other insurance-to-value provisions, and deductibles. This chapter has examined valuation, policy limits, coinsurance, and deductibles as isolated topics. This final section of the chapter shows how they can be combined in several different situations.

Except as noted, these examples are based on the ISO Building and Personal Property Coverage Form. The coinsurance provision in that form was quoted earlier, but is repeated here and referred to in the examples:

Coinsurance

If a Coinsurance percentage is shown in the Declarations, the following condition applies.

We will not pay the full amount of any loss if the value of Covered Property at the time of loss times the Coinsurance percentage shown for it in the Declarations is greater than the Limit of Insurance for the property.

Instead, we will determine the most we will pay using the following steps:

(1) Multiply the value of Covered Property at the time of loss by the Coinsurance percentage;

(2) Divide the Limit of Insurance of the property by the figure determined in Step **(1)**;

(3) Multiply the total amount of loss, before the application of any deductible, by the figure determined in Step **(2)**; and

(4) Subtract the deductible from the figure determined in Step **(3)**.

We will pay the amount determined in Step **(4)** or the limit of insurance, whichever is less. For the remainder, you will either have to rely on other insurance or absorb the loss yourself. [18]

The deductible provision is also relevant in determining amounts payable:

Deductible

In any one occurrence of loss or damage (hereinafter referred to as loss), we will first reduce the amount of loss if required by the Coinsurance Condition or the Agreed Value Optional Coverage. If the adjusted amount of loss is less than or equal to the Deductible, we will not pay for that loss. If the adjusted amount of loss exceeds the Deductible, we will then subtract the Deductible from the adjusted amount of loss, and we will pay the resulting amount or the Limit of Insurance, whichever is less.

When the occurrence involves loss to more than one item of Covered Property and separate Limits of Insurance apply, the losses will not be combined in determining application of the Deductible, but the Deductible will be applied only once per occurrence. [19]

ACV Valuation/Adequate Insurance Example

Company A's building is covered on an actual cash value (ACV) basis under an ISO Building and Personal Property Coverage Form.

At the time of the loss, the assumptions in this case are shown in Exhibit 14-10.

EXHIBIT 14-10	
Company A	
ACV of Company A's building	$275,000
RC value of Company A's building	$375,000
Coinsurance percentage	80%
Limit of insurance	$250,000
Deductible	$500
Amount of loss (ACV)	$40,000
Amount of loss (RC)	$50,000

The steps in determining the amount payable are as follows:

Step 1:   Determine if a coinsurance penalty applies. In this case, the minimum amount of insurance to meet coinsurance requirements (the "should" in the coinsurance formula) on an ACV basis is 80% × $275,000, or $220,000. The $250,000 limit of insurance (the "did" in the coinsurance formula) exceeds the $220,000 requirement. Because the coinsurance requirement has been met, the amount of loss is not reduced by the coinsurance condition.

Step 2:   Determine the coinsurance penalty. In this case, there is no coinsurance penalty. However, the deductible provision still applies.

The steps in determining the deductible provision are as follows:

Step 3:   Determine the adjusted amount of loss by subtracting the coinsurance penalty from the amount of loss:

$40,000 – $0 = $40,000

Step 4:   Subtract the deductible from the adjusted amount of loss:

$40,000 – $500 = $39,500

Step 5:   Pay the resulting amount or the limit of insurance, whichever is less:

$39,500 (the resulting amount) is less than the $250,000 limit, so the insurer will pay $39,500.

Note that the insurer does not pay $40,000 and absorb the deductible. As mentioned earlier, a deductible can be absorbed only *when a property loss exceeds the coverage limit by at least the amount of the deductible.* In this case, the $40,000 property loss does not exceed the coverage limit.

RC Valuation/Underinsurance Example

If Company A's building had been insured on a replacement cost (RC) basis, the coinsurance requirement would not be met, and the computations would produce this result, based again on the assumptions in Exhibit 14-10.

Step 1: $375,000 × 80% = $300,000.

This is the minimum amount of insurance to meet coinsurance requirements *on an RC basis*; a coinsurance penalty applies.

Step 2: $250,000 ÷ $300,000 = .83 (rounded here to two decimal places)

Step 3: $50,000 × .83 = $41,500 ($50,000 is the *RC value* of the loss)

Step 4: $41,500 – $500 = $41,000

The insurer will not pay more than the amount determined in Step 4 or the limit of insurance, whichever is less, so the amount payable by the insurer is $41,000.

Blanket Insurance/Underinsurance Example

The assumptions in this case are presented in Exhibit 14-11.

EXHIBIT 14-11

Company B

ACV of Company B's building at Location 1	$75,000
ACV of Company B's building at Location 2	$100,000
ACV of Company B's personal property at Location 2	$75,000
Coinsurance percentage	90%
Blanket limit of insurance for buildings and personal property at Locations 1 and 2	$135,000
Deductible	$1,000
Amount of loss to building at Location 1 (ACV)	$30,000
Amount of loss to personal property at Location 1 (ACV)	$20,000

The steps in the coinsurance provision are applied as follows:

Step 1:   The total value of all insured property is:
$75,000 + $100,000 + $75,000 = $250,000
$250,000 × 90% = $225,000.

This is the minimum amount of insurance to meet coinsurance requirements on an ACV basis and avoid the penalty shown below; a coinsurance penalty applies.

Step 2: $135,000 ÷ $225,000 = .60

Step 3:   The total amount of loss is:
$30,000 + $20,000 = $50,000
$50,000 × .60 = $30,000

Step 4: $30,000 – $1,000 = $29,000 (the deductible is applied once per occurrence)

The insurer will not pay more than $29,000. The remaining $21,000 is not covered.

When To Apply the Deductible

Property insurance policies can differ in the ways in which they combine coinsurance and deductibles, and these differences affect the amount an insured will recover for a loss. Using the set of assumptions presented earlier, the next example will use the AAIS counterpart to the ISO policy to illustrate a policy form that applies the deductible before coinsurance computations.

The coinsurance provision in the AAIS Building and Personal Property Coverage Part uses a set of steps slightly different from the ISO approach:

    a.   Multiply the value of the covered property at the time of the loss by the coinsurance percentage.

    b.   Divide the **limit** for covered property by the figure determined [in a.] above; and

    c.   Multiply the total amount of loss, after the application of any deductible, by the figure determined [in b.] above.

The most **we** pay is the amount determined in 4.c. above or the **limit**, whichever is less. **We** do not pay any remaining part of the loss.[20]

Applying this formula to Company A in Exhibit 14-10 produces these results, assuming coverage applies on a replacement-cost basis:

Step a: $375,000 × 80% = $300,000 (minimum limit needed to meet coinsurance requirements)

Step b: $250,000 ÷ $300,000 = .83 (rounded)

Step c: $50,000 – $500 = $49,500

       $49,500 × .83 = $41,085

The difference between the ISO and the AAIS commercial property forms is that the deductible in the AAIS form is subtracted from the loss before the coinsurance computation. When the deductible is applied as specified in the AAIS provision, the insured recovers $85 more.

In the insurance-to-value provisions of the ISO Homeowners Policy, the deductible is also subtracted from the loss before any adjustment is made for underinsurance.

Some insurance policies do not specify where in the computation the deductible should be subtracted. When the issue is not addressed, the adjustment usually hinges on the practices of the insurance company or on the claim representative handling the case.

SUMMARY

Various factors affect the amount payable under a policy providing property insurance coverage. Insurance to value is an important concept. It ensures that sufficient funds will be available in the event of a total loss.

Valuation provisions that specify the method to be used in establishing the value of insured property at the time of the loss. The major valuation methods are replacement cost, actual cash value, and actual loss sustained. Other valuation approaches include the repair or replace option, valued policy laws, the agreed value approach, the stated amount approach, functional valuation, selling price clauses, cost of reproduction, pair or set clauses, use value of improvements and betterments, and money and securities valuation.

A range of methods is used to establish limits of insurance for property coverages. Terminology and categories overlap, but limits examined here included scheduled limits, unscheduled limits, specific limits, blanket limits, sublimits, per item limits, per occurrence limits, limits in additions and extensions of coverage, variable limits, and non-dollar limits.

Coinsurance and other insurance policy provisions address insurance-to-value issues. These provisions might reduce the amount payable and are designed to provide an incentive to insure to value. Different approaches for avoiding coinsurance penalties include maintaining insurance to value or using alternative approaches such as flat policies, agreed value, monthly limit of indemnity, or maximum period of indemnity.

Deductibles also can reduce the amount payable. By requiring the insured to share in the loss, deductibles can reduce attitudinal hazards and encourage loss control, eliminate the need to process small claims, and reduce premiums. A variety of straight deductibles, percentage deductibles, time deductibles, aggregate deductibles, and the no-deductible approach are used in property insurance. A few examples illustrate applying coinsurance and deductible computations to various losses involving actual cash value, replacement cost, adequate insurance, and underinsurance.

The amounts payable under liability insurance policies, which are largely determined by standards established through the courts, are discussed in Chapter 15.

CHAPTER NOTES

1. J. J. Launie, J. Finley Lee, and Norman A. Baglini, *Principles of Property and Liability Underwriting*, 3d ed. (Malvern, Pa.: Insurance Institute of America, 1986), p. 91.

2. Form CP-12, Ed 1.0, Copyright, American Association of Insurance Services, 1994.

3. Form PP 00 01 06 98, Copyright, Insurance Services Office, Inc., 1997.

4. Form PP 00 01 06 98, Copyright, Insurance Services Office, Inc., 1997.

5. Form CP 00 32 10 00, Copyright, Insurance Services Office, Inc., 1999.

6. Form HO 00 03 10 00, Copyright, Insurance Services Office, Inc., 1999.

7. A minor exception involves some personal property items pertaining to the maintenance of the building. Fire extinguishers, for example, could be classified as either "building" or "personal property." Because these items are covered in one place or the other, the distinction is moot unless the limits under "building" or "personal property" coverage are inadequate.

8. In practice, one would probably purchase a lower limit, say $720,000 of coverage subject to a 90 percent coinsurance clause. Coinsurance is discussed later in the chapter.

9. Form HO 00 04 10 00, Copyright, Insurance Services Office, Inc., 1999.

10. Form IM-70000, Ed 1.0, Copyright, American Association of Insurance Services, 1994.

11. Exceptions would be unusual, custom, or antique autos covered on a stated amount basis.

12. Copyright © 2001, Independent Insurance Agents of Texas. All rights reserved. E-mail Webmaster@iiat.org to comment on this material.

13. Form CP 00 10 10 00, Copyright, Insurance Services Office, Inc., 1999.

14. Form CP 00 30 10 00, Copyright, Insurance Services Office, Inc., 1999.

15. Form CP 00 10 10 00, Copyright, Insurance Services Office, Inc., 1999.

16. If the deductible is large enough, even two occurrences could result in quite a substantial retained loss.

17. Some scratches or chips are repairable. Sometimes a large, expensive pane of glass, broken on one side, can be cut in half and repaired by adding another matching half and a frame. Plate glass insurance can also cover signs painted on windows, and damage to the paint can be repaired. But for the most part, plate glass is either broken or intact.

18. Form CP 00 10 10 00, Copyright, Insurance Services Office, Inc., 1999.

19. Form CP 00 10 10 00, Copyright, Insurance Services Office, Inc., 1999.

20. Form CP-12, Ed 1.0, Copyright, American Association for Insurance Services, 1994.

Direct Your Learning

Amounts Payable: Liability Insurance

After learning the subject matter of this chapter, you should be able to:

■ Identify the types of coverages found in a liability insurance policy that affect amounts payable after a loss.

■ Identify and describe three types of liability coverage limits and how these limits dictate amounts payable after a loss.

■ Explain how deductibles and self-insured retentions in liability insurance determine amounts payable after a loss.

Develop Your Perspective

What are the main topics covered in the chapter?

The amount that should be paid for a loss under a liability insurance policy depends on the function, type, and amount of policy limits; the loss valuation methods; and the role of deductibles and self-insured retentions.

Review a liability policy from your personal insurance portfolio.

- Identify the types of policy limits listed.
- Consider the loss exposures that would fall under each of those limits.

Why is it important to know these topics?

Knowing this information will help you understand how amounts payable differ under liability insurance and property insurance and how to interpret a policy to determine the available coverage and the process for evaluating losses.

Consider the different methods for valuing losses under liability insurance versus property insurance.

- Why might the methods for valuing losses differ under each policy?

How can you use this information?

Consider a liability loss exposure your organization might face. Investigate the coverage that applies to the loss.

- Do the policy limits provide adequate coverage for the possible loss exposures?
- How might you determine the amount that would be paid for the loss?

Chapter 15

Amounts Payable: Liability Insurance

This chapter emphasizes the difference between amounts payable in property and liability insurance and explores policy limits, valuation, deductibles, and self-insured retentions.

ADEQUATE LIMITS

Adequate limits of insurance are important in both property and liability insurance in order to cover losses as fully as possible. For property insurance, this is accomplished by insuring to value. Insurance to value is a limit of insurance that approximates the maximum potential loss. The maximum potential loss can be estimated based on the replacement cost, actual cash value, or other insurable value of tangible property plus its use value.

Insurance to value is not relevant for most exposures covered by liability insurance, because an organization's maximum potential liability loss usually cannot be determined.

Big businesses and those engaging in hazardous activities might be the most vulnerable to large losses, but almost any person or organization could cause an accident resulting in large damages. An unfortunate example occurred in February 2001 when the driver of a Land Rover sports utility vehicle lost control and drove off a highway in the United Kingdom, causing a chain reaction of collisions involving the Land Rover, a passenger train, and a freight train and resulting in massive property damage, injuries, and casualties.[1] Chances are that the driver of the Land Rover, if found liable, did not have enough liability insurance.

Some liability exposures can be insured to value. The maximum potential loss for liability exposures involving possible damage or destruction to specific property items can be determined. An example would be fire legal liability coverage, which protects a tenant against its potential liability to a landlord for fire damage to a building that the tenant occupies. The maximum possible covered loss is the value of that building plus its use value.

Liability insurance is often purchased in layers. A primary insurance policy provides what might be called a *working layer* of coverage. Most losses are likely to fall within the limits of this working layer. For an individual or a family, the working layer might involve $100,000 of personal liability coverage under a homeowners policy; for a business, it might involve $500,000,

$1 million, or more, of coverage. One or more layers of excess or umbrella insurance cover unusually large "shock" losses that exceed coverage available in the primary policy.

Individuals and businesses must determine their potential losses and then decide how much liability insurance to purchase.

VALUATION OF LIABILITY LOSSES

As discussed in Chapter 14, *property* insurance loss valuation is based on actual cash value, replacement cost, or another valuation provision appearing in the insurance contract. With liability insurance, policy provisions provide information on the maximum amount payable, but how to determine the amount payable is affected by many factors outside the contract.

Relevant Policy Provisions

The liability insurance contract has relatively little to say about *how* the amount of a loss is determined. Under most circumstances, the maximum amount the insurer will pay is the lesser of the following:

1. The applicable policy limit (liability policy limits are discussed later in this chapter) or
2. The compensable amount of the loss.[2]

The extent of the insured's liability to the claimant is based on legal principles. When a jury trial is involved, the compensable amount of the loss is the amount the jurors decide to award to the plaintiff as damages. Subject to policy conditions and limits, the insurer will pay that amount on behalf of the insured. On rare occasions, the judge exercises the power to reduce or set aside an award that "shocks the conscience of the court."

Although policy limits cap the insurer's liability, neither the jury nor the judge is bound to confine an award to the limits of the policy. If the court awards a judgment that exceeds the policy limit, paying the excess award becomes the responsibility of the insured/defendant.

Most cases do not go to a formal trial, and the compensable amount of the loss is determined by negotiations between the liability insurer (or its attorney) and the claimant (or the claimant's attorney). Both parties try to anticipate what a court would do if presented with the same facts. Both parties have an incentive to reach an out-of-court settlement, because they recognize the uncertainty, time, and expense involved in a formal trial.

Most liability insurance policies give the insured/defendant no right to prohibit the insurer and the claimant from reaching a settlement within policy limits. Often, an insured wants its insurer to mount a vigorous defense and vindicate the insured, but the insurer has other priorities. The insurer's goal is usually to minimize its total costs for defense or damages. Sometimes the insurer pays a claim that might successfully have been defended. In some cases, defending a claim would cost more than paying damages. In others, the insurer does not want to risk losing a suit that would set a dangerous precedent for other, similar claims.

For claims exceeding policy limits, the insured has a right to its own legal counsel, usually at the insured's expense, to protect the insured's interests. Otherwise, the liability insurer usually has control over defense costs and the amount it wishes to offer as a settlement.

Other Factors Affecting Loss Valuation

When the insured is clearly liable for damages, the key issue affecting a liability claim valuation is what amount of monetary compensation will reasonably repay the injured person for the loss. How much money will it take to place him or her in a condition equivalent to the condition he or she occupied before the loss? A jury may decide this question of fact, but many settlements are negotiated out of court.

The United States common-law system requires payment of damages to compensate the claimant for loss caused by the insured's negligence in an amount determined as of the trial date. This rule presents no problem when all damage has been repaired by the date of the trial or settlement. In some cases, such as those involving permanent disability, damages must be based in part on an estimate of future expenses.

The claimant usually has the burden of proof. It is up to the claimant to establish what damages were proximately caused by the insured. The claimant also has a duty to mitigate damages and may not recover for damages that result from the claimant's lack of care following the accident. Where the collateral source rule applies by law, the insured's liability to pay damages is not reduced by any recovery the claimant might receive from health insurance or other sources.

Property Damage Liability Claims

When property is damaged, the owner may recover for the reasonable cost to repair the property or to replace the property if it cannot economically be repaired. When property must be replaced, the owner is entitled to the property's reasonable market value before loss or destruction. Generally, the owner may also recover damages to compensate for the loss of use of the property for a reasonable time period. For example, a claimant could claim the cost of renting a substitute car while the damaged car is in the shop.

Under certain circumstances, a claimant may also recover for profits lost from the inability to use the property. The owner of a damaged truck or tractor-trailer might lose revenue, especially if the owner cannot rent a substitute vehicle to make deliveries. The owner of a damaged building might lose rent from tenants or sales from customers while the building is out of use.

A few jurisdictions permit third-party damages for diminution in value of property that has been damaged and repaired.

Bodily Injury Liability Claims

Bodily injury claim evaluation takes into account a broad range of damage elements for the claimant, such as the following:

- Reasonable and necessary medical expenses incurred and those expected to be incurred in the future
- Type of injury
- Wage loss or loss of earning capacity because of the injury
- Other out-of-pocket expenses, such as household help
- Current and future pain and suffering resulting from the injury
- Extent and permanency of disability and impairment
- Disfigurement resulting from the injury
- Preexisting conditions that could have contributed to the injury

Death claims fall into two categories, which affect their evaluation:

1. In a survival action, the person representing the decedent makes a claim for what the decedent could have recovered if he or she had lived. These include the same elements of damages for bodily injury listed above.
2. A wrongful death action is based on the survivors' monetary economic loss. Most states also permit recovery for non-economic losses such as mental anguish, loss of consortium, loss of counseling, and other types of damages.[3]

POLICY LIMITS

Liability insurance policies have policy limits for the same reasons that property insurance policies have limits. The limits do the following:

- Cap the insurer's obligations
- Accommodate consumer preferences
- Reflect insurer capacity
- Substitute for exclusions

Liability Coverage Limits

Liability coverage involves the insurer's agreement to pay, usually on the insured's behalf, sums that the insured becomes legally obligated to pay as damages for bodily injury or property damage. Liability insurance policies' fault-based coverages fall into four categories of limits, discussed next.

Per Event Limits

Per event limit
A single limit, sometimes called a combined single limit, that applies to all incidents (per accident/occurrence/claimant/claim) resulting in injury to one person or several persons, in property damage, or in any combination thereof.

Liability insurance policies typically contain limits that apply (1) per accident, (2) per occurrence, (3) per claimant, or (4) per claim. With a **per event limit**, a single dollar limit, sometimes called a **single limit** or a **combined single limit**, applies to all incidents (per accident/occurrence/

claimant/claim) resulting in injury to one person or several persons, property damage, or in any combination thereof.

Per Accident

Forty years ago, general liability insurance was most commonly written on an accident basis, and **accident** was defined as a sudden, unforeseeable event. Because an accident, as defined, had to happen at a definite time, gradual damage was not considered an accident. For the most part, accident policies have now been replaced with policies covering on a "per occurrence" basis.

The 1998 edition of the ISO Personal Auto Policy, like many other policies, includes a single per accident limit, expressed in these words:

> The limit of liability shown in the Declarations for this coverage is our maximum limit of liability for all damages resulting from any one auto accident. This is the most we will pay regardless of the number of:
>
> 1. "Insureds";
> 2. Claims made;
> 3. Vehicles or premiums shown in the Declarations; or
> 4. Vehicles involved in the auto accident.[4]

Accident is not defined in the Personal Auto Policy. However, this provision makes it clear that, no matter how many insureds or vehicles are involved, no matter how many claims are made by separate parties, and no matter how many times a charge for liability insurance appears in the declarations, a Personal Auto Policy with a combined single limit of $500,000 would provide no more than $500,000 in coverage for any one auto accident. This limit applies for up to $500,000 for liability arising out of bodily injury, property damage, or any combination of the two.

Per Occurrence

For example, the current ISO Commercial General Liability (CGL) Coverage Form has several limits and sublimits, including an each occurrence limit that reads as follows:

> ...the Each Occurrence Limit is the most we will pay...because of all "bodily injury" and "property damage" arising out of any one "occurrence".

The same policy defines occurrence this way:

> "Occurrence" means an accident, including continuous or repeated exposure to substantially the same general harmful conditions.[5]

Clearly, **occurrence** is broader than the usual definition of "accident." Occurrences include adverse conditions that continue over a long period of time and eventually result in bodily injury or property damage, as well as events that happen suddenly and result in immediate bodily injury or property damage. Suppose, for example, an insured repeatedly drives her three-ton recreational

Accident
A sudden, unforeseeable event.

Occurrence
An event that happens suddenly and results in immediate bodily injury or property damage; also includes adverse conditions that continue over a long time period and eventually result in bodily injury or property damage.

vehicle across a private bridge with a two-ton load capacity, and the bridge eventually collapses. The collapse is not an accident as the term is commonly defined outside the business auto form, but it is an occurrence.

Sometimes determining whether a given set of circumstances involves a single occurrence or a series of occurrences is difficult. To illustrate this dilemma, suppose the tailgate of a gravel truck traveling down the highway is not completely closed, and gravel falling from the truck damages the windshields of many cars. Is this a single occurrence, or is each broken windshield a separate occurrence? Cases like this raise questions of fact for the courts to decide.

Per Claimant

Some liability insurance policies cover intentional torts, such as libel and slander, that do not technically qualify as accidents or occurrences because of their intentional nature. In the commercial general liability policy, for example, these "offenses" are subject to a separate personal and advertising injury limit that applies on a per claimant basis:

> ... the Personal and Advertising Injury Limit is the most we will pay under Coverage B for the sum of all damages because of all "personal and advertising injury" sustained by any one person or organization.[6]

The policy limit applies to each person or organization sustaining injury or damage. Several claimants can be injured in a single occurrence. For example, the publication of a single magazine article can offend a number of people, each of whom presents a libel claim.

Per Claim

A single occurrence injuring one person can generate multiple claims. Some policies, notably professional liability policies, provide coverage on a per claim basis. Typical policy wording might read as follows:

> **Limit of Liability/Each Claim**
>
> The liability of the Company for loss payments and claim expenses against each Insured for each claim shall not exceed the amount stated in the Declarations.

Split Limits

In contrast to the per event or single limits approach just described, the **split limits** approach uses separate limits for bodily injury claims and for property damage liability claims. For example, a policy might provide a $500,000 bodily injury liability coverage limit and a $100,000 property damage liability coverage limit. In the customary shorthand of the business, they might be written as "500/100 limits" or orally expressed as "five hundred, one hundred limits."

Split limits
Separate limits for bodily injury and for property damage liability; most policies also include a bodily injury sublimit applicable to each injured person.

Personal auto policies and other split limit policies usually contain three limits:

1. A bodily injury sublimit applicable to each injured person
2. A bodily injury limit—usually larger—applicable to two or more injured persons
3. A property damage limit

The first is a sublimit; the second and third are separate limits. These limits are illustrated in Exhibit 15-1.

EXHIBIT 15-1

Split Limits Example

Assume that Audrey is an insured under an auto policy with 25/50/10 ("twenty-five, fifty, ten") limits. Three examples illustrate how these limits apply:

1. Audrey negligently causes a covered accident resulting in no injuries but in $15,000 damage to another driver's car. The insurer would pay no more than $10,000—the property damage liability limit—for this damage. Audrey could not apply any of the separate bodily injury liability limits to cover the property damage liability claim.

2. In a separate accident, Audrey negligently causes $27,000 in bodily injury to Mrs. Smith and $4,000 to Mr. Smith. Audrey's insurer would at most pay $25,000 to Mrs. Smith (the per person sublimit) and $4,000 to Mr. Smith.

3. In another accident, Audrey is responsible for $134,000 in bodily injury to all five members of the Jones family, as well as $15,000 in property damage to the Joneses' car. The insurer would pay the claimants no more than $60,000; that is, $50,000 for bodily injury and $10,000 for property damage. Sixty thousand dollars is the maximum amount payable for any one accident under a policy with 25/50/10 limits.

Aggregate Limits

An **aggregate limit** is a specific limit on the maximum amount an insurer will pay for total damages from all covered events during the covered period. An aggregate limit typically is two or three times the per event limit (per accident/occurrence/claimant/claim), and it usually is expressed as an annual limit for each policy year. See Exhibit 15-2 for an example.

Aggregate limit
A specific limit on the maximum amount an insurer will pay for the total damages from all covered events during the covered period.

Aggregate limits are common in commercial liability policies. Personal insurance coverages, such as personal auto and homeowners policies, usually do not contain aggregate limits. As a practical matter, an individual or a family rarely incurs two or more separate, substantial liability losses during a single policy term (typically a year or less).

> ### EXHIBIT 15-2
>
> ### Aggregate Limits Example
>
> Liability Policy A has a single limit of $100,000 per occurrence and an annual aggregate limit of $300,000. Three covered losses occur in the following amounts during the first six months of the policy term, which begins on February 1:
>
> 1. February 15: $ 50,000
>
> 2. April 11: $120,000
>
> 3. June 5: $200,000
>
> The insurer would pay $50,000 for the first loss and $100,000 each for the second and third losses for a cumulative total of $250,000 during the first six months. At this point, the insured has accumulated $250,000 in insured losses and has only $50,000 of coverage available for the remaining six months of the policy period because the policy has an aggregate limit of $300,000 per year. Another separate occurrence with $50,000 or more in damages would exhaust the $300,000 annual aggregate limit. Once this aggregate limit has been used to pay claims, the insured is without further protection.

Limits on Defense Costs and Supplementary Payments

A liability insurance contract contains more than the insurer's agreement to pay damages on the insured's behalf. The insurer also agrees to pay the costs of defending the insured, and the insurer often contributes substantial experience and expertise to the defense process. Many insurance buyers consider the insurer's defense services to be one of the most important reasons to buy liability insurance.

Courts have consistently held that the liability insurer's duty to defend is broader than its duty to pay damages. Even if a suit appears to be groundless, false, or fraudulent, the insurer must defend an insured whenever the plaintiff alleges facts that could conceivably fall within the policy's coverage. Even if a single allegation among many would be covered, the insurer in most states is obligated to defend the insured. The insured might be found not liable, meaning that no damages would be paid; however, the insurer must defend the insured.

Knowing whether defense costs are paid *within* or *in addition to* policy limits is important because the amount of insurance available to pay damages can be significantly reduced when defense costs are paid as part of the policy limits. See Exhibit 15-3.

Is an insurer likely to spend $40,000 defending a claim for $90,000 in damages? Situations like this occur. The claimant might originally seek a much higher damage amount, and the insurer's vigorous defense might reduce the amount ultimately payable. Or the claimant might be seeking $90,000 in damages, and the insurer might think it can successfully defend the case and receive a favorable judgment for the insured, with no damages payable. Or perhaps the claimant refused to accept a reasonable settlement offer, leaving the insurer with no practical choice but to defend the claim.

EXHIBIT 15-3

Limits on Defense Costs Example

Suppose an insurer has issued a professional liability insurance policy covering a beautician with a $100,000 policy limit. The insurer incurs $40,000 in costs to defend a professional liability claim, and the trial court holds the insured liable for $90,000 in damages.

- If defense costs are within limits, the insurer will pay $40,000 in defense costs and $60,000 in damages, consuming the entire $100,000 limit. The insured will be responsible for the other $30,000.

- If defense costs are payable in addition to policy limits, the insurer will pay the $40,000 in defense costs plus the full $90,000 in damages. Additionally, if the claimant appeals the case to a higher court, the insurer would probably pay the costs of defending the appeal, and its defense obligation would not end until it had *paid* $100,000 in *damages*.

Under the vast majority of liability insurance policies, defense costs are payable *in addition to* the maximum amount payable for damages. *No dollar limit* is placed on the amount the insurer might be required to pay in defending the insured against a claim for covered damages. However, the insurer's obligations are not entirely limitless. A typical liability insuring agreement stipulates that the insurer's obligation to defend against any given claim for damages terminates when the amount it *pays* for *damages* equals the specified limit of liability. For example, the ISO Commercial General Liability Policy states:

> Our right and duty to defend end when we have used up the applicable limit of insurance in the payments of judgments or settlements under Coverages A or B or medical expenses under Coverage C.[7]

What about serious cases in which the damages clearly exceed the policy limits? Can the insurer just pay or "tender" the limits and bow out of the case? No. In policies with this wording, the insurer's duties do not end until it has *paid* the full policy limits *in fulfilling a judgment or settlement*. If the claimant is not willing to settle for policy limits, the insurer is obligated to continue defending the insured until a final court judgment has been rendered or a settlement has been reached.

Although the insurer's defense obligation is theoretically unlimited, practical constraints apply. Most policies give the insurer the exclusive right to control the defense. The insurer can select its own defense counsel, monitor the case, and attempt to negotiate a settlement if costs threaten to become disproportionately high.

The Importance of Defense

The benefits of a sound legal defense including the following:

- Often a strong defense results in a judgment favoring the insured and requiring neither the insurer nor the insured to pay damages.
- A legal decision in the insured's favor may establish good case law and discourage similar claims.
- A strong defense signals plaintiffs' attorneys and would-be claimants that the insurer will vigorously defend similar claims rather than pay to dispose of them.
- The amount of damages payable can be substantially reduced because of evidence introduced through a sound, if costly, defense.

Because litigation involves a dispute between parties with different viewpoints, the outcome can never be predicted with complete confidence. Insurers do not always prevail when they choose to defend a case, and defense costs sometimes are incurred on claims that could have been reasonably settled out of court by paying the claimant's original settlement demand.

Rather than incur defense costs, insurers sometimes pay small, questionable "nuisance" claims—even those that they could probably win—to avoid defense costs or the possibility of a large adverse judgment.

Limits for Non-Fault-Based Coverages

Other coverages in a liability policy that affect amounts payable are the non-fault-based coverages. Many insurance policies that cover liability arising out of bodily injury include "medical payments" coverage for some of the same elements of loss, but without requiring liability on the part of the insured. Because these coverages are provided without regard to who caused the injury, they are called non-fault-based coverages. This section examines a few of these medical payments coverages, along with a comparable "damage to property of others" coverage in homeowners policies.

Nominal limits of medical payments coverage enable an insurer to pay small claims in a way that eliminates the need for litigation and preserves the insured's goodwill, while preserving the insurer's defenses in the event of a larger liability claim. Consider the following example:

Doris injured her knee and incurred medical expenses of $500 when she fell in her friend Jim's driveway. Doris asked Jim to pay her medical expenses because she believed they were caused by a hazard in his driveway. Jim notified his homeowners insurer, and it readily paid Doris's claim under that policy's "medical payments to others" coverage. Consider what might have happened if Jim had liability coverage but did not also have medical payments coverage:

- The insurer might have attempted to defend Jim, at some expense, by showing that Doris's fall was caused by her own clumsiness and not by Jim's negligence.

- Jim's insistence that he was not negligent might have cost him Doris's friendship.

- Rather than lose Doris's friendship, Jim might have agreed with her side of the story to help her recover her expenses from his insurance company.

- Recognizing that defense could be costly, the insurance company might pay Doris's expenses of $500. Doris might later be encouraged to bring a larger claim for additional expenses or disability.

The standard *homeowners* limit for medical payments to others is usually $1,000 *per person* as the result of one accident. Subject to this limit, the insurer agrees to pay "necessary medical expenses that are incurred or medically ascertained within three years of the date of an accident causing 'bodily injury.' " Coverage does not apply to injuries of the named insured or to regular household residents, and most policies contain no per accident limit.

As with homeowners policies, medical payments coverage is automatically built into *commercial general liability* policies, usually with a limit of $5,000. The stated limit is the most the insurer will pay for all medical expenses because of bodily injury sustained by any one person due to an accident on the insured's premises or because of the insured's operations. Covered expenses must be incurred and reported within one year from the date of the accident. Coverage does not apply to an insured or its employees.

Auto medical payments coverage differs sharply from homeowners or commercial general liability medical payments coverage. Auto med pay, as it is commonly called, covers the named insured's injuries and those of family members, in addition to covering passengers' injuries. Limits are offered in modest amounts such as $5,000. Coverage for the insured and family members provides a first-party benefit that does not overlap with the liability policy's coverage. Coverage for the others' injuries is comparable to the medical payments coverage of homeowners policies.

In some states, auto liability insurance policies are endorsed to include *auto no-fault* ("personal injury protection," or PIP) coverages. Generalizing about PIP coverages is difficult because these coverages vary by state. Nearly all PIP endorsements provide specified amounts of insurance, restricted solely to losses resulting from auto accidents, regardless of who is negligent. The typical endorsement provides at least some coverage for medical expenses, funeral expenses, survivor benefits, loss of income, and replacement of essential services.

A $1,000 limit is printed in the body of standard ISO homeowners policies for damage to the property of others. This "additional coverage," which applies to damage to the property of others caused by an insured, is subject to additional policy provisions. The insured need not be legally responsible for the property damage for the insurer to pay a claim. Like homeowners medical payments to others coverage, this additional coverage, coupled with a nominal limit, allows the insurer to pay small claims without determining liability or implying that the insured was liable for the property damage.

Workers Compensation Limits

No dollar limits appear in the workers compensation coverage of a workers compensation and employers liability policy. The workers compensation insuring agreement is simple:

> We will pay promptly when due the benefits required of you by the workers compensation law.[8]

The states or territories with workers compensation laws that are referenced are listed in the policy's declarations, referred to in the policy as an information page. The policy itself is not required to include dollar limits, because state workers compensation statutes indicate the applicable limits. These legally specified limits become the amounts payable.

Increasing Policy Limits

Keeping limits in line with insurable values is essential in property insurance. With liability insurance, this requirement is unnecessary because many costs, such as defense costs, are not subject to policy limits.

Insureds must be careful to stay adequately insured because coverage limits are not usually adjusted unless the insured actually selects a new policy limit. Unlike workers compensation limits that are changed by statute or as necessary, liability limits do not automatically change according to inflation or peak season. Therefore, a $100,000 policy from ten years ago might not adequately cover an exposure now worth $1 million.

Although property insurance costs are directly proportional to the insurance limits, liability insurance is not. The premium for a policy with a $1 million liability limit is only a little more than the premium for a policy with a $500,000 limit, but it provides twice the coverage.

This section has shown the different types of coverages available on a liability insurance policy and how these coverages determine amounts payable in the event of a loss. The next sections show how deductibles and self-insured retentions (retaining risks) affect amounts payable.

DEDUCTIBLES AND SELF-INSURED RETENTIONS

By requiring the insured to share in the loss, deductibles do the following:

1. Reduce attitudinal (morale) hazards and encourage loss control
2. Eliminate the insurer's need to process small losses, thereby reducing insurers' loss costs and loss adjustment expenses
3. Reduce the premium cost to the insured

Although deductibles serve these purposes well with most types of *property* insurance, they are much less effective with *liability* insurance.

With liability deductibles, insureds might not report seemingly minor incidents until the situation has escalated. Insurers want to be involved in small liability claims. Liability claim investigation involves not only the nature and extent of damages but also who is legally responsible for paying them. That is why insurers need to control liability claims from the outset.

With most coverages, liability deductibles would not noticeably reduce premiums. One reason is that relatively few liability claims involve small amounts. More important, unlike property insurance, under which the insurer usually is not involved in small claims below the deductible, the liability insurer is involved in all claims. Even with a deductible, the liability insurer usually pays "first dollar" expenses for investigation and defense coverage, just as it does for policies without deductibles. Usually the deductible applies only to the amount paid to the claimant in settling the claim, not to defense costs.

With property insurance, the insurer simply subtracts the deductible to determine the amount payable to the insured. To get a third-party liability insurance claimant to settle a claim and sign a release, the insurer usually must pay the agreed-upon settlement in full, without reduction for any deductible. The insurer then has the right to recover the amount of the deductible from the insured. The value of that right depends on the insured's ability and willingness to pay—after the insurer has mounted an unsuccessful defense. In light of these factors, insurers are sometimes selective in choosing the insureds for whom they will even consider a liability deductible.

Deductibles are not usually found in standard general liability, personal liability, or auto liability policies. However, large deductibles are common with some specialty liability coverages, such as those involving professional liability or directors and officers liability. By involving the insured in each loss, these large deductibles are used primarily to encourage loss control. Deductibles are also common in bailee legal liability coverages, such as those for warehouses and garagekeepers. These forms provide property damage liability coverage against loss to a specified category of property, and the deductibles function similarly to those used with property insurance.

Self-Insured Retentions (SIRs)

Some liability insurance policies include a self-insured retention (SIR). An SIR closely resembles a large deductible, but a fundamental difference exists between an SIR and a deductible. See the following box.

> ### Deductibles Versus Self-Insured Retentions
>
> - With a liability insurance deductible, the insurer defends on a first-dollar basis, pays all covered losses, and then bills the insured for the amount of losses up to the deductible.
> - With an SIR, the insurer pays losses only once they exceed the self-insured retention level. The insurer does not defend claims below the amount of the SIR. Consequently, the organization is responsible for adjusting and paying its own losses up to the SIR level.

To compensate for its lack of control over self-insured claims, a policy with a self-insured retention usually requires strict reporting to the insurer of any claims that have the potential of exceeding the self-insured retention level.

SIRs are common in professional liability insurance policies and some specialty policies. SIRs are also commonly found in the "drop-down" coverage of umbrella policies. The drop-down coverage of an umbrella policy provides primary coverage, subject to the SIR, on claims that are not covered by an underlying primary insurance policy and not excluded by the umbrella policy.

The specific details of SIRs vary widely. Donald S. Malecki and Pete Ligeros have identified the following "points to consider" when evaluating any given SIR. By implication, these points also summarize some of the important variations among SIRs.

- Who has the right or obligation to designate the claims servicing organization?
- Is the entity utilizing the SIR endorsement (to be referred to as the "self-insured") entitled to select legal counsel to protect its interests?
- Is the self-insured or the insurer responsible for providing defense of suits within the SIR?
- If the self-insured is responsible for defense, is there any limit on the amount of legal costs that must be paid by the SIR?
- Is the self-insured required to accept any reasonable offer of settlement within the SIR?
- Can the insurer to whose policy the SIR endorsement is attached settle without the self-insured's permission, if the amount of settlement is within the SIR?
- If the SIR endorsement describes the scope of defense coverage to be provided within the SIR, is the defense provision of the policy to which the SIR endorsement is attached automatically deleted, or is it modified to reflect the scope of defense coverage provided by the endorsement?
- To what extent, if any, is the insurance company involved required to share defense expenses incurred by the self-insured?

- When and under what conditions is the self-insured obligated to notify the insurer of the policy containing the SIR endorsement of any occurrence, claim, or suit?

- Is the amount of the SIR deducted from the policy limit, or is the policy limit payable in full once the SIR is exhausted?

- Does the wording of the SIR endorsement being used create a deductible or a true self-insured retention?

- If the policy or its SIR endorsement includes an arbitration clause, is the venue (location) for settling a dispute mandated by the arbitration clause? If so, is that venue convenient to the self-insured?

- Is the self-insured obligated to provide periodic reports to the insurer of occurrences, claims, and suits?

- Is the SIR endorsement limited to bodily injury and property damage coverages, or does it encompass personal injury, advertising liability, and other coverages provided under the policy?

- Can the self-insured reinsure the SIR amount or does the endorsement specifically prohibit this or require the insurer's permission to do so?

- Can the insurer advance settlement costs on behalf of the self-insured?

- Is the assistance and cooperation condition applicable to the respective parties clearly stated to apply under both the terms of the policy and the SIR endorsement?

- Does bankruptcy, insolvency, receivership, or inability of the self-insured to pay within the SIR relieve the insurer of its obligations?[9]

SUMMARY

This chapter examined how liability insurance policies specify amounts payable. Substantial differences exist between liability insurance and property insurance, in which the amount payable depends on the valuation of covered property using the valuation approach specified in the policy and adjusted for policy limits, deductibles, and coinsurance or other insurance-to-value provisions. With liability insurance, the amount payable as damages depends largely on legal principles as they are, or would be, as applied by the courts, and on the negotiation of the parties involved. Policy limits can cap the insurer's obligations; defense costs are usually, but not always, covered in addition, even if the full policy limit is payable as damages. Also, insurance-to-value provisions are virtually nonexistent in liability insurance. Deductibles are uncommon, and an SIR may be used instead of a deductible.

In addition to the policy provisions, the amount payable under either a property or liability insurance policy can be further adjusted if other insurance covers the same loss, which Chapter 16 discusses.

CHAPTER NOTES

1. World Wide Web: http://www.policestop.org.uk/Selby.html.

2. Occasionally, an insurer is held to payments in excess of the policy limit when the insurer is found guilty of bad faith or negligence in failing to settle the claim for less than the policy limit.

3. Morton Daller, *Tort Law Desk Reference 2000, a Fifty-State Compendium* (New York: Aspen Law and Business, 2000).

4. Form PP 00 01 06 98, Copyright, Insurance Services Office, Inc., 1997.

5. Form CG 00 01 07 98, Copyright, Insurance Services Office, Inc., 1997.

6. Form CG 00 01 07 98, Copyright, Insurance Services Office, Inc., 1997.

7. Form CG 00 01 07 98, Copyright, Insurance Services Office, Inc., 1997.

8. Form WC 00 00 00 A, Copyright, National Council on Compensation Insurance, 1991.

9. Donald S. Malecki and Pete Ligeros, J.D., "Self-Insured Retentions: An Examination of the Uses and Problems, Part II," *Malecki on Insurance*, vol. 3, no. 1, November 1993, Malecki Communications Company, Cincinnati, pp. 1–10.

Chapter 16

Direct Your Learning

Amounts Payable: Other Sources of Recovery

After learning the subject matter of this chapter, you should be able to:

■ Explain why policies include "other insurance" provisions.

■ Identify and describe the five other sources of recovery that affect amounts payable.

■ Identify and describe the three types of "other insurance" provisions.

■ Given a loss situation and an "other insurance" provision, explain how the primary insurer might determine amounts payable.

Develop Your Perspective

What are the main topics covered in the chapter?

This chapter describes the characteristics and types of "other insurance," the policy provisions that determine how to settle coverage conflicts in the face of other sources of recovery, and how other sources of recovery can affect the amounts payable under a policy.

Review the provisions in an insurance policy.

- What types of other insurance provisions are included?

Why is it important to know these topics?

By knowing the policy provisions that deal with other insurance, you will understand why it is important to check for other possible sources of recovery when determining the amounts payable, and how the policy provisions regarding other insurance work to limit an insurer's obligation in certain coverage situations.

Review the policy provisions again.

- How is coverage affected if another possible source of recovery is available?

How can you use this information?

Consider a loss exposure facing your organization.

- Are there multiple insurers who would cover the loss?
- Would they pay for the loss?
- How much would they pay?

Chapter 16

Amounts Payable: Other Sources of Recovery

The amount an insurer is obligated to pay under a property or liability insurance policy can be affected by other insurance covering the same loss. That amount can also be affected, under some circumstances, if the insured has a legal right to recover from a noninsurance source. This chapter explains how these situations are handled according to policy provisions.

Most insurance claims are covered by a single insurance contract, and the contract's wording, usually drafted by the insurer, governs the insurer's obligations. An insurer cannot control the wording of contracts written by other insurers, and conflicts regarding payment obligations sometimes result. This chapter reviews some of the ways in which these conflicts are resolved.

SOURCES OF MULTIPLE RECOVERY

Insurance coverage analysis generally begins with the premise that one insurance policy or coverage, standing alone, covers a given loss. However, in some cases, the insured might also have access to additional sources of compensation covering all or part of the same loss. A fundamental assumption of insurance is that people should not be indemnified more than once per loss.

In response, insurers developed ways to manage situations in which multiple recoveries may be possible. A "multiple recovery" rule applies only to other sources against which the insured has a legally enforceable right, including the following:

- Other insurance in the same policy
- Other insurance in a similar policy
- Other insurance in a dissimilar policy
- Noninsurance agreements
- Negligent third parties

Some other sources of recovery involve noninsurance agreements. However, multiple sources of recovery generally involve an "other-insurance" situation. An **"other-insurance" situation** exists when more than one insurance source provides recovery for the same interest, cause of loss, and dollars of loss.

"Other-insurance" situation
A situation in which more than one insurance source provides recovery for the same interest, cause of loss, and dollars of loss.

Other Insurance in the Same Policy

Unless specific policy provisions state otherwise, property-liability insurance policies often cover a given loss under two or more coverages of the same contract. Consider these examples:

- A scheduled personal property endorsement (personal articles floater) attached to a homeowners policy provides coverage for scheduled items, many of which are also covered under the unscheduled personal property coverage of the homeowners policy.

- A crime insurance form, as well as a special-form building and personal property insurance on a building, can both be parts of a commercial package policy, and both might provide coverage against building damage by burglars.

- Personal property used to maintain or service a building—such as fire extinguishing equipment, outdoor furniture, or refrigerators—is specifically covered under the "building" coverage of many commercial property insurance forms. The same items also qualify for coverage as personal property under another insuring agreement of the same form.

- An auto insurance policy includes a separate premium charge for uninsured motorists coverage for each of two cars. One might argue that an insured, when driving a nonowned auto, has twice as much uninsured motorists coverage as another insured who owns only one car.

- A passenger injured in an auto accident involving an uninsured motorist, who was partly at fault, might have medical payments coverage for medical expenses regardless of who was at fault; he or she might also bring a bodily injury liability claim against the driver (who was partly responsible for the accident); and might also have a right of action against the uninsured motorist who was driving the other car. Coverage might apply under the liability, medical payments, and uninsured motorists coverages of the car owner's personal auto policy.

Each of these examples might appear to involve a distinction without a difference. Because the insured's loss is covered, it might not seem important to know which coverage applies. But some questions remain:

- Does some policy provision make only one coverage apply?

- Do the *limits* of insurance "stack," giving the insured the combined limits of both coverages to handle a large loss? Or does the policy include an anti-stacking provision?

- Is payment under one of the coverages more advantageous to the insured because of different valuation provisions or deductibles? If so, can the *insured* choose which coverage to apply?

- Are fire extinguishing systems, refrigerators, or other items subject to duplicate coverage included in the building value, the personal property value, or both when applying the coinsurance clause?

The answers to these questions can vary by policy, so they are best resolved by analyzing the policy that applies.

Other Insurance in a Similar Policy

Sometimes, overlapping coverage exists because the same party is protected by two or more policies, as in the following examples:

- ABC Realty's property exposures exceed the capacity of any single insurer, so several insurance companies issue policies that, together, provide adequate limits of coverage.

- Fred moves to a new home, buys a new homeowners policy, and does not cancel the homeowners policy on his old home, which is still for sale. Both policies simultaneously cover some of Fred's exposures.

Other-insurance situations like these can involve more than one insurance company. The question then is not which coverage applies, but which insurer will pay. To answer that question, the language of two or more policies must be examined. Even similar policies are not always in agreement.

Other Insurance in Dissimilar Policies

A loss is sometimes covered by more than one type of insurance, often from two or more insurers, as the following examples show:

- Isabel owns a utility trailer. Under some circumstances, liability claims involving the trailer might be covered by both her homeowners policy and her personal auto policy.

- Pizza Palace offers valet parking, using its back lot. The valet parking activity might be covered under both Pizza Palace's general liability policy *and* its commercial auto liability policy.

- Pizza Palace offers a delivery service for which employees use their own cars. Pizza Palace's liability for an employee's acts or omissions might be covered under both the employee's personal auto policy *and* Pizza Palace's commercial auto policy.

- A Pizza Palace employee injured in an auto accident on the job might be able to recover under the employee's auto insurance; the employer's auto insurance; individual or group medical expense or disability insurance purchased by the employee, the employer, or the employee's parent; or workers compensation insurance.

Dissimilar insurance policies do not necessarily include provisions that clearly coordinate coverage with other policies, especially when the policies are of different types or issued by different insurers.

Noninsurance Agreements

People often have a contractually enforceable source of recovery that does not involve insurance. The following are examples:

- A lease contract or bailment agreement might make a tenant, equipment lessee, or bailee responsible for damage to leased or bailed property that is also covered by insurance.

- A credit card enhancement might protect the cardholder against claims for damage to a rented car, partially duplicating auto physical damage coverage in the renter's personal auto policy.

- A credit card enhancement might protect property purchased with the card against theft or accidental damage. The same property would probably be covered under a homeowners policy.

- An extended auto warranty, home warranty, appliance service agreement, or other plan can provide yet another contractually enforceable source of recovery.

Credit card enhancements are often underwritten by an insurance company, operating behind the scenes. However, the benefit itself is provided through a contract between the credit card company and the cardholder. The cardholder is contractually entitled to the benefits promised by the credit card organization. As indicated, these benefits often duplicate insurance benefits. Even if the property is also insured, a cardholder might find it desirable to claim benefits from the credit card company. Unlike property insurance, the credit card benefit generally is on a first-dollar basis with no deductible.

For example, the 2000 revision of the property section of the ISO Homeowners Policy includes a provision reflecting the growing popularity of service agreements:

> If a loss covered by this policy is also covered by...a service agreement, this insurance is excess over any amounts payable under such agreement. Service agreement means a service plan, property restoration plan, home warranty or other similar service warranty agreement, even if it is characterized as insurance.[1]

The last line of this provision reflects the fact that service agreements are sometimes described as "insurance" when they are marketed, even if they do not meet a legal definition of insurance.

Third-Party Liability

Another source of recovery affecting amounts payable is third-party liability. As a matter of law, a party who is injured or whose property is damaged by a negligent third party generally has a right to recover damages from the third party—whether or not the third party has liability insurance. The recovery from a third party (or the third party's liability insurance) could overlap with any first-party property insurance benefits. Although two types of insurance might be involved, the relevant policy language is not captioned "other insurance," but "subrogation," as illustrated by the following example.

Bonnie's car is struck and damaged by Dave, a careless driver. Dave has liability insurance; an insurer has agreed to pay liability claims on his behalf. Bonnie has a right under tort law to seek recovery from Dave; Dave will turn the claim over to his insurer. Bonnie also has a contractual right to recover from her own insurer's collision coverage. Does Bonnie's insurance reduce or eliminate Dave's obligation to pay damages to Bonnie? Or is Bonnie's insurance company off the hook because Dave caused the accident?

The answer to both questions is "No."[2] Whether or not a careless driver like Dave has liability insurance, his legal obligation to pay damages does not affect the contractual obligations of the insurer providing first-party property coverage—unless the insurance contract specifies otherwise. Dave is legally obligated, and Bonnie's insurer is contractually obligated, to pay for the damage to her car.

That does not mean Bonnie will recover twice as much as she lost. According to the subrogation provision in Bonnie's personal auto policy, if she recovers from her own insurance company, that company can attempt to recover from Dave or his insurer. If Dave's insurer also pays Bonnie directly, she is required to reimburse her insurer.

GENERAL CHARACTERISTICS OF "OTHER INSURANCE" PROVISIONS

Broadly speaking, "other insurance" provisions include all policy provisions, regardless of their caption, that attempt to specify in advance of a loss how an insurer's obligations (amounts payable) will be affected by other insurance applying to the same loss. Several characteristics of other insurance provisions, such as the following, are worth noting:

- Other insurance provisions are not necessarily labeled other insurance. An "excess clause" or a "subrogation provision," among others, might address other-insurance situations.

- Other insurance provisions, regardless of their title, are usually found in the conditions section of an insurance policy.

- Policies with more than one distinct coverage section often contain more than one other insurance provision.

- A single other insurance clause often includes more than one other insurance provision. For example, the clause might address several possible types of other-insurance situations.

- Two other insurance provisions of the same general type are not necessarily consistent with one another.

- Applying an other insurance provision literally can be impossible. For example, the only two policies covering a particular loss might both state that they are excess over other applicable policies.

- Even when other insurance provisions are consistent, other coverage differences (nonconcurrencies) in the same policy might make them difficult to apply. For example, one property insurance policy might provide coverage against the basic causes of loss while a similar policy is written on a special-form basis.

A subrogation provision often qualifies as an other insurance provision by this definition. So do provisions labeled "other insurance." Group medical insurance policies include a "coordination of benefits" provision that addresses other-insurance situations.

TYPES OF "OTHER INSURANCE" PROVISIONS

Most other insurance provisions fall into one of three broad categories:

1. Primary/excess provisions
2. Proportional provisions
3. Escape clauses

Primary/Excess Provisions

An insurance policy might specifically indicate that it provides either primary coverage or excess coverage. **Primary coverage** pays before other applicable policies until its own limits are exhausted. **Excess coverage** pays the amount over the primary coverage.

For example, Mitch owns property insured under two policies:

- Policy A with a $6,000 limit states that it is primary coverage.
- Policy B with a $10,000 limit states that it is excess coverage.

Mitch has a $10,000 loss covered by both policies. The insurer with Policy A will pay its $6,000 limit of coverage. The insurer with Policy B will then pay $4,000, the amount of the loss over $6,000.

An excess other insurance clause should not be confused with an excess insurance policy. An excess policy covers losses over either underlying insurance or a large self-insured retention (deductible) amount. An excess other insurance clause is usually found in a primary insurance policy that provides payment only after the coverage of other primary policies is exhausted.

Proportional Provisions

What happens when two policies both state that they are primary, or when both state that they are excess? Such situations are often addressed by a proportional other insurance provision.

Proportional "other insurance" provisions limit the insurer's obligations to a portion of the overall loss. Losses may be proportioned among insurers in two common ways:

1. Proration by policy limits
2. Contribution by equal shares

Primary coverage
A policy that pays for covered losses before other applicable policies until its own limits are exhausted.

Excess coverage
A policy that pays the amount over the primary coverage.

Proportional "other insurance" provisions
Provisions that limit the insurer's obligations to a portion of the overall loss.

Proportional provisions might be said to prescribe an equitable way for two or more insurers to *share* in a loss. Equitable loss sharing is the *result* only when every applicable policy has the same type of other insurance provision. The *purpose* of any proportional provision is to limit the obligations of the insurer issuing that policy.

Two important points should be remembered throughout the discussion on proportional other insurance provisions:

1. *An other insurance provision affects only the contract in which it appears.* One insurer's contract cannot specify the coverage that will be provided by another insurer.

2. *A proportional provision limits an insurer's obligations, but it does not subtract coverage.* If losses exceed the total limits of coverage available, each insurer will pay its full limit, barring contraindications elsewhere in the policy.

Proration by Policy Limits

Proration by policy limits caps the insurer's maximum obligations at the proportion of the loss that the insurer's policy limit bears to the sum of all applicable policy limits. An example of proration by policy limits appears in the AAIS Building and Personal Property Coverage Part:

> **Insurance Under More than One Policy – You** may have another policy subject to the same plan, terms, conditions, and provisions as this policy. If **you** do, **we** pay **our** share of the covered loss. **Our** share is the proportion that the applicable **limit** under this policy bears to the limit of all policies covering on the same basis.[3]

The concept may be expressed as a formula:

$$\frac{(A's\ limit)}{(A's\ limit + B's\ limit + C's\ limit + \ldots)} \times Loss = A's\ maximum\ obligation$$

The following is an example. Two insurers are involved. Insurer A's limit is $90,000, Insurer B's limit is $10,000, and a $40,000 loss occurs.

- A is contractually obligated to pay no more than $36,000:
  $$(\$90,000 \div (\$90,000 + \$10,000)) \times \$40,000.$$

- If B's policy has a similar proration by policy limits provision, B's obligation is limited to $4,000:
  $$(\$10,000 \div (\$90,000 + \$10,000)) \times \$40,000.$$

  But even if B's policy does not have a similar provision, A's obligation is still limited to $36,000 because the insured also had coverage under Policy B. A's policy cannot prescribe the amount payable by Policy B.

- If a loss of $100,000 or more occurred, Insurer A would pay $90,000. If Policy B had a similar proration by policy limits provision, Insurer B would pay $10,000. These amounts would not change if the loss is greater than $100,000, because an insurer is not obligated to pay more than its policy limits.

Proration by policy limits is commonly used in property insurance policies. It provides an equitable way of allocating losses in situations in which each insurer's premium is directly proportional to policy limits.

Contribution by Equal Shares

Contribution by equal shares
A method of paying losses in which both policies pay the loss equally until one policy is exhausted; then the other policy alone pays.

Under **contribution by equal shares**, both policies pay the loss equally until one policy is exhausted; after that, the other policy alone pays.

Here is how payment by equal shares would apply in the previous example. Two insurers are involved, and both policies specify contribution by equal shares. A's limit is $90,000, B's limit is $10,000, and a $40,000 loss occurs.

- A and B would pay equal shares until A has paid $10,000 and B has paid its $10,000 limit. A would also pay the remaining $20,000. Therefore, A would pay $30,000 of the loss ($10,000 + $20,000), and B would bear $10,000.

Contribution by equal shares is often used in liability insurance policies, in which each insurer's premium is not directly proportional to policy limits. In other words, the first $100,000 layer of liability insurance generally costs much more than the next $100,000 layer of insurance, and so forth. Under these circumstances, contribution by equal shares tends to distribute losses among insurers in proportion to the premium they collected for the risk.

Escape Clauses

Escape clause
An "other insurance" provision that relieves the insurer of any obligation to pay a claim when other insurance applies.

An **escape clause** is an "other insurance" provision that relieves the insurer of any obligation to pay a claim for which other insurance applies. See the following box.

Escape Clauses

An escape clause might function in one of four ways:

1. *Prohibition*—Forbidding other insurance
2. *Exclusion*—Excluding property or activities covered by other insurance
3. *Disclaimer*—Denying responsibility if other insurance applies
4. *Offset*—Reducing the coverage limit by the amount of other insurance

---

Prohibitions

Other insurance prohibitions forbid the purchase of other insurance. An insurer may deny coverage to any insured who fails to comply with a policy condition that prohibits other insurance.

For example, the ISO Personal Auto Policy contains an escape clause based on a prohibition. The "automatic termination" provision begins by stating that the policy ceases to provide further coverage at the end of the policy period if the insured does not accept the insurer's renewal offer. This statement is followed by the escape clause:

> If you obtain other insurance on "your covered auto", any similar insurance provided by this policy will terminate as to that auto on the effective date of the other insurance.[4]

People usually do not buy extra auto insurance on purpose. In most cases, this provision reflects the intent of the insured who decided to replace one policy with another. The provision also addresses the rare insurance fraud situation in which duplicate claims are filed with two or more insurers. Of course, the provision is effective only when the insurer knows a duplicate claim has been filed with another insurer.

Another example of prohibition appears in some liability policies involving a large self-insured retention (SIR) or deductible. For example, one directors and officers (D&O) liability policy includes these words:

> This policy shall pay only the excess of such retention…and such retention shall be uninsured.

A large deductible or SIR in a liability insurance policy is intended to encourage loss control by making the insured participate substantially in any loss. Other insurance covering the deductible would defeat this purpose.

Exclusions

Insurers try to avoid covering exposures in one policy that should be covered by another type of insurance. Often, they clarify their intentions by excluding property or activities that would be better covered in another policy. These exclusions are not other insurance provisions, because they apply even when the other insurance does not exist. For example, the liability coverage of homeowners policies excludes coverage for most auto-related losses. The exclusion applies even if a particular homeowner does not have an auto policy.

Other exclusions negate coverage only if other insurance applies. These do function as other insurance provisions, even if they appear in an exclusions section of the policy. For example, the personal property coverage of an ISO homeowners policy specifically excludes:

> Articles separately described and specifically insured, *regardless of the limit for which they are insured*, in this or other insurance.[5] [emphasis added]

The italicized phrase was added in the 2000 policy edition to make it clear that this is an exclusion, not an offset. Coverage is completely excluded for items covered in the homeowners policy, an endorsement to the homeowners policy, or a separate policy such as a personal articles floater. Suppose a diamond ring worth $10,000 is destroyed in a house fire and the ring has $5,000 of scheduled coverage under a scheduled personal property endorsement. Without the endorsement, the homeowners policy would provide

$10,000 coverage on the ring (assuming its value could be proven).[6] However, the endorsement provides only $5,000 of coverage, and the homeowners policy will not pick up the difference. This exclusion and others like it shift all responsibility for the loss to the policy that has generated a premium coverage on that valuable item, and it also encourages insurance to value on scheduled items.

Exclusions in some policies give back coverage to the extent other insurance is inadequate. These exclusions are properly categorized as excess provisions.

Disclaimers

Disclaimer escape clauses provide coverage only if no other insurance applies. Disclaimers usually involve fringe or supplemental coverages rather than the policy as a whole. For example, a state no-fault law might prohibit stacking of coverages and prescribe the order in which insurance applies. To illustrate, insurance "on the car" might be the first to pay for injuries to any occupant, but if there is no insurance "on the car," a guest passenger's own personal injury protection would apply.

Offsets

An offset escape clause applies when the available policy limit is reduced by the policy limit of other insurance that applies to the same loss. Two scenarios are possible:

1. If the other insurance's policy limit equals or exceeds the limit of Policy A, which has this provision, the insurer pays nothing under Policy A.
2. If Policy A's limit is higher than the other insurance's limit, the insurer with Policy A pays no more than the difference in limits.

For example, part of the uninsured motorists coverage other insurance provision of the ISO Personal Auto Policy functions as an offset:

> If there is other applicable insurance available under one or more policies or provisions of coverage that is similar to the insurance provided under this Part of the policy…any recovery for damages under all such policies or provisions of coverage may equal but not exceed the highest applicable limit for any one vehicle under any insurance providing coverage on either a primary or excess basis.[7]

RESOLVING CONFLICTS AMONG "OTHER INSURANCE" PROVISIONS

Sometimes insurers disagree about each insurer's obligations for payment when overlapping coverage exists, especially when neither policy's other insurance provision clearly addresses the situation. The most common approach is an agreement or a compromise between the two companies. In cases of severe disagreement, arbitration might be used. Other procedures that can be used to resolve such differences include application of the Guiding Principles and resolution in court.

Guiding Principles

The Guiding Principles were developed by industry-wide associations in the 1960s to resolve conflicts among multiple insurers covering the same loss. The Guiding Principles apply when other insurance clauses are contradictory or when other insurance clauses do not exist. They operate only when more than one policy covers a loss and none of the other policies' insurance clauses resolve how the respective coverages should apply.

The Guiding Principles indicate when policies are primary to or excess over one another, and they provide a method of proration for policies that are neither primary nor excess to one another. In establishing priority, the Guiding Principles make policies that cover more specifically described property at more specifically described locations primary over more general policies.

The Guiding Principles are complex, and adherence to them is voluntary. Arbitration can resolve disputes where the insurers disagree with the outcome resulting from applying the Guiding Principles.

Court Resolution

When large amounts of money are involved, insurers sometimes find it necessary to take the case to court. Predicting the outcome in such cases is difficult because the courts have inconsistently ruled on overlapping coverage issues.

SUMMARY

Other sources of recovery can affect the amounts payable under a given insurance policy. Multiple sources of recovery can involve other insurance in the same policy or a similar or dissimilar policy, noninsurance agreements, and third parties who might be legally obligated to pay damages for loss also covered by first-party insurance.

Other insurance provisions usually limit an insurer's obligation when other insurance applies. Other insurance provisions can state whether a policy provides primary coverage or is excess over other policies. A proportional other insurance provision applies when two or more policies are at the same level (e.g., both are primary), and it specifies how a loss will be shared by the policies, usually based either on proration of the policy limits or contribution by equal shares. Escape clauses operate to prohibit other insurance, exclude activities or property covered by other insurance, deny responsibility if any other insurance applies (disclaimer), or reduce coverage by the amount of other insurance (offset).

Other insurance provisions cannot possibly address every situation. Insurers resolve other conflicts by reaching a compromise agreement, by applying the Guiding Principles, by seeking arbitration, or, as a last resort, by taking the case to court.

Other-insurance situations result from external sources of recovery that are not part of the insurance contract itself. Various other external factors can also affect coverage under any given policy, as explained in Chapter 17.

CHAPTER NOTES

1. Form HO 00 03 10 00, Copyright, Insurance Services Office, Inc., 1999.
2. This statement is not true where a state no-fault law applies to property damage. The vast majority of no-fault laws apply only to bodily injury.
3. Form CP-12, Ed 1.0, Copyright, American Association of Insurance Services, 1994.
4. Form PP 00 01 06 98, Copyright, Insurance Services Office, Inc., 1997.
5. Form HO 00 03 10 00, Copyright, Insurance Services Office, Inc., 1999.
6. Homeowners coverage on jewelry is limited to $1,500 on loss by theft, but this is a fire loss.
7. Form PP 00 01 06 98, Copyright, Insurance Services Office, Inc., 1997.

Chapter 17

Direct Your Learning

External Factors Affecting Insurance Contracts

After learning the subject matter of this chapter, you should be able to:

■ Explain why external factors can affect insurance contract interpretation.

■ Identify and describe the twelve external factors affecting policy interpretation.

■ Given a claim scenario, identify possible external factors and how they might affect how the terms of the policy are applied.

Develop Your Perspective

What are the main topics covered in the chapter?

This chapter describes some of the external factors or major variables that can affect how an insurance contract is interpreted and analyzed.

Examine an insurance policy.

- Does it contain language that addresses unknowns such as undefined perils and unissued policies?

Why is it important to know these topics?

Knowing the external factors outside the contract language that affect the insurance contract's interpretation will help you determine whether coverage applies to a given situation and how that coverage might apply.

Consider the use of settlement options such as negotiation, structured settlements, and rehabilitation services.

- Why are these considered external factors to the insurance contract?
- How can they affect the coverage provided for the loss?

How can you use this information?

Consider the use of noninsurance contracts such as pre-loss waivers.

- Assuming the role of an insurance advisor, imagine a situation in which you might use a pre-loss waiver or another noninsurance contract to affect the terms of an insurance policy.

Chapter 17

External Factors Affecting Insurance Contracts

The previous chapters deal mainly with the information written in insurance policies. However, much that is *not* written in an insurance policy can affect policy interpretation. Each major topic in this chapter deals with an area outside of the written insurance contract that can affect the contract's interpretation or application to a situation. In this chapter, these areas are called "external factors."

External factors must be considered when analyzing an insurance policy to determine whether or how coverage applies.

This chapter explains why insurance contract analysis involves many factors outside the contract language and explains some major factors, which are outlined in the following box.

Twelve External Factors Affecting Insurance Contracts

1. Role of the courts
2. Procedures to resolve coverage disputes
3. Legal doctrines
4. External factors invoked by policy provisions
5. Coverage for the unknown
6. Unwritten rights to continue protection
7. Burden of proof
8. Overlapping sources of recovery
9. Noninsurance contracts
10. Unlisted settlement options
11. External factors affecting the amount payable
12. Damages or other penalties assessed against the insurer

ROLE OF THE COURTS

The United States legal system clearly affects the interpretation of insurance contracts. Generally, courts resolve questions about four types of insurance-related issues that are not necessarily resolved by insurance contract language:

1. Questions of liability
2. Questions of coverage
3. Questions of law
4. Questions of fact

Questions of Liability Versus Questions of Coverage

Questions of liability and questions of coverage can easily be confused. Courts often resolve the questions as follows:

- *Questions of liability.* For liability claims, the courts can apply the law to determine if the *insured* is legally obligated to pay damages to a third party.

- *Questions of coverage.* For both property and liability claims, the courts can apply the law to interpret the insurance contract and to determine whether the *insurer* is obligated to pay the claim to, or on behalf of, the insured and, if so, to what extent.

As illustrated in the following box, the *insurer's* liability to pay damages on the insured's behalf can depend on the *insured's* liability to pay damages to an injured third party.

Questions of Coverage Versus Questions of Liability

A commercial tenant operated a restaurant in a rented building. A fire originated in wiring inside the building's walls. The restaurant owner immediately filed a claim under her commercial general liability policy, which included liability coverage for "damage by fire to property rented to you." An insurance company representative declined to pay the claim, explaining that the tenant could not be held legally responsible for a fire caused by the building's wiring. The tenant became angry. Although the claim representative had said, "You are not liable," the tenant heard, "You are not covered."

Suppose the landlord—or the landlord's property insurer—sues the insured tenant to recover the cost of repairing fire damage to the building. The insurer would defend the insured tenant and attempt to prove the insured was not *liable*. If the court finds that the insured is liable for damages (perhaps the landlord would prove that the tenant had installed 30-ampere fuses in a 15-ampere circuit), then the insurer would pay the claim unless another basis existed for holding that the claim was not *covered*.

Declaratory Judgment (DJ) Action

A **declaratory judgment (DJ) action** resolves questions of *coverage* apart from questions of *liability*. In a DJ action, the insurer presents a coverage question to the court and asks the court to declare the rights of the parties under an insurance policy. A DJ action could involve questions about whether there has been an "occurrence," whether a given exclusion applies, or whether the insurer has an obligation to defend the insured against a specific set of allegations.

DJ actions are particularly useful when an insurer faces a substantial third-party claim involving a serious coverage question. If handled promptly, a declaratory judgment provides a decision on the *coverage* issue before the question of *liability* is litigated. If the court declares that coverage applies, the insurer can decide how best to fulfill its obligations. If the court declares the insurer has no duty under the policy, the insurer may close the claim. The defendant must then arrange its own defense. An example appears in the following box.

Declaratory judgment (DJ) action
The resolution by a court, at the insurer's request, of a coverage question.

Declaratory Judgment Action Regarding an Ambiguity

Excluded Watercraft in HO Policy Includes Jet Ski[1]

James McGinnis was killed when a jet ski operated by seventeen-year-old Jeremy Wittekind collided with a jet ski on which James was a passenger. Jeremy's parents, Roger and Jane Wittekind, had a homeowners policy issued by Nationwide; however, it excluded bodily injury arising out of a watercraft owned by or rented to an insured if the watercraft had inboard or inboard-outdrive motor power of more than 50 horsepower (HP). In this case, both jet skis had 60 HP power plants.

Nationwide filed this action for a declaratory judgment to determine its liability, if any, to the insureds arising out of James's death. The trial court granted Nationwide's motion for summary judgment based on the policy exclusion. The insureds appealed.

The insureds contended that the term "watercraft" was ambiguous and should be construed in their favor. The higher court pointed out that the accepted meaning of the word is a vessel used on water. It said that the term was not ambiguous simply because it included all boats, ships, and other vessels that travel on water. In this case, the policy excluded liability arising out of the insured's use of a "watercraft" and, therefore, excluded the use of a personal watercraft.

The appeals court affirmed the summary judgment entered in the trial court in favor of Nationwide.

Questions of Law Versus Questions of Fact

Court decisions apply the law to the facts. In cases with no jury, the trial judge determines the law, finds facts, and applies the law to the facts. In jury trials, the jury hears the evidence and decides the facts. The jury decides all questions of fact, and the judge decides all questions of law. Judges do not make factual determinations in jury trial cases, and juries do not answer legal questions.

A *question of law* in a negligence case, for example, might be whether a defendant owed a plaintiff any duty. A *question of fact* in the same case might be whether the plaintiff suffered any harm. In a property insurance case, a *question of law* might involve the issue of whether a valued policy law applies. A *question of fact* in the same case might involve the cash value of the damaged or destroyed property.

Public Policy Issues

Questions of law sometimes involve issues of public policy. Public policy considers the well-being of society as a whole and is reflected in common law, statutes, administrative regulations, and prevailing ideas relating to safety, health, morals, and the public's general welfare.

Courts have found coverage exceptions based on public policy considerations rather than on explicit policy provisions. For example, punitive damages claims are considered uninsurable in a number of states because allowing an insurer to absorb the punishment intended to penalize a wrongdoer is against public policy. Likewise, courts have supported insurers' rights to deny claims based on wear and tear or known losses.

Courts sometimes must reconcile a clash between these two important public policy issues:

1. An insured should not profit from the insured's wrongdoing.
2. Victims of wrongdoing should be compensated.[2]

Such issues arise in "innocent co-insured" cases (which have nothing to do with coinsurance) in which one insured, often an estranged spouse, intentionally destroys property jointly owned with the other spouse, who is also an insured. If an insurance policy exclusion for an insured's intentional damage is enforced, the "innocent spouse" becomes an uncompensated victim. If the exclusion is not enforced, the other spouse is permitted to profit from his or her wrongdoing.

Unenforceable Insurance Contracts

Before analyzing an insurance contract's coverage, one should know whether the contract is enforceable. The contract's enforceability depends on variables outside the policy. Regardless of what an insurance policy says, no court will enforce a contract that is void or voidable.

- A *void* contract never legally existed because an essential element was missing.
- A *voidable* contract legally exists, but one or both parties can legally reject or "void" it.

Mandatory or Prohibited Policy Provisions

Courts may choose to ignore a prohibited provision that appears in a written insurance contract, or they may construe the policy to comply with requirements.

Despite their best efforts, insurers can find it difficult to comply with a range of state statutes and regulations requiring certain provisions in insurance policies and prohibiting others. An insurer is usually permitted to provide more liberal coverage than that legally required. But a court may read mandatory language into a policy lacking such language. Even approved forms and mandatory policy language are not immune from claims that are ambiguous or that violate public policy.

PROCEDURES TO RESOLVE COVERAGE DISPUTES

Insurance policies generally say nothing about what an insurer should do for claims that might not be covered. The procedures insurers follow in these cases are external factors that affect the contract's application.

Insurance policies describe the insurer's duties in the event of a loss, but they do not explicitly state an insurer's four available options:

1. *The insurer may accept the claim or defend the insured against the suit.* For a property claim, the insurer agrees to pay the claim. For a liability claim, the insurer either pays the claim or agrees to defend the insured and, if necessary, to pay damages up to policy limits.

2. *The insurer may disclaim any obligation under the policy.* The insured or a third-party claimant might sue the insurer, and the insurer might ultimately be found to have breached its contractual duties. When an insurer denies coverage, it also loses some defenses; for example, the insurer cannot later use the defense that the insured did not file a proof of loss.

3. *The insurer may issue a reservation of rights letter or a nonwaiver agreement if a question about liability and/or coverage arises.* With either procedure, the insurer agrees to investigate the claim (and, for liability cases, to provide a defense) but reserves its rights to disclaim coverage later, depending on the investigation's results.

4. *The insurer may seek a declaratory judgment.* As previously explained, the insurer asks the court to declare the parties' rights.

The following section examines what can happen when the insurer chooses not to immediately treat the claim as an insured event.

Insurer Denies Coverage

When denying a claim, an insurer faces the possibility of a suit from either the insured or a third-party claimant.

Suit by an Insured

When an insurer denies a claim, the insured may sue the insurer to recoup both damages and costs. The insurer might also face allegations of bad faith, leading to ramifications that are discussed later in this chapter. A suit could also result in a judgment requiring the insurer to pay not only the original claim but also punitive damages.

Property and liability policies generally contain provisions describing the circumstances under which an insured can sue an insurer to enforce the policy. "Suit" provisions usually require that the insured first comply with other policy provisions. Property insurance policies usually also stipulate that the legal action must be initiated within a specified time (one year or several years) after the date of the loss. Liability policies do not carry time limitations but prohibit the filing of any suit against the insurer until the insured's obligation is determined by final judgment or settlement; this can involve a long delay.

Suit by Third-Party Claimant

A third-party claimant has no contractual relationship with the insurance company of the party who injured the claimant or damaged the claimant's property. Therefore, a third-party claimant usually has no basis on which to sue the insurer. However, a few jurisdictions have enacted **direct action statutes** that permit such actions.

Direct action statutes
Statutes that permit third-party claimants to sue an insurer directly.

Preserving the Insurer's Rights

Whether coverage applies to a claim is sometimes unclear. When an insurer even implies that a loss is covered, the insurer might be prohibited from disclaiming coverage later. Insurers use reservation of rights letters and nonwaiver agreements to preserve their ability to disclaim coverage if the facts reveal that there should be no coverage under the policy.

Reservation of Rights Letter

Reservation of rights letter
A letter signed and issued by an insurer to indicate that it is handling a claim with the understanding that it might later deny coverage when more information is available.

An insurer might mail a **reservation of rights letter** to the insured if a question arises about whether coverage applies to a given claim. An insurer issues a reservation of rights letter to specify that it is handling a claim with the understanding that it might later deny coverage when more information is available. A reservation of rights letter has two purposes:

1. *To protect the insurer's* right to deny coverage later, if warranted, without facing the accusation that its earlier actions waived that right

2. *To inform the insured* that a coverage problem might exist and give the insured an opportunity to protect the insured's interests

To prevent bad-faith actions, the insurer should send a reservation of rights letter to the insured immediately on identifying a potential problem. The letter should be specific and concise, clearly stating the insurer's position and quoting pertinent policy language. Many claim representatives send reservation of rights letters by certified mail return receipt requested, so that they have proof that the insured has received it. A sample letter appears in Exhibit 17-1.

EXHIBIT 17-1

Reservation of Rights Letter

Notice of Reservation of Rights

Date:

RE: Policyholder

Claimant

Date of Loss

Policy Number

We have received notice of an occurrence that took place at (location) on (date), for consideration under policy number _____ , which was issued to (policyholder) by (insurance company). In order that the company may continue to handle this matter, we want you to know that we are proceeding under a reservation of rights. We are reserving our rights under the policy for the following reason(s):

(Specify reasons, identifying actual policy provisions.)

Our continued handling of this matter does not constitute an admission of any kind on our part. No act of any company representative while investigating, negotiating settlement of the claim, or defending a lawsuit shall be construed as waiving any company rights. The company reserves the right, under the policy, to deny coverage to you or anyone claiming coverage under the policy.

You may wish to discuss this matter with your own attorney. In any event, we would be pleased to answer any questions you have concerning our position as outlined in this letter.

Very truly yours,   By

INSURANCE COMPANY   FOR THE COMPANY

A reservation of rights letter implies a conflict between the insured's interests and the insurer's interests. Although the insurer must defend the insured as long as it is handling the case, the insurer might at any time deny coverage and cease handling the case. The insured who receives a reservation of rights letter often hires its own legal counsel to protect its interest.

Nonwaiver Agreement

Like a reservation of rights letter, a **nonwaiver agreement** signifies that the insurer does not waive its rights to later deny coverage. A reservation of rights *letter*, like other letters, is a one-way communication from the sender to the recipient, signed by the sender. Like other agreements, a nonwaiver *agreement*

Nonwaiver agreement
An agreement indicating that the insurer does not waive its rights to later deny coverage; becomes effective when signed by both parties to the agreement.

signifies a two-way understanding, and it becomes effective when it is signed by both parties. A sample nonwaiver agreement appears in Exhibit 17-2.

EXHIBIT 17-2

Nonwaiver Agreement

It is agreed between (insurance company) and (policyholder) involving policy number _____that a claim has been filed with the company for consideration under the policy with respect to claims arising out of an accident and/or occurrence on or about (date) at or near (location). It is further agreed that there may be no coverage for part or all of the damages claimed from this occurrence because:

(Specify reasons, identifying actual policy provisions.)

It is further agreed that the policyholder desires the company to complete an investigation of the facts and damages arising out of this claim and/or defense of these claims as seems expedient to the company. It is the intention of this agreement to provide for that investigation of the accident or occurrence and to determine the damages resulting therefrom without in any way affecting, impairing, or adding to the liability of the company under the policy or under any statute or the common law, and no action taken by the company hereunder shall be construed as an admission of liability or coverage. Such action shall not waive any right the company may have to deny any obligation under this policy and shall not waive any of the rights of the policyholder.

Signed this (date) day of (month), Year (20xx).

INSURANCE COMPANY   POLICYHOLDER

The strength of a reservation of rights letter or a nonwaiver agreement depends on the circumstances. For example, evidence that an insured received a reservation of rights letter and understood it might outweigh any argument against its validity. On the other hand, the insured can refuse to sign a nonwaiver agreement, in which case the insurer might deny a defense and ask a court to resolve the coverage question through a declaratory judgment action, or the insurer might simply send a reservation of rights letter.

LEGAL DOCTRINES

Many legal doctrines and principles, external to the insurance contract, can affect the contract's interpretation. See the following box.

Legal Doctrines That Affect Insurance Contract Interpretation

1. Contract of adhesion
2. Reasonable expectations

3. Unconscionable advantage

4. Substantial performance

5. Waiver and estoppel

6. Fortuity

Contract of Adhesion Doctrine

Insurance policies are contracts of adhesion. Ambiguities in a contract of adhesion are interpreted in favor of the party that did not draft the contract, usually the insured.

Standard insurance policies are sometimes constructed to take advantage of the doctrine of adhesion. If an insurance contract can be interpreted in two different ways and the insurer is satisfied with either interpretation, no expansion of the contract is necessary to make it more precise. The following box illustrates:

Acceptable Ambiguity

Insurance policies are often ambiguous when there is no need to become more precise and the interpretation most generous to the insured is acceptable to the insurer.

For example, the ISO Building and Personal Property Coverage Form's definition of "Building" in the "Building" insuring agreement includes some items of personal property:

Personal property owned by you that is used to maintain or service the building or structure or its premises, including:

(a) Fire extinguishing equipment;

(b) Outdoor furniture;

(c) Floor coverings; and

(d) Appliances used for refrigerating, ventilating, cooking, dishwashing or laundering....[3]

Some building owners rent a building to others and do not purchase insurance on its contents. Yet most landlords own some personal property in connection with their buildings. Apartment building owners often own appliances that are rented to tenants along with the apartments.

The policy is written this way so that a landlord automatically has coverage for such personal property items, even if the landlord has not recognized that personal property loss exposure. The same standard policy form is used by parties that occupy their own buildings. If the owner-occupant of a building purchases both "building" coverage and coverage on "your business personal property," both coverages would apply to these items.

Continued on next page.

> The writers of this policy could have added a provision to clarify how this situation would be handled, but the ambiguity is acceptable. It usually does not matter whether a loss to these personal property items is paid as a building loss or as a personal property loss. But sometimes it does matter. For example, suppose outdoor furniture was stolen and the building coverage was written on a special-form basis including theft, while the personal property coverage applied to broad named perils (without theft). Any insured who understood the policy would claim the theft as a "Building" loss, and the insurer would pay it. In this case, the insurer is ethically obligated to pay the claim under the building coverage, where coverage applies, even if the claim is submitted as a personal property loss that would not be covered. The policy is ambiguous as to whether this is a covered building loss or a not-covered personal property loss, and the ambiguity would be resolved in favor of the insured.

Whether a contract is ambiguous is a question of fact. In many states, whether ambiguities in a case are interpreted against the insurer depends on (1) who drafted the policy provision and (2) the insured's level of sophistication in insurance matters.

- *Unsophisticated insured.* Usually, a sophisticated seller (the insurance company) has drafted a ready-made contract that is sold to an unsophisticated buyer (the insured) who has little or no control over the contract's wording. Ambiguities in this case are interpreted against the insurer.

- *Sophisticated insured.* In a minority of cases, the insurance buyer and its representative draft all or part of the insurance contract, or the insurance company and a sophisticated insurance buyer negotiate the contract wording. In these cases, the contract of adhesion doctrine might not apply.

The courts often consider factors like these when determining whether an insured falls within the "sophisticated insured" rule:

1. Size of the insured organization
2. Insured's employment of a professional risk manager
3. Involvement of counsel on insured's behalf
4. Insured's retention of a sophisticated insurance broker
5. Use of a manuscript policy
6. Relative bargaining power of the parties.[4]

Reasonable expectations doctrine
A doctrine that interprets an insurance policy as providing the protection that the insured might reasonably have expected, even though that expectation is not clearly expressed in or supported by the policy.

Reasonable Expectations Doctrine

The **reasonable expectations doctrine** is triggered, not by policies' ambiguity, but by the insured's surprise at how the policy provisions are said to apply. Not all courts recognize the doctrine of reasonable expectations, but when courts do apply it, they interpret the policy to provide the protection that the insured might reasonably have expected, even though that expectation is not clearly expressed in or supported by the policy's wording.

The reasonable expectations doctrine is sometimes applied to renewal policies that contain a change. Unless an oral or a written explanation accompanies the renewal policy, the insured can "reasonably expect" that the renewal policy is the same as the expired contract.

Unconscionable Advantage Principle

The **unconscionable advantage principle** has been described in these words:

> An insurer will not be permitted an unconscionable advantage in an insurance transaction even though the policyholder or other person whose interests are affected has manifested fully informed consent.[5]

Unconscionability has not been clearly defined. But generally, the courts have sided with the insured in cases in which the insured is trying to preserve the contract but finds some provision objectionable, difficult, or almost impossible to fulfill. Whether the courts explicitly recognize unconscionable advantage, it often is the only rationale for a decision.

In one case, an insured suffered a property loss and filed a written claim under a property insurance policy that required a proof of loss. The insured's written claim included much more detail than that required by the proof of loss, and the insurer never requested a completed proof of loss form. After paying the mortgagee its interests under the policy, without any proof of loss form, the insurer denied the insured's claim for failure to file the proof of loss form. A court prevented the insurer from taking unconscionable advantage of this insured.

Unconscionable advantage principle
A principle that prevents an insurer from taking unfair advantage of an insured.

Substantial Performance Doctrine

The **substantial performance doctrine** recognizes that, even though insurance policy conditions must be met, something short of literal performance may sometimes be acceptable. In the preceding example illustrating unconscionable advantage, the insured did not literally complete a proof of loss form but provided the same information in a different format. The insured *substantially performed* its duties and could *reasonably expect* that it had met the insurer's requirements; failure to recognize this substantial performance would be taking *unconscionable advantage* of the insured.

The substantial performance doctrine applies to insureds who have attempted honestly and faithfully to perform their contractual duties. Whether a given insured meets this standard is a question of fact. The insured must be able to demonstrate no willful omission or departure from the contract.

In the past, strict compliance with all insurance contract provisions was required. Today, the doctrine of substantial performance has become the minimum standard required of the insured. As long as the insured has acted

Substantial performance doctrine
A doctrine that allows the insured, under some circumstances, to meet policy conditions through something short of literal performance.

honestly and in good faith, substantial compliance with policy provisions usually is adequate. The insurer will not be allowed to deny liability on grounds that the insured failed to abide by a narrow interpretation of policy requirements.

Waiver and Estoppel

Waiver and estoppel are closely related legal doctrines under which an insurer might provide benefits not specified in the insurance contract:

Waiver
The intentional or voluntary relinquishment of a known right.

Estoppel
A legal principle that prevents a party from enforcing a present claimed position because it is inconsistent with that party's past conduct.

- **Waiver** is the intentional or voluntary relinquishment of a known right. For example, an insurer accepts Tanya's renewal premium twenty days after the date when coverage would normally terminate. By accepting the renewal premium, the insurer waives (voluntarily relinquishes) its right to terminate Tanya's policy for nonpayment of the renewal premium.

- **Estoppel** exists when a party's present claimed position cannot be enforced because it is inconsistent with that party's past conduct. For example, suppose the insurer accepted Tanya's renewal premium twenty days late several times in the past but now refuses to pay a claim for a loss occurring ten days after the due date of this year's renewal premium, on the basis that coverage had terminated. Tanya insists that she intended to maintain continuous coverage this year by paying the renewal premium within the twenty-day period, as she was allowed to do last year.

Because it *waived* its rights to terminate the policy when it accepted the late premium last year (past conduct), the insurer may be *estopped* from enforcing the termination (its present claimed position) during a subsequent year. Waiver and estoppel can apply to many other insurance situations beyond policy renewal.

Fortuity

Fortuity means that an event occurs by accident and is unexpected and unintended from the insured's standpoint. A fundamental principle of insurance law holds that insurance contracts do not provide coverage when a loss is not fortuitous. Insurance contracts carry an implied exception for losses that are not fortuitous. Usually, fortuity is considered from the insured's standpoint.

Even without a specific exclusion, the concept of fortuity would preclude property coverage against loss resulting from ordinary wear and tear, inherent vice, or defect. Even if wear and tear itself is not fortuitous, loss or damage ensuing from wear and tear may still be covered. For example, an electrical fire caused by a worn extension cord would not be excluded on the basis that the cord suffered ordinary wear.

Known-loss or loss-in-progress situations are closely related to the issue of fortuity. Traditionally, insurers did not need to cite an explicit policy exclusion to successfully deny coverage where the policyholder had purchased insurance knowing of an ongoing situation likely to result in a loss. However, many recent policies now explicitly exclude coverage for known losses.

EXTERNAL FACTORS INVOKED BY POLICY PROVISIONS

Sometimes, insurance policies refer to external documents that must be consulted to fully interpret and apply the policy's coverage. Some relevant rights are not defined in the policy itself but instead are invoked by the policy. For example, liberalization provisions, conformity with statute provisions, and workers compensation benefits illustrate this concept. Other insurance policy provisions also invoke external factors, such as insurer's rules and rating manuals.

Liberalization

Many policies contain liberalization clauses that incorporate non-policy documents into policies. The liberalization clause automatically amends an existing policy, as of the date an insurer implements a change without introducing a new policy edition, to incorporate broadened features. Consequently, sometimes the insured is entitled to coverage that does not appear anywhere in the insured's contract.

Liberalization clauses vary in their effect. Some apply to all revisions that would broaden coverage. Others apply only to changes in the same edition of the policy.

Liberalization Applies to Policy Condition[6]

In Mazur v. Truck Insurance Exchange, Mazur's apartment building sustained earthquake damage on January 17, 1994, but his property insurance claim was not submitted until July, 1995, because he initially thought the earthquake damage was minor.

The insurer initially denied Mazur's claim because his insurance policy at the time of loss required that claims be reported within one year. However, the policy also included a liberalization clause, providing, "If the form of policy being issued by the Company shall later be revised to extend or improve coverage afforded the insured under this original policy, such extension shall inure to the benefit of the insured hereunder."

On January 1, 1994, the insurer had begun to cycle in new policy forms in California. The new forms included a two-year contractual limitation of action provision. The court concluded, "the clause is not ambiguous because objectively reasonable expectations of the insured require that the clause be interpreted to afford Mazur the benefit of the expanded two-year suit limitation provision as of January 1, 1994, when Truck began to make that provision available."

Insurance company representatives are ethically obligated to provide policyholders with all the benefits to which they are legally entitled. The liberalization clause provides contractual rights to which insurance buyers are entitled, even though the rights are based on documents external to the contract.

Conformity With Statute

Conformity with statute provisions require that coverage specified by statute be provided even if not the coverage provided by the policy. Some insurance policies incorporate a specific *conformity with statute* provision like this one in an AAIS Homeowners Policy:

> **Conformity With Statute** — "Terms" in conflict with the laws of the state in which the premises shown on the "declarations" as the described location is located are changed to conform to such laws.[7]

The conformity with statute provision enables insurers to use a countrywide form despite conflicting state statutes. Even without a conformity provision, state statutes still control insurance policies, and insurance policyholders are entitled to benefits applicable under current statutes. The conformity with statute provision also prevents the entire policy from being voided because certain clauses do not comply with applicable state law.

Workers Compensation

Workers compensation benefits are prescribed by state law, not by policy provisions. For example, the workers compensation insuring agreement of the NCCI Workers Compensation and Employers Liability Policy simply states:

> We will pay promptly when due the benefits required of you by the workers compensation law.[8]

The policy's workers compensation coverage and limits cannot be determined by the policy itself. Applicable state laws must be examined to determine how to interpret the policy.

COVERAGE FOR THE UNKNOWN

Insurance policies often cover exposures that could not readily be anticipated and are not specifically described in the policy. Because they are not specifically described, these unknowns are considered external factors.

Many insurance policies provide coverage to unnamed insureds, on nonowned property, for unidentified exposures, or for undefined perils. Obviously, none of these unknowns are specifically identified in the policy, and coverage is not as obvious as the coverage for named insureds, scheduled property, scheduled activities (in a liability policy), or named perils.

Another type of unknown involves delayed policy issuance. Before a policy issuance, some assumptions must be made about the coverage that is being provided. Additionally, insurance can cover emerging risks not known or anticipated when the policy was drafted.

Unnamed Insureds

Generally, only a party named in a contract can enforce it. However, some unnamed parties have rights because they are included by reference in property and liability insurance policies. Unnamed insureds include, for example, those who fall into a generic class description such as "spouse" or "employee" or those who serve as a legal substitute for a named insured.

Nonowned Property

Coverage for owned property scheduled or described in a property insurance policy is usually clear. Nonowned property can also be the subject of a covered property loss. Some nonowned property is covered because of a relationship between the named insured and the property owner. Other situations are based on a contractual obligation. Examples of nonowned property include the following:

- *Property in the possession of a bailee.* Dry cleaners, laundries, warehouses, and repair shops have within their care, custody, or control the property of customers for which they might or might not be legally liable.
- *Leased property.* Autos, computers, photocopy machines, and other equipment are leased under written contracts that prescribe responsibilities of both lessor and lessee.
- *Property on consignment.* Property belonging to others may be on the premises of a distributor or retailer awaiting sale, generally subject to a written contract between the parties specifying who is to be responsible for loss or damage to the property.
- *Employees' property.* Tools, clothing, and other items owned by employees might be situated on their employers' premises. Some union contracts make the employer responsible for the loss of tools.

Often, a property owner has protection without being named in an insurance policy. For example:

- Homeowners forms commonly cover loss to personal property of others in the care, custody, or control of the insured.
- Homeowners forms generally also cover, at the named insured's option, personal property on the insured's premises owned by a guest or domestic employee.
- Some inland marine floaters for dry cleaners and other bailees cover damage to customers' goods even if the bailee is not legally liable for the loss.
- ISO's Building and Personal Property Coverage Form, under "your business personal property," covers leased property that the named insured has a contractual obligation to insure. An additional coverage, for a limited amount, applies to personal effects and personal property of others. Coverage for personal property of others in the named insured's care, custody, or control also may be included under a separate insuring arrangement.

Unidentified Exposures

Automatic coverage for new exposures not necessarily known to the insurer is often specified in policy provisions. In other cases, automatic coverage is a matter of custom or practice developed, in part, to minimize paperwork.

Insurance contracts commonly cover new exposures that develop during the policy period, even if the insurer is not immediately notified. Some policies provide automatic coverage until the end of the policy period, while others provide automatic coverage if an exposure is reported within a specified time period. For example:

- The ISO Personal Auto Policy defines "newly acquired auto" and describes the automatic coverage that applies.
- Commercial property insurance policies commonly offer automatic coverage on both newly constructed and newly acquired buildings and structures. Coverage is generally subject to limitations on the amount of coverage and the period during which the insurer must be informed of the exposure.
- Subject to other policy terms, commercial general liability policies automatically cover all operations and activities initiated after the policy is developed, even if they are not of a type listed in the policy declarations. The insurer will make an appropriate charge at the end of the policy term when the policy is audited. Although new operations and activities of the named insured are automatically covered, automatic liability coverage does not necessarily apply to new organizations or to those resulting from mergers, acquisitions, or newly formed partnerships or joint ventures.

Undefined Perils

Some covered property insurance perils, such as sinkhole collapse, are defined in detail while some of the most common and serious perils, such as fire and lightning, are merely named. Even though insurance policies appear to cover "fire" without qualification, some named-peril fire losses are not covered. Courts have upheld the general understanding that "fire" coverage does not apply to loss of covered property by a so-called friendly fire—a fire that remains within its intended place. A hostile fire, one that is accidental or leaves its intended place, generally is considered a covered peril. If sparks from a fireplace land on a carpet and set a house on fire, a hostile fire has occurred, and the damage is covered.

Nothing within a typical property insurance policy makes the distinction between friendly and hostile fires. However, the difference is widely understood and applied, and it rarely becomes an issue.

Fire is not the only peril that is not defined in a typical property insurance policy. The ISO Homeowners Policy, for example, provides no definition of five perils:

1. Fire or lightning
2. Explosion
3. Riot or civil commotion
4. Vehicles
5. Vandalism or malicious mischief

Unissued Policies

Sometimes, a written insurance policy does not exist, and coverage questions must be based on other evidence. Claims often occur when no written insurance contract exists. Because of processing delays, insurance coverage often goes into effect before a complete, written insurance policy is formally issued, and the only written contract the insured receives might be a one-page binder that serves as a policy summary.

Binders

A *binder* is a temporary contract indicating the type of coverage provided. An oral binder is an enforceable insurance contract. However, the exact terms of an oral binder can easily be disputed. Insurers routinely issue written binders to assure the insured that the specified coverage is in effect despite the lack of a complete, written contract. Binders, like the one in Exhibit 17-3, are usually one page. Although they might contain form names or numbers, binders do not contain all the provisions that ultimately appear in the complete, written contract.

When a loss occurs before the actual policy is issued, the insurer and the insured might dispute the actual coverage they agreed to. No single rule applies to all disputes, and each must be considered on its own merits. State law sometimes has a bearing. The terms of a standard policy form usually prescribe the extent of coverage even when the policy has not yet been delivered.

Certificates of Insurance

A **certificate of insurance** is a document issued by an insurer or an authorized representative of the insurer as evidence that a policy has been issued providing coverage in a certain amount. Certificates of insurance are used in many situations. Mortgagees require evidence that property subject to a mortgage is properly insured and that the mortgagee's interests are protected. Businesses that engage a contractor require the contractor to demonstrate that it has liability insurance. A sample certificate of liability insurance is shown in Exhibit 17-4.

Like binders, certificates of insurance summarize coverage. If the certificate and the policy differ, courts usually enforce the policy.

Certificate of insurance
A document issued by an insurer or an authorized representative of the insurer as evidence that a policy has been issued providing coverage in a certain amount.

EXHIBIT 17-3

Acord Insurance Binder

ACORD™ INSURANCE BINDER		DATE

THIS BINDER IS A TEMPORARY INSURANCE CONTRACT, SUBJECT TO THE CONDITIONS SHOWN ON THE REVERSE SIDE OF THIS FORM.

PRODUCER | PHONE (A/C, No, Ext):

COMPANY | BINDER #

	EFFECTIVE				EXPIRATION	
	DATE	TIME		AM	DATE	TIME
				PM		12:01 AM
						NOON

THIS BINDER IS ISSUED TO EXTEND COVERAGE IN THE ABOVE NAMED COMPANY PER EXPIRING POLICY #:

CODE: | SUB CODE:

AGENCY CUSTOMER ID:

DESCRIPTION OF OPERATIONS/VEHICLES/PROPERTY (Including Location)

INSURED

COVERAGES
LIMITS

TYPE OF INSURANCE	COVERAGE/FORMS	DEDUCTIBLE	COINS %	AMOUNT
PROPERTY CAUSES OF LOSS				
[ ] BASIC [ ] BROAD [ ] SPEC				
GENERAL LIABILITY		EACH OCCURRENCE		$
[ ] COMMERCIAL GENERAL LIABILITY		FIRE DAMAGE (Any one fire)		$
[ ] CLAIMS MADE [ ] OCCUR		MED EXP (Any one person)		$
		PERSONAL & ADV INJURY		$
		GENERAL AGGREGATE		$
	RETRO DATE FOR CLAIMS MADE:	PRODUCTS - COMP/OP AGG		$
AUTOMOBILE LIABILITY		COMBINED SINGLE LIMIT		$
[ ] ANY AUTO		BODILY INJURY (Per person)		$
[ ] ALL OWNED AUTOS		BODILY INJURY (Per accident)		$
[ ] SCHEDULED AUTOS		PROPERTY DAMAGE		$
[ ] HIRED AUTOS		MEDICAL PAYMENTS		$
[ ] NON-OWNED AUTOS		PERSONAL INJURY PROT		$
		UNINSURED MOTORIST		$
				$
AUTO PHYSICAL DAMAGE DEDUCTIBLE	[ ] ALL VEHICLES [ ] SCHEDULED VEHICLES	ACTUAL CASH VALUE		
COLLISION:		STATED AMOUNT		$
OTHER THAN COL:		OTHER		
GARAGE LIABILITY		AUTO ONLY - EA ACCIDENT		$
[ ] ANY AUTO		OTHER THAN AUTO ONLY:		
		EACH ACCIDENT		$
		AGGREGATE		$
EXCESS LIABILITY		EACH OCCURRENCE		$
[ ] UMBRELLA FORM		AGGREGATE		$
[ ] OTHER THAN UMBRELLA FORM	RETRO DATE FOR CLAIMS MADE:	SELF-INSURED RETENTION		$
WORKER'S COMPENSATION AND EMPLOYER'S LIABILITY		[ ] WC STATUTORY LIMITS		
		E.L. EACH ACCIDENT		$
		E.L. DISEASE - EA EMPLOYEE		$
		E.L. DISEASE - POLICY LIMIT		$
SPECIAL CONDITIONS/ OTHER COVERAGES		FEES		$
		TAXES		$
		ESTIMATED TOTAL PREMIUM		$

NAME & ADDRESS

	[ ] MORTGAGEE	[ ] ADDITIONAL INSURED
	[ ] LOSS PAYEE	
	LOAN #	
	AUTHORIZED REPRESENTATIVE	

ACORD 75-S (1/98)   **NOTE: IMPORTANT STATE INFORMATION ON REVERSE SIDE**   c ACORD CORPORATION 1993

CONDITIONS

This Company binds the kind(s) of insurance stipulated on the reverse side. The Insurance is subject to the terms, conditions and limitations of the policy(ies) in current use by the Company.

This binder may be cancelled by the Insured by surrender of this binder or by written notice to the Company stating when cancellation will be effective. This binder may be cancelled by the Company by notice to the Insured in accordance with the policy conditions. This binder is cancelled when replaced by a policy. If this binder is not replaced by a policy, the Company is entitled to charge a premium for the binder according to the Rules and Rates in use by the Company.

Applicable in California

When this form is used to provide insurance in the amount of one million dollars ($1,000,000) or more, the title of the form is changed from "Insurance Binder" to "Cover Note".

Applicable in Delaware

The mortgagee or Obligee of any mortgage or other instrument given for the purpose of creating a lien on real property shall accept as evidence of insurance a written binder issued by an authorized insurer or its agent if the binder includes or is accompanied by: the name and address of the borrower; the name and address of the lender as loss payee; a description of the insured real property; a provision that the binder may not be canceled within the term of the binder unless the lender and the insured borrower receive written notice of the cancellation at least ten (10) days prior to the cancellation; except in the case of a renewal of a policy subsequent to the closing of the loan, a paid receipt of the full amount of the applicable premium, and the amount of insurance coverage.

Chapter 21 Title Paragraph 2119

Applicable in Florida

Except for Auto Insurance coverage, no notice of cancellation or nonrenewal of a binder is required unless the duration of the binder exceeds 60 days. For auto insurance, the insurer must give 5 days prior notice, unless the binder is replaced by a policy or another binder in the same company.

Applicable in Nevada

Any person who refuses to accept a binder which provides coverage of less than $1,000,000.00 when proof is required: (A) Shall be fined not more than $500.00, and (B) is liable to the party presenting the binder as proof of insurance for actual damages sustained therefrom.

EXHIBIT 17-4

Acord Insurance Binder

ACORD™ **CERTIFICATE OF LIABILITY INSURANCE**		DATE (MM/DD/YY)

PRODUCER	THIS CERTIFICATE IS ISSUED AS A MATTER OF INFORMATION ONLY AND CONFERS NO RIGHTS UPON THE CERTIFICATE HOLDER. THIS CERTIFICATE DOES NOT AMEND, EXTEND OR ALTER THE COVERAGE AFFORDED BY THE POLICIES BELOW.
	INSURERS AFFORDING COVERAGE
INSURED	INSURER A:
	INSURER B:
	INSURER C:
	INSURER D:
	INSURER E:

COVERAGES

THE POLICIES OF INSURANCE LISTED BELOW HAVE BEEN ISSUED TO THE INSURED NAMED ABOVE FOR THE POLICY PERIOD INDICATED. NOTWITHSTANDING ANY REQUIREMENT, TERM OR CONDITION OF ANY CONTRACT OR OTHER DOCUMENT WITH RESPECT TO WHICH THIS CERTIFICATE MAY BE ISSUED OR MAY PERTAIN, THE INSURANCE AFFORDED BY THE POLICIES DESCRIBED HEREIN IS SUBJECT TO ALL THE TERMS, EXCLUSIONS AND CONDITIONS OF SUCH POLICIES. AGGREGATE LIMITS SHOWN MAY HAVE BEEN REDUCED BY PAID CLAIMS.

INSR LTR	TYPE OF INSURANCE	POLICY NUMBER	POLICY EFFECTIVE DATE (MM/DD/YY)	POLICY EXPIRATION DATE (MM/DD/YY)	LIMITS	
	GENERAL LIABILITY				EACH OCCURRENCE	$
	COMMERCIAL GENERAL LIABILITY				FIRE DAMAGE (Any one fire)	$
	☐ CLAIMS MADE ☐ OCCUR				MED EXP (Any one person)	$
	_____				PERSONAL & ADV INJURY	$
	_____				GENERAL AGGREGATE	$
	GEN'L AGGREGATE LIMIT APPLIES PER:				PRODUCTS - COMP/OP AGG	$
	☐ POLICY ☐ PRO-JECT ☐ LOC					
	AUTOMOBILE LIABILITY				COMBINED SINGLE LIMIT (Ea accident)	$
	☐ ANY AUTO					
	☐ ALL OWNED AUTOS				BODILY INJURY (Per person)	$
	☐ SCHEDULED AUTOS					
	☐ HIRED AUTOS				BODILY INJURY (Per accident)	$
	☐ NON-OWNED AUTOS					
	_____				PROPERTY DAMAGE (Per accident)	$
	GARAGE LIABILITY				AUTO ONLY - EA ACCIDENT	$
	☐ ANY AUTO				OTHER THAN EA ACC	$
					AUTO ONLY: AGG	$
	EXCESS LIABILITY				EACH OCCURRENCE	$
	☐ OCCUR ☐ CLAIMS MADE				AGGREGATE	$
						$
	☐ DEDUCTIBLE					$
	☐ RETENTION $					$
	WORKERS COMPENSATION AND EMPLOYERS' LIABILITY				WC STATU-TORY LIMITS	OTH-ER
					E.L. EACH ACCIDENT	$
					E.L. DISEASE - EA EMPLOYEE	$
					E.L. DISEASE - POLICY LIMIT	$
	OTHER					

DESCRIPTION OF OPERATIONS/LOCATIONS/VEHICLES/EXCLUSIONS ADDED BY ENDORSEMENT/SPECIAL PROVISIONS

CERTIFICATE HOLDER	ADDITIONAL INSURED; INSURER LETTER: ___	**CANCELLATION**
		SHOULD ANY OF THE ABOVE DESCRIBED POLICIES BE CANCELLED BEFORE THE EXPIRATION DATE THEREOF, THE ISSUING INSURER WILL ENDEAVOR TO MAIL _____ DAYS WRITTEN NOTICE TO THE CERTIFICATE HOLDER NAMED TO THE LEFT, BUT FAILURE TO DO SO SHALL IMPOSE NO OBLIGATION OR LIABILITY OF ANY KIND UPON THE INSURER, ITS AGENTS OR REPRESENTATIVES.
		AUTHORIZED REPRESENTATIVE

ACORD 25-S (7/97)   © ACORD CORPORATION 1988

IMPORTANT

If the certificate holder is an ADDITIONAL INSURED, the policy(ies) must be endorsed. A statement on this certificate does not confer rights to the certificate holder in lieu of such endorsement(s).

DISCLAIMER

The Certificate of Insurance on the reverse side of this form does not constitute a contract between the issuing insurer(s), authorized representative or producer, and the certificate holder, nor does it affirmatively or negatively amend, extend or alter the coverage afforded by the policies listed thereon.

©ACORD. Used with permission.

Unknown Risks

Changes in science; technology; and the physical, political, legal, and social environment produce risks that are not contemplated when insurance policies are drafted.

Applying old insurance policy language to new exposures is challenging.

- For example, during the early 2000s, the rapid changes in electronic communication and use of the Internet produced risks, such as the computer virus threat, that needed to be specifically addressed.

A recent survey of 1,500 U.S. and European risk managers in large corporations, as well as U.S. agents and brokers, showed that businesses do not adequately understand the risks posed by technology, have difficulty identifying potential risks, and lack the tools to manage the risks effectively. The survey found that, although businesses do not fully understand the implications of new technologies, respondents do consider computer, Internet, and e-commerce risks among the most important risks companies will be facing.[9]

UNWRITTEN RIGHTS TO CONTINUE PROTECTION

An insurance policy's protection often does not end when the written contract says it does. Sometimes, continued protection is mandated by external factors such as a state statute. In others, coverage is extended because of external factors such as insurance company procedures.

Statutory Protection

During the 1960s, insurers embarked on a wave of policy cancellations because of poor underwriting results. In response, most states introduced legislation to limit insurers' cancellation and nonrenewal rights. Although these statutes originally applied only to auto liability insurance, most states now also apply cancellation—and sometimes nonrenewal—restrictions to property and liability insurance covering both individuals and businesses.

Insurance policies, like other contracts, invariably contain cancellation provisions that state how, when, and under what conditions both the insurer and the insured can end the contract. Often, a standard insurance form is modified by a state-specific endorsement that includes cancellation terms required by the state laws. Even if the policy does not match the law, applicable law always takes precedence over policy provisions. If an insurer fails to follow at least the statutory provisions or provides late notice of an intent not to renew, the insurer will likely be required to continue insurance for the full policy term or for another term.

An insurer might, for example, agree in the policy to provide a longer advance nonrenewal notice than the minimum required by statute. If policy provisions are more liberal than what the statute requires, then the policy provision favoring the insured would prevail.

Cancellation Practices

Because of insurance company cancellation practices, insureds sometimes can obtain coverage that otherwise might not apply. For example, if a premium installment is not paid when due, one might assume that coverage has terminated. However, laws or policy provisions often require the insurer to give the insured a certain number of days of advance notice before cancellation takes effect. Until this time period has elapsed, the insurer is obligated to fulfill its promises just as though no notice of cancellation had been issued.

Billing and payment cycles, as well as bills and checks crossing in the mail, regularly create murky situations. Complications develop when the insurer establishes a pattern by sending a notice of cancellation, followed by reinstatement when a late payment is received. Having repeatedly waived its rights to cancel for nonpayment, the insurer might be estopped from denying coverage for a claim following nonpayment of a renewal premium.

Even when coverage terminates due to nonpayment of a renewal premium, insurers routinely reinstate coverage back to the renewal date after receiving payment, once they are assured that no claims have occurred. This expedient custom is convenient for all parties and produces a paper trail showing continuous coverage without a gap. However, it raises some interesting ethical questions whenever an insurer certifies that continuous coverage has been in effect even though it might have denied coverage between the premium-due date and the premium-received date.

Burden of proof
A legal principle that requires a party to establish by evidence the facts necessary to prove that party's case.

BURDEN OF PROOF

Burden of proof is a legal principle that requires a party to establish by evidence the facts necessary to prove that party's case. The party with the burden of proof can lose a case because it cannot produce enough evidence to prove its position.

Who has the burden of proof in an insurance claim? Is a claim covered unless the insurer can prove coverage does not apply? Or is the burden on the insured to prove that a claim qualifies for coverage? Few, if any, insurance policies specifically address this question.

Generally, the burden of proof is on the *insured* to show that coverage applies. For example, if a third party makes a claim against the insured because of bodily injury or property damage resulting from the insured's products, the insured must show that it had purchased enforceable products liability insurance and that the alleged injuries meet the policy definition of bodily injury or property damage. The burden of proof then shifts to the insurer, which, to preclude coverage, must demonstrate that one or more exclusions apply.

With property insurance, the issue is often not whether covered property has been damaged but whether it was damaged by a covered peril. Although neither type of policy specifically says so, named-perils policies place the burden of proof on the insured, but all-risks (special-form, open-perils) policies place it on the insurer. From the insured's standpoint, "all-risks" special-form property policies have two important advantages. First, they cover more causes of loss than named-peril forms cover. Perhaps more important is the fact that they implicitly shift the burden of proof to the insurer, and the party with the burden of proof is more likely to lose any dispute.

OVERLAPPING SOURCES OF RECOVERY

An insurance company is not necessarily aware of all the other insurance or noninsurance sources of recovery that might be available to its policyholder. Many cannot possibly be identified until after a loss. Yet an insurer's obligation under its insurance contract may be affected by legal rules such as the collateral source rule, other insurance policies, and other noninsurance sources of recovery—all of which are "external factors," outside the insurance contract.

Each insurance policy attempts to explain how the insurer will address a loss for which other sources of recovery are also available. However, a provision in one insurer's policy cannot directly clarify the responsibility of another insurer that issued another policy.

Collateral Source Rule

Generally, a tortfeasor (the wrongdoer, the one who commits the negligent act) is liable for the damages sustained as a result of the tortfeasor's wrongful act or omission without regard to other actual or possible sources of compensation available to the wronged party. The collateral source rule, discussed in Chapter 8, is a legal rule of evidence that bars the introduction in court of any information indicating that the plaintiff has been compensated or reimbursed by any source other than the defendant. Where the collateral source rule applies, liability claims are adjudicated on the presumption that the defendant provides the only source of recovery for the plaintiff. The result is that a claimant can collect from both the insurer and other collateral sources for the same elements of loss.

About one-third of the states have approved tort-reform laws that would significantly change the collateral source rule. The approaches taken include permitting consideration of compensation or payments received from some or all collateral sources and requiring that any award be offset by the amount of collateral source payments.[10]

First-Party Versus Third-Party Claims; Subrogation

Property insurance policies generally do not explain that the insured has two choices when covered property is damaged through the negligence of a third party. These two choices are the following:

1. The insured can bypass its property insurance and attempt to recover directly from the negligent third party (or its liability insurer). This approach can be expedient when the third party is clearly responsible for the damages and willing to cooperate in settling the claim. It also involves no deductibles.

2. The insured can make a first-party claim under its property insurance policy, subject to any applicable deductible. After indemnifying its insured, the first party's insurer is subrogated to the insured's rights of recovery against the negligent third party and will seek to recover its payment from the third party (or its liability insurer). The insurer will also attempt to recover the deductible and, if successful, will reimburse the insured in the amount of the deductible.

In either case, the loss is ultimately borne by the party responsible for causing the loss (or its liability insurer). Subrogation shifts the ultimate cost of a first-party loss to the responsible third party.

Although most property insurance policies contain a subrogation provision, the insurer has a right to subrogation independent of policy provisions, based on common law and statutes. Subrogation actions are usually based on negligence of a third party. If the insured suffers property damage but has no right to recover from another party, the insurer cannot subrogate.

Self-Insurance

Many liability insurance policies refer to other *insurance* and do not specifically address the question of whether a retention arrangement is actually a form of insurance. Where the policy is not specific, the courts may decide the question. A growing number of insurance contracts now specifically address the issue.

NONINSURANCE CONTRACTS

Another type of external factor affecting an insurer's obligations under an insurance policy involves the side agreements that shift liability from one party to another. Liability is transferred daily under the terms of construction contracts, lease agreements, easements, purchase order and sales agreements, and countless other types of contracts. They are not insurance, but they resemble insurance in that they are contracts providing for some transfer of risk. Indemnity and hold-harmless agreements are discussed in Chapter 3.

The main reason for most noninsurance contracts is not to force one party to retain the loss, but rather to indicate in advance of any loss whose insurance is expected to cover it. Although they are not a part of the insurance contract, these side agreements can play a major part in determining whether the insurer will pay a given loss.

Pre-Loss Waivers

A typical property insurance policy permits the insured, *before a loss occurs,* to waive its rights of recovery against a third party that might be responsible for the loss. Pre-loss waivers, which are common, therefore present one type of noninsurance contract that might affect recovery under that policy.

The subrogation provision in most property insurance policies transfers to the insurer, following a loss, the insured's rights to recover from any third party responsible for the property damage. Clearly, it is in the insurer's interests to preserve these rights of recovery. Therefore, subrogation provisions in many policies forbid the insured from doing anything after a loss that would adversely affect the insurer's right of subrogation.

Specifically, the typical subrogation provision prohibits the insured from waiving any of its rights of recovery *after a loss.* After a loss, the insured would, in effect, be waiving not its own rights, but the insurer's. *Before the loss,* the situation might be different. The purpose of a pre-loss waiver, sometimes referred to as a waiver of subrogation, is to prevent an insurer from exercising its right of subrogation against someone whom the insured has released from liability.

For example, a landlord (lessor) may give her tenant (lessee) a waiver only to the extent that the lessor's property policy provides coverage. In other words, both parties agree that the tenant is not responsible (is exculpated) for any damage to property covered by the landlord's insurance.

Although the subrogation provisions in most property insurance policies permit waivers of subrogation before loss, not all policies do. In some cases, the existence of a pre-loss waiver could void the entire policy.

UNLISTED SETTLEMENT OPTIONS

Many insurance policies contain specific language explaining how claims are to be settled. Yet, in many instances, both parties may agree to a settlement that does not directly conform to any of the alternatives presented by the policy. Obviously, some additional alternatives—external factors—not mentioned in these policies are available. Three examples include negotiation, structured settlements, and rehabilitation.

Negotiation

Claim settlement often involves some give and take by both parties. For example, an insurer providing auto physical damage coverage agrees to pay for the loss in money or to repair or replace the damaged vehicle, after subtracting any applicable deductible. The insurance policy covers the actual cash value of the vehicle without stating a dollar amount. To determine any car's value at the time of the loss, the insurer will have to consider the make and model, age, and condition, as well as the extent of damage. Any diminution in value of the repaired auto might also be considered in some cases. Whether the repair uses the original equipment manufacturer's new parts, aftermarket parts, or used parts might also be an issue, as well as which body shop will perform the repairs. If the insured is reluctant to accept the insurer's initial offer, further negotiation might be necessary until both parties reach an acceptable figure.

The same kind of negotiation may take place with liability insurance claims. It is not unusual for the insurer's claim representative to negotiate with an injured third party over the amount of damages that will be paid. In more serious cases, much of the negotiation occurs between the attorneys representing both parties.

Structured Settlements

Liability and workers compensation insurance policies imply that the insurer will settle claims by paying a single lump sum, but not all claims are paid that way. In cases involving large awards, a lump sum settlement gives the claimant or his or her family a large sum of money to budget and/or invest to meet their future needs.

Structured settlement
A series of periodic future payments lasting either for the injured person's life or for a stated period.

Under a **structured settlement**, the insurer agrees to make a series of periodic future payments lasting either for the injured person's life or for a stated period. Structured settlements were developed to provide a more stable income or cash flow over an extended period. The insurer typically arranges funding by purchasing an annuity. Considerable flexibility and creativity may be exercised in structuring payout schedules to match the claimant's needs.

Rehabilitation Services

Rehabilitation services are another settlement option that insurers often provide that most insurance policies do not formally recognize. (Some no-fault endorsements to auto insurance policies explicitly provide for rehabilitation expenses.) Rehabilitation focuses on helping an injured person to recover from the injuries and return to some form of gainful employment, rather than emphasizing money damages as a substitute for physical well-being.

Many insurers employ rehabilitation specialists or purchase rehabilitation services from specialty organizations. Insurers have been leaders in conducting rehabilitation programs for disabled workers and third-party claimants, often providing rehabilitation benefits well beyond those required by law.

Rehabilitation services
Services to help restore an injured or ill person to his or her optimum physical, mental, vocational, and economic usefulness.

EXTERNAL FACTORS AFFECTING THE AMOUNT PAYABLE

A property or liability insurance policy, by itself, usually does not include enough information to indicate the exact dollar amount payable by the insurance company for an insured loss. Additional information is usually needed to determine the amount payable for any given loss.

Valuation of Property Losses

A property insurance policy's valuation provision usually indicates *how* the loss amount will be computed, and the policy limit generally states the maximum dollar amount of insurance payable under a specific coverage. For many reasons, such as the following, the insurer is not necessarily required to pay the maximum amount, even for a total loss:

- The policy limit might exceed the property's insurable actual cash value or replacement cost value.

- The property might be underinsured and subject to a coinsurance penalty, factors that can be determined only by establishing the property's insurable value at the time of the loss.

- The amount of recovery might be limited by the extent of the insured's insurable interest in covered property. This amount cannot be determined without knowing the nature and extent of the insured's property interests.

- The replacement cost value of covered property is not stated in the policy but is based on the amount actually required to repair or replace the property at the time of the loss, factors determined only when the repair or replacement has been completed or when a contractor has agreed to complete the work for a guaranteed amount.

- When coverage applies on an actual cash value basis, both the replacement cost and applicable depreciation must be determined.

- In some cases, especially those involving auto physical damage, diminution in value, betterment, and the type of replacement parts used might also have a bearing on the amount payable by the insurer. State laws, another external factor, might have a bearing on these issues.

- Regardless of the property's replacement cost value or actual cash value, and regardless of coinsurance clauses or other policy provisions, a minority of states have a valued policy law that might require the insurer to pay the policy limit when fire totally destroys a covered building.

- An additional limits of liability endorsement to a homeowners policy increases coverage available to reflect the full current replacement cost of the dwelling, even if it exceeds the policy limit.

Valuation of Liability Claims

Determining the amount of damages payable in a *property damage* liability claim is similar to determining the amount payable in a first-party property insurance policy, because it is based on the value of the damaged or destroyed property plus any damages associated with its loss of use. The main differences are (1) property damage liability claims usually involve no deductible, and (2) emphasis is placed on the amount that will indemnify the third-party claimant rather than on property items, perils, and consequences covered by insurance and by relevant provisions affecting the amount payable.

In a limited sense, the amounts payable for *bodily injury* liability damages might be compared to the first-party coverage provided by accident and health insurance policies covering medical expenses and disability income. However, many additional variables clearly affect amounts payable, such as damages for pain and suffering. Liability insurance covers defense costs, which are not an issue with most first-party coverages. Also, charges for the same medical services can vary widely depending, in part, on any managed care arrangements between the insurer and the provider. In addition, liability insurance may pay claims for general damages, punitive damages, and possibly even treble (triple) damages awarded under some statutes.

Defense Costs

As discussed earlier, the insurer's duty to defend is broader than the duty to pay damages. As long as any potential exists that the insured might be liable for damages to which coverage would apply, the insurer has an obligation to defend the insured. This obligation exists even if some of the allegations are groundless, false, or fraudulent, and even if some of the allegations are not covered by the policy. However, the insurer is obligated to pay damages only for liability arising from an event insured under the policy. The insurer is not obligated to provide a further defense once the entire policy limit has been *paid* for damages.[11]

Defense costs can be incurred in handling both property damage and bodily injury liability claims, as well as those involving personal injury, wrongful acts, errors and omissions, or other offenses. An insurer might incur defense costs, including the costs of investigating a claim, even when it ultimately has no obligation to pay damages, possibly because the defense was successful and the insured was found *not* legally responsible for the damage or injury. Most liability insurance policies place no dollar limit on covered defense costs, although some policies include defense coverage within policy limits.

Special Damages

Special damages include specific out-of-pocket expenses and income losses such as hospital expenses, doctor and miscellaneous medical expenses, ambulance charges, prescriptions, and lost wages for time away from the job during recovery. Because they are specific and identifiable, special damages are easier to calculate than general damages. Still, it is not always easy to determine the proper level of treatment, proper charges for that treatment, the appropriate length of a disability period, or the extent and duration of future medical care.

General Damages

General damages include compensation for pain and suffering; disfigurement; loss of limbs, sight, or hearing; and loss of the ability to bear children. These items are not tied to specific measurable experiences, and establishing their value is arbitrary at best. However, a value must be established either through negotiation or through a court award.

Punitive Damages

The treatment of punitive damages is yet another factor, often outside the scope of policy language, that can affect an insurer's obligations under a liability insurance policy. A court may award punitive damages in addition to special damages and/or general damages when it finds the conduct of the insured particularly reprehensible.

Treble (Triple) Damages

In cases involving racketeering or violation of antitrust statutes, any court-awarded damages may be automatically tripled by law. Unless treble damages are specifically excluded, insurers' liabilities can substantially increase in such cases.

Organized activities may be subject to the Racketeer Influenced and Corrupt Organizations Act (RICO). Although originally intended to apply to organized crime, RICO is now pleaded in a wide variety of cases, including lawsuits against insurance companies. Treble damages may also be mandated under the Sherman Antitrust Act and the Clayton Act.

The Application of Policy Limits

For a variety of reasons, including the following, the limit of insurance on a policy's declarations page does not necessarily equal the maximum amount the insurer might pay under that policy:

- Some policies include additional or supplemental coverages that expand the scope of protection and provide additional coverage limits.

- Some forms provide several coverages that could easily be involved in a single loss event. For example, a typical $200,000 homeowners policy provides not only $200,000 coverage on the dwelling building, but also $20,000 on detached appurtenant structures, $100,000 for personal property, and $60,000 for loss of use. If a house, a separate garage, and all contents are destroyed, the amount payable could be not $200,000, but $380,000. An additional coverage or coverage extension might provide additional coverage.

- Unless policy provisions or laws specifically prohibit stacking, a single incident might lead to more than one policy coverage of some claims. For example, an injured passenger could conceivably collect under two or more of the liability, medical payments, or uninsured motorists coverages of an auto policy.

Policy provisions directly or indirectly address most of the examples just mentioned. However, the application of limits can also be based on other information that does not appear in the policy, including the following:

- Many liability insurance policies are subject to an aggregate limit. Once the insurer has paid the aggregate amount in damages because of one or more occurrences, the policy provides no further protection. The amount of protection remaining at any point—if any—is not specified in the policy.

- Even when an aggregate limit applies, the insurer may end up paying several times the aggregate limit if more than one policy was in force, or if the same policy was in force for several policy periods, during the time when coverage was triggered. Under some trigger theories applied by the courts, the limit of each policy year during the entire exposure period might be payable, and the amount of damages payable could be several times the current policy's aggregate limit.

DAMAGES OR OTHER PENALTIES ASSESSED AGAINST THE INSURER

Most of this chapter has involved the question of what is covered by insurance policies and the external factors that determine how the insurer fulfills its contract. Any payment the insurer must make is directly associated with its obligations under an insurance contract, as determined or enforced by the courts, if necessary. In addition, noncontractual situations can arise that obligate an insurer to pay damages to an insured or third-party claimant. These damage claims might or might not relate directly to an underlying loss subject to an insurance policy the insurer issued.

Such damages or penalties can cause an insurer's ultimate payment to sometimes far exceed any applicable policy limits. These situations arise when a claim or suit is made alleging that the insurer mishandled a claim. On the basis of these allegations, an insurer might be found liable to pay compensatory damages for breach of contract, to pay punitive damages for bad faith, or to pay fines or penalties assessed by regulatory authorities.

Compensatory Damages for Breach of Contract

An insurer that has breached its contract with the insured might be required to pay compensatory damages. A general rule of contract law permits the recovery of compensatory damages for breach of an implied covenant of good faith and fair dealing.

Both the insurer and the insured are subject to this implied covenant, which is not expressly stated in an insurance policy. The insured, for example, owes a duty to the insurer to provide truthful underwriting and claim information, and the insurer has an obligation to be fair and reasonable in handling claims.

In many cases an insured can show that the insurer's breach of the contract caused a definite financial loss. Suppose, for example, the insurer fails to pay a valid $500,000 property insurance claim when business property is destroyed, and the business fails as a result. The businessowner might convince the court that, as a direct result of the insurer's failure to fulfill its obligations, the insured lost not only the $500,000 value of the building, but also $2 million the business would have earned if insurance proceeds had permitted prompt reconstruction of the building. In such situations, courts sometimes award damages that far exceed the limits of the original policy. The goal of the suit is not to enforce the coverage provided by the insurance contract itself, but rather to seek damages for the breach of the insurance contract created by the insurer's failure to pay the claim.

Punitive Damages for Bad Faith

Punitive damages may be awarded against an *insured*, not to compensate the third-party claimant for monetary damages, but to punish the insured defendant. Punitive damages can also be awarded *against an insurer*. If an insured proves that an insurer has committed fraud, malice, or oppression, the insured might be entitled to receive punitive damages that often greatly exceed the compensatory damages.

Awarding punitive damages against insurers raises their overhead costs and drives up insurance rates. However, the threat of punitive damages awards can serve to discourage insurers from any action that even appears to involve bad faith.

Policyholders, claimants, and excess insurers can bring bad-faith claims against insurers.

Penalties Under Unfair Claim Practices Acts

An insurer that violates unfair claim practices acts might be fined or sanctioned by the state. Unfair claim practices acts are not intended to change coverage, exclusions, or loss settlement provisions in insurance policies. However, a state insurance department can assess penalties and sanctions against an insurer who is found to have violated a provision of an unfair claim practices law with such frequency as to indicate a general business practice. As noted earlier, the claimant can also bring a separate tort action against the insurer alleging bad faith. In some cases, the results of the unfair claim practices act proceeding can be used as evidence in the insured's bad-faith action.

State unfair claim practices acts address many aspects of claim handling, including insurers' responsibility for prompt communications with their insureds, adequate investigation, detailed explanations of coverage denials, and so on. Generally, these laws require that insurers handle claims promptly, which requires prompt investigation, timely evaluation, and, where warranted, prompt settlement.

Possible penalties and sanctions include the following:

- Fines
- Interest on an overdue claim payment
- Payment of other fees and costs
- Injunctions or cease-and-desist orders
- Suspension of a claim representative's or insurer's license
- Revocation of a claim representative's or insurer's license

If insurers have been penalized or sanctioned, they usually take corrective action to prevent further violations. Insurers pay fines to the state department of insurance, not to the policyholder. Suspension and revocation of licenses are extreme measures, usually imposed only after other penalties have proven ineffective.

SUMMARY

This chapter discussed matters that are outside of the insurance contract and that affect the contract's interpretation and analysis:

- The courts play a role in answering questions of liability, questions of coverage, questions of law, and questions of fact.
- Procedures exist to resolve coverage disputes, including suit by an insured, suit by a third-party claimant, and two measures to preserve the insurer's rights: reservation of rights letters and nonwaiver agreements.

- Legal concepts the courts apply include contract of adhesion, reasonable expectations, unconscionable advantage, substantial performance, waiver and estoppel, and fortuity.

- The policy provisions that invoke external factors include liberalization, conformity with statute provisions, and reference to workers compensation statutes.

- Insurance policies often cover the unknown by providing coverage for unnamed insureds, nonowned property, unidentified exposures, undefined perils, unissued policies, or unknown risks.

- Insurance policies sometimes provide protection even after their expiration date because of statutory restrictions on cancellation or because of cancellation practices that insurers use.

- Insurance policies rarely mention burden of proof, yet a decisive factor in many claims revolves around the question of which party has the burden of proof. This is an important, but subtle, reason why "all-risks" or special-form policies provide better protection for the insured than named-peril policies: in "all-risks" cases, the burden of proof is on the insurer.

- Some sources of recovery might overlap with insurance, leading to such issues as the collateral source rule, subrogation, and the question whether self-insurance qualifies as "other insurance."

- Noninsurance contracts can affect the coverage provided by insurance contracts. For example, a pre-loss waiver by the insured might effectively eliminate an insurer's subrogation rights.

- Although insurance policies imply lump sum payment of an easily identifiable sum, settlement can actually involve negotiation, structured settlements, and rehabilitation services that are not mentioned in the policy.

- Many external factors affect the valuation of property and liability losses.

- Insurers sometimes are required to pay damages and fines because of failure to fulfill the insurance contract. Insurers who fail to uphold their responsibilities under an insurance contract can be held liable for damages for breach of contract. When the insurer's failure is the result of bad faith, the insurer can also be held liable for punitive damages. Finally, an insurer who is guilty of unfair claim practices can face regulatory penalties.

TEXTBOOK SUMMARY

This textbook examined key insurance and risk management issues:

- Risk is an inescapable and important part of business and everyday life. Sound risk management practices increase a business's value and positively contribute to people's welfare.

- Insurance functions as both a risk management technique and a business for dealing with insurable risks, but insurance is not the only means of financing risks. Various risk financing alternatives are also available.

- An insurance contract is formed when the required elements of an enforceable contract exist. An insurance contract can be enforced only by an insured party with an insurable interest in the losses covered by insurance. One must examine the common provisions in an insurance policy to determine whether any have a bearing on a specific claim. One must also determine whether an insured event has occurred.

- If the policy covers the loss, then the amounts payable to cover the loss must be determined. Some losses may be covered by more than one coverage, policy, or insurer.

- Finally, insurance coverage in many situations depends on factors not appearing in the insurance contract.

CHAPTER NOTES

1. Nationwide Mutual Fire Insurance Company v. Wittekind et al., Ohio Ct. App., 4th Dist. 730 NE. 2d. 1054 (1999).
   Source: "Court Decisions," From case reports published in the *North Eastern Reporter 2d*, St. Paul, Minn.: *West Publishing Co.*, and *Rough Notes*, April 2001, p. 8.

2. Kenneth S. Wollner, *How to Draft and Interpret Insurance Policies* (West Bloomfield, Mich.: Casualty Risk Publishing, L.L.C., 1999), p. 169.

3. Form CP 00 10 10 00, Copyright Insurance Services Office, Inc., 1999.

4. Stephen M. Hoke, "Contract Interpretation in Commercial Insurance Disputes: The Status of the Sophisticated Insured Exceptions and Alternatives to the Ambiguity Rule," *Federation of Insurance & Corporate Counsel*, Quarterly/Spring 1990, p. 264.

5. Robert E. Keeton, *Insurance Law* (St. Paul, Minn.: West Publishing Co., 1971), p. 348.

6. Unpublished opinion in Plaintiff v. Defendant, Mazur v. Truck Insurance Exchange, Los Angeles County, Superior Court no. SC048679, Court of Appeal Second District.

7. Form 3, Ed 2.0, Copyright American Association for Insurance Services, 1995.

8. Form SC 00 00 00 A, Copyright National Council on Compensation Insurance, 1991.

9. Phil Zinkewicz, "Survey Shows Cyber-Risk Little Understood," *Rough Notes*, April 2001, pp. 50–51. The referenced survey was conducted by the New York-based opinion research firm of Schulman, Ronca & Bucuvalas, Inc., on behalf of the St. Paul Companies.

10. Ruth Gastel, ed., *Insurance Issues Update*. Insurance Information Institute, April 2001, p. 16.

11. The insurer also is relieved from the duty to defend when all counts that the policy may cover have been eliminated. In some cases, insurers have been able to apportion the cost to defend between covered and non-covered allegations.

Index

SPLENDOURS OF SOUTHERN AFRICA

Splendours of Southern Africa

GERALD S. CUBITT

Mr. Brown
With our very Best Wishes
Janet & Gerald

January 1974

CAPE TOWN

C. STRUIK (PTY) LTD

1972

© C. Struik (Pty.) Ltd.
Africana Specialist and Publisher

ISBN 0 86977 017 9

English text written by Gerald S. Cubitt
Edited by Ursula Kingwell
Afrikaans translation by Madeleine van Biljon
Title suggested by Greta den Hartog and George Francois Laurence
Dustjacket design by James Giles
Monochrome Bromide Prints produced by Gale Daniels, Johannesburg

Lithographical positives by Hirt & Carter (Pty.) Ltd.
Text printed letterpress, illustrations printed offset
Paper: Focus Matt Art 135 gsm
Bound in Scholco Bookcloth
Printed and bound by Gothic Printing Company Limited,
Printpak Building, Dacres Ave., Epping, Cape

For Janet,
and to the memory of her brother David

The Publishers wish to acknowledge the financial assistance received
from the undermentioned with the production of this book:
Van Reekum Papier-Gepacy (S.A.) (Pty) Ltd
South African Tourist Corporation

INTRODUCTION

Africa is many things to many people; to some it is a rising colossus, where the once neat and tidy colonial entities have burgeoned into a host of new, self-conscious nations, each in its own way striving to cope with problems of internal development, but at the same time confronting the rest of the world with a loud voice and a powerful vote that cannot be ignored.

To others Africa represents simply a vast economic potential, a continent still relatively underpopulated and underdeveloped, and yet rich in the minerals and natural resources that are demanded by modern industrial technology.

In some, however, the concept of Africa arouses a deep nostalgia, an awareness of and appreciation for the wide open spaces – the great plains, mountains, deserts, forests and lakes. Much has changed, and is still changing, as the inevitable result of man's technological conquest over nature. Cities, towns and highways have mushroomed forth out of the dust and deserts; but the continent is huge, and with just a little effort, it is possible to leave behind city life and enter the wilds of Africa, where man may move in harmony with nature.

This book is about Southern Africa. It comprises a selection of photographs that, I hope, capture at least some of the atmosphere of natural Africa. Intentionally, there are no pictures of city life, industry or other signs of the modern world.

Moreover, to do full justice to the title chosen, many volumes would have to be filled instead of just one, and there are consequently and inevitably many gaps. The photographs are of subjects which have particularly appealed to me as a photographer.

For many people visiting Southern Africa, Cape Town is the port of arrival. When Sir Francis Drake first caught sight of the Cape in 1580 he referred to it as "the fairest we saw in the whole circumference of the earth".

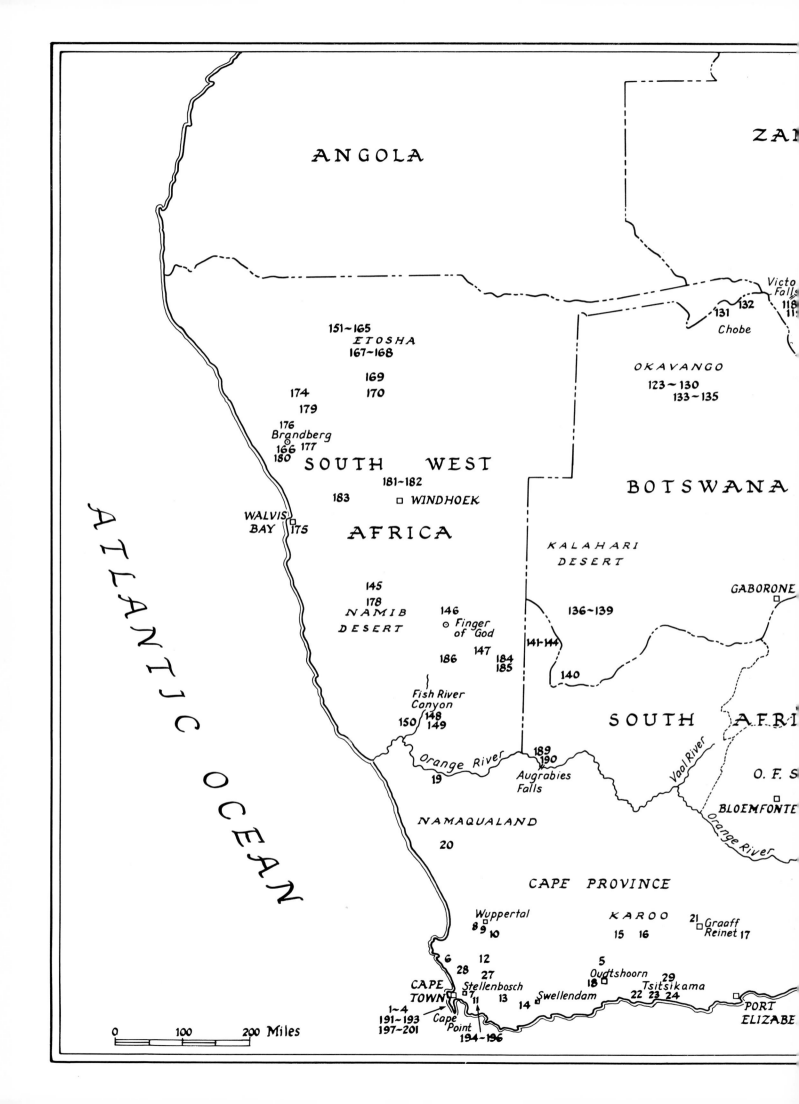

ANGOLA

ZAM

Victo Falls

131 132 118 11

Chobe

151~165
ETOSHA
167~168

169

170

174

179

176

Brandberg

166 177

180

SOUTH WEST

181~182

183 □ *WINDHOEK*

AFRICA

WALVIS □
BAY 175

OKAVANGO

123~130

133~135

BOTSWANA

KALAHARI
DESERT

136~139

GABORONE □

145

178

NAMIB

DESERT

146

○ *Finger*
of God

141-144

140

186

147 184
185

Fish River
Canyon

148
150 149

Orange River

189
190

19

Augrabies
Falls

Vaal River

O. F. S

BLOEMFONTE □

Orange River

NAMAQUALAND

20

CAPE PROVINCE

Wuppertal

8 9 □
9 10

KAROO

15 16

21 □ *Graaff*
Reinet 17

6

28

12

27

5

Oudtshoorn

29

Tsitsikama

CAPE □ 7
TOWN 11

Stellenbosch

13 14 *Swellendam*

18

22 23 24

□

PORT
ELIZABE

1~4
191~193
197~201

Cape
Point

194~196

ATLANTIC OCEAN

0   100   200 Miles

SOUTH AFRI

MALAWI

122

120
121

MOÇAMBIQUE

RHODESIA

SALISBURY

111

BULAWAYO

109
110

113-114   Zimbabwe

Matopos
Hills

112

116·117

Gorongosa
103~108

BEIRA

W

R

E

S

101

KRUGER

98   PARK

Blyde River
Canyon   94   89

99   95

TRANSVAAL   100   96

Pilgrims Rest   97

102

PRETORIA

JOHANNESBURG

92 93

SWAZI~   LOURENCO
                MARQUES
90 26
LAND
          77 78
        Ndumu

58~60   Mkuzi   72~76
                            82~85
          87   Hluhluwe
          ZULULAND   79~81
Golden
Gate   88   Umfolozi
        Drokensberg   86
62   NATAL   63 66
71   67

ESOTHO   69 61   PIETERMARITZBURG
70   Sani   DURBAN
        Pass
      68   25

64

RANSKEI   33
Umtata
0~32
4~56
57

EAST LONDON

INDIAN OCEAN

0   100   200   300   400   500   Kms.

Ralph Taylor

Dominated by the majestic Table Mountain that rises above Cape Town, the Peninsula stretches a rocky spine some 50 kilometres southwards to Cape Point. A magnificent marine drive along the western flank of the Peninsula takes in most of the scenic beauty that is characteristic of the south-western Cape.

The Cape mountains were formed by a buckling or crumpling of the earth's crust, which gave rise to a series of vertical and near vertical formations. With their steep crenellations and sparsely vegetated slopes, these mountains provide a rugged contrast to the fertile green valleys at their foot. The natural vegetation of the region consists of varieties of low, hardy shrubs and indigenous proteas which are able to survive the hot, dry summers and wet winters.

Over 20 000 species of flowering plants flourish in the Cape, and in springtime, in September, the countryside is transformed into a kaleidoscope of colour. The greatest concentration of wild flowers occur around Springbok in Namaqualand, about 500 kilometres north of Cape Town. For most of the year the semi-desert land is arid and bleak, but when the flowers burst into bloom, it is as though a collection of exotic and beautiful Persian carpets had been spread out on a bare floor.

Both the indigenous fauna and flora of the Cape have suffered from the advent of the early settlers. The animals that survive are mainly the smaller species of antelope such as grysbok, rhebok, mountain reedbuck and duiker, as well as baboon and hyrax that take advantage of the low-growing and often dense bush which provides a measure of camouflage and protection. Leopards still live in the remote reaches of the mountains, but they are rarely seen and their numbers are dwindling.

To get some idea of the natural forests that once covered a wide area, one must travel east to Knysna, on the Garden Route. In the Tsitsikama Forest are superb specimens of yellowwood and stinkwood, as well as many other indigenous trees. This forest is also the last refuge for the small herd of Knysna elephants. Were it not for the dense and often impenetrable tangle of vegetation, these few survivors would have been hunted down decades ago.

Inland, to the north and north-east of the Cape mountains, lies the Karroo. In the Hottentot language, this word means "an arid desert", and it is an apt description. Rainfall is low, and provides scant moisture for the stunted bush that is prolific throughout. It is a monotonous landscape, usually brown and dry, mostly flat, with occasional solitary flat-topped hills that are remnants of ancient volcanic pipes.

In the harsh glare and heat of midday, the Karroo is a place to traverse as quickly as possible, but in the early morning soon after dawn, and especially towards dusk in the evening, the colours of the veld are warm and beautiful. The softer light brings out the delicate tints of the bush, contrasting with the vivid pink and purple hues reflected from the hills.

Few areas in Africa have been so completely devastated as a result of man's activities, as has the Karroo. The original vegetation included many varieties of grasses and bush, which provided food for large nomadic herds of antelope. Over the last hundred years, widespread over-grazing by sheep, and the elimination of almost all wild life, have resulted in the predominance of shrub with a low nutritional value.

The destruction of wild life in the Karroo was an incalculable loss. The English traveller George Thompson, in his book *Adventures in Southern Africa*, published in 1827, wrote of the Karroo as it was in his time, as follows:

"As we proceeded along the plains gently declining from the Sneeuw-berg we discovered thousands of antelope, quaghas and gnoos. . . . Hundreds of them were now playing round us, and ever and anon a troop of these fantastic animals would join a herd of quaghas, and all sound off helter-skelter across the plains, throwing up clouds of dust from the arid ground, which is here quite a karroo. . . .

The numbers and variety of game formed, indeed, the only feature of animation and interest throughout this desolate region. . . .

In an hour we remounted and proceeded on our course, over extensive plains, sprinkled with numerous herds of game – quaghas, elands, gnoos, koodos, hartebeest, gemsboks, and smaller antelopes, the movements of which helped to relieve our lonely journey. . . .

Travelling through the Karroo . . . I passed through prodigious flocks of springboks, spread over the plains as far as the eye could reach. The number it is impossible to estimate with any nicety but I suppose I saw at least 100,000 in the course of fifty miles. They were migrating from the great desert towards the Colony."

The Mountain Zebra National Park near Cradock today harbours the remnants of the wild life that once flourished in the Karroo. The unfortunate quagga, however, fought a losing battle and the last known specimen died at Berlin Zoo in 1875.

One has only to glance at the place-names on a modern map of the Karroo, to find haunting reminders of the animals that once roamed across the plains: Leeuberg, Elandskloof, Buffels River, Hartbeesvleiberg, Gemsbokkop, Kwaggaskop, to name but a few.

The greater part of Southern Africa consists of an elevated plateau which varies in altitude between 600 and 2 000 metres, and is rimmed by mountain ranges which form the Great Escarpment. The plateau slopes gradually from east to west, and includes both the Karroo and the Kalahari desert.

The highest and most dramatic section of the Escarpment culminates in the Drakensberg around Lesotho. These mountains divide the Natal grasslands from the Highveld of the southern Transvaal and the Orange Free State.

When looking up at the Sani Pass, or towards the summits of Champagne Castle, Cathedral Peak, Mont-aux-Sources and other towering landmarks of the Drakensberg, one may imagine that these are the first of a series of mountain ranges. Yet, on reaching the top of the spectacular Sani Pass, at 2 750 metres, instead of seeing further rising peaks and valleys, one is confronted by the high, treeless Lesotho Plateau.

In the east the Escarpment is for the most part very steep, forming a rain trap for the Transkei and the coastal lowlands, while in the west the gradient is less pronounced. The Orange River, rising in the Maluti Mountains, gathers much of the rain that falls near the crest of the Escarpment and then flows westwards on its 2 000-kilometre journey to the Atlantic coast.

The Highveld of the Orange Free State and the Transvaal lies to the west of the Drakensberg and varies in altitude from 1 200 to 1 800 metres. This area is rather flat and featureless and has few distinctive natural landmarks. Like the Karroo, it also was once thickly populated with wild animals. The few that remain today are protected in small reserves and on private farms.

Soil erosion is a scourge in the Transkei and the grasslands of Natal, and in places the land is deeply scarred. Over-grazing and deforestation have exacerbated the problem, and in many areas the poor quality of the soil has severely restricted agricultural potential.

North of Durban, in the coastal regions of Natal, there are four wonderful game reserves: Umfolozi, Hluhluwe, Mkuze and Ndumu. These are mere remnants of the formerly huge game trails of Zululand, but in spite of their small size, they are Edens of wild life for the enthusiast. White and black rhino, buffalo, wildebeest, zebra, nyala, kudu, and impala are abundant, and the bird life is rich and varied. Each reserve has its own character and appeal and is quite distinct from the other. Mkuze is particularly worth while; here, from the two game hides at the Bube and Msinga waterholes, the animals may be seen at close range as they come down to drink.

Ndumu has a special charm because of its beautiful setting. Situated in the northernmost part of Natal and bordered by the Usutu River, this reserve consists of forests, lakes and bush. Fringed by graceful yellow-barked fever trees, the lakes are a paradise for pelicans, flamingoes, storks, herons and many other water-birds, as well as for crocodiles.

A continuation of the Drakensberg range in Swaziland and the north-eastern Transvaal separates the Highveld plains from the dense bush country of the Lowveld. The Limpopo with its tributaries, the only other major river system in South Africa besides the Orange, drains much of central and northern Transvaal, before flowing into the Indian Ocean north of Lourenço Marques.

In the north-eastern Lowveld of the Transvaal lies the famous Kruger National Park, a superb ecological entity which provides sanctuary for thousands of wild animals.

Although this was formerly well-known hunting country, the animals were for years protected by the prevalence of malaria and sleeping sickness, which acted as deterrents to the settlement of man. The terrain is mainly flat, bordered on one side by the Drakensberg, and on the other by the Lebombo Mountains. The region is crossed by rivers, notably the Sabie and the Olifants, the latter of which joins the mainstream of the Limpopo in the east. These rivers offer marvellous opportunities for game-viewing. In the dry winter months, from May to October, the need for water drives many animals out of the thick bush to the banks of the rivers, where they can be seen more easily.

Elephant, giraffe, buffalo, zebra, wildebeest, waterbuck, tsessebe, eland, kudu, sable and roan antelope and impala are among the species that browse or graze in an unspoilt environment. Both species of rhinoceros have been re-introduced and their numbers are increasing. Lions, leopards, cheetahs, hyenas, jackals and wild dogs roam freely, following their predatory instinct. Baboons and vervet monkeys, ever inquisitive and curious, are plentiful throughout the park.

North of the Limpopo River, Rhodesia provides a contrasting landscape, ranging from the mountain peaks of the eastern highlands, culminating in Inyangani (2 521 metres), to the low-lying plateau that embraces the basins of the Zambezi, Limpopo, Sabi and Lundi Rivers. Much of the country lies at an altitude of 900–1 500 metres and comprises grasslands and mopane woods, broken by granite koppies. In the Matopos National Park near Bulawayo, some of the most striking of these koppies can be seen: huge boulders balanced precariously one upon the other as though by a giant's hand. They are a favourite haunt of leopards, as well as of their prey: hyrax and baboons.

In the heart of Rhodesia lies the mysterious ruined city of Zimbabwe. The origins of the strange acropolis, temples and other stone buildings remain almost as obscure today as when first discovered, in 1868. The atmosphere is brooding and haunted, especially at dawn, when the blackness of night gives way to the first rays of the morning sun, and the cold, grey ruins pose their unanswered challenge to another day.

The mighty Zambezi River rises in Angola, travels south and then east, gathering on its way the waters of countless rivers and streams. At the Victoria Falls the "Great River", nearly 2 kilometres wide at this point, pours into a deep, narrow gorge. The impact of the cascading waters is so great that a cloud of spray rises hundreds of metres into the air. Viewing the falls from the lush tropical forest that borders the precipice, one is drenched by the spray as if by rain. David Livingstone has described his first impressions of the falls on the 21st November, 1855, thus: ". . . after twenty minutes sail from Kulai, we came in sight, for the first time, of the columns of vapour appropriately called 'smoke', rising at a distance of five miles, exactly as when large tracts of grass are burned in Africa. Five columns now rose, and bending in the direction of the wind, they seemed placed against a low ridge covered with trees. The tops of the columns at this distance appeared to mingle with the clouds. They were white below, and higher up, they became dark so as to simulate smoke very closely.

"The whole scene was extremely beautiful. The banks and the islands dotted over the river are adorned with silvan vegetation of great variety of colour and form. These trees have each their own physiognomy. There, towering over all, stands the great burly baobab each of whose enormous arms would form the trunk of a large tree; besides, the groups of feathery shaped leaves depicted in the sky lend beauty to the scene. No one can imagine the beauty from anything in England. The Falls are bounded on three sides by ridges, three or four hundred feet high, which are covered with forest, with red soil, appearing through the trees."

From the Victoria Falls the Zambezi flows into the Kariba Dam, the largest man-made lake in the world, 280 kilometres long and 65 kilometres wide. The river then continues east, entering Moçambique for the final stretch before reaching the sea north of Beira.

Gorongoza National Park, a short distance north-west of Beira, is one of the finest game parks in Africa. It is a gem. As a result of many months of patient research by Ken Tinley, a leading South African ecologist, the boundaries of this park will soon be extended to form an ecological unit that will accommodate the migratory movements of its animals.

The coastal grasslands of Gorongoza, with its scattered doum, borassus and ivory palms, conjures up visions of a prehistoric landscape, out of which dinosaurs and other long-extinct creatures could emerge.

Rising in the western highlands of Angola, the Okavango River crosses the Caprivi Strip and flows into north-western Botswana, where it is split into myriads of channels and small streams that comprise the Okavango Swamps. The maze of crystal-clear waterways and verdant marsh divides thousands of small islands from one another. This pristine corner of Africa, still to a great extent unexplored, is a paradise for wild life. Near Chief's Island, I have watched a herd of about 300 lechwe move through the marsh at speed, the sound of their hooves reminding me of an express train thundering through a railway station. Hippo, buffalo, tsessebe, impala, waterbuck, sitatunga and kudu are some of the larger animals that flourish on these swamp islands. There are also lions, leopards, cheetahs and other predators. The lagoons and rivers are inhabited by crocodiles, as well as tiger-fish, bream and barbel. Bird life is both varied and interesting: pelicans, storks, ibis, herons, geese, ducks and lily-trotters are but a few of the species that abound. The distinctive cry of the fish-eagle is frequently heard.

The vegetation of the swamps varies from lush grass and papyrus to thick forest. The trees that flourish on the islands are superb; tropical palms compete in profusion with huge wild fig, "sausage" and motsodi trees. The ubiquitous termite hills are towers of greyish brown in a sea of green.

Tsetse flies and malarial mosquitoes have helped preserve the swamps from the intrusion of man; except for a few scattered pockets of River Bushmen, the vast swamps remain uninhabited. Because of the lack of distinctive landmarks it is almost impossible to walk for any distance without becoming hopelessly lost.

Despite an annual rate of evaporation that exceeds 2 metres, some of the delta waters re-converge in the south. In years of high rainfall the surplus waters reach Lake Ngami via the Nghabe River, and Lake Xau via the Botlele River. The future of the Okavango Swamps depends largely upon the policy to be adopted by the new Orapa Diamond Mine which will require about 11 megalitres of water daily. It is a complex and controversial issue, and one hopes that it will somehow be resolved without long-term detriment to the unique ecology of the swamps.

Concentrations of wild animals are also found in the Moremi Reserve bordering the Okavango Swamps, in the Chobe National Park in northern Botswana, and in the vicinity of the great Makarikari Pan between Francistown and Maun. The Makarikari Pan is a flat mud desert, devoid of vegetation and usually dry. In 1972, however, there were exceptionally good rains and the Pan was covered with a steel-grey sheet of water. The area is well known for its vast migratory herds of wildebeest, zebra and springbok, which rival those of the Serengeti plains in Tanzania.

West of the Transvaal, the Southern African plateau slopes gradually into the Kalahari basin. The Kalahari is only a semi-desert, since some form of vegetation covers almost the entire area. Rainfall is very low, rarely exceeding 12 centimetres a year, but when it does rain, moisture is absorbed by plants which in turn provide nourishment for the nomadic animals of the desert.

Gemsbok, springbok, kudu, wildebeest and hartebeest traverse vast tracts of desert each year, moving from one pasture to the next. The Kalahari Bushmen likewise live a nomadic life. Their specialized metabolism, the result of centuries of acclimatization and adjustment to their harsh environment, enables them to survive a life of appalling hardship.

Most of the Kalahari lies in Botswana and is virtually inaccessible, but the Kalahari Gemsbok National Park, in the south-east corner, in South Africa, consists of typical desert terrain: dry riverbeds, lined with hardy acacias, and dunes scattered with shrub, thorn-trees and tsamma melons. Temperatures vary enormously, especially in winter when the days are warm but the nights bitterly cold. During the summer months it is uncomfortably hot.

Besides the larger animals, I found the ground squirrels and sociable weaver birds in this beautiful national park particularly interesting. The squirrels, attractive little creatures, gregarious and always curious, pop in and out of their holes, scampering along the ground in search of food, every now and then standing up on their hind legs to look about.

The name of the sociable weaver birds defines their chief activity: the building of their enormous communal nests. These are lined and woven with grass and small twigs and look like miniature haystacks into which holes have been driven. They usually last for many years and provide a refuge for other birds besides the weavers. Sometimes the weight becomes too great for the tree to bear and the nest tumbles to the ground, perhaps taking with it a torn-off branch or even uprooting the tree itself.

South West Africa covers a huge area. It is a land of great beauty and vivid colour.

The Namib Desert, stretching for 1 600 kilometres along the coast and with a width of 60 – 160 kilometres, is one of the oldest deserts in the world, and one of the least explored. Its ferocious climate and huge, forbidding sand dunes are effective barriers against man's intrusion, and with the exception of diamonds, the Namib has as yet yielded few of its secrets. The annual rainfall rarely exceeds 10 centimetres and hence the vegetation that exists is scant and seasonal. Along the west coast the cold Benguela current causes mist, but not rain.

The Namib gives way in the east to the escarpment and the plateau which is mountainous, and fertile in places. Most of this highland of South West Africa consists of open grassland interspersed with low bush. Water is scarce and valuable. Wild animals are encouraged and protected on many of the farms, especially browsing antelopes, which help prevent the bush from overwhelming the heavily grazed pastures upon which depend large herds of sheep and cattle.

In the south, the Great Fish River snakes its winding way through a fissure over 300 metres deep in the rocky crust.

The Fish River Canyon is surpassed in grandeur only by the Grand Canyon in Arizona. From the edge of the steep walls, a magnificent panorama is revealed. My first sight of the canyon was at dawn, when the rising sun tinted the walls a soft, alluring pink. Later, as the day progressed, the colours hardened to a deep yellow and finally became a uniform greyish brown, contrasting with the green, stagnant waters of the river far below.

The famous Etosha Pan in the north is one of the finest game parks in Africa. The Pan itself, like the Makarikari, is flat and devoid of vegetation, but the surrounding grasslands and bush are a haven for many species of animals and birds. It is wild, hot, and very dusty; this is the real Africa where nature reigns supreme, and where man is but a passing guest.

1   A peaceful sunset at the Cape Peninsula. Bartholomew Diaz, the Portuguese navigator, was the first European to round the Cape, in 1488. A treacherous coast with strong currents and a rocky, jagged shoreline, the Peninsula was first known as the "Cape of Storms". King John of Portugal, however, soon appreciated the significance of the Cape for opening up the sea route to India and renamed it the "Cape of Good Hope".

2   One of the world's most famous landmarks and a welcome sight to generations of sailors: Table Mountain, rising to a height of 1 086 metres, stands majestically facing a great bay. First climbed in 1503 by Antonia da Saldanha, the mountain provided a rich source of timber as well as water for the early European settlers. Cape Town, founded by Jan van Riebeeck in 1652, lies within the shadow of the dramatic mountain cliffs.

3   Lion's Head seen from the scattered boulders of Oudekraal along Victoria Drive. A prominent peak flanking Table Mountain, it was for many years used as a position from which signals were given to passing ships, and a flagpole stood at the highest point. The signalman lived at Kloof Nek and used a ladder to make his daily ascent to the summit.

4   Black-backed Gulls (*Larus dominicanus*), are common sight along the
    south and west coasts of Southern Africa. Notorious scavengers, these
    gulls are a scourge to sea-bird colonies, where they will swoop down to
    seize either egg or chick. One of their favourite foods is a sand-mussel
    known as Donax, which they find in shallow waters. In order to break the
    mussels open, the gulls drop the shells from a height to splinter
    on the rocks.

5   A Cape Coloured family cottage in the foothills of the Swartberg
    Mountains.

6   Grey Herons (*Ardea cinerea*) and little Egrets (*Egretta garzetta*), at rest
    in the early hours of the day on a jetty along the south-western coast.

7   Rising above autumnal vineyards in the Helshoogte Pass, the majestic
    Wemmershoek Mountain holds court between a fringe of wispy clouds.

8   Linked by only one road to the outside world, the Coloured village of
    Wupperthal shelters in a verdant, fertile valley surrounded by the rust-
    coloured mountains of the Cedarberg range. The hamlet owes its origin
    to a Rhenish Mission founded at the site in 1830.

9   The thatched, white-washed cottages at Wupperthal are laid out in
    neat rows against the hillside on the bank of the Tra-Tra River. Peaches,
    grapes, figs, Rooibos tea and tobacco are among the crops grown in
    the valley, while above the cottages, are pens for donkeys, pigs,
    sheep, goats and a multitude of chickens.

4

5

6

8

9

10 Wupperthal is a peaceful place, with an atmosphere somehow reminiscent of the nineteenth century. The village has retained its unique charm and character, partly as a result of its relative inaccessibility and isolation and partly because the small community wishes to accept from the modern world only essentials while rejecting many of its materialistic values.

11 The rich colours of autumn highlight the beauty of the Jonkershoek Valley near Stellenbosch. The "Twins" (1 494 metres), the highest and most dramatic peaks of the surrounding mountain range, stand like lofty sentinels guarding the secrets of the Eerste River with its cascading waterfalls and thick forests of oak and pine.

12 In the remoter parts of the Cape mountains a Coloured family travelling by donkey-cart blends in harmony with the uncluttered landscape; a poignant reminder of an age when travel was a leisurely business.

13 Thick Protea bushes and the rounded slopes of the Riviersonderend Mountains near Villiersdorp catch the last soft rays of the sun.

14 Good rains and a full river: The Breë River winds its way through fertile plains beneath the Langeberg Mountains near Swellendam.

15 It is dry and hot in the Karroo. An endless expanse of hostile, barren soil, dotted with clumps of Renosterbos, lies beneath the blue canopy of the sky. In the glare of the day it is a bleak landscape, but as evening approaches the setting sun suffuses the scene with glowing colour.

16 Although hardly any surface water exists in the Karroo and rainfall is scant, the windpumps introduced in 1885 tap resources of water deep below the ground. This makes sheep-ranching a practical proposition. Often the immediate vicinity of a waterpump is like an oasis where green grass and trees flourish. It is in such surroundings that one may see the beautiful walnut tree (*Juglans nigra*) with blossoms of bright, dazzling yellow.

17 From the Kranskop heights in the Mountain Zebra National Park near Cradock, a superb view unfolds of the Bankberg Mountains. In the early hours of a wintry morning, a thick mist clings to the valley floor, and the mountain ridges rise above it like islands in a sea of white.

18 The Little Karroo, a 100-kilometre-wide plain, lies between the Outeniqua and Swartberg Mountains. Perennial mountain streams and a dry climate provide conditions ideal for large-scale ostrich farming. This commenced in the 1860's and for years fortunes fluctuated according to the whims of fashion. Today prices are good, and some 25 000 birds thrive on fields of lucerne in the many large farms of the area.

17

18

21

22

23

19   The muddy waters of the Orange River reflect the sky in the glare of midday. The Orange flows 2 000 kilometres from the high Lesotho plateau to the Atlantic coast at Alexander Bay. Together with its main tributaries, the Vaal and the Caledon, it forms the most important river system in South Africa. To the Bushmen and Hottentots it was known simply as "The Great River". The present name was bestowed by the explorer Captain Gordon in 1779, in honour of the Prince of Orange.

20   Springtime in Namaqualand — the semi-desert landscape, dry and barren for ten months each year, suddenly comes alive in a profusion of orange *Ursinia*.

21   The Valley of Desolation near Graaff-Reinet: the spectacular result of natural erosion. Jagged teeth of crumbling red sandstone stand out from the main massif in a weird jumble of shape and size. From the mountain summit, at 1 405 metres, these strange rocks provide a dramatic contrast to the distant Karroo Plain.

22   From the summit of the Spitskop, north of Knysna, the Tsitsikama Forest covers the mountain slopes with a dark blanket of vegetation.

23   Indigenous trees in the foreground, Australian Eucalyptus behind and Monterey Pines in the distance: a cross-section of the Tsitsikama Forest. Only 1 per cent of South Africa is covered with forest and the greater part lies between George and Humansdorp. For many years the great indigenous trees were cut down at random; ancient hardwood was especially prized for ship building and for railway sleepers. Serious control began in 1886 and denuded areas were planted with exotics, but effective action came too late to restore the Tsitsikama to its original grandeur.

24 In the deep gorge cut by the Groot River near Plettenberg Bay, lush tropical vegetation thrives in the humid climate. Wild Banana trees (*Strelitzia alba*) flourish in these surroundings.

25 A wild Hibiscus (*H. tiliaceus*) displays a wondrous crown of yellow petals. This is a small shrub that occurs along the coasts of southern Natal and the Transkei. There are some 40 different species of Hibiscus in Southern Africa and all have brilliantly coloured flowers.

26 *Androcymbium striatum*, a wild liliaceous plant found only in the Eastern Transvaal and in Swaziland. The name *Androcymbium* literally means "a boat-full of stamens" and refers to the prominent stamens, each of which is held by a large, white, boat-shaped bract. About 30 other species of *Androcymbium* occur throughout Southern Africa.

27 "Pin Cushion" Proteas (*Leucospermum cordifolium*) adorn the Cape mountain slopes.

28 Wild *Ursinia* in the fields near Darling.

29 A huge Outeniqua Yellowwood tree (*Podocarpus falcatus*), its branches hung with silvery lichen (*Usnea*), in the green depths of the Groot River Valley. The steep cliffs of the gorge act as a barrier to the rays of the sun and cast strong shadows along the valley floor. It is a world of mysterious twilight, pierced at intervals by shafts of sunlight.

30 A Xhosa hut has one entrance and one tiny window. Inside, there is a place in the middle for a fire to provide warmth and a means for cooking. When the weather is fine, a fire is kindled outside and the three-legged iron cooking-pot is placed over the embers. On one side of each hut there is usually a small stock pen, fenced in for protection against marauders and predators.

25 ▲   ▼ 27   26 ▲   ▼ 28

30

31

31 A group of African huts in Pondoland surround a central enclosure that is used as a stock pen. These round huts consist of a framework of wooden poles, with wattle branches woven between. Both exterior and interior surfaces are plastered with mud. The roofs are lined with wattle brush and thatched with grass.

32 The Xhosa are a sociable people and there is always a lively chatter in and around the kraals.

33 The Umzimvubu River flows between two thickly forested ridges, known as the "Gates of St. John", before it reaches the sea near Port St. Johns on the Wild Coast.

34 A Xhosa mother, with baby wrapped securely on her back, puffs away contentedly at her pipe.

35 A coy little girl steals a glance at the intruder.

36 Xhosa girls can carry enormous loads on their heads. Sometimes, as in this case, a helping hand is needed to position the pile of wattle wood on the head of the carrier, but once in place it is carried, often for many miles, with a superb balance. This wood is used in the construction of the simple huts, and is woven around a circular framework of stakes.

37 Rounding up cattle on horseback; a common sight in the Transkei where it is the responsibility of the men to see to the welfare of livestock while their women in the kraals attend to domestic chores.

38 By wearing a rough skirt fixed above the bosom and the traditional folded turban on her head, this Xhosa woman reveals that she is married.

39 A Xhosa woman with painted face displays her arms brightly decorated
with bead bracelets. These are fitted tightly, one next to the other.
If with age she puts on weight, they could cause great discomfort; for
once in place, it is the custom that they should never be removed.

40 Homeward bound from the day's pasture. The Xhosa are a pastoral
people, whose wealth is measured in terms of livestock; hence their
animals are tended with lavish care.

41 A young Xhosa maiden in the warm evening sunlight. Only when she
is married will tribal custom compel her to cover her bare bosom
with a garment, to signify her new status in life.

42 In the years before initiation into manhood by the Ukwalusa circumcision ceremony, young Xhosa boys live a carefree, happy life. One of the few responsibilities is to tend the family's livestock—an important task in a rural community.

43 Laden donkeys on the road to Port St. Johns carry provisions from a nearby trading store to a distant kraal.

44 Known to the local Africans as "Esikhaleni" (Place of the Sound), the "Hole in the Wall" is a prominent feature of the Wild Coast. A massive island cliff rising precipitously above the turbulent surf, it is named for the great gash that pierces its flank, allowing the ocean swell to pound through the cavern with a mighty roar.

45 A bastion of reddish rock, known to the Pondo as "Mlengani" (Hanging One), and to Europeans as "Execution Rock", dominates the valley of the Umgazi River (Place of Blood) — so named for the savage tribal battles that occurred here in former years).

44

45

48

49

50

46 A mischievous group of African children in the Transkei near
Ngcwanguba. Two of them carry long "knopkieries", a favourite but
dangerous weapon in the hands of older boys.

47 Three little Xhosa boys with their mother. The Xhosa usually have
large families and each new addition is warmly welcomed. Family ties are
strong and meaningful from the start and remain so for life.

48 Destruction of the natural forest and the fierce action of sun, wind and
water have caused extensive erosion and rendered large areas of the
Transkei useless for cultivation. Deep crevices in the earth mark
the paths of tempestuous seasonal streams.

49 A sweeping Transkeian landscape of green grassland dotted with kraals.
In the distance, a mountain ridge terminates the level plain.

50 Sweets for a little girl—the joy of giving is matched by the evident
joy of receiving—along the road to Coffee Bay.

51 A Xhosa woman with her traditional long-stemmed pipe.

52 Xhosa women usually carry their possessions on their heads. Even an umbrella can be wedged into the bundle. The weight hardly impedes movement, and the constant attention to balance helps to develop the erect carriage and graceful walk possessed by these women.

53 Donkey-cart on the highway.

54 Among the Xhosa the man's role within his family is paramount; he is the master. The husband, comfortably mounted on horseback, with his wife striding in front on foot, graphically illustrates this custom.

53

54

58

59

55 In the Transkeian plains trees are few and far between. Wood is a necessity, however, both as a building material and as fuel, and sometimes it has to be collected from far afield. This is a task for the women of the tribe who walk many miles, balancing on their heads huge bundles of sticks bound with cord.

56 A picture typical of the rural life in Pondoland: a small field of maize and a number of African huts protectively surrounding the communal stock pen. Maize, meat and milk are the staple foods, and life revolves around their bounty.

57 A Xhosa woman, her face painted with white clay, rests beneath a shady Eucalyptus near the Great Kei River.

58 Seen from the summit of Cathedral Peak (3 005 metres), the Drakensberg Mountains appear as a high plateau, with jagged cliffs falling away steeply to the rolling foothills far below.

59 Beneath a 1 200-metre mantle of basaltic lava the Drakensberg Mountains consist of richly coloured layers of sandstone. The many caves in these softer strata were once a haven for mountain Bushmen, and their rock paintings are vivid records of their chief pursuits.

60 From the valley of the Mlambonja River a great mountain ridge, culminating in Cathedral Peak, reaches towards the sky. The lofty Bell (2 922-metres), standing apart from the other peaks, is easily recognizable by its distinctive shape.

61 Evening shadows descend upon a peaceful mountain landscape at the foot of the Sani Pass.

62 The splendour of the mighty Ampitheatre at awakening day. Sunlight highlights the ripples of the Tugela River which flows at ease after a tortuous, cascading journey from the heights of Mont-aux-Sources, the "Mountain of Springs".

63 The summits of Cathkin Peak and Champagne Castle shimmer in the midday sun.

64 A shepherd drives his flock along a dusty mountain road in the Barkly Pass and passing motorists must surrender their right of way.

65 A lonely path in the Drakensberg foothills.

63

64

68

69

66 A fertile valley in the Drakensberg area with the towering summits of the Bell and Cathedral Peak obscured by a veil of cloud.

67 Bearing remarkable resemblance to the map of Southern Africa, a cleft in the mountain ridge near Cathedral Peak, frames a section of the Drakensberg, including the summits of Cathkin Peak and Champagne Castle.

68 Precipitous cliffs rising above the Sani Pass form the edge of the high Lesotho Plateau.

69 The bleak and cold Lesotho Plateau, at 2 750 metres, seems an anticlimax after the hair-raising twists and turns of the Sani Pass. Except for coarse, hardy grass this plain is devoid of vegetation, and stone is used as the building material in the local African kraals.

70   Basuto boys in a sandstone cave that once served as studio to a
      Bushman artist. Brightly coloured blankets are draped across the shoulders
      in traditional fashion. Though decorative, they also serve as a
      protection against the biting cold that grips the Lesotho highlands for
      much of the year.

71   An African homestead near Teyateyaneng. The circular wall is
      plastered with a thick layer of brown clay to help trap the warmth
      within, while the overlapping, conical roof is reinforced with layers of
      finely plaited grass.

72   A Woolly-necked Stork (*Dissoura episcopus*), a skilled fisherman with
      razor-sharp, pointed beak, holds aloft a frog it has just speared. A
      migratory bird, this stork is often found in the vicinity of waterholes in
      which abound its favourite food: small fish, frogs and insects. —
      At Mkuze in Zululand.

73   During the winter, when water is scarce, herds of Impala (*Aepyceros
      melampus*) file down to the Msinga Waterhole in the Mkuze Reserve.
      Constantly on the alert for danger, the graceful creatures bend
      down to quench their thirst.

74   A Nyala bull (*Tragelaphus angasii*) at the Msinga Waterhole in the
      Mkuze Reserve. This elegant, gregarious antelope has a limited
      distribution in Southern Africa, but is fairly common in the game reserves
      of Zululand, where it thrives in thick bush country, rarely far from water.

75   The horny armour-plating of a log-like Crocodile (*Crocodylus niloticus*)
      protrudes above the muddy waters of a Mkuze waterhole. As if in an
      hypnotic trance, the watchful reptile awaits an unsuspecting prey.

72

73

74

76 A Hammerhead (*Scopus umbretta*), showing off the profile that explains his name. The brown crest, of the same colour as the feathers of the body, can be neither raised nor lowered at will. This curious bird is fairly common throughout Southern Africa, and is usually found in pairs, in the vicinity of water; wading through the shallows, the Hammerhead searches for small frogs and fish.

77 One of the most beautiful game Reserves in Southern Africa, Ndumu is situated in north-eastern Natal, near the border of Mozambique. Primeval indigenous forest, thick bushland and graceful fever trees surround a series of reed-fringed lakes fed by the seasonal overflow of the Pongola and Usutu Rivers.

78 One way to face the world is to turn your back on it, but if you do, it is best not to leave a reflection in the water, even if you are Big Game.

79 After the Elephant, the White or square-lipped Rhinoceros (*Ceratotherium simum*) is the world's largest land mammal. Named "white" from the Afrikaans word "wyd", meaning wide, this massive beast stands nearly 2 metres high and weighs more than 2 721 kilograms. Whereas the smaller "black" cousin browses habitually on low bush, the "white" species is essentially a grazer, consuming vast quantities of grass during the twilight hours and at night. Once prolific throughout much of Southern Africa, both hunter and poacher have sadly reduced their numbers. The White Rhino is today mainly confined to the game reserves of Zululand, although successful efforts have been made to reintroduce them to several sanctuaries elsewhere.

80 Burchell's Zebra (*Equus burchelli*) are the most numerous members of this genus. Sociable animals, they are, however, highly strung and contagiously nervous. At the slightest disturbance, the zebra throws back his head with a shrill neigh and charges off into the bush. Only when completely reassured will he return to drink in peace.

81 At a waterhole in Hluhluwe, a group of female Kudu (*Tragelaphus strepsisceros*) timidly approach for a drink. In days gone by, due to the high quality of their meat, these attractive antelopes were mercilessly shot, in many areas to a point of extermination. Today, more sense fortunately prevails, and their distribution is once again widespread.

82 A Nyala cow at Mkuze steps daintily across a sunny glade. The female bears little resemblance to the handsome bull; she is much smaller, has no horns and her coat is a soft reddish brown, lined with vertical white stripes.

83 Mirrored in the glassy water of the Msinga Waterhole at Mkuze, two Impala, oblivious of possible danger, enjoy a long, cool drink.

81

82

84   The ecstasies of a mud bath: a Warthog (*Phacochoerus aethiopicus*) revels
     in the mire. Not exactly favoured with good looks these wild pigs make up
     for this shortcoming with an abundance of character. As they are
     shortsighted creatures, it is often possible to approach downwind quite
     close to a family group before the "paterfamilias" detects something amiss.
     With a snort he sets off at a trot with family in tow behind, all with tails
     erect like miniature flagpoles. A warthog's courage has to be seen to be
     believed. Recklessly, and with total disregard for consequences, the plucky
     pig will charge the source of danger whether large or small, often
     with surprising results.

85   A gathering of Blue Wildebeest (*Connochaetes taurinus*) in the shallow
     reaches of the Msinga Waterhole. Somewhat ungainly in appearance,
     these shaggy animals can move with remarkable energy. If they are
     surprised at the waterhole, all hell breaks loose. Snorting with indignation
     they beat a noisy retreat, churning the water with their hooves,
     before stampeding to the safety of the bush.

86   White Rhino mother and calf, at Umfolozi. Rudely disturbed from
     the pleasures of a roll in the mud, they strike a tank-like pose with horns
     upraised and sniff the threatened air.

87   Hadeda Ibis (*Bostrychia hagedash*) perched on the branches of a
     dead tree. Relatively inconspicuous while at rest, when in flight they
     announce their whereabouts with a piercing cry: "ha-de-dah, ha-ha".

88 Traditional beehive huts merge with more modern dwellings in a Zululand landscape.

89 A young Vervet Monkey (*Cercopithecus aethiops*) in the Kruger Park. These neatly marked primates are common in many parts of Southern Africa, especially in heavily wooded areas. They usually travel in orderly troops that can sometimes number up to 50 members. They search the woodland pastures for birds' eggs and nestlings, fruit, nuts and seeds, supplementing their diet with an occasional raid on a farmer's field of maize.

90 An inquisitive grey Meerkat (*Suricata suricatta*). These endearing little animals, common throughout the Southern African veld, live in holes burrowed in the earth. During the early morning and late evening they can often be seen scampering along the ground, hunting for insects or small edible succulents. Every now and then they stop, sit bolt upright on their haunches, and peer about with a keen, searching eye.

91 A Chameleon (*Chamaeleo dilepsis*) patiently awaits a tasty insect. Though slow-moving and non-poisonous, this curious reptile is an expert marksman; with split-second timing and lightning speed it unleashes its long, coiled, sticky tongue at an unsuspecting prey. When alarmed, the Chameleon puffs up its throat menacingly and emits an angry hiss.

92 A Sibaca dance near Piggs Peak in the Swazi mountains. Teams of dancers compete with each other for the prize of a fatted calf. With flamboyant gyrations and a fast rhythmic tempo, the participants elicit an excited response from the spectators.

93 Dressed in gowns of brightly patterned calico and wearing the traditional hairpiece, two Swazi women brave the gloom of a rainy day.

94 A panoramic vista of outstanding grandeur: the Blyde River Canyon in the north-eastern Transvaal. The distant river snakes along a tortuous passage 760 metres below the massive cliffs of the "Three Rondavels".

95 With regal nonchalance a Serval (*Felis serval*) reclines in the warmth of the evening sun. This elegant cat has a powerful, streamlined body and is an adept nocturnal hunter.

96 From a grassy hillock in the Kruger Park, a magnificent bull Waterbuck (*Kobus ellipsiprymnus*) surveys the thorny veld. These antelopes usually graze in herds near water-courses and flood plains where the grass is lush. If danger threatens they make for the water.

97 An Elephant (*Loxodonta africana*), ambles down a well-worn track in the Kruger Park. As far back as 1884 President Kruger advocated the establishment of game sanctuaries in the Northern Transvaal, where wild life would be able to recover from the depredations of hunting, but only in 1898 was the Sabie Game Reserve established. After the Anglo-Boer War in 1902, the Reserve was re-proclaimed by Lord Milner, and Colonel James Stevenson Hamilton was appointed as first Game Warden, a post he held with great distinction until his retirement in 1946. The Borders of the Reserve were subsequently increased by the inclusion of private land between the Sabie and Letaba Rivers. Finally, in 1926, a National Parks Board was appointed and the Reserve was proclaimed as the Kruger National Park.

98 A view from the heights of the Wolkberg (Cloud Mountain) near Tzaneen.

99 The waters of the Treurrivier, just before its confluence with the Blyde River, hurtle down in a froth of dazzling white foam.

100 Bourke's Potholes, a curious sculpture moulded by the Blyde River.

101　A Ground Hornbill (*Bucorvus leadbeateri*) in the Northern Transvaal Lowveld, flutters long eyelashes and peers down its broad beak as if to ask "What's next"? Small groups of these birds spend most of the day searching for insects, reptiles and rodents. At night they roost in trees.

102　In the mountains above Pilgrim's Rest the air is crisp and cool after summer rains.

103　In the Gorongoza National Park a herd of Hippopotamus (*Hippopotamus amphibius*) wallow in a shallow lake. Every few moments a huge head emerges above the floating mass, to emit a grunt and open its mouth in a gaping yawn.

104　At Gorongoza, beneath the fan-like fronds of the tall Borassus Palms, a young elephant makes his way across the Savanna, pausing here and there to uproot a tasty shoot.

105 The King of Beasts (*Panthero leo*) rests from the fierce heat of day beneath a shady palm.

106 A tiny Steenbuck (*Raphicerus campestris*) peers from a sea of high grass.

107 With a backdrop of lowering storm-clouds, the tropical vegetation of Gorongoza is illuminated by the last rays of the setting sun.

108 Sunset at Gorongoza.

109 Colourful earthenware jars line the roadside in neat rows, watched over by three little salesmen. Near Lundi in Rhodesia.

110 The Lundi River, so named from a corruption of the African name "Runde", meaning "a river liable to great floods", is here spanned by a low-level bridge. In summer a heavy downpour will suddenly transform the placid river into a wide, muddy torrent.

105

106

109

110

111   A lonely African hut in the arid bushveld of eastern Rhodesia. This is a hard, stony land, plagued by drought for most of the year, where the raising of crops is a constant struggle.

112   An African kraal in the hills south of Umtali.

113   The Matopos: a weird landscape of isolated boulders and crenellated koppies. Erosion has gradually worn away the mantle of softer rock to expose bizarre formations of hard plutonic granite.

114   Sable Antelope (*Hippotragus niger*) in the Matopos National Park. The Sable's distinctive features are its huge scimitar-shaped horns, white facial markings and a shiny black coat with tufted mane.

115   Portrait of a Chacma Baboon (*Papio ursinus*). These intelligent primates, common in hill country throughout Southern Africa, travel in troops under the leadership of one or more dominant males. They feed, during the daytime, upon wild fruits and berries, roots, insects, scorpions, and small mammals. Occasionally they raid a farmer's crop of maize or wheat. In the Cape Peninsula a local troop has even taken to fishing for mussels from the rocky beaches. Baboons are very protective towards their females and young. In the event of danger, the adult males will often fight a desperate rearguard action to enable others to escape to safety.

116   The mysterious ruined city of Zimbabwe, near Fort Victoria. For long a source of endless speculation and controversy, it is now generally accepted that the mass of stone buildings are walled settlements built for defence purposes by successive generations of the African Karanga Rozvi tribal group. None of the buildings appear to have been roofed and it is likely that the familiar type of African hut made from mud and thatch sheltered within the stone enclosures. Nearly one million chippings were used in the construction of the "Temple", a massive circular construction that probably housed the palace of the Great Chief. The strange conical tower within was perhaps symbolic of his authority and status.

117   The "Acropolis" at Zimbabwe: a huge granite koppie that forms a perfect natural fortress. Stone chippings were used to build a series of walls and platforms around existing boulders.

20

21

118 A cloud of spray obscures the mighty Zambezi River as it plunges into the gorge far below with a thunderous roar.

119 The Victoria Falls: one of the natural wonders of the world. Along a front more than 1 km wide, an endless sheet of water pours over the precipice, at the rate of 550 megalitres per minute.

120 The Shiré River in southern Malawi, in full flood after heavy summer rains.

121 From a clearing in the Malawi bush, an African child stares wistfully at a passing car.

122 Seen from a rocky tree-lined cove, the serene waters of Lake Malawi glisten in the morning sun. This great lake extends for 580 kilometres along the eastern flank of Malawi, and marks the southernmost arm of the Great Rift Valley.

123 The Okavango Swamps in north-western Botswana — a huge expanse of untamed Africa. The great Okavango River, emerging from the Angola highlands, is split into a maze of countless streams, forming a vast inland delta. Reeds and papyrus thickets hem the waters, and during the seasonal floods, small forested islands provide the only landmarks in the marshy wilderness.

124 A "Lily Trotter" (*Actophilornis africanus*) in the Okavango Swamps steps lightly across the floating reeds in search of insects and choice lily seeds.

125 A massive termite hill on Chief's Island bears silent witness to the industry of countless tiny workers.

126 Striding out with long, powerful legs, an Ostrich foursome (*Struthio camelus*) makes speed across the Nxai Pan.

127 A flock of Ostriches competing in an African Derby.

123

124

126

127

128 From their lofty perch in a wild fig tree, a pair of majestic Fish-eagles (*Haliaetus vocifer*) keep a watchful eye on the surrounding swamps. These birds, which feed on fish and small mammals, usually hunt in mated pairs, swooping with lightning speed to seize their prey with strong, curved talons. From time to time, their wild and piercing cry — "kue kue kuekuekue" — shatters the brooding silence of the lonely swamps.

129 Seen from the air, the vast unfettered swamps of the Okavango delta stretch from one horizon to the other. Here and there, tall Borassus Palms (*Hyhaene ventricosa*) show as glints of silver in an ocean of green.

130 A Lilac-breasted Roller (*Coracias caudata*), at rest on a thornbush in northern Botswana. The name "Roller" is derived from the rollicking, noisy aerobatics that the male bird engages in while courting.

131 A small group of Puku (*Kobus vardoni*) in the marshy flood-plains of the Chobe River.

132 Buffalo (*Syncerus caffer*) graze peacefully near the banks of the Chobe River. These sturdy beasts converge on the grass-covered flood-plains in the early morning and late afternoons. During the heat of the day they usually rest in the shade of dense bush.

133 A Batawana family group near the Boro River. The Mokoro, a dugout craft hewn from a single log of wood, is pulled up on the bank.

134 Musical interlude at Txatxaba camp on the Boro River in the heart of the Okavango Swamps. The finger instrument is known as the "Selikani", while the string accompaniment is a "Tsworoworo".

135 As the sun sinks low in the sky, the waters of the Thamalekane River, at the edge of the Okavango delta, are transformed into molten gold.

136 In the Kalahari Desert, a Bushman, clad in a loin-cloth and with bow in hand, surveys an expanse of orange dunes. The enlarged posterior, a condition known as steatopygia, is a natural endowment which offsets the effects of prolonged famine. These remarkable people once roamed over large areas of Southern Africa, but the southward migration of Bantu tribes and the expansion of the Cape Colony forced the Bushmen into the inhospitable wastes of the Kalahari, where life is a constant struggle for survival.

137 The Bushmen of the Kalahari are great story-tellers. Old traditions and stories of the past are handed down to each successive generation by the elders of the tribe, who are held in high esteem.

138 A Bushman shelter is a temporary dwelling which provides shade from the heat of day and warmth from the bitter cold of night. Signs of increasing contact with the outside world are previously unknown items such as cloth and a metal bucket.

37

38

42

43

139 With bonneted infant clinging to her back, a woman of mixed descent visits a Bushman shelter. In the background, small skins, strips of meat, and tobacco leaves are hung out to dry.

140 A single Kokerboom (*Aloe dichotoma*) in a wide expanse of treeless desert.

141 In the Kalahari Gemsbok National Park, tufts of coarse grass and scattered Camel-thorn trees thrive in a harsh environment. Against the background of a dry riverbed and rising sand dunes, a Gemsbok (*Oryx gazella*) is well camouflaged. Because of the great scarcity of water, these animals seek nourishment from wild cucumbers, Tsamma melons and certain bulbs that store water within their husks.

142 A group of Springbok (*Antidorcas marsupialis*) in the stony veld of the Kalahari. These gregarious antelopes are well adjusted to desert life and can travel for great distances without need of water. The name derives from the curious jumping motion that is a characteristic: with head down and body arched they jump up to 3 metres into the air in a series of stiff-legged leaps.

143 A herd of Wildebeest kick up the soft sand with their hooves as they move in slow formation towards a cluster of shady Acacia trees. Blue Wildebeest, like the Gemsbok and Springbok, have adapted themselves well to the parched, semi-desert condition of the Kalahari.

144 A Ground Squirrel (*Xerus inauris*) poses for his portrait. These attractive
little creatures live in colonies of deep burrows. When they emerge
for food they scurry along the ground in search of seeds and small bulbs,
stopping every now and then to sit up erect and motionless, to
make sure the coast is clear.

145 On the fringe of the great Namib Desert in South West Africa
yellow dunes of shifting sand beneath an azure sky.

146 The "Mukurob", or "Finger of God", is an eroded tower of rock some
30 metres high. The head-piece of layered sandstone is joined to the main
pedestal of Karroo slate by a slender neck.

147 An old man gives rein to his horses as they trot briskly along a
dusty track near Koes.

148 The Great Fish River Canyon, a deep, spectacular gorge carved by
the unbridled forces of nature. Some 550 metres below, the Fish River
meanders towards its eventual confluence with the Orange River.

147

148

152

153

149   A diminutive Kokerboom clings precariously to a rocky ledge deep within the Fish River Canyon. Great boulders lie around in profusion to impede the progress of the weary climber. The steep walls of the canyon trap and reflect the heat of the sun, turning the valley floor into an inferno.

150   The Fish River twists and turns like a sluggish green serpent in the barren depths of the great canyon.

151   A flock of starlings in flight across the pink sky of dawn. — From Namutoni Fort in the Etosha Game Park.

152   Disturbed at the waterhole, a Giraffe (*Giraffa camelopardalis*) raises his long neck to observe the uninvited guest.

153   Large herds of Elephant roam the plains that border the vast Etosha Pan. A full-grown bull will eat up to 300 kilograms of food a day, a proportion of which, in the Etosha area, consists of bulbs, roots and tubers. These he digs out of the ground with his tusks, which sometimes splinter in the process.

154 An elegant Gemsbok strides across the Etosha plains, displaying its distinctive, symmetrical markings. When seen in complete profile, the long, tapered horns appear as one, which accounts for the fact that in former days this antelope was sometimes mistaken for the legendary unicorn.

155 A herd of Springbok in the sun-bleached Etosha grasslands.

156 Beneath the shady foliage of a thick thornbush, a Cheetah (*Acinonyx jubatus*) rests from the heat. Formerly well distributed over most of Southern Africa, their habitat today is restricted to the remote bushveld of the northern and eastern Transvaal, parts of Zululand, the Kalahari and South West Africa. In the Etosha Game Park they are fortunately still fairly numerous. The cheetah is reputed to be the fastest of all land mammals, attaining speeds of up to 90 kilometres an hour in the final sprint to achieve a kill.

157 Thorny scrub country with scattered Acacias is well suited to the Kudu. A bull with fine, lyre-shaped horns pauses for an instant before joining his cows in a dash for the thicket.

158 A Black Tree Agama (*Agama atricollis*), climbing the bark of an Acacia, suddenly stops to glance around with an inquisitive stare.

56

57

162

163

159 During the dry winter months in the Etosha Game Park, herds of Zebra congregate at waterholes to indulge themselves in the cool, refreshing water.

160 When a herd of elephant pass by, it is taken for granted by one and all that their's is the right of way.

161 Giraffe thrive in the open bushland of the Etosha Park where they browse on the leaves of the abundant Acacia trees. Palatable foliage is stripped from the upper branches of a tree by the combined use of a long flexible tongue, mobile upper lip and strong lower incisors.

162 A Zebra "mother-to-be" seems to enjoy the company of her attendants.

163 Namutoni Fort—a well-known landmark in the Etosha Game Park. Built by the Germans in 1901, it was attacked on 28th January 1904 by a force of some 500 Ovambo tribesmen. The tiny garrison of 7 men kept the besiegers at bay for a whole week before running out of ammunition. Under cover of night they succeeded in escaping and made their way to the main column of soldiers. Shortly afterwards the Fort was recaptured. Today Namutoni is a rest camp for visitors to the Park, but it still retains a romantic atmosphere reminiscent of the turbulent past.

164 The "Haunted Forest" near Okaukuejo: a copse of weird Moringa trees (*Moringa ovalifolia*). The contorted branches of these strange trees look like upturned roots grasping for nourishment. The Moringa is found only in South West Africa and usually grows on isolated ridges in mountainous areas.

165 His thirst slaked at last, a Gemsbok splashes his way through an Etosha waterhole to reach the opposite bank.

166 Like the aftermath of a devastating landslide, gigantic boulders cover the slopes of the Brandberg. These mountains rise dramatically out of the semi-desert plain to culminate in the Königstein peak (2 740 metres)—the highest summit in South West Africa.

167 In the Etosha Park, wherever water is to be found, wild life abounds.

168 Daintily spreading out his forelegs, a giraffe lowers his long neck to reach for an evening drink.

167

168

170

171

169 The "Vingerklip", south-west of Outjo, a remarkable thumb-shaped rock, completely dwarfs the approaching figures.

170 A huge sandstone boulder keeps lone vigil over an expanse of scrub and thornbush — Some 95 kilometres south-west of Outjo.

171 Flat-topped, eroded hills are the only landmarks in the featureless plateau that stretches to the distant horizon.

172 A tall Aloe (*Aloe littoralis*), protected by a base of spiky leaves, presents a joyful spectacle with its thousand tiny blooms of vivid red.

173 A Blister Beetle (*Mylabris*) feeds upon the limp petals of a yellow desert flower (*Tribulus terrestris*) growing beside a white, egg-shaped fungus (*Podaxis pistilaris*).

174 A tall termite hill points a gaunt finger 5 metres up into the air. —
Near Welwitschia.

175 Silhouetted against the evening sky, a flight of Pelicans (*Pelecanus onocrotalus*) wings its way to a nocturnal roost; a frequent sight along the misty coast of South West Africa.

176 The "White Lady", a famous rock painting reputed to be some 3 000 years old. This masterpiece of Bushman art was discovered in 1917 in a shallow cave within the Tsisab Gorge of the remote Brandberg Mountains.

178

179

181

177 Water is a rare sight in the Brandberg. Only in years of exceptional rainfall do the mountain springs gush forth their precious bounty. Green tufts of grass and brightly hued wild flowers cluster beside the flowing stream, while numerous shiny tadpoles wriggle about in the quiet pools.

178 A female Welwitschia plant (*Bainesii*) sprawls upon the desert floor in an untidy tangle of green leaves. This strange plant is a primitive coniferous gymnosperm which has adapted itself to the harsh climatic conditions of the Namib Desert. The flowers are pollinated by both wind and insects. In a mature plant, the leaves can reach 10 metres in length. The age of the largest plants is estimated to be about 2 000 years.

179 The "Petrified Forest" near Welwitschia: fossilized tree trunks some 200 million years old. These blackened logs were probably uprooted elsewhere and swept to their present site by an ancient flood. Thickly encrusted with mud, they successfully withstood decomposition, and with the passage of time the wooden grain was gradually replaced by silica.

180 A Damara woman in a long dress poses in the stony veld near Uis. The origins of the Damara people are obscure and its members differ in many ways from the other Bantu groups in South West Africa. Prior to German colonization, they were enslaved by the dominant Herero and Nama tribes.

181 Wearing the traditional turban of folded cloth and a woollen shawl, a Herero woman stops in her path to flash a cheerful smile at the photographer.

182 The mode of attire introduced by Christian Missionaries of the Victorian era has continued to this day as the height of fashion. Oblivious of the heat, Herero women proudly drape themselves in full-length, long-sleeved dresses of gaily patterned material.

183 North-west of Usakos, the imposing massif known as "Spitzkoppe" (1 700 metres in height) looms eerily above the plain.

184 A Sociable Weaver Bird (*Philetairus socius*) dives from the gigantic nest, atop a dead tree, that it shares with a flock of feathered cousins. These amazing nests are not used just for breeding, but serve as permanent residences. They last for many years, each successive generation effecting repairs as well as new additions to the intricate structure.

182

185 Resembling a suspended haystack, a Sociable Weaver Bird's nest dwarfs a trio of residents. The birds depart and return through the communal entrance with an interminable twittering chatter.

186 The "Kokerboom Forest", a congregation of tree aloes near Keetmanshoop. In English the name means "Quiver Tree". In former days, Hottentots and Bushmen used to cut the thick stems, remove the soft core of pith, and then cover one end with a piece of leather to fashion a perfect quiver for their poison arrows. Simon van der Stel, on his journey to the Copper Mountains of Namaqualand in 1685, was the first European to record his impressions of these strange plants and their interesting usage.

187 A brightly marked Rock Agama (*Agama atra*) basks in the sun atop a smooth boulder. These insectivorous lizards have the habit, when disturbed, of bobbing their heads up and down in a most comical manner.

188 The Black-backed Jackal (*Canis mesomelas*) is common in most regions of Southern Africa. Besides feeding on small mammals and birds, it is also partial to carrion, and is thus a useful scavenger in the bush.

189 Two subsidiary waterfalls join the main stream of the Orange River as it races through a deep ravine below the Augrabies Falls. The great granite trench, carved by the furious action of the Orange, extends for 10 kilometres and has an average depth of 160 metres.

190 With a mighty roar, the great Orange River hurtles over the narrow lip of the Augrabies Falls.

191 Poised like statuettes, a group of Grey Herons greet the chilly advent of a misty morning.

192 As twilight descends upon the still waters of Rondevlei, a flock of Lesser Flamingo (*Phoenicopterus minor*) wade through the shallows, their bills skimming the surface in a methodical search for algae.

90

197

198

193 "Groot Constantia", one of the most beautiful and the best known of all Cape Dutch mansions. Simon van der Stel was granted the site by the Dutch East India Company in 1685, and he built the Manor House soon after his appointment as first Governor of the Cape, in 1692. Extensive alterations and additions were made by a subsequent owner, Hendrik Cloete, during the 1780's. Among these were the wide, embellished gables and lofty thatched roof that are the outstanding features of the house.

194 The "Kruithuis" or Arsenal at Stellenbosch was constructed in 1777 for the storage of gunpowder. It is a solid building with an unusual vaulted roof, designed as a precaution against the hazard of fire. On one of the stout walls, the monogram of the Dutch East India Company: "V.G.O.C.", is clearly imprinted.

195 "Schoongezicht", a gracious Cape Dutch dwelling in a superb setting. Against the backdrop of the Simonsberg Mountains, it lies surrounded by the fertile fields of Ida's Valley.
The house dates from the early 1800's, while the main gable was built in 1814 by Hendrik Cloete, similar in style to the one at Groot Constantia.

196 "Old Nektar" as it stands today was built in 1814, on a site that was originally granted by the Dutch East India Company to two freed slaves, Marquart and Jan van Ceylon.
It is well known for what is considered to be the first example in the Cape of a neo-classical gable on a small façade.
The house stands in a magnificent position, surrounded by mountains, near the head of the Jonkershoek Valley.

197 A Cape Sugarbird (*Promerops cafer*) perched in the branches of a Silvertree (*Leucadendron argentium*) on the lower slopes of Table Mountain.

198 Viewed from the flat summit of Table Mountain, Lion's Head and the timber-clad slopes of Signal Hill divide Cape Town in two.

199 The "Fairest Cape"— a view from the top of Table Mountain, looking south towards Cape Point.

200 Van Riebeeck named Hout Bay for the abundance of wood found in the locality. The rough mountainous terrain, however, proved an obstacle in transporting the timber to the Dutch Settlement in Cape Town. Today, the sheltered bay is the centre of the flourishing and prosperous fishing industry.

201 At the southernmost tip of the Peninsula, a steep cliff plunges into the restless sea: this is Cape Point. Beyond lies only the empty Atlantic Ocean.

NOTES

My wife Janet and I first came to South Africa in 1968 after four years spent in Kenya, where we were married. Well attuned to the magnetic atmosphere of the wilds of Africa after many extensive travels, we were delighted when the opportunity eventually arose for us to travel south to explore a land of wide new horizons.

Even with a lively imagination, it is always hard to picture a new country before arrival. We knew that South Africa was a land of enormous economic and agricultural potential, with fast-spreading, modern cities and flourishing industries, and we were, of course, aware of the topical problems associated with the contentious race policies. But we did not realize, at first, the amazing variety and contrast that exist for those addicted, like ourselves, to the wilder trails of Africa.

Though circumstances dictated our residence and participation in city life, we have used every opportunity to explore the natural beauty of the country.

While in South Africa we lived in Johannesburg and Cape Town, and from these two centres we started on many travels. Setting out from Johannesburg, we covered the northern and eastern Transvaal, Natal, Lesotho, Swaziland, Botswana, Rhodesia, Moçambique and Malawi, while from Cape Town we explored the Cape mountains and coast, the Karroo, the Garden Route and the Transkei in the east, as well as Namaqualand and South West Africa in the north.

Distances are vast in Africa. To someone living in Europe, a journey of 300 kilometres represents a long, frustrating day's drive through an almost endless succession of built-up areas where traffic jams are part of daily life. Flying high above Southern Africa, in a modern jet, one is struck by the great open spaces that stretch as far as the eye can see. Here and there, small dots and symmetrical patterns on the ground show evidence of man and his activities, but the main centres of population are separated one from the other by scores, and sometimes hundreds, of kilometres. When one travels by road, these impressions are confirmed, and one can often motor from one horizon to the next without seeing a human being. Three hundred kilometres in these circumstances represents about three hours of smooth driving on roads where the sight an oncoming car is almost a welcome diversion.

Our first journey out from Johannesburg was to Swaziland, a week before that country's independence. With the inexperience of the uninitiated, we relied upon a small-scale map and hopelessly misjudging the distance and condition of the road, we found ourselves at dusk driving along a rough, muddy track, made dangerous by torrential rain, towards Goedgegun. We eventually arrived late at night, very tired but wiser for the experience.

During the course of several visits to the north-eastern Transvaal, we explored the Kruger Park as well as the superb mountain country in the vicinity of Pilgrim's Rest, Graskop and Tzaneen, that in variety and splendour rivals the Cape mountains.

In order to appreciate fully the beauty of Southern Africa, we have always used our car simply as means of getting to a predetermined destination. On arrival, we have, whenever possible, taken to our feet to walk for miles in the bush and mountains. Only thus can one really learn to appreciate nature and savour the atmosphere of the wilds.

The Drakensberg has always been one of our favourite haunts. There are endless opportunities for walking and riding in these beautiful mountains. Our first visit to the Royal Natal National Park nearly landed us in trouble when, in the dark of the night, and in pouring rain, we took a wrong turning. Suddenly, on rounding a sharp corner on a steeply descending hill, the road disappeared and we were faced by the raging waters of the Tugela River in full flood. We were able to pull up just in time, but then became stuck in the mud. African rivers are deceptive and dangerous; in a matter of minutes, after heavy rain, an insignificant stream over which one can easily pass will become a treacherous torrent, sweeping away everything and everybody that obstructs its turbulent passage.

The high plateau and mountains of Lesotho have a beauty of their own, whether in the dry heat of summer or in the snows of winter. A personal friendship with King Moshoeshoe II, with whom I was at school in England, has enabled us to explore several little-known parts of this small, delightful country.

The game reserves of Zululand are my favourites in South Africa. For the wild-life enthusiast they offer superlative opportunities for the close observation of many species. On one visit to Umfolozi, we were fortunate enough to witness the amazing courage of a warthog. Two of these stocky wild pigs, with a young family in tow, were being chased through the bush by a pair of cheetahs; suddenly they whirled around to face the enemy. Not content with a mere last-ditch stand, the gallant warthogs then proceeded to charge the two cheetahs, who, with tails between their legs, made a speedy departure from the scene.

We spent two successive Christmas holidays camping at the Victoria Falls, a long day's car journey from Johannesburg. In spite of its being the rainy season in Rhodesia, December is perhaps the best time to make this trip, as the Zambezi is then in full flood, and in consequence the falls are at their most spectacular. Walking through the rain forest overlooking the great chasm, we were drenched by the soft, soaking spray – an exhilarating experience.

Blantyre, in Malawi, is only 1 760 kilometres from Johannesburg and, from a map, the journey may seem straightforward and easily accomplished in two days. This, however, is not the case. There are no problems until after Salisbury, where the tarmac ends. The main road then cuts through the western neck of Moçambique to reach the town of Tete. Here one crosses the Zambezi by ferry to rejoin the road which leads into Malawi. This is indeed a 650-kilometre "hell run" through some of the loneliest and most inhospitable bush country in Africa. The rough, dusty road is in terrible condition, deeply rutted and with bare rock protruding in places, which necessitates a snail-like pace. We made this journey in October 1970, just before the onset of the rainy season. We passed very few vehicles, saw hardly any people or dwellings, and everything seemed completely lifeless. It was, moreover, fiendishly hot.

We eventually arrived in Malawi completely exhausted and covered in dust from head to foot. That night, a bath was our idea of heaven.

On the return journey, we travelled via Tete to Gorongoza and Beira. This was another long day's ordeal on an impossible "main" road, through endless, monotonous bush, again for the most part devoid of all signs of habitation.

To reach the Okavango Swamps, a wonderful expanse of untamed Africa in northern Botswana, we flew by regular air service from Johannesburg, via Francistown, to Maun. In this small "outback" town on the edge of the great inland delta, we chartered a Cessna that flew us into the depths of the swamps to a place known as Txatxaba, where Lloyd Wilmot, son of the famous crocodile hunter, runs a delightfully casual tented safari camp. For anyone who wants to get "right away from it all", this must surely be one of the finest places to go to.

From Txatxaba I set out on two long treks through reeds and marsh to explore a number of thickly wooded islands. It was impossible to keep a sense of direction as, to my untrained eye, one island and stretch of marsh looked identical to the next. Without the company of an African guide, with his intimate knowledge of the swamps, I would have been lost within minutes. In such wild surroundings, one has to admire the courage possessed by the early explorers in Africa who set out on their travels literally "into the blue", with no idea of what might lie ahead.

We returned from Txatxaba to Maun in a small open boat powered by an outboard motor, a journey of some 130 kilometres down the Boro River, that really made us aware of the vastness and splendour of the Okavango Swamps.

At about 8 o'clock at night, some 30 kilometres from Maun, we ran out of petrol. With the use of a couple of rough branches cut by our African boatman we paddled for several miles to an island, where we made camp beneath the stars and a spreading fig-tree. A roaring fire soon warmed the chill night air, as we put up our tent and cooked a welcome meal.

Cape Town is the ideal starting-point for exploring the southern and western coasts, with many places of interest in the immediate environs of the city.

South West Africa is linked to Cape Town by an excellent road that passes through the arid hills of Namaqualand before reaching the border at Vioolsdrif. Many of the most interesting places in South West Africa lie off the beaten track, and one has to travel great distances over rough and stony roads or, even worse, over treacherous, sandy tracks, where a great deal of skill is required to prevent the car from getting bogged down.

Our travels in South West Africa were plagued with car problems. A hole developed in the petrol tank while we were crossing the Namib Desert, but we were fortunate to reach a karakul ranch, where the tank was repaired in the farm workshop. Our main tribulations, however, stemmed from the automatic gearbox. Time after time we found ourselves stuck in remote areas, with nothing to be done but wait for help.

One day, near Welwitschia, we were travelling on a reasonable road, when we were suddenly confronted by a 100-metre-wide dry riverbed. The road on the other side looked deceptively close, and we were loath to retrace our steps and waste many hours by taking a different route. We took the plunge, but ground to a halt about a third of the way across. It was a gruelling battle in the searing heat, trying to get the wheels out of the soft sand. Eventually a truck appeared on the scene, and with a few extra hands and a great deal of digging and pushing, we reached the far bank to continue our journey.

Another inconvenience and a terrible nuisance is the all-pervading, powdery dust, which penetrates every nook and cranny of the car, to the great discomfort of its occupants.

In spite of these minor hardships, however, South West Africa is a wonderful and exciting country, and very rewarding to explore.

There is really quite a story behind most of the photographs depicted in this book. Travelling in Africa does require a certain amount of endurance; it is generally hot and dusty, and there is always the hazard of the car breaking down in some remote place off the beaten track. Although this has happened to us on numerous occasions during our travels, we have rarely returned home disappointed with our safaris.

The photographic equipment I now take on my travels is the result of eight years' experience of the bush and veld of Africa. My cameras and accessories have to put up with a hard life, being bounced about not only in the car, but also in the sling-bag to which I transfer equipment when setting off on a hike.

I go to great lengths to make sure that my equipment is at all times protected from direct heat. Not only can the penetrating African sun irreparably damage film emulsions, but the heat may result in an excess of oil spilling between the camera shutter-blades, thereby causing them to stick.

For the storage of films, I use an insulated cooler-bag, and a bag of silica crystals to absorb any humidity. Cans or bags of dry ice are useful for short safaris, but the cooler-bag does suffice for longer journeys, provided it is kept out of the direct sunlight.

I always take plenty of polythene bags of various sizes, to keep out the dust. I use these not only to pack items for later use, but also to protect the camera which I keep at hand for quick action.

A blower lens brush and a packet of lens tissues are two other useful items that I carry around; the former to remove the odd specks of dust that invariably settle on the lens in spite of the polythene bag; and the latter to clean the lens, eye-piece, and view-finder, at the end of a day's photography.

A tripod is, of course, indispensable for certain types of work, but it is a bulky item to convey, and whenever possible I try and make do without it, by using low speeds and even time-exposures, with the camera balanced against a tree or other immovable object.

For colour work, I am addicted to the 6×6 cm transparency format, and use a Hasselblad with the standard 80 mm and 250 mm lenses. The former I find adequate for general use, whereas the latter is ideal for wild-life studies. I have recently acquired a 500 mm lens for specialized telephoto effects; but in this book only one picture, that of a lilac-breasted roller, was taken with this lens.

On all occasions I find it advisable to use a lens shade to cut out extraneous rays of sunlight. This is, of course, particularly important for back-lit effects, when one is pointing the camera in the direction of the sun.

To facilitate a rapid succession of photographs without the chore of changing films, I use two magazines, each of which holds a spool of 12 exposures. With the Hasselblad these are completely interchangeable.

The prismatic view-finder is an accessory I find useful, particularly when using a telephoto lens, as it magnifies clearly, and without distortion, the image on the ground-glass screen.

All the black-and-white photographs illustrated were taken with a Pentax SV camera, now about eight years old. I use the normal 55 mm lens as well as the light and handy 200 mm telephoto lens. As with the Hasselblad, the lens shade is a constant appendage when shooting.

An ultraviolet filter is usually affixed to my Pentax and provides additional protection for the lens. To bring out the drama of cloud effects, and to soften somewhat the harsh contrasts of an African landscape, I often make use of a yellow-green filter.

For colour work, I use relatively low-speed Agfa 50 S "transparency" film, which, in my opinion, brings out natural colours with a superb radiance and depth of tone. As regards black-and-white shots, I use Ilford FP4, and all the photographs in this book were taken with this film, which I have developed in Ilford ID11.

For accurate exposure readings, a Weston V Meter has been my constant companion.

When it comes to the finished photographs, much depends on the skill and judgement of the printer. For this, I am indebted to Gail Daniels, who has put in many hours of dedicated work to produce the high-quality black-and-white prints reproduced in this book.

In the belief that the beauties of Southern Africa, as described and illustrated in this book, may well have created a desire to travel amongst many of our overseas readers, we suggest that they contact any of the following offices of the South African Tourist Corporation for additional information on the tourist attractions of the Republic of South Africa: . . .

SOUTH AFRICAN TOURIST CORPORATION

SATOUR BRANCH OFFICES:

BRITAIN: 13 Regent Street, London SW1Y 4LR. Tel. 01–839–7462. Telegraphic: Satour London SW1.

GERMANY: 6 Frankfurt/Main, Alemannia-Haus, An der Hauptwache 11. Tel. 28–1505 and 28–1593. Telegraphic: Satour Frankfurt/M.

FRANCE: Rue de Richelieu 104, Paris 2e. Tel. 742–1871 and 742–1872. Telegraphic: Satourist Paris.

ITALY: Quarto Piano, Via Barberini 86, 00187 Rome. Tel. 476–778. Telegraphic: Satour Rome.

HOLLAND: Leidsestraat 64–66[11], Amsterdam C. Tel. 020–24 30 07. Telegraphic: Satour Amterdam.

UNITED STATES: Rockefeller Center, 610 Fifth Avenue, New York, N.Y. 10020. Tel. 245–3720. Telegraphic: Satourist New York.
Suite 721, 9465 Wilshire Boulevard, Beverly Hills, California 90212. Tel. 275–4111. Telegraphic: Satourist Beverly Hills California.

CANADA: Suite 1512, Proctor and Gamble Building, 2 St. Clair Avenue West, Toronto 195, Ontario. Tel. 922–5121. Telegraphic: Satourist Toronto.

AUSTRALIA: 10th Floor, Bankers and Traders' Building, 115 Pitt Street, Sydney, N.S.W. 2000. Postal Address: G.P.O. Box 4889, Sydney, N.S.W. 2001. Tel. 25–6165. Telegraphic: Tourepsa Sydney.

RHODESIA: Mercury House, Gordon Avenue, Salisbury. Postal Address: P.O. Box 1343, Salisbury. Tel. 6–1161. Telegraphic: Satour Salisbury.

HEAD OFFICE: 8th Floor, President Centre, 265/9 Pretorius Street, Pretoria. Postal Address: Private Bag X164, Pretoria. Tel. 2–5201. Telegraphic: Satourist Pretoria.